IMAGINING CHINA IN
TOKUGAWA JAPAN

Imagining China
in Tokugawa Japan

LEGENDS, CLASSICS, AND
HISTORICAL TERMS

Wai-ming Ng

SUNY
PRESS

Cover image: "Nanking in Chingku," by Utagawa Yoshikazu, 1861.

Published by State University of New York Press, Albany

© 2019 State University of New York

For information, contact State University of New York Press, Albany, NY
www.sunypress.edu

Library of Congress Cataloging-in-Publication Data

Names: Ng, Wai-ming, 1962- author.
Title: Imagining China in Tokugawa Japan : legends, classics, and historical terms / Wai-ming Ng.
Other titles: Dechuan Riben de Zhongguo xiang xiang. English
Description: Albany : State University of New York, [2019] | Translation with substantial revisions of: Dechuan Riben de Zhongguo xiang xiang. | Includes bibliographical references and index.
Identifiers: LCCN 2018015531 | ISBN 9781438473079 (hardcover ; alk. paper) | ISBN 9781438473086 (e-book)
Subjects: LCSH: Japan—Civilization—Chinese influences. | Japan—Civilization— 1600-1868.
Classification: LCC DS821.5.C5 N4 2019 | DDC 952/.025—dc23 LC record available at https://lccn.loc.gov/2018015531

10 9 8 7 6 5 4 3 2 1

TO MIHO AND MASASHI

CONTENTS

ACKNOWLEDGMENTS

This is my second English academic book on Tokugawa intellectual history. After the publication of *The I Ching in Tokugawa Thought and Culture* through the University of Hawai'i Press in 2000, I conducted research on *Yijing* studies in East Asia, Japan–Hong Kong relations, and Japanese popular culture. I was happy to return to my original path of Tokugawa studies a few years ago.

I have always been fascinated by the ways in which Tokugawa Japanese adapted Chinese culture into their own systems of thinking. My previous study on the *Yijing* in the Tokugawa period provides a good example of the indigenization of Chinese culture in Japanese thought. This study adds depth and dimension to this important theme in Sino-Japanese studies by examining the imagination of China and the localization of Chinese culture among Tokugawa Japanese from three different angles, namely, Chinese legends, Confucian classics, and historical terms.

My years at Princeton University and the University of Tokyo were truly rewarding and unforgettable. In the making of my academic career as a historian of Tokugawa Japan, I am deeply indebted to the late Marius Jansen, who has always been a source of inspiration to me. His idea of studying China and Japan from an East Asian context has become my own academic vision. Watanabe Hiroshi and Kurozumi Makoto have taught me how to define and conceptualize key issues in Tokugawa thought. My gratitude also extends to Joshua Fogel, Richard Smith, Martin Collcutt, Tam Yue-him, Douglas Reynolds, Shyu Shing-ching, Kevin Lam, Lin Shao-yang, and Wang Yong for their encouragement and support of my research on Tokugawa intellectual history.

This book first appeared in Chinese in 2015 and was published by the Tsinghua University Press, to whom I am grateful for allowing me to retain the copyright on the English edition. I have made substantial revisions in this English edition. Earlier versions of some chapters were published in the *Journal of Asian History*, *Sino-Japanese Studies*, and *East Asian History*. I am also thankful to the editors of these journals for permission to revise these articles and turn them into chapters in this book. My gratitude also goes to Christopher Ahn, Chelsea Miller, Jenn Bennett-Genthner, and the editorial staff and the production and marketing team at SUNY Press, as well as the two anonymous reviewers.

This book is dedicated to my wife, Miho and my son, Masashi, who are always by my side. My life would not have been so fulfilling without them.

Many things have happened in my middle adulthood, but my passion for research has never diminished. I feel so blessed to have chosen a career path that fulfills me in so many ways. To quote "The Road Not Taken" by Robert Frost:

> Two roads diverged in a wood, and I—
> I took the one less travelled by,
> And that has made all the difference.

This book serves as a record of footprints in my academic journey. You will see my hesitation and disorientation, but I am coming back to where I belong.

—Wai-ming Ng

A NOTE ON ROMANIZATION

This book uses the Hepburn system for Japanese and the Pinyin system for Chinese. All Japanese and Chinese words are italicized, with diacritical marks included where necessary. Certain Japanese words or place names that have been incorporated into the English language are left without italics or diacritics. All English translations of original Japanese and Chinese texts, unless stated otherwise, are my own. Original Japanese and Chinese characters are provided when necessary. Following the East Asian practice, Japanese and Chinese surnames precede given names, except for those Asian authors who have published their works in English.

INTRODUCTION

The China Factor in Tokugawa Culture

Although the Edo *bakufu* (military government) never established formal political ties with Qing China and trade with China was restricted to the port of Nagasaki, the Tokugawa period (also known as the Edo or early modern period, 1603–1868) was the heyday of Sino-Japanese intellectual and cultural exchanges. Tokugawa scholars engaged in Chinese learning mainly through imported classical Chinese texts, rather than direct person-to-person interaction.[1] To Tokugawa Japanese, China was a unique entity that played an important role in shaping Japanese thought and culture. Without China, Tokugawa intellectual life would not have been so flourishing and creative. Current scholarship on Tokugawa Japan tends to see China as either a model or "the Other." This study aims to provide a new perspective by suggesting that China also functioned as a collection of building blocks. In other words, the people of the Tokugawa period appropriated and transformed Chinese elements to forge Japan's own thought and culture. They selectively introduced and then modified Chinese culture to make it fit into the Japanese tradition. Chinese culture was highly localized in Tokugawa Japan. Chinese terms and forms survived, but the substance and the spirit were made Japanese. Hence, Sino-Japanese cultural exchange in the early modern period should be perceived as the interplay of the Japanization of Chinese culture and the Sinicization of Japanese culture. The three perceptions of China reflect different attitudes of Tokugawa intellectuals toward Chinese culture. These images of China could coexist in the same individual or intellectual school, serving as a reminder of the diversity and ambiguity in Tokugawa thought.

CHINA AS ROLE MODEL

Sinophilia was by no means a minor intellectual current among Tokugawa intellectuals, as it was not only embraced by Confucians and Sinologists, but prevalent in different schools of thought and culture as well.[2] Traveling to China was almost impossible, and Tokugawa Confucians and Sinologists could only visit China in their dreams. China became a nostalgic and blissful cultural homeland and utopian imaginary place. Fujiwara Seika (1561–1619) yearned to make a cultural pilgrimage to China, but the long distance and rough seas made the journey impossible. He wrote: "I always admire Chinese culture, and I want to see its cultural relics for myself."[3] In 1600, he paid a visit to Tokugawa Ieyasu (1543–1616) wearing his own homemade Confucian-scholar costume. Kumazawa Banzan (1619–91) and Kaibara Ekken (1630–1714) praised China as the *shi-kuni* (teacher-nation), expressing gratitude to China for enlightening different aspects of Japan. Banzan argued that the impact of Chinese culture on Japan was all-encompassing and far-reaching:

> China is the teacher-nation for the four seas and has contributed tremendously to Japan. Rites, music, books, mathematics, architecture, costumes, transportation, agricultural tools, weapons, medicine, acupuncture, officialdom, rankings, military codes, the ways of archery and riding, and miscellaneous skills and technologies were all imported from China.[4]

Ekken also acknowledged Japan's indebtedness to China for introducing morality and etiquette:

> Japan is pure and awesome in its social customs and is indeed a very fine nation. It is appropriate to refer to it as a nation of gentlemen. However, in uncivilized antiquity, Japan had neither etiquette nor law. There was no dress code, either. Wearing one's hair down, folding the clothes to the left, and marrying one's own sisters or nephews were very common. In the middle ages, Japan communicated frequently with China, learning from it and changing its customs. One can refer to the national histories to understand this. Although Japan has never been subordinated to China, it has been extensively adopting Chinese customs and teachings. Hence, China can be called the teacher-nation. We must not forget the foundations of China and should not look down upon it.[5]

Ogyū Sorai (1666–1728) expressed his passion for all things Chinese as follows: "I have been indulging in the study of Chinese classics and admiring Chinese civilization ever since I was a child."[6] The Chinese civilization that he admired was the way of the Sages of the Three Dynasties. He referred to China as *Chūka* (Central Efflorescence or Central Civilization) and *Chūgoku* (Central Kingdom), and to himself as a *Nihonkoku ijin* (barbarian of the nation of Japan) and *tōi no hito* (eastern barbarian). He regretted very much that he was not born in the land of the sages and that "no sages were born in the Eastern Sea."[7] Sorai was not alone with regard to his attitude toward Chinese culture. Basically, Tokugawa intellectuals from different Confucian schools all enthusiastically introduced Chinese morality and etiquette.[8] What Tokugawa Japanese admired was not the Qing Dynasty ruled by the Manchus, but the Three Dynasties under the sage-kings and the great Han and Tang dynasties. Their tendency to emphasize the past and belittle the present was salient.[9] Tokugawa Sinophiles demonstrated a high level of confidence and nativist consciousness,[10] and some believed in the concept of *kai hentai* (the transformation from civilized to barbarian and vice versa), seeing Japan as the new center of Confucian order in East Asia.

The Edo *bakufu* and some of its domains promoted Chinese learning.[11] The fifth Tokugawa *shōgun* (head of the *bakufu*), Tokugawa Tsunayoshi (1646–1709), and the second *daimyō* (domain lord) of the Mito domain, Tokugawa Mitsukuni (1628–1701), were both representative Sinophiles. Tsunayoshi was engrossed in the study of the *Yijing* (Classic of Changes). Over a period of eight years, he chaired the *Yijing* public lecture series two hundred and forty times, inviting courtiers, retainers, Confucians, Buddhist monks, Shinto priests, merchants, and commoners to attend.[12] Mitsukuni treated the Ming refugee scholar Zhu Shunshui (1600–82) with great respect, following his advice to promote Confucian education, start the wearing of Ming court costumes, build a Confucian temple, and construct the "West Lake embankment" in Edo's Koshikawa Kōrakuen Garden.[13]

Tokugawa Confucians were confident in their ability to read Confucian classics, but they sought advice and recognition from Chinese scholars in the areas of *kanshi* (Chinese-style poetry), calligraphy, and drawing. Composing *kanshi* was a common pastime in the Tokugawa period, and Japanese wrote more Chinese-style poems than Japanese-style poems.[14] Arai Hakuseki (1657–1725), a *bakufu* advisor and historian, attempted to send his Chinese poems to China for suggestions on how to improve them. Most Tokugawa calligraphers preferred *karayō* (Chinese style) to *wayō* (Japanese style), and model calligraphy inscriptions from the Tang and Song dynasties were the most popular. Some went to Nagasaki to study calligraphy under Chinese monks or scholars. Works by Chinese Ōbaku Zen monks were highly esteemed.[15]

To most Tokugawa Japanese, China was unreachable. Their only sources of contact were Chinese immigrants, including monks, merchants, and *Tōtsūji* (Chinese interpreters), in Nagasaki. Chen Yuanyun (1587–1671), Yinyuan Longqi (1592–1673), Zhu Shunshui, and Shen Nanping (1682–?) were little known in Ming-Qing China, but etched their names into Japanese history. Chen Yuanyun was invited by Tokugawa Yoshinao (1600–50), the first *daimyō* of the Owari domain, to move to Edo, where he taught samurai martial arts. Yinyuan Longqi was the founder of the Ōbaku school of Zen Buddhism in Japan. The emperor, courtiers, *bakufu* retainers, *daimyō*, and merchants all came to study Buddhism under him. Zhu Shunshui was an influential figure in Tokugawa Confucianism and historiography. Though not a man of letters, he was often asked by Japanese scholars to comment on their Chinese-style poems. His *hitsudan* (written dialogues) contain many discussions of Chinese-style poetry. Shen Nanping taught the Japanese bird-and-flower painting during his two-year stay in Nagasaki.

When Tokugawa Japanese could not find Chinese sojourners in Nagasaki, they knocked at the doors of Chinese interpreters descended from Chinese immigrants. For example, Ogyū Sorai learned modern colloquial Chinese from Okajima Kanzan (1674–1728).[16] Kumashiro Yūhi (1713–72), the most important disciple of Shen Nanping in Nagasaki, became a leading figure and influential teacher of painting. Hayashi Dōei's (1640–1708) calligraphy and Ga Chōshin's (1628–86) seven-stringed zither skills also attracted students.[17] Although Chinese interpreters were low-ranking officials, they were respected as the spokespersons for Chinese culture.

The interest in China among Tokugawa intellectuals was genuine and ardent. Chinese culture continued to inspire the Japanese in all walks of life. In particular, many Tokugawa Confucians regarded the Chinese as their mentors, sharing a common identity with the Chinese as members of the Confucian tradition in East Asia.

CHINA AS "THE OTHER"

China meant different things to different people in the Tokugawa period, being regarded as a model by Sinophiles, and as "the Other" by nativists. The attitudes of Tokugawa Japanese toward China were often complicated and ambivalent. Confucians worshipped the ways of the ancient Chinese sages, but tended to look down upon the Qing dynasty under the Manchus. Many believed that Confucian traditions were faithfully implemented in Tokugawa Japan, whereas they had been forgotten in Qing China. According to the concept of *kai hentai*, Japan had replaced China as the center of Confucian civilization. Yamaga Sokō (1622–85), a Confucian and strategist, pointed out that Japan had surpassed China in terms of its geography, political morality, religion, literacy, and military arts, and thus only Japan deserved to be called *Chūka* and *Chūgoku*. He explained:

> Regarding the movement of heaven and earth and the four seasons, if these reach a balance, wind and rain and cold and heat will not disappear. The soil will turn fertile and the people will become clever. One may then speak of *Chūgoku*. In the whole world, only *honchō* [our dynasty] and *gaichō* [foreign dynasty, i.e., China] have achieved this balance. In the Age of the Gods, Ame-no-Minaka-Nushi-no-Kami [the God of Creation] and the two divinities of creation [Izanami and Izanagi] shaped our nation in the [area of the] central pillar. Hence, it is natural to call our nation *Chūgoku*. This is why our nation has the divine and unbroken lineage of the imperial family and enjoys superiority in literacy and military arts. [18]

Likewise, Tokugawa Mitsukuni also maintained that the Japanese political tradition of maintaining the unbroken lineage of the imperial family reigning over the nation was superior to Chinese political tradition of revolution, and therefore only Japan would deserve to be called *Chūka*. He said: "According to *Morokoshi* [China], the Chinese call their nation *Chūka*. We Japanese should not follow that. We should call the capital of Japan *Chūka*. Why do we call a foreign nation *Chūka*?"[19]

Tokugawa Confucians were torn in their views of China between seeing it as a model and as "the Other," and scholars of *kokugaku* (nativist learning),

Shinto, the Kimon school, and the late Mito school often saw China in a negative light. By condemning China as "the Other," they constructed their own nativist identities. Unlike Tokugawa Confucians, who remained respectful to ancient Chinese sages, they denied the entire cultural heritage from the Three Dynasties to the Ming-Qing. For example, the *kokugaku* scholar Kamo Mabuchi (1697–1769) demonized China to underline the supreme quality of Japan:

> China is the land of evil intentions. Education can make it look good on the surface, but it remains evil inside. Social unrest is unavoidable. Japan is a simple nation. Although our people receive little education, they are obedient. Following the principle of heaven and earth, our people can do without education.[20]

The *kokugaku* master Motoori Norinaga (1730–1801) condemned the ancient Chinese sages for establishing Confucian morality and profound philosophy to fool the people and to rule over them. In his comparison of the political traditions in Japan and China, China served as "the Other" to underscore the superiority and uniqueness of Japan's nationality. For instance, he pointed out that the unbroken lineage of the imperial family brought peace and stability to Japan, whereas revolution caused chaos and social unrest in China. Sharing the same Chinese character, the Japanese term *shintō* and the Chinese term *shentao* invited comparison. Norinaga differentiated the two terms as follows:

> A book of the Tang [*Yijing*] reads: "The sages established *shentao*." Some people thus believe that our nation borrowed the name "Shinto" from it. These people do not have a mind to understand the principles of things. The meaning of our deities has been different from that nation from the beginning. In that nation, people apply the concept of *yin* and *yang* to explain deities, spirits, and the universe. Their discussion is only empty theory without substance. Deities in our imperial nation were the ancestors of the current imperial emperor, and thus [Japanese Shinto] is by no means empty theory.[21]

Sasaki Takanari, a scholar of the Kimon school, referred to China as a *kakoku* (inferior nation): "The customs of *Seido* [Western Land] are radical and dirty. It is an inferior nation in which *yin* and *yang* are either excessive or insufficient. It has been a land of beasts since its foundation. Our nation is a land of deities, having moral standards and a good balance between *yin* and *yang*."[22]

Fukagawa Yūei (1695–1768), a Shinto priest, looked down upon the Chinese, calling them *Hani* (Han barbarians) because they did not implement the ways of loyalty and filial piety. He held that only Japan was entitled to the name *Chūgoku* or *Chūka*:

> That nation calls itself *Chūka* and our imperial nation a barbarian [nation]. Indeed, only our nation deserves to be called *Chūka* and *Chūgoku*. That nation is nothing but barbaric.... We should uphold the dignity of our imperial nation. However, many Confucians nowadays call the nation of *Hani Chūka*, *Chūgoku*, or a nation of sages and gentlemen, but refer to our imperial nation as a nation of barbarians without manners and principles.[23]

It is interesting to note that in Tokugawa discourse, China was an amorphous concept, being an imaginary model for Tokugawa Sinophiles and a metaphor of otherness in the eyes of the nativists.[24] Throughout Tokugawa history, China was gradually marginalized in the worldview of the Japanese.[25] In the last decades of the Tokugawa period, Qing China became a negative example. China and the Chinese were disdainfully called *Shina* (derogatory term for China) and *chankoro* (derogatory term for the Chinese), respectively. De-Confucianization and de-Sinicization were in full swing, smoothing the way for the rise of the notion of *datsu-A ron* (escaping from Asia) in modern Japan.[26]

CHINA AS A SET OF BUILDING BLOCKS

Seeing China as a role model or as "the Other" were two major Tokugawa perceptions of China. Regarding the role of China in the making of Tokugawa thought and culture, China served as a collection of building blocks. Rather than copying faithfully from the Chinese, Tokugawa Japanese used Chinese elements to build and enrich their own thought and culture. Naitō Konan (1866–1934), a leading Sinologist in prewar Japan, used the making of tofu as a metaphor to describe how Japanese elements (soybean milk) and Chinese elements (coagulant) were mixed to forge Japanese culture (tofu):

Japanese scholars use a tree to explain the birth of Japanese culture. The seed has been there for a long time. Chinese culture provides the nutrients for the tree to grow. I would like to compare it to making tofu. The bean liquid is there, but it requires something to condense. Chinese culture is the coagulant that can make it firm.[27]

Konan argued that many things have existed in Japan for a long time, but they did not have a name or concept, and thus the Japanese use Chinese terms and ideas to explain Japan's indigenous culture. He used loyalty and filial piety as an example:

Undoubtedly, *chū* [loyalty] and *kō* [filial piety] are terms imported from China, but Japan already possessed the virtues of loyalty and filial piety. There is a tendency [for the Japanese] to use imported Chinese terms to explain what Japan already has.[28]

Takeuchi Yoshio (1886–1966), a disciple of Konan, expressed a similar view in his discussion of the nature and function of Confucianism in Japan. He suggested that Confucianism provided a platform for Tokugawa scholars to explain and elaborate upon Japanese values.[29] For example, Tokugawa Japanese put emphasis on the virtue of *cheng* (sincerity) because it was in accordance with the spirit of Shinto. Bitō Masahide (1923–2013), a scholar of Tokugawa intellectual history, pointed out that Tokugawa Confucianism was actually Japanized Confucianism that used imported Chinese terms to promote indigenous thought.[30]

Aside from cultural appropriation, another use of Chinese culture as a set of building blocks was hybridization. Inoue Tetsujirō (1856–1944), a semi-official philosopher who published Tokugawa Confucian writings to promote traditional values, identified early Tokugawa Confucianism as an eclectic synthesis that fused the Cheng-Zhu school, the Lu-Wang school, Confucian classics, history, literature, Buddhism, Shinto, Daoism, and *wagaku* (Japanese learning) together.[31] Kurozumi Makoto, a specialist in Tokugawa intellectual history, has also highlighted eclecticism as the major feature of Tokugawa thought, seeing its history as the process of fusing Chinese, Shinto, Buddhist, and Western elements.[32]

In the processes of cultural appropriation and hybridization, Chinese culture, together with Western, Indian, and indigenous cultures, provided

Tokugawa Japanese with building blocks to construct their own thought and culture. The same Chinese terms could mean different things in Qing China and Tokugawa Japan. This can be observed in the ways in which Tokugawa Japanese reinterpreted Chinese legends, Confucian classics, and historical terms. These three components constitute the basic narrative structure and analytical framework of this research.

Part 1 of this book examines the naturalization of Chinese legends in Tokugawa Japan. Wu Taibo, Xu Fu, and Yang Guifei (719–56) were household names in Japan. Their images and legends in Japan were different from their prototypes in China, used to glorify Japan rather than China, showing a rise of nativist consciousness among Tokugawa Japanese.

Wu Taibo was transformed from a Chinese sage into the ancestor of the Japanese imperial family. This idea was supported by Fujiwara Seika, Hayashi Razan (1583–1657), and Nakae Tōju (1608–48). Hayashi Gahō (1618–80) praised Taibo for preserving the way of the sages in Japan as the imperial ancestor. Kumazawa Banzan speculated that Taibo was the Sun Goddess, Amaterasu-Ōmikami, the most important Shinto deity and the divine ancestor of the imperial family:

> Descended from Zhou, Japan is thus named *Tōkai himeshi no kuni* [nation of Ji in the Eastern Sea]. It is the name for females, and in Japan we call females *hime*. *Hime* is the honorific term for women and the surname of Zhou. Amaterasu was Taibo. The statue of Uhōdōji [Rainmaking Boy] was made in the image of Amaterasu, reflecting the image of Taibo and the haircutting customs of Wu. Japanese clothing is called *gofuku* and utensils are *goki*. These are all related to the state of Wu [*go* in Japanese].[33]

The advocates of Wu Taibo as the imperial ancestor sought to give Japan a respectable place in the Confucian order, as the Japanese were no longer eastern barbarians, but descendants of an ancient Chinese sage and preservers of the way of the sages. Associating Taibo with Shinto legend was an expression of the syncretism of Shinto and Confucianism in the Tokugawa period.

The legend of Xu Fu reached its apex in the Tokugawa period. More than twenty places in Japan claimed to have legacies of Xu Fu, and many Tokugawa writings mentioned Xu, who was merely a Qin sorcerer in the eyes of the Chinese. Tokugawa Japanese regarded him as either the transmitter of

Chinese culture or a political refugee. These two views seem to have represented the competition between Sinophiles and nativists, but they were indeed only differing expressions of Japanese identity. Hayashi Razan, Kumazawa Banzan, and Arai Hakuseki saw Xu as the transmitter of ancient Chinese culture, praising him for bringing pre-Qin texts, morality, and advanced technologies to Japan. Banzan remarked: "Xu Fu introduced Confucian morality, public manners, and various institutions. He found refuge in Japan and settled down here with thousands of followers. Although some Chinese classics disappeared in China, they survived overseas."[34] Matsushita Kenrin (1637–1703), Ono Takakiyo (1747–1817), and Satō Setsudō (1797–1865) portrayed Xu as a political refugee who found his ideal nation in Japan. Kenrin wrote: "Xu Fu saw the national glory of Japan and came to settle down there. He escaped from the Qin, the land of tigers and leopards, and died in Japan as a deity."[35] The use of Xu Fu to glorify Japan was a very original idea, and represents a good example of the localization of Chinese culture. The Xu Fu legend was mixed with Japanese Shinto mythology and folklore in Tokugawa writings.

The Chinese beauty Yang Guifei was seen as the manifestation of a Shinto deity. According to some medieval and early modern Japanese texts, Shinto deities sent Atsuta Myōjin to take the form of Yang Guifei to infatuate Emperor Xuanzong of Tang (685–762) so that he would forget his plan to invade Japan. When Yang died, the spirit of Atsuta Myōjin returned to Atsuta Shrine. The *jōruri* play *Yōkihi monogatari* (1663) fabricated a dialogue between Emperor Xuanzong and the great poet Bai Juyi (772–846). Bai chastised the emperor in the following terms:

> Your Majesty, you are the cause of this misfortune. Your obsession with Yang Guifei's beauty has caused all of the chaos. There is a country called Japan in the East. Yang Guifei was its Atsuta Myōjin. She was born in our nation as a woman provisionally to create troubles. Shame on her![36]

Kanō school painter Kanō Einō (1631–97) further added that many evil characters in Tang China were indeed Japanese deities who transformed into Chinese in order to save Japan from invasion. He wrote:

> It is said that, in the Tang era, Japan frequently paid tribute to China. When the gifts were few, the Chinese killed the Japanese envoys,

Xuanzong sought to annihilate Japan. Atsuta Myōjin was Yamato-Takeru-no-Mikoto. This deity transformed into Yang Guifei, Sumiyoshi Myōjin turned into An Lushan, and Kumano-no-Ōkami turned into Yang Guozhong. They went to Tang China to destroy Xuanzong.[37]

Yang Guifei as the manifestation of a Shinto deity was the Shinto version of the doctrine of *honji suijaku* (Japanese deities were manifestations of the Buddha or bodhisattvas) and an expression of *gokoku* (the protection and prosperity of the state). Yang was considered an evil beauty in the eyes of the Chinese, but was respected by some Japanese as a guardian deity or protector of Japan.

Part 2 looks into the appropriation of Confucian classics among Tokugawa scholars to advocate Japanese ideas. Confucian classics were popular readings among Tokugawa scholars from different schools of thought and religion. In order to accommodate Confucian values into the Tokugawa system and Japanese tradition, Tokugawa Japanese interpreted Confucian classics in their own ways to promote Japanese indigenous values, rather than original Chinese teachings.

The *Mengzi* (Sayings of Mencius) was not held in high esteem among Tokugawa scholars, as its ideas were not always in agreement with Japanese political tradition and the Tokugawa system of government. In particular, the notions of revolution and regicide were considered incompatible, dangerous, and disloyal. The Kimon school, the Sorai school, *kokugaku*, and the late Mito school were critical of the text. Although the *Mengzi* contains many relatively liberal political ideas, it was used by Yoshida Shōin (1830–59) to advocate con-servative political ideology. For instance, he reinterpreted *tenmei* (mandate of heaven) as "the order of the *tennō* [Japanese emperor]." Receiving the mandate of heaven meant being appointed by the imperial family to be the *shōgun*, and the emperor could take this mandate away if the *shōgun* failed to carry out his duties. Shōin gave the Edo *bakufu* a most serious warning: "Posts like that of *shōgun* are appointed by the imperial court only for those who can carry out the duties of those posts. If the *shōgun* shirks his duties like the Ashikaga house did, he should be sacked immediately."[38]

The *Xiaojing* (Classic of Filial Piety) is a book about filial piety, but it was used to promote loyalty in Tokugawa Japan. Tokugawa samurai ethics put loyalty before filial piety. The *bakufu* preferred the *guwen* (old-script edition) of the *Xiaojing*, which underlines the absolute authority of the ruler. Hayashi

Razan, in his *Kobun kōkyō genkai* (Colloquial Explanation of the *Xiaojing* in the Old-Script Text), restated the famous saying in the preface by Kong Anguo: "Even if the emperor does not behave like an emperor, his minister cannot be disloyal. Even if the father does not behave like a father, his son cannot be unfilial." In terms of *wulun* or *wujiao* (the order of the five constant relations), many Zhu Xi school scholars and Mito school scholars put the ruler-subject relation prior to that of the father-son relation.[39]

The *Yijing* was localized in Tokugawa Japan, used by nativists to expound Shinto ideas. The Shintoist Watarai Nobuyoshi (1615–90) explained the history of the Age of the Gods and Shinto thought in terms of *Yijing*-related concepts such as *taiji* (the Supreme Ultimate), *yin-yang wu-xing* (two primal forces and five phases), *sancai* (three spheres of nature), and the hexagrams. The *kokugaku* thinker Hirata Atsutane (1776–1843) and his disciples turned the *Yijing* from a Confucian classic into a Shinto text, maintaining that Fu Xi, according to tradition the creator of the eight trigrams, was the manifestation of the Shinto deity Ōmononushi-no-Kami, who went to China in antiquity to cultivate the Chinese:

> Paoxishi is also called Taiho Fu Xi Shi. He was actually Ōmononushi-no-Kami, a deity of our divine nation of Fusō. He went to ancient China to exploit its land and became the emperor. He taught its foolish people the ways of heaven, earth, and humanity. By observing the changes of the universe and everything, he created the eight trigrams.[40]

Atsutane saw the *Zhouyi* as a corrupt version of the *Yijing*, condemning King Wen for distorting the text and changing the order of the sixty-four hexagrams and the number of yarrow stalks to justify the revolution that overthrew the Shang dynasty. His academic mission was to restore the original *Yijing*. Regarding the *Yijing* as a Shinto text, scholars of the Hirata school used its related ideas to explicate Shinto and carry out divination for agriculture.

Part 3 documents how Chinese historical terms were redefined in Tokugawa Japan. Many imported Chinese terms were interpreted and used differently. Names for China, *bakufu*, and *shōgun*, as well as the discussion of legitimacy in Tokugawa historiography, are all examples of how meanings of Chinese terms could be adjusted to express Japanese values and feelings.

Following the rise of the theory of *kai hentai* and the Japanese version of the Sinocentric world order, some Tokugawa Japanese applied honorific names originally reserved for China to Japan. Yamaga Sokō, in his last years, referred to Japan as *Chūka*. He remarked: "How foolish I was! Born in *Chūka* [Japan], but failing to understand its beauty, I was absorbed in the classics of *gaichō* [China] and admired its people. How absent-minded I was! How lost I was!"[41] The historian Rai Sanyō (1781–1832) called Japan *Chūgoku* and *Chūchō* (Central Dynasty) in his *Shinsaku* (New Proposal; 1804). The Mito scholar Aizawa Seishisai (1781–1863) referred to Japan as *Chūgoku* and *Shinshū* (Divine Land) in his *Shinron* (New Thesis; 1825).

Honorific titles for the Edo *bakufu* and *shōgun* (such as *kōgi, kubō, chōtei, taikun, denka,* and *kinchū*) were mostly imported Chinese terms that at first applied to the Kyoto court and the emperor. In the last decades of the Tokugawa period, many titles that the *bakufu* and *shōgun* had acquired from the court were restored to their original meanings and usage. The Mito scholar Fujita Tōko (1806–55) insisted that titles for the imperial court should not be applied to the Edo *bakufu*: "The innocent people refer to the *bakufu* as the *chōtei* [central court government], and some even use the word *ō* [king]."[42]

Tokugawa historians created their own concepts of legitimacy (such as the imperial regalia theory) and redefined imported Chinese concepts (such as heaven's mandate) to rationalize Tokugawa political realities. The *Dai Nihonshi* (History of Great Japan; started in 1657 and completed in 1906) claimed legitimacy for the Southern Court because it was the holder of the three imperial regalia. The regalia theory had a very strong impact on the Kimon school and the Mito school. Tokugawa Harutoshi (1773–1816), the seventh *daimyō* of the Mito domain, argued: "The conflict between the East and West, the civil war between the North and South, and the legitimacy of the imperial line can all be settled by the regalia."[43] Also, the mandate of heaven was used in Tokugawa historical writings primarily to discuss the right to govern, and denied a Chinese-style system of "revolution" and dynastic change. This Japanese version of heaven's mandate became an ideological tool to legitimize the *bakufu* as the de facto central government. Ironically, the same theory was applied to challenge the legitimacy of the *bakufu* in the *bakumatsu* period (late Tokugawa era, 1853–67). Yoshida Shōin warned: "The descendants of the Sun Goddess in our heavenly dynasty shine on the universe. If the *bakufu* does not follow the order of the heavenly dynasty and does not carry out its duty to repel the barbarians, the situation is called 'using the state of Yan to fight against the state of Yan.'"[44]

BEYOND A MODEL AND "THE OTHER"

China in the Tokugawa imagination was complicated and multifaceted. In understanding the China factor in Tokugawa culture, we should think beyond the traditional dialectical framework of model and "the Other." China also functioned as a set of building blocks to construct Tokugawa culture. This tripartite conceptual framework helps to achieve a holistic understanding of the nature of Tokugawa culture. Sino-Japanese cultural exchange in the early modern period should be perceived as the process of interplay between the Japanization of Chinese culture and the Sinicization of Japanese culture. Tokugawa Japanese selectively introduced and then modified Chinese culture to make it fit into the Japanese tradition. Used largely as a collection of building blocks to construct Japanese culture, Chinese culture was highly localized and hybridized in Tokugawa Japan. In the name of *wakon kansai* (Japanese spirit and Chinese scholarship), Chinese terms and forms survived, but the substance and spirit became Japanese. Hence, it is simplistic and even misleading to see Tokugawa Confucianism or Chinese learning as an overseas branch of Chinese culture. Characterized by eclecticism and pragmatism, Chinese scholarship in Tokugawa Japan was different from Song-Ming neo-Confucianism or Qing textual criticism. Moreover, the China factor was influential in Tokugawa thought and culture in the sense that it was used extensively by the Japanese to express and reinforce Japanese ideas and values.

Part I

NATURALIZATION OF CHINESE LEGENDS

XU FU AS CHINESE MIGRANT

The story of xu fu has long stimulated and fed the imaginations of artists and discussions among scholars in both China and Japan. It is interesting to note that the Japanese have held very different images of Xu Fu, having generated more images and ideas than the Chinese. In China, Xu Fu is remembered as a court sorcerer who cheated the founding emperor of Qin and escaped from the tyranny of the Qin Dynasty (221–207 BCE). In Japan, Xu Fu has played a more important role in history, having been associated with several identities, namely, the transmitter of Chinese culture, a political refugee, and "the Other." Xu Fu became a building block for the Japanese people to construct their own national identity.

Xu Fu has become a metaphor in Sino-Japanese intellectual and cultural exchange, being used by Chinese and Japanese intellectuals to discuss their bilateral cultural ties. Throughout East Asian history, scholars in China and Japan have made use of the Xu Fu legend for political and intellectual reasons. As time passed, more and more stories about Xu Fu were created in both nations. This study of the Xu Fu legend, I believe, has important intellectual implications in terms of understanding the development of national consciousness in Japan and the changing cultural relationship between China and Japan. Through a textual analysis of Tokugawa writings about Xu Fu, this chapter aims to examine how Tokugawa intellectuals overcame the dilemma of accepting Chinese culture without compromising their national and cultural identity.[1]

THEORIES ABOUT XU FU BEFORE THE TOKUGAWA PERIOD

It is highly debatable whether or not Xu Fu, a half-historical and half-legendary figure mentioned in the *Shiji* (Records of the Grand Historian; compiled by

Sima Qian, 145–90 BCE), ever journeyed to Japan. The legend of Xu Fu appeared in Japan in the latter half of the Heian period (794–1186), and its associated texts and legacies increased gradually during the medieval period (1186–1603). The Xu Fu boom reached its peak in the Tokugawa period, when scholars, writers, and artists were actively engaged in this discourse, illustrating the rise of national consciousness and the complicated feelings toward China among Tokugawa Japanese.

After his first appearance in the *Shiji*, Xu Fu attracted the attention of Chinese historians and scholars. His story was retold and expanded in the *Huainanzi* (The Masters of Huainan) by Liu An (179?–122 BCE), *Hanshu* (Book of Han) by Ban Gu (32–92), *Sanguozhi* (Records of the Three Kingdoms) by Chen Shou (233–97), *Hou Hanshu* (Book of Later Han) by Fan Ye (398–445), and *Zizhi tongjian* (Comprehensive Mirror to Aid in Government) by Sima Guang (1019–86). In these writings, the story of Xu Fu's preparation for his journey during the Qin period became increasingly detailed. None of these official histories, however, clearly states that Xu Fu travelled to Japan.

Beginning in the tenth century, a few Chinese prose writings and poems began to speculate that Xu Fu went to Japan with boys and girls, crew-members, and artisans. Interestingly enough, these Chinese writers seem to have been influenced by the Japanese. Many Japanese Zen monks, merchants, and officials came to China during the Tang (618–907) and Song (960–1279) periods and introduced stories about Xu Fu. They maintained that Xu Fu and his people settled in ancient Japan, where they had a strong impact on Japanese culture, religion, and customs. Japanese before the Tokugawa period created three major theories about Xu Fu in Japan—the Mount Fuji, Kumano, and Atsuta Shrine theories. As Hayashi Razan (1583–1657) summarized: "Regarding Penglai [the legendary immortal mountain where Xu Fu supposedly landed] mentioned in Chinese texts, three places in Japan claim the title: Kumano in Kii, Fuji in Shunshū, and Atsuta in Bishū."[2]

The Mount Fuji theory was perhaps the earliest version of the Xu Fu legend originating in Japan, and it was later introduced to China. Formulated in Japan by no later than the late Heian period, the Mount Fuji theory came to China during the Five Dynasties period (907–60). A Chinese Buddhist monk named Yi Chu recorded what he heard from the Japanese Shingon monk

Kōjun about the legend of Xu Fu in Japan in his *Shishi liutie* (Six Models of Buddhism; 955, also known as *Yichu liutie*). Kōjun told Yi Chu that Xu Fu and five hundred pairs of boys and girls landed in Japan, after which they moved northeastward and settled in the area around Mount Fuji.[3] The narrative demonstrates the utopian imagination of Japan, seeing it as a "lost horizon" for people seeking peace and harmony. Yi Chu wrote:

> The nation of Japan is also called Yamato no Kuni. It is located in the Eastern Sea. Xu Fu brought five hundred pairs of boys and girls to this nation in the Qin period. Nowadays, its people and culture are like those in Chang'an.... More than a thousand miles in the Northeast, there is a mountain called Fuji, also named Mount Penglai. The mountain is high and is surrounded by sea on three sides. It is very high and smoke and fire come out from its top. In the daytime, treasures run down. At night, treasures run up. Music is often heard. Xu Fu settled down there and called it Penglai. Now, his descendants are named Hata [秦]. This land has never been invaded, and is protected by the dragon deity. Its laws have no capital punishment and criminals are exiled to an island. There are many scenic places and famous mountains in this area, but I have no time to introduce them.[4]

In the Muromachi period (1336–1573), the Tendai monk Gentō wrote about the legend of Xu Fu on Fuji in his *Sangoku denki* (Legends of the Three Nations; c. 1407): "Penglai refers to Mount Fuji. Xu Fu lived in seclusion there. His descendants have become known as Hata."[5]

In the late Heian period, the second theory—Xu Fu in Kumano— was created and became prevalent. Records of the Xu Fu Shrine in Kumano appeared in Japanese literature as early as the eleventh century. The *Kumano gongen engisho* (Book on the Origins of the Avatars of Kumano; 1075) mentions the Xu Fu Shrine and Penglai Island. This theory was prevalent in the medieval period and it is recorded that several Japanese spread this theory in China. For instance, a Japanese Zen monk told the Yuan poet Wu Lai (1297– 1340) that Xu Fu landed in Kumano, a port in the southeastern part of Japan's Kii province, where a Xu Fu shrine was built. Wu composed a poem entitled "Tingkehua Xiongyeshan Xushimiao" (Listening to the Visitor about the Xu Shi [another name for Xu Fu] Shrine on Mount Kumano):

In ancient Kii province on Japan's shore,
There were thousands of rocks in the sea.
Xu Shi wanted to be immortal, but died there,
The aged purple ganoderma made people sad.[6]

Mugaku Sogen (1226–86), a Chinese monk who fled to Japan after the fall of the Song, visited the Xu Fu Shrine in Kumano. In "Xianxiang yu Jizhou Xiongye lingci" (Presenting Incense at the Shrine in Kumano of Kii Province), he found parallels between himself and Xu Fu:

Xu Fu came here to gather herbs, but did not return.
His motherland has undergone several rounds of changes.
Today I am presenting incense to remember my nation so far away.
This old monk also came here to escape from the Qin.[7]

The most famous advocate of the Kumano theory was a Japanese *Gozan* (Five Mountain) Zen monk named Zekkai Chūshin (1336–1405), who told the Ming founding emperor, Taizu (reigned 1368–98), the same story about Xu Fu in Kumano, pinpointing for Taizu the location of Kumano on a map.[8] At the request of the emperor, he composed this poem:

The Xu Fu Shrine is located in front of Mount Kumano.
The mountain has plenty of herbs and the soil is fertile.
Now, the sea is calm.
For ten thousand miles, the gentle wind blows for an early return.[9]

It seems that, in the Ming and Qing periods, the legend of Xu Fu in Kumano was well known in both Japan and China. Many Japanese believed that Xu Fu brought Chinese herbal medicine and agricultural skills to Kumano. Xu Fu became a metaphor of Sino-Japanese friendship, used by Japanese and Chinese monks and scholars to open up dialogue and find areas of commonality. Korean minister Shin Suk-ju (1417–75) wrote the *Haedong jegukgi* (Chronicle of the Countries in the Eastern Sea; 1471) to record his visits to Japan, China, and the Ryūkyū Kingdom. On a trip to Kumano, he found that the local people treated Xu Fu as a Shinto deity:

In the seventy-second year of the reign of the Kōrei emperor [218 BCE],
the founding emperor of Qin sent Xu Fu to look for a miracle medicine

at sea. Xu Fu eventually arrived and settled in Kumano. In the seventeenth year of the Sujin emperor [81 BCE], Kumano Daigongen emerged. After his death, Xu Fu became a Shinto deity. He continues to be worshipped by the villagers to the present day.[10]

The Kumano theory added Shinto elements to the Xu Fu discourse. Xu Fu found a miracle medicine in Kumano and was worshipped as a local deity after his death.

The third theory—Xu Fu at Atsuta Shrine—appeared in the Kamakura period (1185–1333). It was not as influential as the Fuji and Kumano theories. In the Kamakura period, Atsuta Shrine was associated with the belief in Penglai (Hōrai). In 1313, Hiezan monk Kōen (1262–1317) wrote in his *Keiran shūyōshū* (Collection of Leaves Gathered in Tempestuous Brooks): "The Penglai Palace refers to Atsuta Shrine."[11] A Muromachi Zen monk named Ishō Tokugan (1262–1317) suggested in his *Tōkai keikashū* (Glorious Stories of the Tōkai Region; 1395) that Xu Fu and his people landed in Bishū, where Atsuta Shrine was built in his honor:

> According to tradition, in the Qin period, Xu Shi wrote to the First Emperor, asking for five hundred pairs of boys and girls to search for elixir in the three heavenly mountains in the sea. He landed on an island and did not return. This marked the beginning of the Atsuta Shrine in Bishū in my country.[12]

Ishō himself did not explicitly identify the legendary Emperor Jimmu with Xu Fu. As Atsuta Shrine worshipped Emperor Jimmu, Ishō nevertheless created the association that Xu Fu was somehow related to the Japanese imperial family. However, this idea was not further developed in medieval and early modern Japan.[13]

These three theories of Xu Fu in Japan were neither fully developed nor widely known in the medieval period. They were used by some Japanese for various purposes on different occasions, such as opening dialogue with the Chinese whom they encountered in China, finding for Japan a respectable place in the Chinese cultural order, or stressing the importance of their home regions.

THE XU FU LEGEND IN THE TOKUGAWA PERIOD

The legend of Xu Fu reached its peak in the Tokugawa period. Xu Fu became a popular topic of discourse in Tokugawa Japan for three main reasons. First, *unidirectional* ✗

the Tokugawa period was an age of Sino-Japanese cultural exchange and intellectual development. Following the large-scale importation of Chinese culture and books, the emergence of a vital and creative intellectual atmosphere, and improvements in publishing, transportation, and material life in the Tokugawa period, more references to Xu Fu appeared in Japanese writings. Different schools of thought and religion emerged and began to compete with each other. Xu Fu became an intellectual battlefield for scholars. Second, the Tokugawa was an age of historiography. The *bakufu*, domains, and individual scholars were enthusiastic about compiling Japanese histories. When they discussed ancient Japanese history concerning the influx of Chinese immigrants, they could not avoid mentioning Xu Fu. Third, the Tokugawa was a period of textual forgery and historical imagination. Tokugawa Japanese produced many fake texts, paintings, maps, and legacies.[14] They also invented many stories about foreigners who supposedly came to Japan, such as Xu Fu, Wu Taibo, Yang Guifei, Jesus, and Moses, as well as Japanese heroes who allegedly found second lives in China, such as Minamoto Yoshitsune (1159–89) and Ōshio Heihachirō (1793–1837). Many authors of *zuihitsu* (miscellaneous writings) penned these kinds of stories to attract readership.

Tokugawa Japanese created material evidence and artworks to reinforce the legend of Xu Fu in Japan. In the Tokugawa period, the three theories about Xu Fu were further expanded upon and a large number of new theories emerged. It was the age of the "Xu Fu boom." All over Japan people competed to determine the place of landing and settlement of Xu Fu and his followers.

The Mount Fuji theory gained a great deal of new textual and material support in the Tokugawa period. Local historical writings and travel records advocated this theory, including the *Tsurutsuka bibun* (Tsurutsuka Epigraph; 1798), *Heishin kikō* (Records of My Trip in the Year of Hinohetatsu; 1616) by Hayashi Razan, *Kōshū sōki* (Miscellaneous Records of Kōshū), *Kaikokushi* (History of Kai Province; 1814) by Matsudaira Sadayoshi (1758–1831), and *Fujisan kitaguchi no ki* (Records of the North Slope of Mount Fuji). Razan, in his *Heishin kikō*, stated that the Mount Penglai at which Xu Fu arrived was actually Mount Fuji in Japan:

> Mount Fuji is not only famous in my nation, but also well known in China. [Yamabe no] Akahito praised it in the *Manyōshū*. Miyako Yoshika mentioned it in the [*Honchō*] *bunzui*. Xu Fu collected

myoh ✓

herbs and reached this mountain, calling it Mount Penglai. It is recorded in the *Giso rokujō*. . . . In the ancient past, righteous men enjoyed happiness [here in Japan]. Why should people look for the immortals in Penglai?[15]

Furthermore, the *Fujisan kitaguchi no ki* links all three theories together, but emphasizes that Mount Fuji was Xu Fu's final destination: "Having wandered around the three mountains in Kumano, Xu Fu went to Atsuta in Owari. He then visited other provinces and finally settled down on the slopes of Mount Fuji."[16] In addition, the *ukiyo-e* master Katsushika Hokusai (1760–1849) drew his *Painting of Xu Fu Looking Up at Mount Fuji* to reinforce this theory.

In terms of material evidence, a small Xu Fu shrine dedicated to Jofuku daimyōjin was built out of stone in Fujiyoshida in the mid-Tokugawa period.[17] Inside Fukugen-ji Temple in Fujiyoshida, a tomb called Tsurutsuka (Crane Tomb) was built in the eleventh year of Genroku (1698). According to the tradition of Fukugen-ji Temple, Xu Fu turned into three cranes after his death, and they lived for more than two thousand years. During the Genroku period (1688–1703), one crane flew to Fukugen-ji Temple and died there. The *Tsurutsuka bibun* reads:

> There is a Tsuru district in Kōshū [now Yamanashi prefecture]. Its south is the slope of Mount Fuji. According to tradition, during the reign of Emperor Kōrei, Xu Fu and his people came to search for medicine. Having crossed the Eastern Sea, they reached this land of blessing and never returned. Later, three cranes flew in this county. People believed that they were manifestations of Xu Fu.[18]

Additionally, Hatashi Shrine within the Sengen Shrine at Lake Kawaguchi worshipped Xu Fu as a god of sericulture. It was believed that Xu Fu introduced sericulture, Chinese textiles, Chinese agriculture, and Chinese herbal medicine to the Mount Fuji region.[19] According to local tradition, Xu Fu could not find an elixir on Mount Fuji and decided to stay in Japan. He married a Japanese woman and settled down on the north slope of Mount Fuji, teaching the villagers how to raise silkworms, spin silk, farm, grow herbs, and make paper. *Bakufu* official Matsudaira Sadayoshi describes Sengen Shrine in his *Kaikokushi* as follows:

This shrine is for the transmission of the God of the Qin. Since Xu
Fu is the subject of worship, this shrine is called the Xu Fu Shrine....
Now, his descendants are the Hata clan living around the Kawaguchi
area and serving as priests in Fujiyoshida. They have several names,
including Hata [秦], Hata [波多], and Hata [羽田].[20]

The Kumano theory continued to be the most popular version of the Xu
Fu legend in Tokugawa Japan, as it was mentioned in a number of Tokugawa
writings, such as the *Kumano nendaiki* (Chronicle of Kumano), *Renshū ryōzai*
(Collection of Best Renga; 1631), *Honchō ressenden* (Biographies of the Immortals
in Japan; 1686) by Tanaka Genjun, *Dōbun tsūkō* (An Investigation of the Theory
of Common Cultural Origins; 1760) by Arai Hakuseki, and *Kumano yūki* (The
Travel Diary about Kumano; 1801) by Kitabatake Kakusai (1731–82).[21] Xu Fu
Shrine was built in Kumano in the medieval period. In the Tokugawa period, a
large number of memorials were created, including Xu Fu's tomb, the tombs of
Xu Fu's seven retainers, *Jofuku no miya* (Xu Fu Palace), Mount Hōrai (Penglai),
Hadasu Village (秦住村), Xu Fu paper, a Xu Fu dance, the Xu Fu saddle, and
pre-Qin documents.[22] Tani Yōryūken included the Xu Fu Palace as one of the
33 Buddhist pilgrimage sites in Western Japan in his *Saikoku sanjūsansho mich-
ishirube* (A Guidebook of Thirty-three Sites in Western Japan; 1690). Xu Fu
Palace is a small shrine dedicated to Xu Fu inside Asuka Shrine in Shingū. It
preserves a bowl allegedly used by Xu Fu. The date of its establishment is far
from clear, but it was mentioned in a Tokugawa text dated 1624.[23] Xu Fu was
given credit for introducing sericulture, rice planting, Chinese herbal medicine,
metallurgy, papermaking, and whaling in this region.

The legend of Xu Fu in Kumano was mentioned in a number of Tokugawa
prose writings and travel records. Hayashi Razan composed a poem entitled
"Wafu" (Prose Poetry about Japan; 1612):

Xu Fu came to search for medicine.
He died here and became immortal.
It is said that he lived in Kumano in Southern Kishū.
People have been worshipping him for a thousand years.[24]

Kitabatake Kakusai (1731–82) introduced Xu Fu's Tomb, the Xu Fu Shrine,
and Mount Penglai in his *Kumano yūki*:

In the east is the Asuka Shrine. The Xu Fu Tomb is in the field. Xu Fu came to look for medicine at the request of the Qin emperor, and finally died there. There is a shrine dedicated to Xu Fu next to the Asuka Shrine. In the west of the shrine there is a hill near the sea named Penglai.[25]

Likewise, Tachibana Nankei (1754–1806) also introduced Mount Penglai, the Xu Fu Shrine, Xu Fu's Tomb, and pre-Qin documents in his *Saiyūki zokuhen* (Sequel to *Records of My Visit to Western Provinces*; 1798). Hirose Kyokusō (1807–63) mentioned his visit to Xu Fu's Tomb in Kumano in his *Nikkan sajiroku* (Records of Miscellaneous Things; 1839). Takizawa Bakin (1767–1848) believed in the Xu Fu legend in Kumano, suggesting that the secret medicine for immortality that he acquired was actually wild ginseng:

> Looking for the medicine for immortality, Xu Fu arrived and settled down here. This is not recorded in official histories. However, based on old tradition, we cannot deny it. On the slope of Mount Kumano in Kii, there is a Xu Fu Tomb in Asuka. In Shingū, Kumano, there is a mountain named Mount Penglai, where we can find the Xu Fu Shrine. The medicine for immortality that Xu Fu found in Penglai was the wild ginseng of Kumano.[26]

Additionally, in the *Chinsetsu yumiharizuki* (The Crescent Moon; 1811), he alleged that Xu Fu introduced Chinese agriculture, textiles, salt-making, fishing, and cuisine to the Kii region.[27]

To a certain extent, the Kumano theory gained semiofficial recognition. In 1629, Empress Meishō (1624–96) prayed for rain at the Xu Fu Shrine. In 1692, Emperor Higashiyama (1675–1710) worshipped at the Xu Fu Shrine. The Kii domain (now Wakayama prefecture and southern Mie prefecture) patronized the Kumano theory. Tokugawa Yorinobu (1602–71), the founding *daimyō* of the Kii domain, built a tomb for Xu Fu in Shingū and asked the Korean Confucian scholar Yi Maegye (1617–82) to write "The Tomb of Qin Xu Fu" in clerical script. In 1635, Yorinobu presented three paintings entitled *Xu Fu Arriving in Kumano* to the Hayatama Grand Shrine. In 1834, the Kii domain erected a Xu Fu memorial at the Nachi Grand Shrine in Kumano.

The Atsuta Shrine theory, compared with the Fuji and Kumano theories, was less influential in the Tokugawa period. It was mentioned in Tokugawa travel writings, such as Hayashi Razan's *Hinotatsu kikō* and Tokugan Yōson's (1632–1703) *Tōyū kikō* (Draft of My Visit to Eastern Provinces), as well as local records such as Naitō Tōho's (1728–88) *Chōshū zasshi* (Miscellaneous Records of Owari) and Amano Sadakage's (1663–1733) *Owari fudoki* (Topography of Owari). Having visited Atsuta Shrine in 1679, Yōson remarked: "I visited Atsuta Shrine in the morning. It is said that Xu Fu looked for an elixir on the three heavenly mountains in the sea. This referred to Atsuta Shrine in Bishū in Japan."[28] Tōho quoted extensively from Japanese and Chinese sources to allege that Xu Fu arrived and lived in Kumano for several years before moving to Owari. For instance, he quoted the following sentences from the *Owari fudoki*: "In front of [Atsuta] Shrine is a forest of pines. It is named Mount Penglai. Was this the same Penglai where the Qin Chinese Xu Fu landed?"[29]

A large number of other theories emerged in the Tokugawa period. More than twenty places claimed to have legacies of Xu Fu, covering the entire nation except for Hokkaido, including Tokyo, Yamaguchi, Hiroshima, Kyoto, Mie, Shizuoka, Akita, Nakano, Yamanashi, Wakayama, and Aomori on Honshū, Saga, Fukuoka, Kagoshima, Ōita, and Miyazaki on Kyūshū, and Kōchi on Shikoku.[30] Here, we will examine two of these cases—Saga and Satsuma (now mostly the western half of Kagoshima prefecture)—to see the formation of the Xu Fu legend in those regions.

In Saga, Mount Hōrai and Hōrai Island were found and many regional sources mention Xu Fu there. The Kinryū Shrine had a painting called *Jofuku Kinryū engi-zu* (The Picture of Xu Fu and the Origin of Kinryū), which described the landing of Xu Fu in Kinryū. It is said that the painting was presented to the Shrine in 1648.[31] According to the *Kinryū jinja ezu engi* (Illustrative Explanation of the Origin of the Kinryū Shrine), Xu Fu was the third son of the First Emperor of the Qin. Having reached the coast of Kyūshū, he looked for a place to land. He put a cup in the water and the current took the cup to Teraitsu in Morodomi-chō, Saga. He followed the cup and landed there. His landing place later became the Kinryū Shrine, and Xu Fu was worshipped as Kinryū Daigongen, or the Great Avatar of Kinryū, a deity of agriculture who could bring rainfall. People in Saga praised Xu Fu for introducing Chinese agriculture, textiles, and medicine to their region, and held a festival for him once every fifty years.[32] The Nikita Shrine in Morodomi-chō worshipped Jofuku Daigongen. Inside the Shrine, there was an old white sandalwood tree allegedly planted by Xu Fu more than two thousand years ago.

Ōki Souemon, in his *Hizen koseki engi* (The Origins of the Legacies of Hizen; 1665), retold the story of how Xu Fu and his seven hundred followers landed in Morodomi-chō. In the Tokugawa period, other legacies of Xu Fu in Saga also became regional attractions, including the Xu Fu Well, a memorial of Xu Fu's landing, the tomb of Xu Fu's Japanese lover, Otatsu, and a Xu Fu hot spring. Their origins are difficult to date.

In Satsuma, people identified four places where Xu Fu had left behind his legacy, and some local sources also supported this theory. For example, according to the *Chōhō-in monjo* (Documents of the Chōhō-in) kept at Chingoku-ji temple on Mount Kanmuri-dake, Xu Fu landed at Kushikino in the west coast of Kagoshima during the reign of Emperor Kōrei. Having stayed for some time, Xu moved to Kumano.[33] It is said that Xu Fu climbed a mountain and took off his official hat when he reached the top. This mountain was thus named Mount Kanmuri-dake (literally, "hat-off mountain").[34] Some local people in Satsuma believed that Xu Fu introduced Chinese herbal medicine to Japan. Many geographical names in the region, such as Hatamura, Hata Sakatome, Hata Yashiki, Tōsen-zuka, Kanmuri-dake, and Ichiki, are all associated with Xu Fu.

In the Tokugawa period, the Xu Fu legend was enthusiastically supported throughout Japan. In some domains, the *daimyō* and regional officials sponsored Xu Fu worship. The Xu Fu legend was used as evidence to bolster the importance of their regions in cultural exchange and to strengthen local economies by promoting tourism. However, the chief supporters of the Xu Fu legend were Shintoists, Buddhists, and local villagers. With the rise in popularity of Chinese culture, many Tokugawa Japanese ardently sought out all things Chinese, including books, paintings, calligraphy works, and poems. The Xu Fu boom was thus a byproduct of the rise of Chinese learning. Less noted, but equally significant, the Xu Fu discourse was fused with Shinto and other Japanese folk traditions, showing a high level of localization in the adaptation of Chinese culture in Tokugawa Japan.

XU FU AS TRANSMITTER OF CHINESE CULTURE

Three differing accounts of Xu Fu are found in Tokugawa writings—Xu Fu as a transmitter of Chinese culture to Japan, Xu Fu as a refugee to Japan, and Xu Fu as "the Other." To a certain extent, these accounts represent different views of Sino-Japanese cultural relationships and attempts to address the psycho-logical conflict generated by Chinese culture among Tokugawa intellectuals.

The first account regarded Xu Fu as a transmitter of Chinese culture to Japan, praising him for cultivating the Japanese and preserving long-lost ancient Chinese culture.[35] Of the three accounts, this one was the most widely accepted, and was particularly influential among Tokugawa Confucians and scholars whose domains had Xu Fu legacies. Xu Fu became a cultural diplomat and a bridge for Sino-Japanese cultural exchange.

Hayashi Razan, a Zhu Xi scholar serving the Edo *bakufu*, was a supporter of the theory that Xu Fu was a transmitter of Chinese culture. The *Honchō tsugan* (The Comprehensive Mirror of Japan; 1670), the official Tokugawa history complied by Razan and his son, Hayashi Gahō (1618–80), clearly records the arrival of Xu Fu in its narrative of the reign of Emperor Kōrei (reigned 290–215 BCE):

> In the thirty-sixth year, the Qin Chinese Xu Fu came with one thousand boys and girls and books of the early kings. Having failed to find the elixir, he stayed and never returned. It is said that he settled down on Mount Fuji. Moreover, there is a Xu Fu shrine on Mount Kumano. His descendants in Japan were named Hata.[36]

The legend of Xu Fu in Japan became the official historical narrative. Razan believed that Xu brought many ancient texts to Japan, but those texts were not extant in Tokugawa Japan. He wrote in a regretful tone:

> Xu Fu came to Japan about six or seven years before the burning of books and the burying alive of Confucians [by the First Emperor of the Qin]. During that time [in Japan], few people could understand the greater seal script and the lesser seal script written down on lacquered or bamboo plates [that Xu Fu brought to Japan]. Due to incessant warfare in later generations, most of these [ancient texts] were lost. I have not heard that they remain intact. How sad it is.[37]

Razan's idea of Xu Fu as a cultural transmitter was not new, and he basically only added a footnote to the Song scholar Ouyang Xiu's (1007–72) famous poem "Ribendao ge" (Song of the Japanese Sword), in which he maintained that Xu Fu and his group brought ancient Chinese classics, skills, and tech-nologies to Japan, that their descendants had become the Hata, and that hundreds of ancient classics remained intact.[38] Razan cited various sources to argue that the three major Japanese versions of the Xu Fu legend had been introduced to China:

> Mount Fuji of my nation is well known overseas. The *Shishi liutie* reads: "The highest mountain in the Kingdom of Japan is Fuji, also known as Penglai. In the era of Qin, Xu Fu went there." In addition, Song Lian's [1310–81] "Ridungqu" [Poems about Japan] also has verses about Mount Fuji. When our monk, Zekkai Chūshin, went to the Great Ming, Taizu of the Ming asked him about Xu Fu. Chūshin then composed a poem to introduce the Xu Fu Shrine in Kumano. The Nanzen-ji monk Ishō said: "There are three places that can be called Penglai: Fuji, Kumano, and Atsuta in Bishū."[39]

Razan is a good example of a Tokugawa Sinophile who had high respect for ancient Chinese culture. He himself even felt favorably disposed toward the theory that the Japanese imperial family originated in China.[40] Although Razan and Gahō believed that the Shang prince Wu Taibo was an ancestor of the Japanese imperial family, they did not also include Xu Fu. This was because Xu Fu, unlike Taibo, was neither a sage nor a prince, and associating the Imperial House with a Chinese low-ranking official would not serve to glorify Japan. To Razan, Xu Fu's historical role was that of a cultural transmitter. Razan's belief in the Xu Fu legend in Japan achieved two purposes: while recognizing the supremacy of Chinese culture in East Asia, Razan was also able to secure for Japan a respectable place in this Chinese cultural order. In other words, Japan had played a crucial role in preserving and inheriting ancient Chinese culture that had been lost in China. In this way, Razan demonstrates how Tokugawa Confucians attempted to pursue Chinese learning without compromising their national identity.[41]

Kumazawa Banzan (1619–91), a Wang Yangming scholar, also gave his support to the legend. He believed that Xu Fu went to Mount Fuji and brought Chinese classics, morality, and various systems to Japan:

> [Xu Fu] escaped from the tyranny of Qin and led several thousand boys and girls to leave China. He saw Mount Fuji and thought that it was Mount Penglai. He came to Japan because he had heard from the Koreans that Japan was a land of benevolence.... He introduced

Confucian morality, public manners, and various systems. Xu Fu found refuge in Japan and settled down here with thousands of followers. Although some Chinese classics disappeared in China, they survived in the foreign land [Japan].[42]

To Banzan, Xu Fu preserved Chinese culture overseas and enriched Japanese culture at the same time. He also praised Japan as a land of benevolence where Chinese and Koreans came to seek peace. This logic was problematic. If Japan was a land of benevolence, why did it need Xu Fu to introduce Confucian ethics? This dilemma can be understood in terms of his attempt to solve an identity crisis when embracing imported Chinese culture.

Arai Hakuseki (1657–1725), a Confucian scholar and *bakufu* statesman, believed in the Kumano theory. He stressed the importance of Xu Fu as a preserver of pre-Qin Chinese texts.[43] His approach was historical and cultural. In the *Dōbun tsūkō*, Hakuseki wrote:

> Now, there is a place near Kumano called Tadasuto, and the Chinese characters are Hadasu [秦住]. Its natives believe that it is the site where Xu Fu resided. Seven or eight miles away, there is a Xu Fu shrine. There are ancient tombs inside the shrine, and it is believed that they are the tombs of Xu Fu's retainers. Since all of these ancient legacies have survived and many families share the name Hata, there should be no doubt that Qin Chinese came [to Kumano].[44]

In addition to the Xu Fu shrine that was mentioned in medieval literature, Hakuseki introduced the legend about the tombs of Xu Fu's retainers and the Hata in Kumano. The idea that Xu Fu had seven loyal retainers who followed their master from China to Japan and were buried next to their master sounds more Tokugawa in tone than ancient Chinese, as it added samurai ethical dimensions to the Xu Fu discourse.

Like Razan, Hakuseki believed that Xu Fu brought pre-Qin texts to Japan. Unlike Razan, however, he maintained that some of these ancient Chinese texts remained intact in the Tokugawa period. One particular episode is especially worthy of note. In 1711, a Korean envoy asked Hakuseki about the legend of Xu Fu in Japan. Hakuseki told him about the sites in Kumano and the lost ancient Chinese texts, including the *Guwen Shangshu* (*The Book of Documents* in old-script texts) preserved at Atsuta Shrine and Izumo-taisha

Grand Shrine (in Izumo Province), that were brought by Xu Fu. However, he turned down the Korean's request to read these texts on the grounds that no sacred texts were supposed to be read or copied in Japan.[45] This was indeed a skillful reply. According to some Tokugawa sources, these ancient texts were destroyed by fire in the early Tokugawa period. It is unclear whether or not he was actually able to ascertain the existence of these texts in the shrines. The early Tokugawa was an age of textual forgery and these Chinese texts, if they ever existed, were most likely forgeries. Hakuseki was nonetheless very skillful in using this issue to emphasis Japan's contribution to preserving Chinese cultural traditions.

In recognizing the cultural role of Chinese immigrants but denying their link with the Japanese imperial family, Hakuseki's position was close to that of the Mito School. In the *Dai Nihonshi* (History of Great Japan) compiled by the Mito domain, Xu Fu is mentioned in the narrative of Emperor Kōrei as follows:

> In the seventieth year of the reign of the Emperor Kōrei, the Qin Chinese Xu Fu came to look for elixir. On behalf of the First Emperor of Qin, he presented the books of three sovereigns and five emperors to the emperor of Japan.[46]

In the late Tokugawa period, after a visit to Kumano in 1797, the physician Tachibana Nankei wrote about the Xu Fu legend in his *Saiyūki zokuhen*:

> Together with five hundred pairs of boys and girls, the seeds of five crops, and agricultural tools, Xu Fu escaped from China and came to Japan by boat. Having reached the coast of Kumano, Xu Fu landed and settled down. He engaged in agriculture and educated the boys and girls. His descendants also became the leaders of Kumano and they enjoyed a life of stability and prosperity.[47]

Nankei went on at length to introduce the Xu Fu Shrine in Shingū, stating that there were pre-Qin ancient Chinese texts kept in the Shrine. He even attempted to retrace the footsteps of Xu Fu in Kumano:

> I have heard that even now Shingū and Hongū in Kumano are called Mount Penglai [Hōrai]. Their treasures are pre-Qin texts. The Tomb of Xu Fu is located in Hamate in Shingū. It has five or six old trees and a stele with the characters "The Tomb of Qin Xu Fu" on it. The place

where he [Xu Fu] landed was Natasu Village which is about six or seven miles east of Shingū. According to tradition, Xu Fu landed in Yaga, a rocky beach in Natasu Village on the thirteenth day of December. He stayed there for a while before moving to Hongū, Shingū, and Nachi [in Kumano].[48]

Nankei did not realize that he had created a new Xu Fu legacy in Kumano. This account helps us understand the making of the Xu Fu legend in Tokugawa Japan. The story was that, when Nankei visited Natasu Village, he wrote a five-character quatrain on a large stone:

> The immortal Xu left with fear.
> Penetrating the clouds of Qin,
> He enjoyed a comfortable life in a borrowed space.
> Who can compare with him in history?

This poem was soon washed away by rain. The villagers asked a mason to carve it in stone. This carved stone became the Xu Fu Lettered Stone, a newly added legacy to reinforce the Xu Fu legend in Kumano. Nankei retold this story:

> Having reached the land with Xu Fu's legacy, I composed a five-character quatrain about Xu Fu. I wielded the brush on a stone and left. As time went by, rain and dew washed away my handwriting. Some local people felt sorry for this and thus they asked a mason to carve it. My poor poem, composed in a hurry, can survive for a thousand years. I feel a bit embarrassed, but also delighted because the world treasures it.[49]

Nankei's travel companion, Momoi Tōu (?–1794), also reinforced the Xu Fu legend in his *Kyūai zuihitsu* (Miscellaneous Writings on Trifles) after his visit to Kumano. Like Nankei, Tōu also stressed the cultural contributions of Xu Fu. He visited the Xu Fu Shrine, the Xu Fu Tomb, and Natasu Village.[50] His most interesting argument was that he saw "Xu Fu paper" in two villages in Kumano. Tōu told his story as follows:

> In the year of Hinoetatsu, a monk of Enshin-ji temple in Tenma of Katsuura in Nachi, Kumano, which is in Kishū Province, presented locally made paper to the owner of Goshōan-in Okazaki. This paper

was different from papers like *hōsho* and *sugiharagami* [both are traditional Japanese handmade papers made from mulberry wood fibers]. It
does not look like *kunigara*, *mino*, or *iwakuni* [all are Japanese papers]
either. It looks different and it is not the kind of paper that we often
see. I asked how much it was and the monk replied: "This paper is not
for sale. It is only used by the villagers. In the ancient past, Xu Fu came
to Japan and settled down in Kumano. He taught the natives to make
paper. Even now, there are two villages in this area that have kept this
tradition. They call it Xu Fu paper. Although it is like Tang paper,
when you tear it apart, it always breaks horizontally." This is evidence
that the legend of Xu Fu is real.[51]

The Xu Fu paper was also called Nachi paper or *otonashikami* (no-sound
paper). Its production method and texture were different from ordinary *washi*
(Japanese paper), and it was probably brought to Japan by Chinese immigrants. The Chinese did not invent paper until the Later Han period, and
thus attributing the introduction of paper to Xu Fu was largely based on historical imagination.

Satō Shigehiro (1762–1848), a late Tokugawa herbal and agricultural
scholar, conducted investigations of agricultural plants in different regions.
Having seen the Xu Fu paddy field and listened to the Xu Fu song in Kumano,
he recognized the contribution of Chinese immigrants. He left a very detailed
observation record of his trip to Kumano. For instance, he wrote about
Shingū as follows:

In the surrounding area of Shingū in Kumano, there is a mountain
called Mount Hōrai. At the south of the mountain, there are several
old camphor trees in a field. It is said that the Xu Fu Tomb is 5 to
7 *ken* [in the Tokugawa period, one *ken* was about 6 *shaku*, or 1.8
meters] under the tree. A monument was built in our era, which is
eight or nine *shaku* tall and has characters reading "The grave of the
Qin Chinese Xu Fu" on it. When people from nearby and far away
come to worship at the tomb, cases of malaria will go away. The
surface of the monument is rough, and the field around the tomb on
four sides is called the paddy field of Xu Fu. On a certain day every
April, the villagers gather to sow seeds and hum the tune of the Xu

Fu song. One night, I listened to the singing of this song and found out that it matches Chinese musical theory, and its sounds are all ancient Chinese sounds. It seems that if Xu Fu himself did not come to ancient Japan, many drifters did arrive.[52]

The late Tokugawa *kangaku* (Chinese learning) scholar and historian Iwagaki Matsunae (1774–1849), in his *Kokushi ryaku* (Brief History of Japan; 1827), also described the arrival of Xu Fu to Japan as history rather than legend. This history introduces Xu Fu in the chronicles of Emperor Kōrei:

> In the seventy-second year, the Qin Chinese Xu Fu arrived. Xu Fu came with a thousand boys and girls as well as the books of three sovereigns and five emperors. Fu did not acquire the medicine and thus did not return. It is said that he settled down on Mount Fuji or in Kumano, where the Xu Fu Shrine was built.[53]

As time went by, people created more stories about Xu Fu. This explains why the Kumano theory became increasingly complicated. Compared with early Tokugawa scholars, such as Razan and Hakuseki, mid- and late Tokugawa scholars like Nankei, Tōu, and Shigehiro were more detailed and concrete in portraying Xu Fu as a transmitter of Chinese culture who enriched the cultural and material life of the villagers in the Kumano region.

XU FU AS POLITICAL REFUGEE

The second account portrayed Xu Fu as a political refugee who found his ideal nation in Japan. The advocates of this view did not believe in or mention the role of Xu Fu in transmitting Chinese culture to Japan. Thus, the Xu Fu legend was used to favor Japan over China. Advocated by scholars under the influence of *kokugaku*, this nativist idea attempted to situate the Xu Fu legend within the Japanese tradition.

Matsushita Kenrin (1637–1703), a Confucian and a forerunner of *kokugaku*, had very interesting and original perceptions about Xu Fu in Kumano. His approach was completely different from that of Nankei or Shigehiro. In his *Ishō Nihonden* (Treatises on Japan under Foreign Titles; 1668), Kenrin attempted to place the Kumano theory within a Shinto framework, stressing that Xu Fu came to Japan due to his admiration of the country, and that he became a Shinto deity after his death. Kenrin wrote:

> I want to add that I, Kenrin, also see Japan as a divine nation. Xu Fu was a god of the Japan Sea and could predict the direction of the wind in Japan. . . . It is said that there is a Xu Fu tomb in Asuka under Mount Kumano in Kii Province, and a Xu Fu shrine in Mount Hōrai in Southeast Shingū of Kumano. The Xu Fu Shrine is also called the Mount Hōrai Shrine. This shrine is dedicated to Kumano Daigongen. Kumano Daigongen is a Shinto deity clearly stated in our official histories. Xu Fu saw the national glory of Japan and came to settle down here. He escaped from the Qin, the land of tigers and leopards, and died in Japan as a deity. He lived among the three mountains in Kumano and was not an ordinary man.[54]

Thus, the Xu Fu legend was used to glorify Japan. According to Kenrin, Xu Fu came to Japan because China was a land of tigers and leopards, whereas Japan was a divine nation. Xu Fu was remembered in Japan not as a transmitter of Chinese culture, but as a Shinto deity. He maintained:

> Ouyang Yongshu, in his "Ribendao ge," wrote: "When Xu Fu made his voyage, *The Book of Documents* had not been burned, so the complete one hundred sections must be preserved [in Japan]." Liu [Zhongda] quoted from the *Yuanshi mishu* [Secret Book of Origins; 1397]: "Knowledge in Japan started from Xu Fu." I think it is fine for us to admire Xu Fu's conduct, but I do not believe that Xu represents the beginning of knowledge.[55]

Kenrin downplayed Xu Fu's role as a transmitter of Chinese culture by pointing out that the Chinese writing system and classics came to Japan long before the arrival of Xu Fu, thus questioning Ouyang Xiu's belief that Xu Fu brought ancient Chinese texts to Japan.[56]

The concept of the Shintoization of Xu Fu can also be found in several mid-Tokugawa period writings, such as the *Wakan rengō* (The Unity of Japan and China). This nationalist approach gained more currency in the mid- to late Tokugawa period. For example, the *kokugaku* scholar Ono Takakiyo (1747–1817) emphasized that Xu Fu came to Japan to find peace and virtues.

Takakiyo categorically denied the conjecture that Xu Fu was somehow related to the Japanese imperial family. He maintained:

> In the reign of Emperor Kōrei, the seventh emperor of Japan, Xu Fu and his people escaped to Japan from the authoritarian Qin regime. They became the subjects of Japan and settled down in the countryside of Kumano. They admired the virtues of my nation and became our officials and people. When foreigners heard of this thing, they said, "[Wu] Taibo was the ancestor of Japan," or "Xu Fu was the ancestor of Japan." They lived in the ancient past. For people who have not examined history carefully, they suggested wrong ideas. Our imperial line started several thousand years before the times of Taibo and Xu Fu. Why did people say that our Japanese are the descendants of the Wu or Qin people? I understand why foreigners advocate this idea. However, Confucians of our nation who support this idea are indeed traitors of our divine nation and deities. They are unpardonable evil-doers! We must be cautious.[57]

In 1834, under the auspices of the Kishū domain, the Confucian Niida Nanyō (1772–1850) wrote an epigraph for the *Jofuku kenshōhi* (Xu Fu Memorial) in Kumano. Using Xu Fu to promote nationalism, Nanyō expressed his wish that Japan would become an ideal nation and that people from different cultures would follow in the footsteps of Xu Fu and find peace in Japan. The latter half of the epigraph reads:

> Alas! It is understandable that the scholar Xu Fu, in order to avoid being killed under the tyranny of Qin, pretended to be a Taoist priest. He advocated the idea of the three divine mountains as a means to seek refuge in a land of happiness. Didn't he know that there was a nation of gentlemen in the East? Confucius said: "[When the Way is not respected], I will take a small boat and let it float away to the sea." Xu really understood the thinking of Confucius. In the Warring States period, Lu Zhonglian spoke with a defiant tone: "If the Qin empire unifies the nation, Lian will jump to death in the Eastern Sea. I will not become its subject." The world respected his morality and appreciated his remark. However, he only said this. He cannot compare with Xu Fu, who actually did it. Although there were billions of people in the Qin,

no one could compare to Xu Fu in terms of morality and good behavior. I am sad that people of later generations do not know the whole story and see him merely as a Taoist priest, criticizing him for being ridiculous. Alas! How foolish they are! In the first year of Genbun [1736], the lord of Shingū Castle, Mizuno Tadaaki [1700–1749] asked me to build a memorial stone for the tomb [of Xu Fu]. It had no epigraph on it. In the year of Kinoe-uma, Yoshifuru [Niida Nanyō] was ordered to visit Kumano. I searched for stories [about Xu Fu]. There were so many legacies there and the picture became clear. Hence, I wrote the epigraph. Alas! In the whole wide world, thousands of nations are now at odds with each other. Ten thousand years later, when people look for Hōrai [heaven on earth], they should come here [Japan]. This is the reason why I wrote the epigraph for this memorial.[58]

In this epigraph, the contributions of Xu Fu in Japan were not mentioned at all. Xu Fu was important only because he set the precedent for non-Japanese to seek refuge in Japan, the land of gentlemen and happiness. Nanyō was confident that Japan would continue to be a haven for peace lovers from all over the world for generations to come.

Saitō Setsudō (1797–1865), a late Tokugawa Confucian, composed a Chinese poem to praise Xu Fu for making the right decision to find refuge in Japan. Like Nanyō, he used Xu Fu to glorify Japan as the land of gentlemen and the Penglai fairyland. The poem reads:

> It is glorious that the immortal left the legacies.
> Remember in the ancient past, he sailed across the ocean to Japan.
> From ten thousand miles away, he found refuge in the land of gentlemen.
> He was willing to become a sage-immigrant.
> Ganoderma and herbal medicine are not particular.
> Penglai Island and Utopia (the Garden of the Peaches) are not unique.
> Escaping from the tyranny of the Qin, you [Xu Fu] went a step further.
> The bird that can choose the tree to perch on is a clever one.[59]

In brief, the view that Xu Fu was merely a refugee gained larger momentum in the mid-to late Tokugawa period, following the rise of nativist consciousness. This attitude represents a powerful and original sub-current. Many of its ideas had never been heard of in China or Japan prior to the

Tokugawa period, serving as examples of the appropriation of Chinese culture to pursue a nativist agenda.

XU FU AS "THE OTHER"

The third account was skeptical of the Xu Fu legend and disapproved of people using Xu Fu for their own intellectual agendas. Xu Fu was negatively viewed as "the Other." Advocates of the Xu Fu legend were criticized as being unfaithful to their own Japanese identity.

In the Tokugawa period, people from different regions found "evidence" to support the legend of Xu Fu in Japan. This practice came under fire by some intellectuals. Kaibara Ekken (1630–1714), a Confucian and physician, was one such critic. For instance, he did not believe in the *Dōnan kanryo iwa* (Stone of Boys and Girls) in Chikugo Province (now the southern part of Fukuoka Prefecture), which was allegedly the landing place of Xu Fu:

> The villagers called it the *Dōnan kanryo iwa*. Now, even old men in the village do not know about this thing. The "boys and girls" refer to the boys and girls who were carried to Penglai by boat with Xu Fu. A so-called *Dōnan kanryo iwa* can be found on the beach in Tango, Kawasaki, in Kamitsuma of Chikugo. It was made by later generations to forge evidence. People merely added the name to the stone.[60]

Amano Sadakage (1661–1733) accepted the assertion that Xu Fu went to Atsuta in Owari, but did not give him credit for introducing the writing system to Japan. He remarked:

> The *Liushi hongshu* [Collection of Sources by Liu; 1611, by Liu Zhongda] attributed the knowledge in Korea to Jizi and the knowledge in Japan to Xu Fu. I think the writing system in my nation started before Emperor Jimmu. How can we believe in the record about the year of Kinoene? Regarding the beginning of the writing system, how can we believe that it started in the reign of Emperor Kōrei?[61]

Yamagata Bantō (1748–1821), a merchant-scholar from Osaka, did not believe in any version of the Xu Fu legend in Japan. To him, Xu Fu was only a religious cheater who left China without a trace, and all legends about him were unfounded. He held:

The theories about Xu Fu in Japan or about Yi Zhou and Chan Zhou [two islands in the Eastern Sea mentioned in the *Sanguozhi*] are all speculations. There is no evidence to support the claim that Xu Fu brought the writing system to Japan. Xu Fu cheated the First Emperor of the Qin, taking his treasures as well as boys and girls away. He left without a trace. All theories about his landing are speculations. Instead of denying them, [some of us] have followed these far-fetched ideas from books and evil monks. I do not believe them at all.[62]

Bantō criticized Japanese Confucians who blindly believed in Chinese books, adding that the writers of those books were misled by Japanese monks who spread false information during their sojourns in China.

The books that have taken the words of Japanese monks as truth are wrong. Even our countrymen make mistakes, not to mention foreigners. Our Confucians, having read unreasonable records of my country in Chinese books, gladly cited them.[63]

Likewise, Yamazaki Yoshishige (1797–1856), a *zuihitsu* writer, did not believe in the Xu Fu legend in Kumano. In the *Kairoku* (Records of the Seas), he argued that, although there was a Xu Fu shrine in Kumano, it was not supported by official histories. He pointed out that the *Tensho* (Book of Heaven) that supports this theory was a forgery.[64]

Hirata Atsutane (1776–1843), the founder of the Hirata school of *kokugaku*, regarded Xu Fu as an unwelcome figure to the Japanese. He maintained that the big fish that tried to stop him from going to Japan was an envoy sent by the Shinto deity Ōwatatsumi-no-Kami, which was a dragon and water god.

The god of the sea is Ōwatatsumi-no-Kami. His envoy was manifested in the form of a dragon. The envoy, the god of sea monsters, looked like a dragon. This was the great shark mentioned in the *Shihuang benji* [The Biography of Qin Shi Huang from the *Shiji*.[65]

He added that Xu Fu did not arrive on Mount Fuji, but only made it to Kumano. He did not bring Chinese classics with him and died in Kumano without making any contributions.[66]

Senke Takazumi (1816–78), a *kokugaku* scholar and Shinto priest, criticized the legend of Xu Fu in Kumano for being too far-fetched. He believed in neither the preservation of pre-Qin texts nor the arrival of Xu Fu in Kumano:

> There was so much hearsay that even the Koreans heard about it. Xu Fu is a topic without substance. The hearsay about Xu Fu finding refuge on an island to escape from the chaos of the Qin and that he went to Kumano of our imperial dynasty is far-fetched.[67]

The most powerful arguments were provided by Ise Sadatake (also Ansai, 1715–84), a historian and *bakufu* retainer who identified many forgeries and discredited superstitious ideas. In the *Ansai zuihitsu* (Miscellaneous Writings of Ise Ansai), Sadatake discredited the belief that Xu Fu came to Japan, condemning his countrymen who used Xu Fu to belittle Japan:

> Someone wrote: "The Qin official Xu Fu went to Japan. The *Shang shu* remained intact." This was recorded in the foreign nation [China], but not in our official historical records, and therefore we should not believe it. Recently, Confucians of our country have evinced respect for that foreign nation, referring to it as the Central Kingdom and belittling Japan as a barbaric nation. They are disloyal people who look down upon Japanese traditions, believing that stories about Wu Taibo and Xu Fu are historically true.[68]

Sadatake did not believe in the Kumano theory and denied Xu Fu's role as a transmitter of Chinese culture. He maintained:

> Ouyang Xiu's "Ribendao ge" reads: "When Xu Fu left for Japan, it was before the burning of books. Even now, hundreds of Chinese classics remain intact in Japan." In order to create evidence to support this conjuncture, they [Tokugawa Japanese] worship Xu Fu as a god who came to Kumano. We should not believe in this kind of folklore.[69]

Obviously, the denial of the Xu Fu legend was not merely an academic conclusion; Sadatake's arguments had an explicit nationalist tone. He did not believe in the Xu Fu legend because it was not written down in Japanese official records, and he even condemned advocates of the Xu Fu legend as disloyal to Japan. Hence, intellectually, this attitude was closer to the second account of Xu Fu as a political refugee. Though discussing Xu Fu from opposite directions, they shared the political and intellectual goal of emphasizing Japan's cultural excellence and uniqueness while downplaying Chinese influence on the country.

SIGNIFICANCE OF THE XU FU LEGEND

Xu Fu was perceived as a Chinese migrant in the eyes of Tokugawa Japanese. Some saw him as a "skilled migrant" who brought advanced civilization to ancient Japan, whereas others regarded him merely as a political refugee who found peace and prosperity in Japan. These two views sound conflicting, but share a common nativist tone.

The mainstream view saw Xu Fu as a cultural transmitter. It seems that most Tokugawa intellectuals respected Chinese culture and praised Xu Fu's role in transmitting and preserving it. However, they never forgot their Japanese identity. They put emphasis on Japan as a place to preserve the culture and classics of the Chinese sages. No one went so far as to suggest that Xu Fu was the ancestor of the Japanese imperial family, as it would have created political and intellectual problems due to undermining of the Japanese identity.[70] An influential alternative view regarded Xu Fu as merely a political refugee to find his second life in the ideal nation. Although he did not make contributions to enrich Japanese culture, he set the precedent for peace lovers to find refuge in Japan. Hence, the Xu Fu legend was used to glorify Japan. Nativist ideas existed in various forms—some even attempted to transform Xu Fu into a Shinto deity or challenged the credibility of the Xu Fu legend and the China worship that it represented. Xu Fu became an intellectual battleground for Tokugawa scholars from different backgrounds and a metaphor used by Tokugawa scholars to define Sino-Japanese relations.

The Xu Fu legend was significant in Sino-Japanese intellectual and cultural exchange and Tokugawa intellectual history. Knowledge of it deepens our understanding of such Tokugawa intellectual developments as the changing attitudes toward China and its culture and the rise of national consciousness. Our inquiry indicates that many Tokugawa scholars were disturbed by their conflicting identities as Confucians and Japanese. Chinese learning did not always fit into the Tokugawa system. A common concern shared by Tokugawa scholars was the question of how to integrate Chinese learning without compromising national identity.[71] These three different accounts of Xu Fu, in a sense, represent responses to overcome this dilemma. Xu Fu thus served as a building block to foster national identity.

YANG GUIFEI AS SHINTO DEITY

Zhongguo ?
妃?

In the last chapter, it was explained how Xu Fu was a building block. Xu was not an exception. Many other Chinese historical figures served the same function. In Tokugawa Japan, legends about prominent Chinese historical figures, such as Xu Fu, Wu Taibo, and Yang Guifei (719–56), finding refuge in Japan became popular. Many Japanese believed that these Chinese individuals moved to Japan and played an important role in Japanese history. Texts about and relics of these Chinese legends were found in many different parts of Japan. Formulated in particular historical settings with different ideologies lying behind them, these legends have important implications for understanding the adaptation and localization of Chinese culture in Japan and the formation of Japanese identity through the practice of consuming and domesticating Chinese culture. Based on textual analysis of late medieval and Tokugawa texts, this chapter examines the formation and cultural adaptation of the Yang Guifei legend in Japan, and aims to discuss its historical significance in Tokugawa intellectual history and Sino-Japanese cultural relations.

The Japanese had distinctive ways of imagining Yang Guifei. Among the many different versions of the Yang Guifei legend created in Japan, I am particularly interested in the Shinto interpretation that transformed her from a great Chinese beauty into a Shinto deity associated with the Atsuta jingū (Atsuta Shrine). By tracing the origins and transformation of the Yang Guifei legend in Tokugawa Japan, this study demonstrates how Chinese ideas were indigenized to enhance Japan's nativist ideology and cultural identity.

THE LEGEND OF YANG GUIFEI IN TOKUGAWA JAPAN

The long narrative poem "Chang hen ge" (The Song of Everlasting Sorrow; 806) by the Tang poet Bai Juyi (772–846) became the main source of inspiration for Chinese and Japanese poets and scholars in developing the Yang Guifei legend.[1] The favorite concubine of Emperor Xuanzong of Tang (685–762, reigned 712–55), Yang Guifei was killed in the wake of the An Lushan Rebellion (703–57).[2] In the poem, a Taoist priest sent by Emperor Xuanzong finally finds Yang in the Penglai Palace, which was built on a divine mountain in the Eastern Sea.[3] The poem states:

> At last the monk heard that in the Isles of the Blessed there was a fairy mountain where numerous immortals dwelt in magnificent palaces on five-coloured clouds. The ex-nun Taizhen lived there, and her snow-white skin and flowery face made him think that she was the one the Emperor was searching for.[4]

Introduced to Japan by no later than the ninth century during the Heian period, the "Chang hen ge" had a very strong impact on Japanese literature, dramas, and art.[5] The poem was well received by emperors and courtiers at the court of Kyoto. For instance, Ōe Koretoki (888–963) quoted some lines from the "Chang hen ge" in his *Senzai kaku* (Splendid Verses of a Thousand Years; c. 950), and Fujiwara Kintō (966–1041) alluded to it in the *Wakan rōeishū* (Anthology of Japanese and Chinese Poems Intended to be Sung).[6]

More significantly, elements of the "Chang hen ge" were incorporated in Heian literature. Murasaki Shikibu (?–1016), in the opening chapter of the *Genji monogatari* (Tale of Genji), paraphrased the "Chang hen ge" and *Chang hen ge zhuan* (Tale of The Song of Everlasting Sorrow), and borrowed some lines and stories from the "Chang hen ge."[7] The tenth volume of the *Konjaku monogatari* (Collection of Tales from the Past) contains the romantic story of Yang Guifei and Emperor Xuanzong based on the "Chang hen ge."[8] In the medieval period, the legend of Yang Guifei dwelling in the Eastern Sea was developed through various artistic expressions including military tales and *nō* plays.[9]

In the Tokugawa period, the legend of Yang Guifei became popularized among the literate masses. Asai Ryōi (1612–91) used *kana* (syllabic Japanese script) to explain the "Chang hen ge" sentence by sentence in his *Yōkihi monogatari* (Tale of Yang Guifei). Yosa Buson (1716–83) cited the "Chang hen ge" in his *haiku*, and he also created a painted hanging scroll of Emperor Xuanzong's journey to Sichuan during the An Lushan Rebellion. Inō Hidenori (1806–77) turned the "Chang hen ge" into *waka* poetry in his *Chōgonka kudaiwaka* (The Song of Everlasting Sorrow in *waka* style).

The Yang Guifei legend also appeared periodically on the *jōruri* puppet theatre and *kabuki* stages over the course of the Tokugawa period, represented by Ki Kaion's (1663–1742) *jōruri* puppet play *Gensō kōtei hōrai tsuru* (Emperor Xuanzong and the Crane in Penglai) and Morishima Chūryō's (1754–1810?) *kabuki* play *Rizan hiyokuzuka* (The Combined Tomb on Mount Li; 1779). Chikamatsu Monzaemon's (1653–1724) *Kōkiden unoha no ubuya* (Cormorant Feather Delivery Room in the Ladies' Quarters at the Palace), a *jōruri* puppet play about Emperor Kazan (968–1008) sending the famous diviner Abe Seimei to search for his lover on a remote mountain, was likely inspired by the "Chang hen ge." The playwright also mentioned Yang Guifei and the "Chang hen ge" in his *jōruri* play *Futago sumidagawa* (Twins at the Sumida River; 1720).[10] As for music, the two *koto* (Japanese zither) masters Yamada Kengyō (1757–1817) and Mitsuzaki Kengyō (?–1853) composed the *Chōgonka kyoku* (Music for *The Song of Everlasting Sorrow*) and *Akikaze no kyoku* (Melody of Autumn Wind), respectively.

In the realm of painting, a sub-genre existed that was known as *Chōgonka zu* (paintings of *The Song of Everlasting Sorrow*). In particular, the Kanō school produced a number of scroll paintings, panel paintings, and illustrations themed on the "Chang hen ge." For example, Kanō Sansetsu's (1590–1651) painting *Chōgonka emaki* (Scroll Painting of *The Song of Everlasting Sorrow*) is considered a masterpiece of Tokugawa art.[11] The history of the "Chang hen ge" in *ukiyo-e* (Japanese woodblock prints) can be traced back to an illustration for the puppet play *Yōkihi monogatari* (Tale of Yang Guifei; 1663, artist unknown, also titled *Gensō kōtei* (Emperor Xuanzong). With the rise of the genre of *bijinga* (paintings of beautiful women), Yang Guifei was featured in the *ukiyo-e* of Okumura Masanobu (1686–1764) and Hosoda Eishi (1756–1829), and in *bunjinga* (literati paintings) by Takaku Aigai (1796–1843).[12]

Thanks to the popularity of the "Chang hen ge," the legend of Yang Guifei dwelling in the Eastern Sea became deeply rooted in Tokugawa thought and culture. More importantly, the Japanese also created unique interpretations of the Yang Guifei legend. There were two main threads of Japanese narratives about Yang, portraying her as a political refugee and a Japanese deity, respectively. The former expanded on an element already present in the Chinese versions, while the latter was an original Japanese creation.

YANG GUIFEI AS POLITICAL REFUGEE

The "Chang hen ge" likely inspired the conjecture that Yang Guifei found refuge in Japan, while some Japanese added details about the fate of Yang after her arrival in Japan.[13] According to this account, Yang was rescued by Abe Nakamaro (698?–770), a Japanese diplomat-student who had been sent to Tang China. On her way to Japan, her ship sank in a storm near the coast of Japan. She finally came ashore on a lifeboat, arriving at a small fishing village called Kuzu (now Yuya-chō, Nagato City, in Yamaguchi Prefecture) at the western end of Honshū.[14] Yang soon died after her arrival and was buried on a slope in Kuzu by the villagers.

Formulated in late medieval times, the Kuzu version of Yang's story gained more momentum in the Chūgoku region (the western region of Honshū, in which Kuzu was located) during the Tokugawa period. In 1766, Eigaku, the fifteenth rector of Nison-in (Temple of Two Buddhist Statues) in Kuzu, wrote two books, entitled *Nison-in yuraigaki* (Book on the Origins of Nison-in) and *Yōkihi den* (Tale of Yang Guifei), which were both based on regional oral traditions and folktales.[15] According to these two books, in 765, Yang landed in Kuzu, and the place where she came ashore was named Tōdoguchi (literally, "the opening through which the Tang [Chinese] come over"). Yang became very sick on the way to Japan and died shortly after her arrival. The villagers buried her on a slope (which later became the site of Nison-in) and built a tomb and a five-story pagoda in her honor. Yang's spirit, the books say, turned into a red bird that appeared in a dream to inform Emperor Xuanzong of her death. The Emperor sent the general Chen An to Japan to search for Yang's body so that a Buddhist ritual could be performed to release her soul from purgatory. Not knowing that Yang landed and died in Kuzu, Chen went to the Kinki area. Before returning to China, he deposited two Buddhist statues at Seiryō-ji in Kyoto. Later, Emperor Xuanzong heard that Yang's tomb was at Tensei-ji in Kuzu, and then requested Seiryō-ji to send the two statues to Tensei-ji. Seiryō-ji refused to return them, and thus created a potential diplomatic issue. The imperial court in Nara did not wish to offend the Tang, and thus asked Japanese carpenters to create two replicas. One authentic statue and one replica were sent to Tensei-ji. The building inside the temple that housed the two statues was named Nison-in. The *Nison-in yuraigaki* reads:

> In the sixth lunar month of the fifteenth year of Tianbao in the Tang era, Yang Guifei, the beloved concubine of Emperor Xuanzong, boarded a small boat, which drifted to our village in Tōdoguchi. She soon died. The villagers buried her inside this temple. In order to make Emperor Xuanzong stop looking for her, the spirit of Guifei went to China and appeared for several consecutive nights in the Emperor's dreams. The Emperor realized that Guifei was dead. Out of affection for her, Emperor Xuanzong sent his minister Chen An to Japan with two statues, namely, those of Amitābha Buddha and Shakyamuni Buddha, and a thirteen-story pagoda to release her soul from purgatory. Failing to find the place of her landing, Chen An deposited the two Buddhist statues at Seiryō-ji in Kyoto before returning to his country. Later, the Emperor knew that the place where Yang landed was Kuzu. As the two Buddhist statues were unique in Japan, Seiryō-ji did not want to return them. Famous carpenters made replicas of the Buddhist statues. Both Seiryō-ji and my temple acquired one old statue and one new statue. Later, the tomb of Yang Guifei and the monument for her maids were built.[16]

In the Tokugawa period, the legend of Yang Guifei's arrival in Kuzu was widespread in the Chōshū domain (now Yamaguchi Prefecture). It was largely an orally transmitted legend with little textual or historical support. Pre-Tokugawa texts do not mention Yang Guifei's arrival in Kuzu. The so-called tomb of Yang Guifei was built in the mid- or late Kamakura period and was not necessarily related to her. There were also skeptics of this legend. The fourteenth *daimyō* of Chōshū, Mōri Takachika (1819–71), questioned it in a book that he edited with the title: *Bōchō fūdo chūshinan* (Draft Report on the Geography of Chōshū; 1842):

> There was someone named Yagi [楊貴] in the imperial court. The tomb of someone with this surname was mistaken as Yang Guifei or Miss Yang Gui. People of later generations associated it with Yang Guifei and therefore a false legend was transmitted.[17]

The *wagaku* (Japanese studies) scholar Amano Sadakage (1663–1733) cast doubt on the authenticity of relics associated with Yang Guifei found in different parts of Japan. In a collection of *zuihitsu* entitled *Shiojiri* (1697–1733), he remarked:

> Most temples in my country own antiques. By claiming that they were once owned or given by a certain person, temples showed them to people and then received a lot of money. Therefore, they associated these items with Yang Guifei.[18]

In addition to Kuzu, many other places in Japan also created their own Yang Guifei legends. Hagi, a port not too far away from Kuzu, also claimed to be her landing place. A stone tomb associated with Yang Guifei was built at Chōju-ji in Ogimachi. A jade statue of Yang was also enshrined in the temple. The Seto Inland Sea and Kyūshū also had candidates for her landing place. Some studies suggest that Yang Guifei landed in a nameless place in the Seto Inland Sea and was later taken to Kyoto to greet Empress Kōken (718–70). Trusted by the Empress, she exercised political influence at the Kyoto court and assisted the Empress in suppressing a rebellion.[19]

Higo (now Kumamoto Prefecture) also had its own legend of Yang Guifei. Villagers of Shinwa in Amakusa believed that Yang landed in Higo and lived in a cave in Ryūtōzan, which was a hill in Shinwa. She lived peacefully with the villagers, and the Chinese medicine that she carried (*Yōkihitō*, or Yang Guifei broth) helped them overcome the plague.[20] One day, a dragon came and took her away, and she left a sachet behind in the cave. Alleged relics of Yang can also be found on the west coast, east coast, and central part of Honshū, including a jade curtain at Shōmyō-ji in Kanazawa, a Yang Guifei Kannon (*Guanyin*, the Bodhisattva of Mercy) statue in Sennyū-ji in Kyoto, Yang's bronze mirror in Hōun-ji in Chichibu, and her pillow at Kagetsurō in Nagasaki.

The image of Yang Guifei as a political refugee was also echoed in Tokugawa literature. The *Honchō suikoden* (Japanese Water Margin; 1773) by Takebe Ayatari (1719–74) suggests that Yang was rescued by Fujiwara Kiyokawa, a Japanese envoy to the Tang. Landing in Matsuura, a port in Nagasaki, they then moved to Chikushi (now Fukuoka Prefecture) in northern Kyūshū. At that time, Kyūshū was under the influence of the evil monk Dōkyō

(?–772). Fujiwara trained Yang to assassinate Asomaru, Dōkyō's subordinate in Kyūshū. He revealed his plan with the words:

> In Tang, her beauty captured the heart of Xuanzong. I wanted to use her as a concubine to approach Asomaru. I meant to proceed rapidly, but she did not understand Japanese. I made her learn the Japanese customs and language.[21]

The story ended tragically. After the failure of the assassination attempt, Asomaru killed Fujiwara and Yang fled to Atsuta in Owari.[22] In the novel, Yang is not presented as a charming and intelligent figure, but rather as a pitiful political refugee from China who became involved in Japan's internal politics.[23] The characters in this novel are projections of actual historical figures. For instance, Fujiwara Kiyokawa (706?–78) was a real Japanese envoy to the Tang Court, while Asomaru's namesake was Nakatomi Suge Asomaro, a senior official in Daizaifu in Northern Kyūshū.

YANG GUIFEI AS SHINTO DEITY

From medieval times onward, the Japanese began to creatively reinterpret the Yang Guifei legend through the lens of Shinto mythology. According to medieval texts, such as the late Kamakura Buddhist text *Keiran shūyōshū* (Collection of Leaves Gathered in Stormy Streams; 1313) and the *Soga monogatari* (Tale of the Soga), Japanese deities gathered to discuss how to stop Emperor Xuanzong from invading Japan. They decided to ask Atsuta Myōjin, the Shinto deity of the Atsuta Shrine who could transform into different human forms, to transform into Yang Guifei.[24] In the guise of Yang Guifei, Atsuta Myōjin was able to distract Emperor Xuanzong so that he then forgot his plans to invade Japan. After the demise of Yang at Mawei Station, the spirit of Atsuta Myōjin returned to Atsuta Shrine (also known as Hōrai Shima). Emperor Xuanzong sent a Taoist priest to look for Yang's soul in Japan and was shocked to realize that she was the incarnation of a Japanese deity.

This Shinto interpretation of the Yang Guifei legend in Japan was an original, captivating, yet far-fetched narrative. During the time of the reign of Emperor Xuanzong, China and Japan maintained a relatively peaceful relationship. The unpleasant memory of the Battle of Baekgang on the Korean

Peninsula in 663 was fading. There are no records showing that military confrontations ever occurred between China and Japan, or that there was a military plan to attack Japan during the times of Xuanzong. The Shinto interpretation of Yang Guifei was formulated in the thirteenth century, about five centuries after the death of Emperor Xuanzong and Yang Guifei, thus showing the rise of nativist sentiments after the Mongol invasions of Japan in 1274 and 1281.

The *Keiran shūyōshū*, was among the earliest sources to popularize the Shinto interpretation of the Yang Guifei legend. It contains the following dialogue:

> Question: How shall we introduce the Penglai Palace in our nation?

> Answer: Emperor Xuanzong of the Tang and Yang Guifei once came to the Penglai Palace together. The so-called Penglai Palace is the Atsuta Shrine of my nation. The rear courtyard of this Shrine has a five-story pagoda.... This pagoda is said to be the tomb of Yang Guifei.[25]

Aside from the five-story pagoda located in the northeastern part of the shrine, Atsuta Shrine had other relics with which to uphold its myth about Yang Guifei. A door in the back of the Kagura-den (Hall for Shinto Music and Dance) was named the Shunkōmon (Coming of Spring Gate), and was supposedly the door on which the Taoist priest knocked while searching for Yang Guifei on Mount Penglai. The Atsuta Shrine also contained ancient texts, such as the *Senden shūi* (Notes on the Biography of the Immortals) and *Gyōfūshū* (Wind Blowing Collection), which maintained that the personage of Yang Guifei was indeed a transformation of the deity Atsuta Myōjin.[26] For instance, the *Senden shūi* states that the Emperor did have plans to invade Japan:

> In the past, Emperor Xuanzong of the Tang ruled over more than four hundred provinces and planned to take over Japan. The deity of this Shrine, appearing to be Yang Guifei, disturbed and eventually spoiled Xuanzong's plan to invade Japan.[27]

The Shinto interpretation of Yang was elaborated in the *Soga monogatari*, a work finished in the same period as or slightly later than the *Keiran shūyōshū*. Its second volume, entitled *Gensō kōtei no koto* (Things about Emperor Xuanzong), cited both the "Chang hen ge" and *Chang hen ge zhuan*, and added new stories about Xuanzong and Yang Guifei as manifestations of Japanese deities.[28] After retelling the story about how the Taoist priest found Yang Guifei in the Penglai Palace and how she asked him to bring her hairpin to the emperor, it adds an interesting episode about the response of Emperor Xuanzong:

> The emperor said: "How true it is! The Taoist priest has made no mistakes." Riding in a flying carriage, the emperor arrived at Owari Province of my nation and transformed into Yatsurugi Myōjin [the God of the Eight Swords]. As Yang Guifei who was Atsuta Myōjin made Xuanzong come. The Penglai Palace refers to this place.[29]

It is interesting to note that Emperor Xuanzong was also regarded in the text as the manifestation of a Shinto deity. Inside the Atsuta Shrine complex, there was a small shrine called Kamichikama Shrine, which was allegedly dedicated to Emperor Xuanzong.[30] An old tomb in the shrine was also associated with Xuanzong.

The Shinto interpretation of Yang Guifei became more influential in the sixteenth century. More details were added in late medieval literature, religious texts, and commentaries. The Shinto text *Unshū hikawa kami-amagabuchi ki* (Records of Kami-Amagabuchi in Hikawa, Izumo Province; 1523, author unknown) traces the route of Yang Guifei from China to the Atsuta Shrine as follows:

> Emperor Xuanzong of the Tang, also known as Li [Longji], wanted to invade Japan with all of his might. Japanese deities, big and small, gathered to discuss this. They asked Atsuta Myōjin to live among the Yang family as Yang Guifei to disturb the heart of Xuanzong so that he would forget to invade Japan. Having disappeared after the Incident in Mawei, Guifei took a boat to reach Utsu Miho in the Chita District of Owari, and then returned to the Atsuta Shrine.[31]

The Sengoku-period *renga* (collaborative poetry) master Tani Sōboku (?–1545) associated the architecture of Atsuta Shrine and scenery of Owari with passages in the "Chang hen ge" and *Chang hen ge zhuan*:

> The Tang wanted to invade my nation. With the power of our deities, Guifei was born over there. The Taoist priest visited this Penglai fairyland. The so-called Dazhen Hall recorded in the *Chang hen ge*

zhuan is the Shunkōmon of this Shrine. It is beyond a doubt that the open sea has been a familiar view from the Shrine since the Age of the Gods.[32]

In his commentary on the "Chang hen ge," the court Confucian scholar Kiyohara Nobukata (1470–1550), introduced a similar story about Yang Guifei's connection with the Atsuta Shrine:

> One theory is that Penglai refers to Atsuta Shrine in Owari in Japan. Xuanzong planned to attack Japan. Atsuta Myōjin turned into a great beauty to seduce Xuanzong. The evidence is the Shunkōmon. It acquired its name because the Taoist priest knocked on the gate in spring.[33]

The Shinto interpretation of the Yang Guifei legend continued to be echoed in Tokugawa texts. For example, Izawa Banryō (1668–1730), a retainer of the Higo domain in Kyūshū, introduced the myth involving Atsuta Myōjin in his *Kōeki zokusetsuben* (A Refutation of Vulgar Legends for the Benefit of the Public; 1715):

> According to tradition, Emperor Xuanzong of the Tang sought to invade Japan. Atsuta Myōjin was reincarnated as Yang Guifei to disturb Xuanzong. She brought troubled times and made him forget his plan to invade Japan. . . . Yamato-Takeru-no-Mikoto put on the clothes of his aunt, Princess Yamato-hime, pretending to be a woman to kill Kawakami Takeru. He died in Nobono in Ise Province on his way back. He became Atsuta Myōjin, who later turned into Yang Guifei to seduce Xuanzong.[34]

Mizuno Sadanobu (?–1688), a retainer of the Owari domain, repeated a similar story in the *Biyō zakki* (Miscellaneous Records of Biyō; 1715).[35]

There were two interesting and somewhat opposite trends concerning the Shinto interpretation of the Yang Guifei legend that occurred in the Tokugawa period. On the one hand, scholars began to question the appropriateness of reinterpreting Yang Guifei as a Shinto deity. On the other hand, the legend of her as a Shinto deity gained greater currency in works by playwrights, novelists, and artists, as well as in the visual arts. In this period, we can thus see a marked discrepancy between scholarly and artistic attitudes toward this legend.

Skeptics were of various backgrounds, and included Confucians, *kokugaku* scholars, *daimyō*, and domain retainers. Hayashi Razan cast doubt on the relics in the Atsuta Shrine in his *Honchō jinjakō* (An Investigation of Shinto Shrines in Japan):

> There is a stone pagoda in the back of Atsuta Shrine. It is more than three *shaku* tall and has an ugly shape. Shinto priests identified it as the pagoda of Yang Guifei. Outside of the Shrine, there is a Xuanzong Shrine. It is said to be the tomb of Xuanzong, the third son [of the Li family].[36]

Razan himself did not count them as credible forms of evidence. The five-story stone pagoda was destroyed in 1686 when the fifth *shōgun* Tokugawa Tsunayoshi rebuilt the Atsuta Shrine. Even people from the Owari domain questioned the authenticity of the relics. Amano Sadakage, a retainer of the Owari domain and *kokugaku* scholar, described the destruction of the five-story pagoda in his *Shiojiri*, but he did not believe that it had anything to do with Yang Guifei:

> Regarding this tomb, there are many different theories. They are all ridiculous. Later generations associated it with Yang Guifei. . . . The Atsuta Myōjin belief goes as follows: "The Penglai Palace was Atsuta Shrine. Yang Guifei was Atsuta Myōjin. There was a five-story pagoda in the back of the Shrine. There were Sanskrit inscriptions on it. This pagoda was the tomb of Yang Guifei." This belief is utterly foolish.[37]

Even the ninth *daimyō* of the Owari domain, Tokugawa Munechika (1733–99), did not believe in the legend of Yang Guifei prevalent in his own domain. He remarked:

> According to old traditions, the Yang Guifei Stone was located on the northern side of the main hall of the Atsuta Shrine. It was a three-*shaku*-tall, five-story pagoda. Covered with moss, its inscriptions could not be read. In the era of Jōkyō [1684–88], when the Shrine was rebuilt, shrine priests decided to destroy it. Now we can see its debris beyond the bamboo fence and buried underground.[38]

While the Yang Guifei legend associated with the Atsuta Shrine showed signs of decline among scholars in the Tokugawa period, its impact on art and literature reached its peak in this period. The *jōruri* play *Kuwateki sengun* (The Battleship of the General Kuwateki; 1660, author unknown), contains interesting episodes based on the theory of *honji suijaku* (Japanese deities were manifestations of the Buddha or bodhisattva). In the play, after the An Lushan Rebellion, Bai Juyi informs Xuanzong that Yang Guifei is the incarnation of Atsuta Myōjin. During a sleepless night, the spirit of Yang Guifei appears in front of Xuanzong in the imperial palace in Changan. Having talked to her, Xuanzong sighs and says:

> Yang Guifei told me that she was originally the Great Sun Buddha Dainichi Nyorai [Mahāvairocana], and then was transformed into Atsuta Myōjin, protecting the imperial palace like a bow and arrow. She disappeared in the form of the Great Sun Buddha.[39]

The *jōruri* play *Yōkihi monogatari* (The Tale of Yang Guifei; 1663, author unknown) dramatized and popularized the Yang Guifei legend.[40] In the latter half of this play, the Taoist priest finds Yang Guifei on Mount Penglai, and demons appear to give him this warning:

> The demons asked: "Who are you? You should not stay in the divine territory any longer. Go away!" The Taoist priest did not understand, and asked why the place was a divine territory. A demon replied angrily: "This lady was once Yang Guifei, and she is now Atsuta Myōjin. This land is an island in Japan. You should never come here again!"[41]

This puppet play gives Bai Juyi, perhaps the most beloved Chinese poet in medieval and early modern Japan, a role in the story. In the end, the Taoist priest brings back Yang's hairpin to the emperor. The saddened emperor happens to meet Bai Juyi on a mountain. Xuanzong asks him why the nation had to go through this misfortune. Bai replies:

> Your Majesty, you are the cause of this misfortune. Your obsession with Yang Guifei's beauty caused all sorts of chaos. There is a country called Japan in the East. Yang Guifei was its deity, Atsuta Myōjin. She was provisionally born in our nation as a woman to create troubles. Shame on her! After the uprising is suppressed, I will go to Japan to challenge its natives.[42]

Coincidentally, in 1663, the early Tokugawa writer of *kanazōshi* (stories in the vulgar script) Asai Ryōi wrote a commentary on the "Chang hen ge" that was also entitled *Yōkihi monogatari*. He used the Penglai belief to link Yang Guifei and Xu Fu together as follows:

Penglai, Fangzhang, and Yingzhou are the three mountains of the immortals. According to legend, people can find the elixir of life in these mountains. These mountains are located in the great ocean. They are in Japan. Japan has Mount Fuji in Suruga, Atsuta in Owari, and Kumano in Kii. In the times of the First Emperor of the Qin, the Taoist priest Xu Fu came to Kumano in search of the fabled elixir. During the reign of Xuanzong, the Taoist priest Yang Tongyou came to Owari to look for Guifei. The world was at peace in the times of Emperor Xuanzong. The emperor wanted to invade Japan. Hence, Atsuta Myōjin turned into Guifei to create troubles and save Japan.[43]

The Kanō school painter Kanō Einō (1631–97) commented on Kanō Sansetsu's *Chōgonka emaki* in his *Chōgonka zushō* (Commentary on the Painting of *The Song of Everlasting Sorrow*; 1677), saying:

It is said that, in the Tang era, Japan frequently paid tribute to China. When the gifts were few, the Chinese killed the Japanese envoys. Xuanzong sought to annihilate Japan. Atsuta Myōjin was Yamato-Takeru-no-Mikoto. This deity transformed into Yang Guifei, Sumiyoshi Myōjin turned into An Lushan, and Kumano-no-Ōkami turned into Guozhong. They went to Great Tang to destroy Xuanzong.[44]

Thus, according to this version of the legend, An Lushan (703–57) and Yang Guozhong (?–756), who were both considered evil characters in China, became Japanese deities. Together with Yang Guifei, they successfully accomplished the divine plan to save Japan.

The *jōruri* puppet play *Tō no Gensō* (Xuanzong of the Tang; 1708, author unknown) added details about the divine plan of the Shinto deities to save Japan. In its story, Fujiwara Kiyokawa, at the request of Empress Kōken, goes to pray at the Atsuta Shrine, asking the deities to protect Japan from China's invasion. Atsuta Myōjin then took the form of Yang Guifei to seduce Emperor Xuanzong. After the suppression of the An Lushan Rebellion, the spirit of Yang appeared in the imperial palace to bid farewell to the Emperor.[45]

Inspired by the *jōruri* play *Yōkihi monogatari*, Ki Kaion's *Gensō kōtei hōrai tsuru* (1723) tells a story about Xuanzong's journey to Mount Penglai to see Yang Guifei. She reveals her real identity as Atsuta Myōjin and explains to Xuanzong: "Your Majesty, you have too much desire. In order to undermine your plan to invade Japan, I assumed the form of Yang Guifei, making use of the means of the *suijaku* [manifestation]."[46]

Seeing Yang Guifei as the manifestation of a Shinto deity was an expression of the *shinpon butsujaku* (Shinto as the substance, Buddhism as the manifestation) theory, a Shinto notion akin to *honji suijaku*. Claiming that Japanese deities were manifestations of the Buddha or bodhisattvas, the original *honji suijaku* theory was started as a means to include Shinto within Buddhism in the Nara period (710–84). For example, the Sun Goddess Amaterasu was associated with the Great Sun Buddha Dainichi Nyorai.[47] In the medieval period, Shinto priests relied on a similar, but inverted, framework to develop the notion of *shinpon butsujaku*, according to which the Buddha and bodhisattvas were manifestations of Shinto deities.[48] The Yang Guifei legend in the Atsuta Shrine was an extension of this *shinpon butsujaku* theory.

The legend of Yang Guifei as a Shinto deity was introduced to China through Japanese merchants, monks, and the texts they carried with them, but it did not have a major impact on local interpretations of the character. The early Ming politician and historian Song Lian (Jinglian, 1310–81) heard about the Shinto version of the Yang Guifei legend from visiting Japanese monks and scholars. In the sixth poem of "Ridongqu" (Poems about Japan), Song mentions that Yang became a subject of worship at the Atsuta Shrine in Japan:

> The evil blood of Yuhuan [another name for Yang] stained the world.
> Why is there a shrine dedicated to her spirit?
> Never say, "The divine mountain looks so far away."
> One can find her white skin and beautiful face in the jade palace.[49]

Song himself did not believe in this legend and saw Yang Guifei as an evildoer. However, when medieval Japanese cited "Ridongqu," they only used it to reinforce the legend of Yang Guifei in Japan, ignoring the negative feelings about her that it expresses. For instance, the *Gozan* monk Ōsen Keisan (1429–93) quoted "Ridongqu" to introduce the myth that Yang was the manifestation of Atsuta Myōjin:

> Emperor Minghuang of Tang asked a Taoist priest to sail across the Eastern Sea. When the priest arrived on Mount Penglai, a maid in green clothes took him to meet Guifei. Guifei told the priest: "On

Tanabata [the evening of the seventh day of the seventh lunar month]
in the Lishan Palace, the Emperor and I remembered the tale of the
cowherd and the weaver girl. We swore that we would be husband and
wife for endless generations." The Atsuta Shrine in Japan was Penglai.
Its deity was Guifei. This was the land that the Taoist priest visited.
Scholar Song, in his "Ridongqu," mentions the Yang Guifei Shrine in
my nation: "Never say, 'The divine mountain looks so far away.' One
can find her white skin and beautiful face in the jade palace."[50]

The mid–Tokugawa Confucian Shinozaki Tōkai (1686–1739) also cited
"Ridongqu" along the same lines, remarking: "Taizu of the Ming composed
the poem about Kumano. It can be found in the *Shōkenkō* [The Draft; by
Zakkai Shōken]. In Song Jinglian's "Ridongqu," the legend associating Yang
Guifei with Atsuta is mentioned."[51]

The Shinto version of the Yang Guifei legend was influential in Japan.
Within the context of both the *honji suijaku* and *shinpon butsujaku* syncretistic
interpretations of cultural and religious traditions, the case of Yang Guifei
was somewhat unique. She was neither a deity nor a sage, but rather a beauty
who ruined the nation. In the eyes of Shinto believers, Yang did evil things
in China for the noble cause of saving Japan. In this version of the legend,
Yang's scheming was interpreted as part of a divine plan created and executed
by Japanese deities.

YANG GUIFEI IN TOKUGAWA THOUGHT

In Japan, Yang Guifei was like a heroine with a thousand faces, presented as
a Chinese court lady, a Japanese deity, a Buddhist bodhisattva, an immortal,
a politician, a political refugee, and an assassin. At first glance, the legend
of Yang Guifei in Japan sounds implausible, but it is very rich in historical
meaning, and provides a good example demonstrating how imported Chinese
traditions were localized in Japan.

Unlike other legendary figures such as Xu Fu or Wu Taibo, who were
respected for their roles as cultural mediators or ancestors of the imperial
family, Yang drew attention and stimulated artistic imagination not only due
to her beauty and the romantic and tragic end of her story, but also because
of her role as a protector or guardian deity of Japan.

Although there was a temple dedicated to Yang Guifei in her hometown of Rongxian in Guangxi, she was not deified in China. In this regard, the making of Yang Guifei into a Shinto deity in Japan was highly innovative and significant.

Like Coxinga (Zheng Chenggong, 1624–62) in Chikamatsu Monzaemon's *Kokusenya gassen* (The Battle of Coxinga; 1715), Yang Guifei was deified and Japanified in Tokugawa literary and philosophical texts. The Shinto interpretation of the Yang Guifei legend in Japan thus provides a thought-provoking example of the complexity of Sino-Japanese cultural relations. As a result of the domesticating processes of *honji suijaku* and *shinpon butsujaku*, Chinese sages were often associated with Japanese deities. For instance, the late Tokugawa *kokugaku* scholar Hirata Atsutane identified Fu Xi as Ōmononushi-no-Kami so that he could use the *Yijing* (Book of Changes) without compromising his national identity.[52] Yang Guifei was said to be the manifestation of Atsuta Myōjin. As a result of her reinterpretation through the lens of Shinto, Yang enjoyed a more positive image in Japan than she did in her homeland. In China, she was considered an evil beauty. Du Fu (712–70), in his five-character ancient verse *Bei zheng* (Campaign in the North), compared Yang to Bao Si and Daji, the two beauties blamed for the fall of the Shang and the Zhou, respectively, and Bai Juyi and Chen Hong did the same. In contrast, Yang Guifei was a respectable figure in Japan, where she was regarded as a protector of Japan in her role as the manifestation of a Shinto guardian deity.

This study demonstrates that the Yang Guifei legend in Japan was a form of cultural adaptation through the lens of national identity. Inspired by Chinese historical and literary texts, the Japanese modified the Chinese legend of Yang Guifei and developed their own versions. Through an examination of the formation and intellectual implications of the Yang Guifei legend in Japan, one can understand that Chinese culture underwent different levels of localization in Japan. Yang Guifei was creatively indigenized into something uniquely Japanese. From the Kamakura period to the Tokugawa period, the Chinese version of Yang Guifei and the Japanese version of Yōkihi (her Japanese name) coexisted in Japan, showing the complexity and diversity of Sino-Japanese cultural exchange.

WU TAIBO AS IMPERIAL ANCESTOR

CHINESE CONFUCIANISM HAS IDENTIFIED MANY ANCIENT SAGE-KINGS (such as Fu Xi, Shenzong, Huangdi, Yao, Shun, Da Yu, King Wen, and King Wu) and sages (such as Wu Taibo, the Duke of Zhou, Yi Yin, Boyi, and Shuqi) as political and ethical models. Confucians in China, Japan, and Korea rated Chinese sages differently according to their own political and intellectual agendas. In Japan, for example, Japanese Confucians did not have a high regard for King Wu, since the Mencian concept of revolution was considered unorthodox in Japanese political thought. Wu Taibo, on the other hand, drew more attention and gained more respect in Japan. Some Japanese Confucians saw him not only as an ancient Chinese sage, but also as an ancestor of the Japanese imperial house.

According to the *Shiji* (Records of the Grand Historian), Taibo was the eldest son of the leader of the Ji clan of Zhou. His father wanted to pass the throne on to his third son, who was prepared to rebel against the Yin dynasty. Taibo, in order to avoid internal strife, fled to the south. He cut his hair and tattooed his body like the southern barbarians. He became the founding king of the Kingdom of Wu.[1] Although praised by Confucius (551–479 BCE), Sima Qian, and Zhu Xi (1130–1200), Taibo was a neglected figure in Chinese historiography and Confucianism.[2] Chinese Confucian scholars seldom mentioned him in their writings. In place of Taibo, Boyi and Shuqi were usually remembered for their unfailing loyalty, and Yao and Shun were praised for their lordly self-abnegation. It should be noted that, in terms of traditional scholarship, Taibo has drawn more attention in Japan than in China, appearing frequently in traditional Japanese sources such as histories and prose writings.

The discussion of Taibo reached its apex in the Tokugawa period when the question of whether Taibo was the ancestor of the Japanese imperial family or merely an ancient Chinese sage became a point of controversy. In the seventeenth century, in particular, three major intellectual schools—the Hayashi school, the Kimon school, and the Mito school—participated in an active intellectual debate regarding the historical role of Taibo in Japan. This chapter examines the controversy surrounding Taibo among early Tokugawa scholars and discusses its political and intellectual significance through a textual analysis of Tokugawa writings about him. It aims to deepen our understanding of issues related to the rise of a national and cultural consciousness, the adaptation of Chinese Confucianism within Japanese sociopolitical realities, and the vitality and creativity of thought and culture in the early Tokugawa period.

WU TAIBO AS IMPERIAL ANCESTOR

According to Chinese sources, the Japanese themselves created the myth that Taibo was their ancestor. Beginning with the *Liangshu* (Book of the Liang; 636) by Yao Silian (557–637) and the *Jinshu* (Book of the Jin; 648) compiled under Fang Xuanling (579–648), a number of Chinese historical writings recorded that Japanese envoys and sojourners claimed to be the descendants of Taibo. The *Liangshu* reads: "The Wa people claimed to be the descendants of Taibo. Tattooing their bodies was their custom." The "Woren zhuan" (Records of Japan) of the *Jinshu* reads: "The Wa people lived in the middle of the ocean to the south of Daifang [around Seoul on the Korean Peninsula]. All men, big or small, tattooed their faces and bodies, claiming to be descendants of Taibo." The *Hanyuan*, a collection of articles on the historical geography of Sino-Japanese relations compiled in the early Tang by Zhang Chujin, cited the lost *Weilue* (Brief History of the State of Wei): "It was the custom for all men to tattoo their faces and bodies. I learned an old saying that they claimed to be the descendants of Taibo." The *Tongjian qianbian* (A Previous Chapter of the *Zizhi Tongjian*) by Jin Luxiang (1232–1303) alleged that the Wu people migrated to Japan after the demise of their nation. It reads: "Nowadays, it is said that the Japanese are the descendants of Wu Taibo. After the demise of the Wu Empire, its branches drifted to the sea and became the Wa people."[3] Unlike the Xu Fu legend, the Taibo discourse did not attract much attention in China. By stressing the racial and cultural similarities between Japan and

China, the Japanese created this myth to show their respect for Chinese culture and to establish for Japan a respectable place in the Chinese cultural order. The message was that they were the descendants of the Chinese sage, and by no means barbarians.

According to the *Jinnō shōtōki* (Records of the Legitimate Succession of the Divine Sovereigns; rev. 1343) by Kitabatake Chikafusa (1293–1343), the idea that Taibo was the ancestor of the Japanese race was introduced to Japan during the reign of the legendary Emperor Ōjin with the importation of the *Jinshu*.[4] The *Shinsen shōjiroku* (New Selection and Record of Hereditary Titles and Family Names; 815) lists more than three hundred clans originating in China and Korea. The Matsuno clan claimed to have descended from Fucha (495–473 BCE), the last emperor of the Wu. It reads: "The Matsuno are the descendants of the Wu king Fucha. This was the beginning of the arrival of the Wu people to my nation."[5] Since Taibo was the founding emperor of the Wu and Fucha was the twenty-fifth and the last emperor, the Matsuno clan, if the *Shinsen shōjiroku* is reliable, was made up of the descendants of Taibo.

In the late Heian and medieval periods, some Japanese began to discuss the meaning of *Jishiguo* (Nation of the Ji), a term allegedly used by the Chinese monk Baozhi (418–514) to refer to Japan. The *Nihon shoki shiki* (My Own Notes on the *Chronicles of Japan*; c. tenth century, author unknown) contains the following conversation:

> Question: This nation is called *Jishiguo*. Have you heard about this?

> Answer from the master: In the times of Liang, the monk Baozhi used the term "*Jishiguo* in the Eastern Sea." Our monk Zenmin Suiki remarked: "*Jishiguo* in the Eastern Sea is the name for the nation of Wa."

> My comments: Amaterasu was the ancestor. She was a goddess. Empress Jingū was a female emperor. Because of these, [Japan] is called *Jishiguo* [the nation of females (*hime*)].[6].

This term became well-known in the medieval period, popularized by the prophetic poem *Yabataishi* (Poem on Yabatai). Attributed to the Chinese monk Baozhi, this poem could be a forgery. Cited since the Kamakura period (1185–1333), the Chinese poem made *Jishiguo* a popular term. It begins with these lines:

The nation of Ji was in the Eastern Sea.

[Its rulers] ruled for a hundred generations.

They made contributions to governance.

Having established the nation based on law and order,

They worshipped their ancestors.

Their branches were everywhere.

The relationship between the emperor and the ministers was set up. [7]

The mid-Kamakura Shintoist Urabe Kanekata, in his *Shaku Nihongi* (Explanation of the *Chronicles of Japan*), paraphrased the *Nihon shoki shiki* to deny the theory about the Chinese origin of the Japanese:

> The Liang monk Baozhi wrote in his prophetic poem: "*Jishiguo* in the Eastern Sea is the name for Japan." My comment is that Amaterasu was the founding goddess. Empress Jingū was also a female emperor. Because of these, [Japan] is called the nation of females, or *Jishiguo*. The Eastern Sea refers to Japan where lies between the Great Tang and the East. This term was used by the Tang Chinese. [8]

The legend of Taibo in Japan was, however, not a popular idea in that country before the Tokugawa period, and definitely did not represent the official position of the Japanese authorities. Prior to the Tokugawa, the main advocate of the Taibo legend was the famous Zen monk Chūgan Engetsu (1300–1375), who traced the ancestry of the Japanese imperial family to Taibo in his *Nihongi* (General History of Japan; 1341), associating Taibo with *Kunitokotachi-no-Mikoto*, the first deity born after the creation of heaven and earth. He believed that the offspring of Taibo landed in Chikushi in Kyūshū and became the ancestors of the Japanese imperial family. This view went against the Shinto belief that Amaterasu, the Sun Goddess, was the ancestor of the Japanese imperial family. Attacked severely by courtiers, the book was banned and destroyed by the central court government.

Two courtiers launched an assault on Engetsu's ideas in their writings from a Shinto perspective—Kitabatake Chikafusa in his *Jinnō shōtōki* and Ichijō Kanera (1402–81) in his *Nihon shoki sanso* (Commentary on the *Chronicles of Japan*)—emphasizing that Japan was a divine nation and that the Japanese were descended from Shinto deities. Chikafusa introduced and then denied Chinese and Japanese sources concerning Taibo in Japan. He cited Shinto mythology to maintain that the Japanese were much closer to the Koreans than the Chinese, and that the Japanese were the descendants of the Shinto deities and thus existed well before the arrival of Taibo and his people.[9] Ichijō Kanera explained *Jishiguo* along the lines suggested in the *Nihon shoki shiki*:

> Both the emperors and ministers of my nation are the descendants of deities. Why did people think they are the descendants of Taibo? This idea came from the prophetic poem composed by Baozhi. According to the *Yunshu* [Book of Phonetics], *ji* is a compliment for women. The Sun Goddess is a female deity and Empress Jingū was a female emperor. Thus, our people adopted this word.[10]

Despite criticisms from Shintoists and courtiers, the discussion of Taibo did not disappear in the medieval period and became a full-fledged debate in the seventeenth century, when Confucian scholars were drawn into the controversy over the sage.[11] This controversy has important implications for understanding the conflicts of ideas and political agendas among various Confucian and historiographical schools and the problem of political and cultural identity.

Most advocates of the idea that Taibo was indeed the imperial ancestor were Confucians associated with the Fujiwara-Hayashi lineage of the Zhu Xi school. Fujiwara Seika (1561–1619) was the first Tokugawa scholar to support the Taibo legend. Influenced by *Gozan* (Five Mountain) scholarship, Seika based his arguments on Chinese texts and history and was also influenced by Chūgan Engetsu. First, he cited certain Chinese sources that referred to Japan as *Jishiguo*. He interpreted this term as "the nation of Ji" and argued that, since Ji was the family name of Taibo, Japan must have been the land of Taibo's descendants. Second, the *Lunyu* praised Taibo for *sanrang* (exercising self-abnegation three times), and the Ise Shrine, the most important Shinto shrine dedicated to the imperial family, had the word *sanrang* (*sanjō* in Japanese) in its epigraph. Seika saw this as evidence that Taibo was the ancestor of the Japanese imperial family, stating:

> Japan is also called the nation of Ji [*Jishiguo*], and is believed to be the land of Taibo's descendants. The Inner Shrine of the Ise Shrine has the word *sanjō* [threefold self-abnegation] in its epigraph, [to remind the people that] Taibo exercised self-abnegation three times. The three

regalia represent the three [Confucian] virtues of wisdom, benevolence, and bravery. The surname of Taibo was Ji, and therefore Japan is called the nation of Ji. Chūgan Engetsu of the East Hill Monastery wrote the *Nihongi* based on the abovementioned arguments. The book was banned by the court and was burned.[12]

Hayashi Razan (1583–1657), a disciple of Seika, further developed Seika's ideas and became the champion of the Taibo legend in the Tokugawa period. Razan was an influential figure in early Tokugawa politics and thought, and thus his support made the Taibo legend a matter of concern in Confucian circles. In the *Jimmu tennōron* (Essay on Emperor Jimmu), he introduced the ideas expounded by Chūgan Engetsu. Identifying many correspondences between the Shinto tradition and the Taibo legend, Razan tried to rationalize Shinto myths and explain them in historical terms:

> The Zen monk, Engetsu, of the East Hill Monastery, built the Myōki-in, where he undertook the compilation of the *Nihongi*. Because the court disapproved of it, his work was cast into the fire. Engetsu's idea, as far as I can gather, was to cite a number of historical records indicating that the Japanese were descended from Taibo. Taibo escaped to the land of barbarians, cut his hair, tattooed his body, and lived with snakes and dragons. His descendants migrated to Tsukushi. Ancient Japanese worshipped Taibo as a deity. This corresponds to [the Shinto legend that] the imperial grandson descended to the summit of Takachiho in Hyūga [in Kyūshū]. During that time, some of our people rejected his rule. Ōnamuchi-no-Kami was one such rebel.[13]

Razan believed that the Japanese were affiliated with the Wu and Yue, two Southern states in China's Warring States period (403–222 BCE), and that, with the fall of the Wu and Yue, their people had fled to Japan. Razan said:

> It is written in the *Jinshu*: "The Japanese are the descendants of Xiahou Shaokang [a Xia king, the legendary founder of Yue]." The son of Shaokang's concubine was appointed the lord of Guiji. He cut his hair and tattooed his body, living with sea turtles, lizards, fish, and turtles. Finally, he built the state of Yue. As we can see, the Wu and Yue were geographically close to our country. Even a small boat could

sail between [Wu and Yue and Japan]. We are not sure whether our imperial family descended from Taibo or Shaokang. If I speculate that the imperial family originated in Taibo or Shaokang, I will definitely be condemned like Engetsu.[14]

Razan then pointed out that the imperial grandson, like Taibo, subdued the barbarians who lived with snakes and dragons. He used various pieces of "material evidence" to support the Taibo legend, such as the *sanrang* epigraph at the Ise Shrine and ancient Chinese scripts found in an old tomb. Moreover, he argued that the three imperial regalia were of continental rather than divine origin, because objects similar to the Three Regalia could be found in China in the times of Taibo. In other words, they were brought to Japan by the descendants of Taibo rather than by the deities in heaven, as suggested by Shinto.

Razan, writing in a private capacity, even challenged the official and Shinto views of the imperial grandson and Emperor Jimmu. He speculated that both were Taibo's descendants, who fought all the way from Kyūshū to other parts of Japan to subdue local chiefs. In his explanation, many Shinto deities were demythologized and were interpreted as being merely ancient tribal leaders. Razan asked:

If the imperial grandson were the son of the Heavenly Gods, how can you explain his descent onto a remote hill of the Western region, instead of onto the rich soil of the central province? Why did the three generations, namely, Ninigi, Hoori, and Ugayafukiaezu, live and die in Hyūga? Why did Jimmu have to overcome such difficulties [on his expedition to the East] if he possessed divine powers in war? The enemy of the imperial grandson was Ōnamuchi and the enemy of Emperor Jimmu was Nagasunehiko. They either resisted or fought. Was it strange? I believe that Ōnamuchi and Nagasunehiko were indeed ancient tribal leaders of our nation.[15]

Hence, he concluded, Japanese emperors were descendants of Taibo. Although the lineage of Taibo disappeared in China following the collapse of the Wu state, it continued to flourish in Japan as the Japanese imperial family. Since the Japanese imperial family enjoyed an unbroken lineage, he averred, the Taibo line would last forever in Japan:

Behold! Jin [Taibo] and his descendants, having already held sway for a hundred generations in succession, will continue their reign for ten thousand generations to come. How glorious they are? The once-powerful Wu may have been overcome [in China] by the Yue state, but their reign in our country is coeval with heaven and earth. I believe in the ultimate virtue of Taibo. If Engetsu comes back to life, I have nothing to tell him.[16]

To a certain extent, the Taibo theory was a product of Sinophilia, using Confucian orthodoxy to uphold the legitimacy of the Japanese imperial family.[17] It should be noted that Razan was not always consistent in his advocacy of the Taibo legend.[18] In his official capacity, he did not accept the legend and even criticized it.[19] No evidence of his personal views can be found in his *Honchō tsugan* (The Comprehensive Mirror of Japan; 1670), the Tokugawa official history compiled by Hayashi Razan and his son, Hayashi Gahō (1618–80).

Some modern scholars (such as Kusaka Hiroshi, Sakamoto Tarō, Noguchi Takehiro, and Hori Isao) have explained that Hayashi and his son adopted official historical views based on the *Nihon shoki* (Chronicles of Japan; 720) and *Kojiki* (Records of Ancient Matters; 712) and avoided expressing their personal views when compiling the official history.[20] Such scholars have found support for their arguments in Gahō, who, in the afterword of the first half of the *Honchō tsugan*, stated that the book was based on Japanese historical records and did not adopt foreign legends such as those concerning Taibo or Shaokang. He said: "Things about Shaokang and Taibo are legends of foreign lands. I am not adopting them here."[21] Others (such as Kurita Hiroshi [1835–99] and Kimura Seiji [1827–1913]) believed that Hayashi and his son first included the Taibo legend in their *Honchō tsugan*, and later replaced it with the Shinto myth under pressure from the *bakufu* and the Mito domain.

Hayashi Gahō had many insightful and original ideas about the legend of Taibo in Japan. For instance, he explained that it was practicable for the descendants of Taibo to travel from Wu to Chikushi in Kyūshū:

Taibo escaped to the land of barbarians and founded the state of Gouwu. The land of Wu was vast, including the land now called Ningbo-fu. Tang people called it Mingzhou. In the past, Japanese

Tsukushi

envoys to the Tang went to the capital via this land. It is not a long
distance from Mingzhou to Chikushi. When the wind is mild and the
waves are small, it only takes four to five days to reach the other side.[22]

He alleged that Taibo was deified as the imperial grandson. Regarding the
problem of mismatched historical dates, he rationalized it in terms of the longevity of early emperors:

> In the primitive era, Taibo came to this nation with ultimate virtue.
> The people admired him, calling him a deity. How can we deny the
> possibility that he might have been Ōhirume-no-Muchi [Sun Goddess
> Amaterasu Omikami]? When Emperor Jimmu was enthroned, it was
> during the reign of King Hui of Zhou, twenty generations after the
> death of King Wen. From Ōhirume to Emperor Jimmu, there were six
> generations. The length did not match that of China. However, early
> emperors of my nation lived long lives. Dungun in Korea outlived Peng
> Zu [in China]. We cannot rule out the fact that many ancient people
> lived long in the beginning of the nation.[23]

Tangun-?

According to tradition, Taibo used collecting herbal medicine for his father
as an excuse to flee to the South. Gahō regarded this record as evidence to
support the Taibo legend in Japan, as Japan was a land of medicine. He said:
"How awesome! Taibo came here using collection of herbal medicine as an
excuse. Did people call Japan Penglai Island based on this? Xu Shi [another
name for Xu Fu] came to Japan to collect medicine. Did he admire Taibo and
follow in his footsteps?"[24] Gahō sought to give Chūgan Engetsu's theory of
Taibo a fair historical treatment:

> Engetsu was a representative monk of our nation. He gained extensive
> knowledge through listening and remembering. He was not only well
> known in Japan, but he also won a reputation in the foreign land
> [China]. His ideas must have been based on something. Although
> I am not a follower of Engetsu, I think his ideas are sound. This
> is a wrong verdict that has stood for a thousand years, and I want
> to defend him.[25]

To Gahō, the significance of Taibo was that he was not merely the ancestor of
the imperial family, but also the transmitter of the way of the sages:

I am thinking that Taibo laid the foundation for our imperial family based on his ultimate virtue. Jizi [a Shang prince] cultivated that territory [Korea] with his benevolence. These are the good deeds of the early sages. It is appropriate to call both [Japan and Korea] the lands of gentlemen. With the exception of China, in this world, I have never heard of any nation that followed the principle of morality and promoted scholarship as well as our nation and Korea. Aren't these the legacies of Taibo and Jizi?[26]

Razan's grandson, Hōkō (1644–1732), as well as many students of the Fujiwara-Hayashi school, also asserted the credibility of the Taibo legend. For instance, Kinoshita Junan (1621–98), who studied under Fujiwara Seika's top disciple Matsunaga Sekigo (1592–1657), supported the Taibo legend in Japan. In his *Taihakuron* (Discourse on Taibo), he held that Taibo's descendants came to ancient Japan and that Taibo served as a political model for the Japanese.[27] Muro Kyūsō (1658–1734), a student of Junan, advocated the Taibo legend implicitly. In a personal letter, he praised the fact that many ancient sages went to foreign lands to cultivate the natives without disrupting the local customs:

> In the past, [some sages] implemented the Way directly. Taibo grew his hair and tattooed his body in order to cultivate the southern barbarians. Jizi drew up the Eight Articles for the ruling of Korea. They followed foreign customs at the same time that they implemented their policies to rule.[28]

Kyūsō did not state explicitly that Taibo and his descendants went to Japan, but since he employed the legend of Jizi in Korea, it was natural that readers would associate Taibo with Japan.

Hori Keizan (1688–1757), the grandson of Seika's disciple Hori Kyōan (1585–1642), associated Taibo with Amaterasu, the Sun Goddess said to be the primordial ancestor of the Japanese, believing that Taibo brought higher civilization from the state of Wu to Japan:

> The saying is "Amaterasu is taken to be a female, this divinity should actually be Wu Taibo." I support this idea. Taibo lived in the Yin [Shang] period, and Yin Chinese believed in gods and ghosts. Due to Yin Chinese influence, the Japanese also worship gods. Many things in

Kuretake

Japan carry "wu" [*go* or *kure* in Japanese] in their names, such as *gotake* [Japanese bamboo] and *gofuku* [Chinese textiles]. All of this evidence supports the [abovementioned] saying.[29]

A number of Tokugawa Confucians who were outside of the Fujiwara-Hayashi lineage also lent support to the Taibo legend in Japan.[30] Wang Yangming scholars such as Nakae Tōju (1608–48) and Kumazawa Banzan (1619–91) gave their strong support to this legend.[31] Banzan explained *Jishiguo* in terms of the surname of Taibo:

> Descended from Zhou, Japan is thus named *Tōkai himeshi no kuni* [nation of Ji in the Eastern Sea]. It is the name for females, and in Japan we call females *hime*. *Hime* is the honorific term for women and the surname of Zhou. Amaterasu was Taibo. The statue of Uhōdōji [rain-making boy] was made in the image of Amaterasu, reflecting the image of Taibo and the haircutting custom of Wu. Japanese clothing is called *gofuku* and utensils are *goki*. They are all related to the state of Wu.[32]

Like Razan, Banzan believed that Taibo landed on the shores of Hyūga Province in Kyūshū. He even speculated that Taibo was Amaterasu and that one his descendants was the Emperor Jimmu. To Banzan, Taibo was the original founder of the Japanese imperial family and, by extension, the nation's civilization. He extolled the fact that the influence of Taibo had survived from the ancient past up to the commencement of warrior rule in the twelfth century. Banzan held that Taibo was the founder of the Japanese imperial house, and accordingly lauded him for introducing Confucian morality, agriculture, industry, hunting, mining, and fishery to ancient Japan.[33] To him, establishing proper human relationships in Japan was the most significant contribution of Taibo:

> Having crossed to Japan, Taibo established the Way of human relations, and through love he taught respect; transferring the attitude of respect toward parents, he determined the categories of superior and inferior; he instituted rituals, and by acknowledging the sources of things he informed people of whence they had come. Finally, there existed the rituals of venerating ancestors and heaven and earth. He systematized the rituals of marriage through go-betweens and emphasized the beginnings of human relationships.[34]

Of all of the virtues, Banzan rated Taibo's self-abnegation most highly by saying: "Taibo of the Zhou exercised self-abnegation three times. The ordinary people did not even know his virtue. This is the highest form of abnegation."[35]

The mid-Tokugawa archeologist and philologist Tō Teikan (1723–97) maintained that Taibo was the ancestor of Emperor Jimmu. He alleged that the leader of the Chinese migrants, an offspring of Taibo, came to Kyūshū via the Ryūkyū Kingdom. He married the daughter of a local clan chief and their son later became Emperor Jimmu:

> Our nation originated from Taibo. Since the surname of Zhou was Ji, our heavenly grandson established the nation of Ji, or the Takeamamijima. Tamayori-hime [the mother of Emperor Jimmu] was the daughter of Toyotamahiko, the chief of this island. The offspring of Taibo came to this island. He married Tamayori-hime and had Emperor Jimmu as his son.[36]

According to his research, Emperor Jimmu actually lived around 60 BCE, about six hundred years later than the time recorded in the *Nihon shoki*. Teikan's idea of Taibo drew criticism from the *kokugaku* scholar Motoori Norinaga (1730–1801).

Hence, we can surmise from these disparate efforts that the issue of how to accommodate Chinese Confucianism without compromising Japanese identity was a common concern among Tokugawa Confucians from different intellectual schools. Tokugawa Confucians were specialists in Chinese learning and held the Chinese classics and official records in high regard. However, such attributes did not make them immune to nationalist feeling. I would contend that they employed the Taibo legend in order to give Japan a more important position in the Chinese cultural order. Thus, because the Japanese were believed to be the descendants of a Chinese sage, Japan had inherited and developed the way of the sages. The Zhu Xi school produced a large number of advocates of the Taibo legend, but it did not monopolize the discussions surrounding it. The advocacy of the Taibo legend also represented an attempt by various scholars and writers to provide a more rational and moral explanation for the origins of the Japanese imperial family in place of the Shinto myths. Although they kept this belief to themselves and only hinted at it in their private writings, they nonetheless soon became the targets of attack from their intellectual and political competitors.

TAIBO AS CHINESE SAGE

In the discourse surrounding Taibo in Tokugawa Japan, the majority of scholars only saw him as an ancient Chinese sage and did not accept that he had anything to do with the Japanese imperial family. The Hayashi school was attacked by its competitors in the fields of neo-Confucianism and historiography, including the Kimon school and the Mito school, for endorsing the Taibo legend in Japan.

Yamazaki Ansai (1618–82) and his Kimon school praised the political virtue of Taibo, but rejected the legend of his relationship with the Japanese imperial house. Ansai launched the most comprehensive criticism of the legend in his *Taihakuron* (Discourse on Taibo) from both textual and historical perspectives. Firstly, he cited the *Shiji* to prove that Taibo had no children and was succeeded by his younger brother. Hence, the Japanese could not have been Taibo's descendants. Secondly, he used various Chinese and Japanese sources to demonstrate that Taibo and his brother were the ancestors of the Wu regime in southern China. With the demise of that regime, some Wu people fled to Japan and became the Matsuno clan, a powerful family in Kyūshū. Since the Matsuno were not a noble family, the Japanese imperial family did not, therefore, have any affinity with the descendants of Taibo. Thirdly, he gave the term *Jishiguo* a different explanation, declaring that this name had been coined not because the Japanese imperial family carried the surname of *Ji*, but because the Sun Goddess and many ancient rulers in Japan were female. *Ji*, or *hime* in Japanese, meant "women," and thus *Jishiguo* should be translated as "the kingdom of female rulers."[3] He explained:

> The monk Engetsu adopted the story of Taibo in the national history he compiled. The book was banned by the central court. According to the *Tongjian qianbian* [The first part of *The Comprehensive Mirror*; by Jin Luxiang, 1232–1303], in the third year of King Yuan of Zhou, Yue destroyed Wu. There were twenty-five generations from Taibo to Fucha. Now, the Japanese are said to be the descendants of Taibo because branch families of the Wu people escaped to the sea upon the fall of their nation and they became the Wa. What Jin [Luxiang] wrote was ridiculous. The third year of King Yuan was the third year of the reign of Emperor Kōshō. The *Manta shōjiroku* [the *Shinsen shōjiroku*;

compiled by the Prince Manta, 788–830] records that the Matsuno clan was derived from the Wu king Fucha. His branch families fled to the sea and became the ancestors of Matsuno.[38]

In other writings, Ansai argued that the *sanrang* epigraph could not be used as evidence to support the Taibo legend, because none of the Shinto classics mentioned it. He also questioned the credibility of Chinese sources in which ancient Japanese claimed themselves as Taibo's descendants:

> The idea that [the Japanese] are the descendants of Taibo came from the *Jinshu*. The Japanese traveled to China and came to know old and new books. Therefore, they fabricated the legend [about Taibo in Japan]. We should not fully believe this kind of saying without question.... The *Yabataishi* used the term *Tōkai himeshi no kuni*, and thus Confucians identified Amaterasu with Taibo based on the poem. They explained the femininity [of Amaterasu] in terms of *himeshi*, and suggested that there was a *sanrang* epigraph secretly preserved [in the Ise Shrine]. How ridiculous they are! These things are absolutely not recorded in books such as the *Ise jingū shoki* [Miscellaneous Records of Ise Shrine] or *Gengenshū* [Collected Articles on the Origins of Shinto]. The *Yabataishi* is also not included in our books.[39]

Ansai compared the Taibo legend, in which a Chinese prince became a Japanese emperor, to the Shingon Buddhist version of *honji suijaku*, or the manifestation of the Buddha and bodhisattvas manifested in the form of Shinto deities, criticizing them for being too far-fetched to believe. He condemned the advocates of the Taibo legend as the enemies of both the Chinese sages and Shinto deities:

> Confused by the word *Jishiguo*, Confucians misleadingly associated Taibo [with the Japanese]. Buddhists associated the Great Sun Buddha with the Sun Goddess. These acts represent the crime of making false statement as stated in the *Zhouli* [The Rites of Zhou] and violate the teaching of straightforwardness of our deities. They are indeed sinners in the eyes of our deities.[40]

Although Ansai and his Kimon school rejected the Taibo legend in Japan, they respected Taibo as a perfect political paragon of absolute loyalty (particularly for his refusal to revolt against the Yin) and filial piety (for giving up the right to succeed the throne in order to fulfill his father's wish). While Confucius regarded Taibo and King Wen as the only two perfect moral models, the Kimon school rated Taibo higher than King Wen.[41] For instance, Asami Keisai (1652–1711) compared them as follows: "If we compare King Wen and King Wu, then King Wen represents the ultimate virtue. If we compare Taibo and King Wen, then Taibo represents the ultimate virtue."[42]

The Mito school criticized the historiography of the Hayashi school on the basis of their reliance on Shinto and Japanese official histories. While the disagreement between the Hayashi and Kimon schools remained essentially an intellectual argument, the Mito school turned this debate into a political issue. Andō Tameakira (1659–1716), a Mito scholar, recorded that Hayashi and his son were obliged to drop the Taibo legend from their *Honchō tsugan* due to opposition from Tokugawa Mitsukuni (1628–1700), the second *daimyō* of the Mito domain. Mitsukuni insisted that the official history should follow the *Nihon shoki* and *Kojiki*, and rejected the Taibo legend because it demeaned the Japanese imperial family by questioning its divine origin, and by implication would have turned Japan into a subordinate of China. He said:

> If we accept the Taibo legend, then our divine nation will become a subordinate of the foreign land [China]. This book [*Honchō tsugan*] would bring humiliation to our country for thousands of years. Hence, I ordered Hayashi [and his son] to delete this evil theory and make changes according to our official historical records.[43]

The late Tokugawa Mito scholar Fujita Tōko (1806–55) retold this story:

> One day, the *daimyō* [Mitsukuni] was in the *bakufu* with the *daimyō* from Owari and Kishū. Someone wrote a history and submitted it to the *bakufu* for publication. The *daimyō* reviewed it. When he read the part about Wu Taibo as the ancestor of our divine nation, he was shocked, saying: "This theory is based on farfetched ideas made by foreigners. It is not recorded in our official histories. In the past, in the reign of Emperor Go-Daigo, an evil monk advocated this idea. The court ordered that his book be burned. Now, we are living in a civilized world. How can we allow such a strange thing to happen? Let us order its deletion as soon as possible." The other two *daimyō* supported him. The book was thus not published.[44]

Mito scholars also respected Taibo as a Chinese sage. Like Ansai, Mitsukuni was an admirer of Taibo. In particular, he identified with the ideal of self-abnegation in Taibo.[45] His pen name, Bairi, was borrowed from the tomb site of Taibo. A Tokugawa work entitled *Tōgen iji* (Things about Tōgen) by Asaka Tanpaku, states: "Bairi [*Meili* in Chinese] is the name of the tomb site of Taibo. His Excellency [Mitsukuni] admired Taibo and took Bairi as his [pen] name."[46]

In addition to the Mito school, a number of Tokugawa historians also attacked the Taibo legend from a historical perspective. In his *Ishō Nihonden* (Treatises on Japan under Foreign Titles; 1668), Matsushita Kenrin (1637–1703) emphasized that the Japanese were the descendants of the Sun Goddess, and thus had a much longer history than Taibo. However, he did not deny that some Wu people might have migrated to Japan after the fall of their regime in China:

> My country has existed since the beginning of heaven and earth, and it was named *Dai Nippon Toyo-Akitsushima*. As descendants of the grandson of the Sun Goddess, our imperial family enjoys an unbroken lineage. The Wu only began with Taibo, who lived thousands of years [after the beginning of Japan]. How could we have been the descendants of Taibo? The "Wushijia" [Wu Family] of the *Shiji* reads: "Taibo died without an heir. His brother Zhong Yong was enthroned." . . . Japan had no connection with the Wu before Fucha. According to our national histories and writings, many aliens admired our culture and entered our country to become our officials and subjects. These families were categorized as *banbetsu* [clans descended from foreign lineage] and there were many varieties among the *banbetsu*. The Matsuno were one such *banbetsu*. The *Shinsen shōjiroku* reads: "The Matsuno traced their origins to Fucha. This was the advent of the Wu people in Japan."[47]

Kenrin pointed out that the similarities in languages and customs between the Wu and ancient Japan were coincidental. He argued that a number of customs thought to be derived from the Wu actually originated in Japan:

> Some people who do not understand the origins of things and do not check sources have said: "The Wu people cut their hair and tattooed their bodies. It is also our custom to cut our hair. We wear *gofuku*

[Chinese textiles] and speak *goon* [ancient Chinese sound system used in the Yangzi River region during the Six Dynasties]. Obviously we are the descendants of Taibo." What a far-fetched idea it is! They even make the big mistake of taking the custom of dyeing teeth among officials as a form of tattooing. Our nation only started dyeing men's teeth with iron in the times of Emperor Toba [reigned 1107–23], as recorded in the *Keimei-in sōjōki* [Records of Keimei-in].⁴⁸

Arai Hakuseki (1657–1725) believed that the descendants of Taibo might have come to establish their regional regimes in ancient Japan, but rejected the conjecture that Taibo was the ancestor of the Japanese imperial family. In the preface of his *Koshitsū* [Understanding Ancient History], Hakuseki stated:

> Today, we can no longer trace when it was that our imperial family established its regime in this land [Japan]. Some people, harboring evil intentions, cite Chinese sources to argue that our nation originated from Shaokang, and that the ancestors of the imperial family were the descendants of Taibo.⁴⁹

To Hakuseki, associating the imperial grandson with Taibo was as ridiculous as the *honji suijaku* doctrine used by the Buddhists to include Shinto within Buddhism. He remarked:

> Books of the foreign nation suggest that my nation was descended from Shaokang of Xia and that my imperial family members are descendants of Wu Taibo. It is like those heretics who associated the Sun Goddess with the Great Sun Buddha, seeing them as the imperial ancestor.⁵⁰

However, he did not completely deny the credibility of the *Jinshu* and other Chinese records. The *Jinshu* records that envoys from the some thirty states in ancient Japan claimed themselves to be the descendants of Taibo, and that they tattooed their faces and bodies. Hence, Hakuseki did not rule out the possibility that some of these thirty-odd nations in ancient Japan might have been ruled by the descendants of Taibo, who migrated to Japan after the fall of the Wu regime in southern China. He wrote:

> What were ancient times like? We do not know the origins of the self-styled "kings" of the thirty or so states [in Japan], which

communicated with Han and Wei [China]. Of these states, we cannot rule out the possibility that some might have been the descendants of Shaokang or Taibo.[51]

He then concluded that, since all of those small states were conquered by Emperor Jimmu, the alleged first Japanese emperor, the Japanese imperial family was not related to Chinese immigrants.

Ise Sadatake (also known as Ansai, 1715–84), a historian and *bakufu* retainer, also criticized the Taibo legend in his *Ansai zuihitsu* (Miscellaneous Writings of Ansai). He observed:

> It is said that Xu Fu, a Qin official, came to Japan with the *Shangshu* [Book of Documents]. This was recorded in the foreign nation [China], but not in our official historical records, and therefore we should not believe it. Recently, Confucians in our nation have evinced [undue] respect for that foreign nation and refer to it as the Central Kingdom, and call Japan a barbaric nation. They are disloyal people who look down on Japanese traditions, believing that stories about Wu Taibo and Xu Fu are historically true.[52]

Sadatake stressed that Japanese historical records were more reliable than Chinese sources regarding Japanese history, condemning the advocates of the Taibo legend as treasonous. He remarked:

> Chinese records [about Japan] must be verified by Japanese sources. We cannot rely on them unless they are also recorded in our *Nihon shoki* and *Kojiki*. Recently some Japanese Confucians have belittled Japan by calling themselves "barbarians," and praised China by calling it "the Central Kingdom." They are the unfaithful traitors of Japan. Having the hearts of traitors, they attribute the imperial ancestry to Wu Taibo. This farfetched and unfounded idea can be found in many writings.[53]

There were many other Tokugawa critics of the Taibo legend in Japan. Most of them merely repeated the arguments of Ansai, Kenrin, Hakuseki, and Sadatake. They rejected the legend either because of their Shinto beliefs or as a result of historical analysis.

Like Ansai, Yamaga Sokō (1622–85) did not accept the Taibo legend in Japan because it was not recorded in Japanese national histories. He remarked:

The beginning of the Central Kingdom [here referring to Japan] is recorded in our old national histories. There are no grounds for doubt. Because of the proximity between Wu/Yue [and Japan], empty voices in secular books, Zen interpretations of words, Confucian explanations of articles, and weird speculations, some people regarded Taibo as our imperial ancestor.[54]

Furthermore, he also compared the Taibo legend to the *honji suijaku* doctrine. By comparing the longevity and talents of the emperors in Japan and China, he discredited the Taibo legend:

Many people of the Central Kingdom [Japan] are wise and physically strong. There were ten generations from the human Emperor [Jimmu] to Emperor Sujin. This lasted for seven hundred years. Many emperors lived for a hundred years. The emperors of the foreign nation [China] had more than thirty generations during this period. The descendants of Taibo only had the lifespan of foreigners. Our emperors were so talented, so how could they give the throne away [to foreigners]? For those who live in our land but forget our land, eat in our nation but forget our nation, and live in this world but forget this world, they are like the people who forget their parents who gave life to them. Is this the way of human beings? Those who create far-fetched ideas about the foreign origin of our nation are traitors and thieves.[55]

The mid-Tokugawa astronomer Nishikawa Joken (1648–1724), in his *Nihon suidokō* (An Investigation of the Water and Land of Japan; 1720), echoed the idea that *Jishiguo* refers to the nation of female rulers and has nothing to do with Taibo:

This nation is called *Jishiguo* because Japan occasionally had female emperors. The foreign nation [China] called us this name. It is wrong to interpret us as the descendants of Taibo. In our tradition, we commonly call females *hime* and men *hiko*. *Hiko* is the Japanese word for Japanese men, whereas *hime* is the Japanese word for Japanese women. All people in this nation are descendants of the Sun Goddess.[56]

Ogyū Sorai (1666–1728), an influential scholar of Chinese studies in the mid-Tokugawa period, praised Taibo for his self-abnegation as follows:

"Thanks to the self-abnegation of Taibo, the people in the next generations were benefited both mentally and physically. How great he was!"[57] He
admitted that the state of Wu had cultural exchange with Japan in the past,
but he did not believe that Taibo was the Sun Goddess or the ancestor of the
imperial family.[58]

The Shingon Buddhist monk Seiō (?–1787) refuted the Taibo theory
expounded by Engetsu and Razan in his *Kochōan zuihitsu* (Miscellaneous
Writings of Kochōan):

> In the reign of Emperor Ōjin, the writing system was introduced.
> We should not adopt far-fetched theories such as those saying that
> the Japanese are the descendants of Wu Taibo or Xiahou Shaokang.
> Hayashi Dōshun [Razan] identified Wu Taibo as Amaterasu, and his
> *Jimmu tennōron* promoted the speculative theory of the monk Engetsu.
> All of these theories disrespect the tradition of our divine nation.[60]

The Osaka merchant-scholar Yamagata Bantō (1748–1821), in his *Yume
no shiro* (In Place of Dreams), citied Chinese sources to prove that Taibo had
no heirs and thus the Japanese could not be his descendants. He maintained:

> Writing was known in China in the time of Wu Taibo. If he came to Japan
> and established the country, why did he not propagate writing? After all,
> it is by means of writing that a state comes into being. After writing has
> become known, it is impossible to conceal its existence. The family history
> of the Wu is perfectly clear in the *Shiji*, which says: "Taibo died without
> heirs. He was succeeded by his younger brother, Zhong Yong.[59]

Basically, Sokō, Joken, Sorai, Seiō, and Bantō merely repeated the ideas
suggested by Ansai. Criticisms of the Taibo discourse can also be found in
the following texts written by Confucians: Maruyama Katsudō's (1657–1731)
Taihakuron (1722), Hatta Tomonori's (1799–1873) *Taihakuron*, Terajima
Ryōan's (1654–?) *Wakan sanzai zukai* (Illustrated Encyclopedia of All Things
Japanese; ch. 81), and Kanzawa Tokō's (1710–95) *Okinagusa* (Writings
of an Old Man).

In addition to the abovementioned Confucians, *kokugaku* scholars also
strongly criticized this theory. Motoori Norinaga, Shirai Sōin (?–1667), Yuasa
Jōzan (1708–81), Ono Takakiyo (1747–1829), and Tsurumine Shigenobu
(1788–1859) challenged the Taibo legend from historical and religious

perspectives. Norinaga, in his *Kenkyōjin* (Madman; 1785) strongly rebuked the Taibo legend as follows:

> The story of Taibo can be traced to the phrase "They [the Japanese] claimed to be the descendants of Taibo" in the *Jinshu woren chuan* [Book of the Jin: An Account of the Wa] in China. In my country, some people believed in this story for a long time, creating the name "Nation of the Ji" to support it. Recently, there are people who argue that Wu Taibo was the Sun Goddess, trying to explain the deities descended from heaven in terms of the migration of the Wu people to Japan. This is a new view suggested by our people. Chinese sources about our ancient past are unreliable and hard to believe.[61]

Takakiyo remarked in his *Taihaku Jofuku ben* (Debating on Taibo and Xu Fu), in a nationalistic and angry tone:

> Our nation and emperors existed several thousand years prior to Taibo and Xu Fu. Why did they say we are the descendants of Taibo? I understand why foreigners buy this theory. Confucians of our nation who support this should be annihilated by our deities. They are unpardonable sinners.[62]

Shigenobu expressed his belief that the offspring of Taibo established the Kumaso dynasty in Kyūshū, but insisted that it had nothing to do with the imperial family.

The discussion of Taibo died down gradually after the seventeenth century. This was mainly because all arguments, both for and against, had been put forth by early Tokugawa intellectuals on the basis of the limited Chinese and Japanese sources available concerning Taibo. It was difficult to contribute anything new to the discussion. In addition, the Taibo legend no longer carried much weight. It lost its support not because the arguments for the legend were less convincing than the counterarguments, but mainly due to the changing political and intellectual climate after the mid-Tokugawa period, as the established forms of neo-Confucian thought became more rigid and orthodox. Since the Taibo legend contained ideas that could be interpreted as disrespect for the imperial family and the nation, its advocates were silenced. The rise of nationalist sentiment and cultural pride in Tokugawa thought and culture also made this legend less acceptable.

THE SIGNIFICANCE OF THE TAIBO DEBATE

The theory of Taibo as the imperial ancestor was created by the Japanese, and this shows the cultural adaptation and localization of Chinese culture in Japan. Was Taibo the ancestor of the imperial family, or merely a Chinese sage? Basically, Tokugawa intellectuals had no major problem with the idea that Chinese sages and historical figures came to Japan in ancient times. Many Tokugawa intellectuals and commoners believed that, in addition to Taibo, Xu Fu and Yang Guifei also came to Japan. Unlike the supporters of the Xu Fu or Yang Guifei myths, however, few people in Japan fabricated evidence in the form of tombs, sites, and texts to support the Taibo legend.[63] The majority did not endorse the Taibo legend because it challenged belief in the divine origin of the imperial family and created an identity crisis for the Japanese.

The seventeenth century was brimming with intellectual vitality and creativity. Various schools of learning, ideas, art, and religion blossomed, influencing and competing with one another. The Taibo legend became an intellectual battleground. Seen superficially, whether or not the Japanese were descendants of Taibo was a topic of disagreement between the Hayashi school and the anti-Hayashi camp, which consisted of the Kimon school, the Mito school, and some historians in the early Tokugawa period. On a profounder level, advocates and critics of the Taibo legend in Japan represented conflicting attitudes toward the relationship between Chinese and Japanese traditions.

What was the nature of the debate? The disagreement was not between Sinophiles and nativists. Both advocates and critics were pro-Japan. They only used different ways to glorify their country. The former did it by accepting a Chinese-sage origin, while the latter upheld the Shinto myths. Scholars from these two camps all respected the virtues of Taibo, only disagreeing over the identity of Taibo, whether he was the ancestor of the Japanese imperial family or just an ancient Chinese sage. Nor was the debate simply between neo-Confucians and Shintoists. Razan was by no means anti-Shinto. He was, in fact, a Shinto ideologue who wanted to fuse Shinto with Confucianism, and his belief in the Taibo legend should be understood in this context.[64] The fusion he envisioned is well reflected in the following poem that he composed:

> My country is spiritual and pure, and is a place of divinity. Surrounded
> by the seas, it enjoys plenty of sunshine. Its name is Japan, and this

name shows the nature of the nation. . . . Gentlemen live here. Our customs are unsophisticated. Taibo came. The son of Shaokang also arrived and did not return.[65]

The case of Razan shows that the fusion of Confucianism and Shinto was a strong current in Tokugawa thought, but their contradictions were also salient. The Taibo debate demonstrates the conflict between two schools of thought. The pro-Confucian school believed that Shinto could include Confucianism, seeing Taibo as the ancestor of the imperial family. The pro-Shinto school was concerned about the foreignness of Confucianism and the divine authority of the imperial family, seeing Taibo as merely a Chinese sage.

To conclude, in my opinion, this debate reflects the larger issue that, while Tokugawa Japanese were engrossed in Chinese culture, they also realized that Chinese Confucian doctrines did not always fit in with the Tokugawa system.[66] Tokugawa intellectuals were in a dilemma as to whether to choose a Chinese Confucian sage or a Shinto deity as the originator of their history and world order. Advocates of the Taibo legend attempted to accommodate Chinese Confucianism within the Japanese tradition, whereas critics of the legend upheld Japanese political orthodoxy and cultural integrity in the face of unwanted Chinese influence. Taibo functioned as a building block for Tokugawa Japanese to express their national sentiments in two different directions.

Part II

APPROPRIATION OF
CONFUCIAN CLASSICS

4

THE *MENCIUS* AND POLITICS

Yoshida shōin (1830–59) was a famous late tokugawa confucian thinker, as well as a leading late Tokugawa (*bakumatsu*) imperial loyalist (*shishi*, literally meaning a man of high aspiration), who has drawn much scholarly attention.[1] His life and thought inspired his fellow countrymen and paved the way for the Meiji Restoration. He trained many brilliant young samurai, some of whom later became leaders of the Meiji Restoration and the Meiji government. Among his writings, the *Kō-Mō yowa* (Additional Notes in Explanation of the *Mencius*; 1856) was particularly influential.[2] It was more important as a treatise detailing Shōin's political ideas than as a commentary of the *Mencius*. As a *Mencius* commentary, it does not deepen our understanding of the teachings of Mencius a great deal. As a political treatise, the *Kō-Mō yowa* was one of the most popular texts among *bakumatsu* imperial loyalists, providing them with ideas for the Meiji Restoration through its advocacy of *sonnō jōi* (revere the emperor, repel the barbarians), *tennōsei* (emperor-state) ideology, *kokutai* (national polity or nationality), and the way of the samurai (*bushido*).[3] It continued to be used to propagate political conservatism in prewar Japan. Shōin interpreted the *Mencius* loosely, appropriating its terminology and rhetoric and applying them to discuss contemporary issues and to advocate his own political beliefs. Thus, the text reflects the political thought of Shōin, not that of Mencius. In other words, the *Mencius* served as a building block for Shōin to develop his own political thinking.

The *Mencius* is a book of political philosophy and ethics. Compared with other Confucian classics, its political ideas are relatively liberal and humanistic. In late Qing and early Republican China, the text was used to promote Western ideas, such as democracy, liberty, equality, free will, constitutional monarchy, social Darwinism, mercantilism, and judicial independence.[4] On the other hand, in late Tokugawa Japan, the *Mencius* was used by Yoshida Shōin to construct a conservative political ethic and ideology, the opposite of the political values that this Confucian classic stands for. The appropriation of the *Mencius* in Tokugawa political thought was a very interesting and unique development in Japan. We can hardly find any parallel in either China or Korea.[5]

Through a historical review of Mencian scholarship and a textual analysis of the *Kō-Mō yowa*, this chapter examines how Tokugawa Japanese perceived and modified the *Mencius* to discuss the Tokugawa political system and thought. The aim is to discover how Mencian political thought was twisted in Shōin's commentary, and whether the *Mencius* and Shōin's commentary had a strong impact on the Meiji Restoration and prewar conservatism.

TOKUGAWA SCHOLARSHIP ON THE *MENCIUS*

The *Mencius* arrived in Japan no later than the eighth century. It was not popular in the Nara and Heian periods, but later drew some attention among Buddhist monks and courtiers in the medieval period.[6] The *Mencius* was a popular but controversial text in Tokugawa Confucianism. Following the rise of the Song school of neo-Confucianism, the Four Books (*Daxue* [Great Learning], *Zhongyong* [Doctrine of the Mean], *Lunyu* [Analects of Confucius], and *Mengzi* [Sayings of Mencius]) were widely read among Tokugawa intellectuals. According to estimates by Hayashi Taisuke (1854–1922) in the *Nihon keikai sōmokuroku* (Complete Index of Confucian Writings), there were 169 books written on the *Mencius* by 126 Tokugawa scholars. In terms of the number of Confucian writings published in the Tokugawa period, the *Mencius* came in only seventh place.[7]

Inoue Junri (1915–2009) has identified the titles of 456 Tokugawa commentaries on the *Mencius*.[8] Based on the *Kokusho sōmokuroku* (Complete Index of Japanese Books; 1963) and books in major libraries, Seo Kunio suggests that Tokugawa commentaries on the *Mencius* should number around 500.[9] Although this is not a small number, when compared with other Confucian classics, the *Mencius* was not particularly popular.[10] The sale of its commentaries was also not particularly good. Tokugawa book merchants bought very few commentaries on it from China.[11]

Controversial and sensitive political ideas in the *Mencius*, such as rev-olution, regicide, the distinction between the *ōdō* (kingly way) and the *hadō* (hegemonic way), relative loyalty, politics for the sake of the people, and support for the imperial court, were all considered incompatible with the Tokugawa ideology. They were subject to reinterpretation and criticism. Following the medieval practice, when scholars lectured on the *Mencius* to the Tokugawa emperor and *shogun*, all problematic passages were cut.[12]

With regard to approaches and areas of concern, Mencian studies in the Tokugawa period can be divided into four major schools: the school of com-mentary, the school of textual criticism, the school of moral thought, and the school of political thought. The school of commentary and the school of textual criticism were concerned with the text itself, whereas the school of moral thought and the school of political thought studied the ideas behind the text. The approach of the school of commentary was explanatory, that of the

CONFUCIAN WRITINGS IN THE TOKUGAWA PERIOD

CONFUCIAN CLASSICS	NUMBER OF BOOKS	NUMBER OF AUTHORS
Yijing	395	212
Lunyu	363	261
Daxue	246	183
Chungiu	224	164
Xiaojing	199	144
Shijing	173	131
Mengzi	169	126
Zhongyong	168	131
Shujing	147	111
Liji	144	91

school of textual criticism was philological, that of the school of moral thought was philosophical, and that of the school of political thought was historical.

The school of commentary was the largest, playing a major role in popularizing the text. Scholars of this school annotated and sometimes even translated the *Mencius* passage by passage to help their students and readers understand the meaning of the text. They came from different Confucian traditions, including the Zhu Xi school (e.g., Hayashi Gahō, 1618–80; Kaibara Ekken, 1630–1714; Nakamura Tekisai, 1629–1702; and Okada Hakku, 1691–1767), the Wang Yangming school (e.g., Kumazawa Banzan, 1619–91, and Satō Issai, 1772–1859), and the eclectic school (e.g., Minakawa Kien, 1735–1807, and Ōta Kinjō, 1765–1825). They produced many commentaries of excellent and careful scholarship, such as Minakawa Kien's *Mōshi shakukai* (An Explication of the *Mencius*; 1797), Ōta Kinjō's *Mōshi seion* (The Essence of the *Mencius*; 1828), and Satō Issai's *Mōshi rangaisho* (Notes on the *Mencius*; 1830).

The school of textual criticism also produced some very scholarly works. Influenced by Qing *kaozheng* (evidential research) scholarship, the scholars of this school were critical of the Song commentaries for being too speculative. They attempted to reconstruct the original text and meanings of the *Mencius* through various research methods, such as philology, phonetics, and textual comparison. They were more interested in restoring Han commentaries than discussing issues of authorship or authenticity. Their representative works include Yamanoi Kanae's (1690–1728) *Shichikei Mōshi kōbun* (Textual Study of the Seven Classics and *Mencius*, with Supplement; 1726), Kaiho Gyoson's (1798–1866) *Mōshi Chōshi gi* (Zhao Qi's [108–201] Interpretations of the *Mencius*), and Ikai Keisho's (1761–1846) *Mōshi kōbun* (Textual Study of the *Mencius*; 1827). They improved the accuracy of the text, which had become corrupted over the ages, and restored some pre-Song commentaries. Yamanoi's work was particularly significant in Mencian scholarship and Sino-Japanese cultural interchange. Based on some Song editions of Chinese books held in the Ashikaga School, Yamanoi restored some fragmentary pre-Song texts, in particular the commentary of Zhao Qi (108–201).[13] Tokugawa Yoshimune (1684–1751), the eighth Tokugawa *shōgun*, had the text edited by Ogyū Hokkei (1669–1754), the younger brother of Ogyū Sorai (1666–1728), and published by the *bakufu* in 1731. Reprinted by the famous official-scholar Ruan Yuan (1764–1849) in China, *Shichikei Mōshi kōbun* became one of the few Tokugawa commentaries to be known by Qing scholars.[14]

The school of moral thought produced the best and most original scholarship. Regarding the *Mencius* as one of the most important Confucian classics, scholars of this school used the text to explain their understanding of Confucian morality and philosophy. They mainly came from the *kogaku* (ancient learning) school (e.g., Itō Jinsai, 1627–1707, and Itō Tōgai, 1670–1736), the eclectic school (e.g., Miyake Sekian, 1665–1730, and Nakai Riken, 1735–1807), and the *shingaku* (mind learning) school (e.g., Ishida Baigan, 1685–1744). The representative works of this school were Itō Jinsai's *Mōshi kogi* (Ancient Meanings of the *Mencius*; 1720) and Nakai Riken's *Mōshi hōgen* (Investigation of the Origins of the *Mencius*). These two works were among the best commentaries on the *Mencius* of the entire period. Jinsai and Riken developed the philosophy of the unity of *li* (principle) and *qi* (force) in their explanations of the *Mencius*. They criticized the metaphysics and epistemology of the Zhu Xi school in their discussion of key concepts in the *Mencius*, such as *zhiyan* (understanding the meaning of words), *yangqi* (nurturance of the vital force), *cunxin* (retaining of the mind), *yangxing* (nurturance of the nature), and *jiyi* (accumulation of righteousness).[15] Many scholars of this school came from merchant backgrounds, and they emphasized the universality of Mencian ethics. For instance, Miyake Sekian, Itō Jinsai, and Ishida Baigan found universal value for both merchants and commoners in the *Mencius*.[16]

The school of political thought was a strange company of critics of Mencius that attacked Mencian political thought in their writings.[17] In Ming and Qing China, while some Mencian political ideas were regarded as controversial, most intellectuals recognized the text's political value and relied on it to develop their political ideas. In Tokugawa Japan, however, the anti-Mencian tradition was much stronger due to Tokugawa cultural policies and censorship. Since many of Mencius's political ideas were considered dangerous, unorthodox, and alien up until the last decades of the Tokugawa period, Tokugawa intellectuals would not endorse the text's sensitive political ideas openly lest they get into trouble with officials. This explains why most people discussed Mencius's political thought only in a negative light.

Many scholars of this school came from the Kimon school, the Sorai school, *kokugaku*, and the late Mito school.[18] Scholars of the Kimon school, the Sorai school, and *kokugaku* criticized certain Mencian ideas, which they believed did not fit in with Japan's political tradition or Tokugawa ideology. Their ideas represented a strong nationalist current in Tokugawa intellectual development and had a strong impact on *bakumatsu* imperial loyalists, including Yoshida Shōin. The Sorai school questioned the authority and value of the *Mencius* in Confucianism. Ogyū Sorai did not regard Mencius as a sage and criticized Itō Jansai for overrating the *Mencius*. In the *Mōshi shiki* (Knowing the *Mencius*), Sorai looked down upon Mencius as a provocative scholar who advocated dangerous ideas such as the distinction between righteousness and profit, and between the kingly way and the hegemonic way. His disciple, Dazai Shundai (1680–1747), attacked several aspects of the *Mencius* to uphold the Tokugawa ideology in his *Mōshiron* (Discourses on the *Mencius*). Like his master, Shundai criticized the distinction between the kingly way and the hegemonic way most strongly. This work created a heated debate over Mencian concepts.[19]

THE *KŌ-MŌ YOWA* IN TOKUGAWA MENCIAN SCHOLARSHIP

How shall we situate Shōin's *Kō-Mō yowa* in Tokugawa scholarship on the *Mencius*? The significance of the *Kō-Mō yowa* does not rest so much with its scholarship or originality, but more with its political implications. Fairly speaking, Shōin broke no new ground in his study of the text and ideas of the *Mencius*. As a Confucian commentary, it was not a work of high scholarship. Although Shōin claimed that he had studied the *Mencius* for twenty years, he did not specialize in it and did not study it seriously until his final years. His interest in the *Mencius* seems to have been inspired by his teacher, Sakuma Shōzan (1811–64), who also studied the text in prison. Shōzan influenced Shōin's understanding of the *Mencius* in two ways. First, he said that the *Mencius* had important political and practical value. Second, he claimed that Zhu Xi's commentary contained many mistakes.[20] Shōin's reading of the *Mencius* was also influenced by the late Mito school, the ancient learning school, the Kimon school, and *kokugaku*. In the *Kō-Mō yowa*, Shōin's political ideas were close to those of the Mito and Kimon schools, and his textual interpretation followed Itō Jinsai's commentary closely.

Obviously, Shōin had little to do with the school of commentary or the school of textual criticism. To him, the only things worth studying were those related to the well-being of the nation and the people. He regarded politics and economics as true learning, and looked down upon philology, phonetics, and textual criticism as heretical learning.[21] In the epilogue, he wrote: "I am not familiar with either textual criticism or philology. I have only expressed my sadness and happiness, joy and anger in the *Mencius*."[22] He was not interested in textual study and did not read many commentaries on the *Mencius* before he wrote his lectures. In his lectures, Shōin cited only three commentaries: Itō Jinsai's *Mōshi kogi*, Zhu Xi's *Meng-tzu chi-chu* (Collective Commentary on the *Mencius*), and Okada Hakku's *Mōshi kai* (Explanation of the *Mencius*; 1762). He liked Jinsai's commentary very much and cited it frequently. Like Jinsai, he was critical of Zhu Xi's commentary, pointing out its numerous mistakes in interpretation.[23] He did not belong to the school of moral philosophy, either. Although Shōin addressed moral issues in his lectures, unlike scholars of the school of moral thought, he was mainly concerned with political ethics and cared less about personal ethics.

Among the four schools of Mencian studies, Shōin belonged to the school of political thought. He shared many ideas with Dazai Shundai and scholars of the Kimon school, and may have been influenced by them in his reading of the *Mencius*.[24] There were two areas in which their views were almost identical. First, they pointed out that the imperial family in Japan enjoyed an unbroken lineage and thus regicide, perhaps the most controversial concept in the *Mencius*, was incompatible with Japan's national polity. They condemned Kings Tang and Wu for setting precedents for traitors in China, stressing that revolution was the evilest political principle, and could never be applied in Japan.[25] Second, they advocated absolute loyalty and criticized the Mencian notion of reciprocity in the ruler-subject relationship. According to the *Mencius*, the relationship between the ruler and the subject is reciprocal and conditional, and, therefore, if the ruler is irrevocably bad, the subject may abandon him. Scholars of this school attacked this idea as disloyal, emphasizing that in Japan the subject should always be loyal to the ruler, regardless of the personal qualities and ethics of the ruler.[26] In addition to these two topics, scholars of this school and Shōin also rejected some other Mencian political ideas that they considered either inappropriate or unrealistic, such as politics for the people, concession of the throne to the capable, and the use of rites and music to rule.[27]

Shōin represented a new direction in this school. His commentary demonstrated the emergence of a more vibrant intellectual climate in late Tokugawa Japan. With the decline of *bakufu* authority, many theretofore illegitimate teachings found space to grow. Mencius's political thought was one

such teaching. Unlike early scholars of this school, Shōin basically upheld
Mencian political ideas, although he did not hesitate to disapprove of some
of Mencius's ideas that he deemed incompatible with Japan's political traditions. He disagreed with Shundai and other early scholars of this school over
certain issues. For instance, Shundai attacked Mencius's distinction between
the kingly way and the hegemonic way to legitimize the Tokugawa *bakufu*,
whereas Shōin upheld the distinction to challenge the *bakufu*. According to
Mencius's definition, a hegemon controls the nation by means of his military
strength, whereas a true king manages the nation by implementing benevolent
rule. Mencius did not give high credit to the former, even though one may
bring peace to the nation. On the contrary, Shundai argued that a military
man who could bring peace to the nation was no longer a hegemon but a true
king. Hence, the Tokugawa *shōgun* were the legitimate rulers.[28] Shōin accepted
Mencius's distinction, but added that true kings were determined not only by
benevolent rule, but also by birth. As a result, only the imperial family could
be true kings and the *bakufu* was only a form of hegemony,

Shōin used the *Mencius* to advocate his own political ideas more than he
used his writing to promote Mencius's political ideas. His work is important
because it provides clues for us to understand the ideological underpinnings of
the Meiji Restoration and some of the nationalist ideas that shaped the history
of modern Japan. An examination of Shōin's commentary also deepens our
understanding of the accommodation and naturalization of Chinese political
thought in Tokugawa Japan.

THE BACKGROUND OF THE *KŌ-MŌ YOWA*

The *Kō-Mō yowa* was Shōin's most representative, comprehensive, and influential work. In it, he expressed his opinions on current issues in Tokugawa
politics, economics, and diplomacy. The work was a collection of Shōin's lectures on the *Mencius* given while he was in prison. He realized that he might
not be able to leave the prison alive, and decided to do something that would
help the nation. In regard to the motive behind his work, he wrote:

> Last year, I offended the law and was imprisoned. I could do nothing in
> prison. I am indebted to the virtues of the emperors of all ages and to
> the care of the *daimyō*. I am nobody, but I feel that my responsibility is

by no means light. Being in high spirits, I see reviving the imperial court and the nation as my responsibility. Hence, I wrote the *Kō-Mō yowa*.[29]

He started reading and lecturing on the *Mencius* from 12 April 1855. Two months later, on 13 June, he began a regular lecture series on the text for his cellmates, relatives, and jailers, which he finished a year later on 13 June 1856. During that year, he gave lectures on the *Mencius* fifty-five times, about four to five times per month on average. Having edited his lectures, he named his work *Kō-Mō satsuki* (Notes on the *Mencius*) and sent a handwritten copy to Yamagata Taika (1781–1866), head of the Confucian academy in the Chōshū domain, for comments. To Shōin's surprise, Taika, a Zhu Xi scholar and supporter of the *bakufu*, gave extremely harsh criticisms of the text, attacking Shōin's work almost passage by passage on the basis of the teachings of Zhu Xi and Tokugawa ideology. Shōin engaged in a heated exchange of ideas with Taika. Due to this unpleasant and unnerving experience, his anti-*bakufu* ideas became even stronger and more explicit in his correspondences with Taika. Although the *Kō-Mō yowa* was not published until 1871, handwritten copies were circulated widely among late Tokugawa scholars and activists. Many ideas in the text represent a strong late Tokugawa nationalist current, shared by *shishi* activists, late Mito scholars, and *kokugaku* scholars.

Shōin was already in prison because of his problematic political attitude, but he continued to comment on current affairs. He was a model *shishi* who always followed his own principles without making compromises or worrying about the consequences. If only he believed it was the right thing to do, he would do it even if his action went against some established teachings or laws. It is overly simplistic to trace the intellectual orientation of *shishi* like Shōin to any single origin, such as the Wang Yangming school, the Mito school, *kokugaku*, ancient learning, or the Kimon school.[30] Shōin was certainly influenced by all of these schools of thought, but he never limited himself to one particular school. Basically, he was only faithful to his own beliefs. In writing the *Kō-Mō yowa*, he actually disobeyed Chinese teachings and the orders of Tokugawa *bakufu*. Although the Chinese believed that people without official positions should refrain from discussing politics, and the Tokugawa *bakufu* censored political speeches and writings, Shōin stressed that it would be a crime for anyone to ignore the crisis of the nation, and therefore he had to write down his lectures to remind the people.[31] He laid out four directions for political reforms in Japan within his work: revering the emperor, repelling the Western intruders, promoting political ethics, and cultivating talented people. He explained: "The points that I am suggesting here mean upholding the national polity by revering the emperor and repelling the barbarians, encouraging the proper political conduct of retainers, and cultivating talented people."[32]

In constructing his anti-*bakufu* and conservative ideology, Shōin interpreted the *Mencius* loosely. He was neither pro-Mencius nor anti-Mencius. He simply used his own political standards to judge the *Mencius*. In general, Shōin respected Mencius as a great Confucian master and had a positive view of Mencian political thought. However, when any Mencian idea was in disagreement with his beliefs, he did not hesitate to reject it. For instance, he upheld the Mencian ideas of distinction between the kingly way and the hegemonic way, the way of the *zhishi* (*shishi*), and the politics of benevolence, but criticized the ideas of revolution, reciprocity in the emperor-subject relationship, and politics for the people.

NATIONAL POLITY IN JAPAN AND CHINA

The basic assumption of the *Kō-Mō yowa* was the oft-repeated Shinto and *kokugaku* belief that Japan had a different *kokutai* (national polity), which was superior to that of China or any other nation. *Kokutai* refers to the political culture, ethics, and institutions of a nation. Shōin's definition of Japan's *kokutai* was similar to that of the Mito school, but his presentation of the idea was more powerful and sensational. He held that Confucian values had their universality, but that each nation had its own peculiarities due to its unique historical and geographical background. The *kokutai* of Europe, America, and India were completely different from that of Japan, and thus should not be adopted. In particular, he rejected Christian and Buddhist ethics. He looked down upon Westerners as barbarians and reminded his readers that they could study Western medicine, weaponry, and logic, but should not admire the Westerners. To him, Western learning was only a means to strengthen Japan so that it could repel the Westerners.[33] Like his teacher, Sakuma Shōzan, Shōin believed in the need to combine Western science and Eastern morality to strengthen the nation.[34]

Shōin put a lot of effort in his lectures into comparing the *kokutai* of Japan and China. While acknowledging that there were similarities in the *kokutai* of the two nations, he emphasized that Japan's *kokutai* was fundamentally different from and superior to that of China:[35]

> The Way refers to the universal principle. This is the commonality.
> National polity is the expression of one nation. This is the uniqueness.
> The orders between emperor and subject, father and son, husband and
> wife, elder and younger brother, friend and friend are the five constant
> relationships. They are all the same throughout the world. The emperor-
> subject relationship in my country is the best among all nations. This
> is unique in one particular nation.[36]

Although admiring Confucius and Mencius, Shōin showed little respect
for China, calling it *Shina*, and referring to the Chinese as *mō-Tōjin* (hairy
Chinamen, namely, uncivilized aliens) with disdain, pointing out that Qing
China was poor and corrupt and the way of the sages no longer existed there:
"Although China has preserved the writings of the sages, the kingly way is no
longer respected. Even the barbarians criticize it. How sad!"[37]

Shōin argued that Japan's *kokutai* was superior because the Japanese
treasured the virtue of absolute loyalty. Influenced by Shinto myth prevalent
among Tokugawa intellectuals, he maintained that Japan had adopted a feudal
system under which the Japanese imperial family enjoyed an unbroken lineage
and ministers were hereditary and unfailingly faithful to the emperor. China,
on the other hand, had abandoned feudalism and the true principle of loyalty:

> In our country, from the imperial court down to the regional domains,
> the succession is uninterrupted. This is something that China cannot
> match. In China the subjects engage themselves only for half a season
> like servants. If their lords are good, they stay with them. If they are
> bad, they leave them. The subjects of our country, however, being
> hereditary, share life and death and joy and sorrow with their lords.
> These subjects will never leave their lords, even when they must die.[38]

Shōin was proud to claim that no one in Japanese history, including powerful
ministers and ambitious warriors, dared to usurp the throne. The thing that
he disliked most about China was that loyalty was conditional and relative,
so that the Chinese switched their loyalty easily for personal interest. In the
strict sense of absolute loyalty, Shōin pointed out that most Chinese sages were
far from perfect. For example, King Tang and King Wu, the founders of the

Shang and Zhou dynasties, respectively, were condemned by him as traitors, because they betrayed their emperors and took the throne. Jizi, a Shang prince, was criticized for giving political advice to his enemy, King Wu.[39] Weizi, also a Shang prince, was considered wrong to have left the Shang emperor when his advice was not taken seriously. Likewise, many famous ministers in Chinese history, in Shōin's point of view, "were nothing but human beings who did not know benevolence and righteousness."[40] Even Confucius and Mencius were not spared. Shōin criticized them for leaving the state of their birth to look for posts and opportunities in other states.[41]

According to Shōin, the Chinese way of leaving one's lord to serve another, even with the aim of bringing good to the whole world, was unacceptable in Japan. He added that, if the lord were bad, the subject should remain loyal to him and even prepare to commit suicide to force his lord to repent.[42] In Japan, the subjects were always faithful to the ruler, but, "in China, the situation is different. Although the relationship between the ruler and the subject is said to be based on righteousness, the subject only obeys when the ruler is right, and disobeys when the ruler is wrong. After reminding the ruler of his mistakes three times in vain, they leave for other domains."[43]

In China, the relationship between the ruler and the subject, as Mencius pointed out, was not always harmonious. Sometimes, the ruler treated his subjects as dogs and horses, and the subjects saw their rulers as enemies. Shōin warned that this must not happen in Japan, and that those subjects who regarded their ruler as an enemy should receive capital punishment.[44] He reiterated that, in Japan, the subject must show absolute respect to the emperor. Unlike their Chinese counterparts, the teachers of the Japanese emperor were not allowed to sit while giving their lectures, because the primary status of the teachers remained rooted in their positions as subjects of the emperor.[45]

THE KINGLY WAY VERSUS THE HEGEMONIC WAY

Shōin was an early advocate of the family-state ideology, an integral part of prewar conservatism, in his definition of loyalty. He regarded this concept as a special feature of Japan's *kokutai*. The family-state ideology meant the inclusion of filial piety within loyalty. As he put it: "Lord and subject are one, loyalty and filial piety are the same. Only my nation is like this."[46] Shōin stressed that the people should treat their ruler as their father and the ruler should treat his people as his children, and the people should never abandon the emperor no matter how he behaves.

> After all, the lord is for us also like a father. To look for a lord in another province, leaving one's country of birth, because the lord is foolish and stupid, is the same as taking an old man from a neighboring house as a father and leaving one's own house, just because one's father is stupid.[47]

He added that, since the Japanese emperor had divine origins, he was more important than the people. He said: "In China, the people are considered more important than the emperor. In my country, the holy emperor comes before the people."[48] Therefore, the imperial family, not the people, should be the center of national politics. Shōin rejected Mencius's idea that the emperor existed for the sake of the people. Obviously, the main purpose of the family-state ideology was to promote the emperor's authority more than the emperor's paternal love for his subjects.

Naturally, Shōin saw the Mencian notion of regicide as a kind of treachery. He argued that, even in China, regicide could only be considered under extreme circumstances. Kings Tang and Wu only used it as the last resort, but it was misused by later generations as a convenient ideological justification for revolt.[49] Shōin denied the application of the entire set of Mencian ideas about regicide, such as heavenly mandate, politics for the people, and revolution of the imperial house. According to Mencius, the nation does not belong to a single family, and heaven appoints a man to rule on its behalf. The ruler should carry out the politics of benevolence. If a ruler does not care about the well-being of the people, he will lose the mandate of heaven and heaven will appoint another man to replace him by means of revolution. Shōin did not accept this concept. To him, the idea of heavenly mandate did not apply to the Japanese imperial family. He explained that the tenure of the Japanese emperor does not depend on his ethics and quality, but on his blood. The imperial family holds the right to rule, and its tenure is for good without any conditions.[50] He remarked:

> The offspring of the Sun Goddess will last forever. The Eight Continents were created by the Sun Goddess, and her offspring were put in charge forever. Hence, billions of people share their fate with the imperial family and they should have no doubts.[51]

Shōin, however, did not completely deny Mencian notions of heavenly mandate, politics for the people, and revolution, suggesting that they could be applied to the *shōgun* and regent who were given the right to govern.[52] Shōin reinterpreted the *tenmei* (mandate of heaven) as "the order of the *tennō* [Japanese emperor]," and thus receiving the mandate of heaven meant being appointed by the imperial house to be the *shōgun*. This is perhaps one of the most original aspects of Shōin's political thinking.[53]

More significantly, Shōin expressed his anti-*bakufu* ideas in his explanation of absolute loyalty. He defined the position of the *bakufu* in his explanation of the Mencian notion of the distinction between the kingly way and the hegemonic way. Shōin, like Mencius, did not give high credit to hegemons, even though some brought peace to the state. He condemned the Taira, the Minamoto, the Hōjō, and the Ashikaga as *gyakuzoku* (rebels), and praised Emperor Go-Daigo (1288–1339) for carrying out the Kenmu Restoration.[54] He pointed out that Japan had had five authoritarian regimes in its history: the Minamoto, the Ashikaga, the Oda, the Toyotomi, and the Tokugawa. In general, he was critical of them, although he gave special credit to Oda Nobunaga (1534–82), Toyotomi Hideyoshi (1536–98), and Tokugawa Ieyasu (1542–1616). In particular, he praised Hideyoshi for respecting the imperial court and expanding Japan's territory.[55] In Japanese history, as Shōin put it, the throne always belonged to the imperial family, whereas the running of the administration sometimes was entrusted to powerful families:

> In Japan, the nation only belongs to one man [the emperor] and no one should take over the throne. The Fujiwara, Taira, Minamoto, Hōjō, Nitta, Ashikaga, Oda, and Toyotomi were in control of the administration for a certain period of time. They committed many mistakes, but also did some good things. The tenure of their administration was based on whether they could do good things.[56]

He added that even the most ambitious people in Japanese history did not dare to take over the throne. Not a single *shōgun* or regent failed to show some respect to the imperial court.

The object of loyalty, in Shōin's mind, was always the emperor and not the *shōgun*. The *shōgun*, to him, was merely a subject of the emperor. Accordingly, the people's support for the *shōgun* was conditional. If the *shōgun* performed his duties of revering the emperor and repelling the barbarians, the entire nation should support him. If he ignored his duties, then he should be over-thrown. Thus, the idea of revolution may be applied to the *shōgun*. He gave the Tokugawa *bakufu* a clear warning: "Posts like that of *shōgun* are appointed by the imperial court only for those who can carry out the duties of those posts. If the *shōgun* shirks his duties like the Ashikaga house did, he should be sacked immediately."[57] At first, Shōin asked the people to support and respect the *shōgun* that was officially appointed by the emperor. If the *bakufu* went wrong, people should try to warn it. He said: "From the *daimyō* to officials and commoners, we must unite to remonstrate and argue with the *bakufu*, to respect the imperial court, and to repel the barbarians."[58] Anyone who failed to do this was disloyal. Obviously, the emperor, rather than the *shōgun*, was the true source of political authority. As he explained: "Up until now, we have only respected the *bakufu*. From now on, we respect the *bakufu* only because we [respect and want to] repay the imperial court."[59]

As time went on, Shōin became more radical in prison and turned to suggesting that the *bakufu* be overthrown for disobeying the imperial order to repel the Westerners. He claimed that all lands in Japan belonged to the emperor and that the *bakufu* was disloyal for giving land to the Westerners without the consent of the emperor.[60] He even dared to question the integrity of the Tokugawa *shōgun*: "Although the feat of Tokugawa Ieyasu was unprec-edented, he was far from perfect. His offspring became the *shōgun*. It goes without saying that they were not loyal. We must say that they were not even filial."[61] Thus, in Shōin's hand, the Mencian notion of revolution killed two birds with one stone, as he denied it to strengthen imperial authority and upheld it to question the legitimacy of the *bakufu*. This was a case of inno-vative naturalization of a Chinese political concept.

THE WAY OF SAMURAI AND THE WAY OF IMPERIAL LOYALISTS

To Shōin, *bushidō* was also evidence of the superiority of Japan's *kokutai*. *Bushidō* teachings emphasized the absolute and unconditional loyalty of the samurai to their lords. Like other *shishi* activists, Shōin also considered himself imbued with the samurai spirit. His *bushidō* ideas seem to have been influenced by Yamaga Sokō (1622–85), an early ideologue of *bushidō*, and his reading of the *Mencius*.[62] Shōin used the *Mencius* extensively to explain the way of the samurai. His pen name was *mōshi* (猛士 fierce warrior), a homonym of Mencius

(*Mōshi*) in Japanese. Even the characters are similar. Like Mencius, Shōin felt that he had a sense of mission to save the nation.[63] The samurai spirit, he suggested, was not only for samurai, but also for every Japanese. In other words, he attempted to turn samurai ethics into national ethics.

Shōin identified death as the most important element in *bushidō*. This was perhaps the most distinctive feature of his political thought. To him, a real samurai must prepare to die for his lord at any time. Like Yamamoto Tsunetomo (1659–1719), the author the *bushidō* classic *Hagakure* (In the Shadow of Leaves; 1716), Shōin was obsessed with death and developed the philosophy of death to the utmost: "I studied the martial arts of the Yamaga school when I was young, and therefore I am imbued with *bushidō*. Death is something that is always on my mind."[64] He encouraged his cellmates and himself, saying: "Although we are in prison and our lives may end soon, we should never forget the quality of the *shishi*."[65] The term *shishi* came from the *Mencius*. Shōin quoted the following sentence from the *Mencius* to emphasize that a *shishi* should prepare to die for the principles he believes in: "A *shishi* [man whose mind is set on high ideals] never forgets that he may end in a ditch; a man of valor never forgets that he may forfeit his head."[66] Shōin's position is different from Mencius's. Mencius only regarded martyrdom as the *last* recourse for fulfilling ethical ideals, while Shōin saw it as the *necessary* recourse.

Shōin regarded death as the fundamental principle in his teaching and stressed its importance throughout his lectures, inspired by the following saying in the *Mencius*: "Life is something I desire; righteousness is also something I desire. If I cannot have both, I will forsake life and select righteousness." He remarked: "Undoubtedly the people of Chōshū should die for the defense of Chōshū, and the people of Japan should die for the defense of Japan. This is the number one principle in my lectures on the *Mencius*."[67] He glorified death as a fulfillment of loyalty that could give the nation the spiritual strength necessary to repel the barbarians: "If retainers are willing to die for their lord, and sons are willing to die for their fathers, we do not have to be afraid of the barbarians."[68] "If the senior ministers and bureau chiefs in the *bakufu* and the ministers and the retainers in the domains are willing to sacrifice their lives for the nation, we can successfully repel the barbarians."[69] He blamed the retainers of the *bakufu* and domains for inviting foreign invasion because they did not want to die for the nation. In Shōin's explanation of the Mencian notion of *cheng-hsin* (correcting one's mind), he noted: "In recent years, we have done a lot of things in front of the foreign barbarians to harm our national polity. The reason is that the retainers and samurai of the *bakufu* and domains do not correct their minds and do not die for the nation."[70] Shōin planned for his own martyrdom in order to fulfill *bushidō* and to awaken the nation.[71] In his last imprisonment in 1859, shortly before his execution, he quoted the *Mencius* to tell his students of his determination to die for the nation:

> [The *Mencius* states:] "Never has there been one possessed of complete sincerity who did not move others." I studied the *Mencius* for twenty years from childhood until now, and yet I did not understand the meaning of this passage. Now, I am going to Edo to receive punishment and will experience this passage with my own body. I am not afraid of death.[72]

This statement was Shōin's lifetime motto, and he quoted it many times on different occasions.[73] *Makoto* (sincerity), a key concept in both Shinto and Confucianism, had a special place in his thought and action. This contributed to a kind of romanticism and moralism that only concerned one's internal principles and will.

Aside from the philosophy of death, Shōin also used the *Mencius* to explain other elements in *bushidō*. First, a samurai must have a constant heart for righteousness. The *Mencius* reads: "Only the gentleman [official] can have a constant heart in spite of a lack of any constant means of support."[74] It also suggests that the gentleman will not become addicted to pleasure in good times, will not change his goals in poverty, and will not bend under military pressure. Shōin believed that these ideals were also applicable to the Japanese samurai. He said that if a samurai could suffer from hunger or even face death without losing his constant heart for righteousness, Japan would fill with spiritual and moral force and could be saved from foreign invasion.[75] Second, a samurai acts according to the principles of loyalty and filial piety, whereas an ordinary person acts according to profit. A samurai seeks the interests of the nation and his lord, but an ordinary person cares only about his own interests. Third, a samurai has a sense of shame: "Samurai in my country talk about shame frequently. Nothing is more shameful than not knowing shame. More than ever before, many present-day samurai do not have a sense of shame. In order to revive *budō* [the way of the warrior], we must first revive the concept of shame."[76]

THE APPROPRIATION OF MENCIAN POLITICAL THOUGHT

In the late Tokugawa period, different Confucian elements were incorporated into a developing conservative ideology. The *Mencius* was only one such element. It was, however, not the original teaching of the *Mencius*, but its Japanese interpretation that had an impact on late Tokugawa politics. As the *Mencius* itself is fairly liberal and open, in the making of a late Tokugawa imperial loyalist and conservative ideology, a large part of its teaching was reinterpreted and distorted. In this process, Chinese political thought was naturalized and became distinctly Japanese. Shōin's *Kō-Mō yowa* should be understood in this political and intellectual context.

Shōin was perhaps the most influential *shishi* thinker.[77] Shōin's political thought, as seen in his *Kō-Mō yowa*, was radical, sensational, eclectic, loosely organized, and sometimes inconsistent. Among the popular readings for *shishi*, the *Kō-Mō yowa* was not as well written and systematic as the *Shinron* (New Thesis) by Aizawa Seishisai (1782–1863) and not as scholarly and ambitious as the *Dai Nihonshi* (History of Great Japan) by the Mito domain. Its ideas were not original, and most were very close to those of the late Mito school and *kokugaku*, representing attitudes and ideas that were prevalent among late Tokugawa activists. The *Kō-Mō yowa* was influential in the late Tokugawa period not because of its scholarship, but because its provocative ideas fit the intellectual needs of the times. People wanted to know what went wrong and what they should do to save the nation. The *Kō-Mō yowa* provided a clear answer and solution: the *bakufu* should be held responsible for not carrying out the imperial order to repel the Westerners, and thus political power should be returned to the imperial court. Shōin's words were forceful, sensational, critical, and penetrating, and they touched the hearts of many late Tokugawa Japanese. His death made him a legend and drew even more attention to his writings.

The *Kō-Mō yowa* was not a faithful commentary on the *Mencius*. Shōin only used the *Mencius* to promote his own ideas.[78] This was perhaps an unwise decision, because in so many ways the *Mencius* stands for opposite political values. The *Mencius*, by traditional standards, contains many liberal and humanistic ideas, and has had a liberalizing effect on East Asian political thought. Using it to advocate conservative ideas was not easy. This is why Shōin was inconsistent in his critique of the text. While supporting some of its ideas, he attacked those liberal and humanistic aspects of the *Mencius*. In his explanation of the *Mencius*,

Shōin made major modifications to pursue his own political agenda. He upheld the distinction between the kingly way and the hegemonic way, but added that true kings were determined by blood. He developed the way of gentleman in the *Mencius* into *bushidō*, stressing that death was necessary and not a last recourse. Regarding the Mencian ideas of reciprocity in the emperor-subject relationship and revolution, he disapproved of their application to discussion of the sovereignty of the emperor, and instead used them to challenge the governance of the *bakufu*.

The images of Yoshida Shōin underwent several changes in prewar times. He was regarded as a leading Restorationist ideologue and a great revolutionary thinker in the late Tokugawa and early Meiji periods. From the late Meiji period to the end of the Second World War, he was used to advocate the emperor-state ideology and other nationalist ideas.

From the *Kō-Mō yowa*, we can conclude that Shōin was neither a creative nor a systematic thinker. He only repeated ideas of the late Mito school, *kogaku*, *kokugaku* and the Kimon school. His ideas were extreme, confrontational, and eclectic. Nevertheless, his nationalist ideas, such as absolute loyalty, *bushidō*, emperor-state ideology, *kokutai*, and imperialism, had a strong impact on late Meiji conservatism and prewar Japanese militarism.

The *Kō-Mō yowa* was not only a popular book in the last years of the Tokugawa period, it was also the main textbook used at his private academy, Shōka Sonjuku (Village School under the Pines). After his release in 1856, Shōin continued to lecture on the *Mencius* and organized the lectures that he gave during his imprisonment to compile them as the *Kō-Mō yowa*. His students, including imperial loyalists and forerunners of the Meiji Restoration (Kusaka Genzui, 1840–64; Takasugi Shinsaku, 1839–67; and Maebara Issei, 1834–76) and Meiji leaders (Itō Hirobumi, 1841–1909; Shinagawa Yajirō, 1843–1900; Kido Takayoshi, 1833–77; and Yamagata Aritomo, 1838–1922), were all familiar with this work. Undoubtedly, it might have exerted a considerable impact on the thoughts and actions of these late Tokugawa imperial loyalists and Meiji leaders. However, the intellectual gap between Shōin and his students was wide. Meiji leaders like Hirobumi and Aritomo were influenced more by Shōin's nationalist and imperial loyalist spirit than by his radical and extremist ideas and actions. Unlike other *shishi* leaders, such as Sakamoto Ryōma (1835–67), Saigō Takamori (1827–77), and Yokoi Shōnan (1809–1869), Shōin did not have a blueprint for the new Japan. Hence, he should be given credit only for contributing to the Meiji Restoration and not to Meiji reforms. He had little to do with

Westernization, although he wanted to go to the United States and approved of people studying Western science and technology.

There was a Chinese *Mencius* versus Japanese *Mencius* scenario in modern Japan. Relatively speaking, the Chinese *Mencius* is liberal, open, and humanistic, whereas the Japanese *Mencius* is conservative, radical, and feudalistic. Due to the basic differences between the *Mencius* and the *Kō-Mō yowa*, they were used by different people in modern Japan to advocate opposite values. Westernizers used the *Mencius* to justify Western ideas. For instance, Nakae Chōmin (1847–1901), a champion of Western philosophy in the Meiji period, found the Western political ideas of liberty, equality, and democracy in the *Mencius*. Mencian political ideas also gave people the strength to demand their rights and to confront the government during the People's Rights Movement in the mid-Meiji period. Yoshino Sakuzō (1878–1933), the spokesman for "Taishō democracy," cited the *Mencius* to uphold the ideal that politics should be for the sake of the people. Uno Tetsuto (1875–1974), a specialist in Chinese philosophy, mentioned in his writings in the Taishō period that the *Mencius* contains the elements of freedom and equality.

By contrast, the *Kō-Mō yowa* was used by conservatives and militarists to promote emperor-state ideology. Passages and ideas from the *Kō-Mō yowa* were included in the official textbooks for ethics and national history in elementary schools during the early Shōwa period.[79] Ōba Osamu, a scholar of Sino-Japanese relations, remembers that, during wartime, he was drawn by an interest in history to join a study group to read the *Kō-Mō yowa*.[80] However, prewar cultural conservatives and the government only promoted the *Kō-Mō yowa* and not the *Mencius*. They even took a critical stance toward the *Mencius*. For instance, in the early Shōwa period (1926–45), conservative scholars, such as Shionoya On (1878–1962) and Nakamura Kyūshirō (1874–1961), attacked the Mencian theory of revolution.[81] In other words, the *Mencius* was remade in Japan, used as a building block to express Japanese ideas. From the late Meiji period to the early Shōwa period, the official ideology embraced only the Japanese or Shōin's interpretation of the *Mencius*, and rejected that of the original Chinese. The Japanese *Mencius* was much more influential than the Chinese *Mencius*. Hence, when we discuss the role of the *Mencius* in the Meiji Restoration, we should know that they were two versions of the *Mencius* in modern Japan. It was the Japanese *Mencius*, not the Chinese *Mencius*, which had a strong impact on the Meiji Restoration and prewar political ideology.

THE *XIAOJING* AND ETHICS

THE DISSEMINATION OF CONFUCIAN VALUES IN JAPAN AND EAST ASIA WAS a long process. Due to geographical and cultural proximity, East Asia has been influenced most strongly by Chinese culture, and is labeled by modern scholars as the "Confucian cultural sphere" or "Chinese character cultural sphere."[1] In China's neighboring countries, such as Japan, Korea, Vietnam, and the Ryūkyū Kingdom, Chinese values were selectively introduced and creatively domesticated. For instance, Chinese Confucianism was highly indigenized in Japan. Confucianism reached its peak during the Tokugawa period, when Tokugawa Confucianism was imbued with national sentiments and Shinto elements.[2]

The relationship between *zhong* (loyalty) and *xiao* (filial piety), two fundamental virtues in Confucianism, has been a subject of concern among Confucian scholars in East Asia for many centuries, and represents the application of Confucian ethics at the family and state levels. Many modern Japanese scholars believe that the main difference between Japanese Confucianism and Chinese Confucianism rests in their preferences for loyalty and filial piety, suggesting that Japanese Confucianism puts loyalty before filial piety, whereas Chinese Confucianism posits filial piety over loyalty.[3] Advocated by nationalist ideologues in prewar Japan, this view argues that Japan has a better *kokutai* (national polity) than that of China.[4] Repackaged as *Nihonjinron*, or discourse on the Japanese, and *Nihonbunkaron*, or discourse on Japanese culture, the discussion of loyalty and filial piety has been declining in postwar Japan. However, it has found a new life in Mainland China, where scholars discuss the differences between China and Japan's loyalty and filial piety in terms of national character and sociocultural structure.[5] The idea that China prefers filial piety and Japan prefers loyalty has become more or less a kind of "common sense" among many Chinese and Japanese. While there is some truth in this, the view is simplistic and ahistorical, and is not useful in understanding the history of Sino-Japanese intellectual and cultural interaction.[6]

Looking back on Chinese and Japanese history, the priority of loyalty or filial piety has been a centuries-old debate. In premodern China and Japan, Confucians never reached a consensus on this issue.[7] The myth about the preference for loyalty over filial piety in Japanese tradition was only forged by right-wing writers from the late Meiji to early Shōwa periods in order to promote national ideology. Whether this moral and intellectual preference for loyalty over filial piety existed in Japanese Confucianism during the Tokugawa period or not is highly debatable.[8] This chapter examines the discourse on the relationship between filial piety and loyalty among Tokugawa Confucians through a case study of Nakae Tōju (1608–48) and his reading of the *Xiaojing* (Classic of Filial Piety) from historical and textual perspectives. It also deepens our understanding of the formation and limitations of Tokugawa state ideology and the adoption and naturalization of Chinese Confucian ethics within the Tokugawa political and intellectual framework.

FILIAL SON OR DISLOYAL SUBJECT

Nakae Tōju established himself as a respectable figure in his own times for setting a high moral standard, earning him the title of the "Sage of Ōmi," and a place in primary school ethics textbooks in the Meiji era.[9] Modern Japanese scholars regard Tōju as a Japanese sage, a paragon of filial piety, and the founder of *Yōmeigaku* (Wang Yangming learning).[10] In his times, Tōju was already a role model in terms of morality and scholarship. However, he committed one highly controversial act. He abandoned his samurai post in the Ōzu domain in Shikoku, returning to his native village in Ōmi (near Lake Biwa) to look after his aging mother. When loyalty and filial piety could not coexist, he chose to be a filial son and a disloyal subject. To him, a mother was more important than a lord.

Tōju's image as a filial son is well documented. According to the *Tōju-sensei nenpu* (Annals of Master Tōju; 1858) by Okada Tsuyoshi (1830–96), Tōju had already showed his preference for filial piety over loyalty at the age of twelve. Tōju is recorded as having said:

One day when I was eating, I could not help thinking about this question: "To whom am I indebted for my daily meal?" [I concluded that,] in the first place, it was the blessing of my parents. Secondly, it was the blessing of my grandparents. Thirdly, it was the blessing of my lord. From that time onward, I swore that I would never forget my indebtedness to them.[11]

Tōju implied that he owed his parents and grandparents more than his lord, and felt much closer to his native village in Ōmi than his workplace in Ōzu domain. Although he began to serve his lord in Ōzu as a low-ranking samurai at the age of nineteen, his heart remained with his family in Ōmi. At the ages of twenty-two and twenty-five, Tōju took leave of his post to visit his mother in Ōmi and repeatedly asked her to join him in Ōzu, but in vain. At the age of twenty-six, he composed the following poem to express his wish that he could quit his post in order to care for his aging mother:

> In the spring, I feel sad, as I am away from home.
> A yellow bird stops in a plum tree.
> The tree may prefer calm, but the wind does not subside.
> For the future, I must quit and go back.[12]

In 1634, at the age of twenty-seven, Tōju wrote a letter to his lord to ask for long-term leave, and promised to resume his duty after the death of his mother. He wrote:

> It is my [moral] duty to take care of four of my family members [grand-parents and parents], but three of them died when I was small. Now, only my mother is still alive. My mother is relying on me, her only son.[13]

The *daimyō* of Ōzu did not want to lose Tōju, and thus ignored his request. When his letter received no replies, Tōju made the most dramatic move in his life, which earned him his reputation as a filial son. Tōju simply abandoned his samurai duty, leaving Ōzu domain and returning to Ōmi without permission. He explained: "Alas! Loyalty and filial piety cannot coexist. Although I am not good, I will not forget to examine myself for a single day."[14] It was no easy task for him to choose between loyalty and filial piety. He felt badly about leaving his lord, but had no alternative for the sake of fulfilling his filial duty. As a gesture of apology, Tōju left some money and crops in Ōzu as a token of returning one year's stipend. Nevertheless, judged on the basis of Tokugawa samurai ethics and legal codes, Tōju committed an illegal and disloyal act. According to samurai ethics, under no circumstances should a samurai betray his lord. A samurai who does not fulfill his duty should commit *seppuku* (cutting one's belly as suicide). The *Hagakure* (In the Shadow of Leaves; 1716), a practical and spiritual guidebook for samurai, records a story about a samurai who went into battle against his parents' will, showing that loyalty to one's lord was regarded as a virtue higher than filial piety to parents.[15] Asami Keisai (1652–1711) of the Kimon school, in his *Chūkō ruisetsu* (Discourse on Loyalty and Filial Piety), also stressed that, when there was a conflict between loyalty and filial piety, a samurai must set his parents aside and be prepared to die for his lord. He even went so far as to suggest that, if a samurai discovered his own father's plot to rebel against the lord, he must report this to the lord, citing Matsuda Hidenao as an example.[16] Disqualified as a samurai, Tōju lost his hereditary samurai status and could have faced the death sentence if arrested. Having returned to his native village, Tōju sold his sword to show his determination to live a new life as a commoner, and earned a living by selling wine, lending money, and lecturing. Fujii Raisai (1618–1709) recorded this event in the *Honchō kōshiden* (Biographies of Filial Sons in Japan; 1684):

> He once served Katō, lord of Ōzu Castle in Yoshū [now Ehime Prefecture in Shikoku]. He wanted to ask his mother to join him so that he could take care of her. His mother said: "I have heard that women should not leave the border of the domain. I want to stay." She refused to join, asking him to quit and return. The lord [of Ōzu] treasured his talents and did not approve his request [to leave]. Korenaga [Tōju] evinced his anger by saying: "Although I am not filial, I will not be constrained by stipends and forget to examine myself." Then, he wrote a letter explaining his determination to live with his mother and left without permission. He lived as a recluse in Ogawa, making his mother very pleased.[17]

The *Tōju-sensei nenpu* provides more details about this significant event:

> Since his aging mother was not being taken care of, he repeatedly asked for work release. His lord respected his personality, but did not endorse [the release]. In March of the same year, he wrote to the

senior administrator, Tsukuda, to express his dilemma, pledging that he would not serve other lords. He received no replies. Finally, he gave up his post and left. He first went to Kyoto and stayed with someone, waiting for the punishments to come. Having waited for more than a hundred days with no punishment, he went to Ogawa. When he left Ōzu, he returned some pecks of rice to the domain's coffers. He spent all of his savings to pay back his debts. From the remaining three hundred copper coins, he gave two hundred coins to lay off his servants. He could not live a life with one hundred coins, and thus sold wine in the market. He also sold his sword and acquired ten silver coins. He lent money for interest. His interest was low, and borrowers always returned the loans.[18]

From the perspective of Tokugawa legal codes and samurai ethics, Tōju was a disloyal and disgraced samurai. However, in light of Chinese Confucian ethics, Tōju was a filial son who sacrificed his career and even jeopardized his own life and good name for his mother. In fact, throughout Chinese history, many Confucian scholars have chosen filial piety over loyalty if compelled to make a choice.[19] Giving up an official post to take care of one's parents was not uncommon or unacceptable among Confucian officials in China. Tōju's act finds support in the *Er Shi Si Xiao* (Twenty-Four Filial Acts) by Guo Jujing of the Yuan Dynasty, a small illustrative book of filial acts in Chinese history. It includes the story of the Northern Song (960–1127) official Zhu Shouchang quitting his job to look for his mother.[20] The *Er Shi Si Xiao* was one of the most popular and influential Chinese readings among Tokugawa intellectuals, reprinted many times by the *bakufu* and commercial publishers and adapted into popular dramas, art, and literature.[21] Although the story of Zhu Shouchang in the *Er Shi Si Xiao* had intellectual implications that were not always in agreement with Tokugawa samurai ethics, the *bakufu* and domains promoted the text without reservations. They reprinted it multiple times without censoring the story. Likewise, Tokugawa Confucians from different schools did not raise any objection against these two stories. This attitude shows that the *bakufu* did not forge a clear and rigid state ideology that promoted loyalty at the expense of filial piety, and that the conflict between filial piety and loyalty was a "gray area" in Tokugawa thought.

In Japan, records of this dilemma between loyalty and filial piety are rare, and Tōju's case serves as a good example to deepen our understanding of the nature of Tokugawa ideology and the naturalization of Chinese Confucian ethics. The tension between filial piety and loyalty in Tokugawa thought indicates that Chinese Confucianism did not always fit into the Tokugawa *bakuhan* (*bakufu*-domain) system, and there was a conflict between indigenous Japanese tradition and imported Chinese ethics.[22] In light of samurai ethics, Tōju was a disloyal and corrupt person. However, he did not face reprimand or prosecution. The preference for loyalty over filial piety was never a very strong state ideology or ethic in the Tokugawa period. Although Tokugawa ideology tended to prefer loyalty, it allowed ambiguity in this issue. The *bakufu* and domains usually did not interfere or ban the various views suggested by Tokugawa intellectuals regarding the relationship between filial piety and loyalty, as long as the discussion carried no anti-*bakufu* implications.

Neither the *bakufu* nor the Ōzu domain showed any keen interest in pursuing Tōju's case, and thus Tōju was given the opportunity to live a new life in his native village as a commoner. Not even Hayashi Razan (1583–1657), a pro-*bakufu* ideologue and critic of Tōju, used this case to attack him.[23] No one labeled Tōju a disloyal subject, and many actually praised him as a *kōshi* (filial son) and *seijin* (sage). For example, Fujii Raisai, a scholar of the Kimon school (founded by Yamazaki Ansai, 1618–82), included Tōju in his best-selling *Honchō kōshi den* (Biographies of Filial Sons in Japan; 1685). Raisai composed a tetrasyllabic verse to praise Tōju as a champion of filial piety and Wang Yangming's teachings:

> Ōzu is blowing the wind of Lu and Wang's Confucianism.
> He taught people to live a moral life and the importance of loyalty.
> For his mother, he gave up his post.
> He made his mother happy by returning to his hometown.
> How filial he was! Did it come from his nature or through learning?[24]

All of these demonstrate that the *tennōsei* (emperor system) ideology and *bushidō* (way of the samurai) ethics were not fully developed and institutionalized in the Tokugawa period, and that the preference for loyalty over filial piety never dominated Tokugawa thought. When there was a conflict between filial piety and loyalty, the choice was left to the individual. Generally speaking, Zhu Xi school scholars tended to favor loyalty, whereas Wang

Yangming school scholars preferred filial piety.[25] There was no consensus reached among Tokugawa Confucians on this issue, but the voices for loyalty increased throughout the Tokugawa period following the rise of national discourse in Tokugawa thought.[26] It goes without saying that late Tokugawa *shishi* (imperial loyalists), who advocated the return of political power to the emperor, stressed the importance of loyalty.

FILIAL PIETY AS THE PRIMARY ETHICS

In the early Tokugawa period, the loyalty-filial piety relationship was a topic of heated intellectual exchange among Zhu Xi school scholars (particularly the Kimon school). The mainstream view was that both could coexist in most circumstances, but in extremes cases when they contradicted each other, it is necessary to choose loyalty over filial piety.[27] In contrast, Wang Yangming school scholars paid more attention to filial piety, of which Nakae Tōju was the champion.

Tōju was a respectable reader of the *Xiaojing*. His ideas of filial piety can be found in two of his major writings—*Kōkyō keimō* (An Introduction to the *Classic of Filial Piety*; 1642) and *Okina mondō* (Questions from an Old Man; 1640).[28] Tōju saw filial piety as something more than a Confucian ethic, more on the order of some kind of religion. To him, everything in the universe is subject to the principle of filial piety. He expounded:

> Filial piety is everything. Although many generations have passed, filial piety in the universe has no beginning or end. There is not a single motion in which filial piety is not in action. There is nothing in the world over which filial piety does not prevail.[29]

Tōju treated the *Xiaojing* with religious respect. From the age of thirty-three onward, he performed a ritual every morning. He took a bath, put on a costume, burned incense, and mediated on the moments when he was inside his mother and when he was a small child before reading the *Xiaojing*. Once a month, he fasted and worshipped the Taoist deity Taiyi Tianzun to express his gratitude to the gods.[30] In addition to Taoist influence, his concept of filial piety also contained Buddhist and Shinto elements. In the *Kagamigusa* (Mirror Plant; 1647), he used stories on karmic causation to promote filial piety. In his poem "Taijingu" (Ise Shrine), he fused Confucianism and Shinto in his praise of filial piety:

The brightness of the *Xiaojing* lasts forever.

It can compare with the feat of Fu Xi.

I pray that the teachings of the sages will shine on the Ise Shrine.[31]

His reading of the *Xiaojing* made him believe that all Confucian virtues, including loyalty, were derived from filial piety. He stated: "Filial piety is the summit of virtue and the essence of the Way in the three realms of heaven, earth, and man. What brings life to heaven, earth, man, and all things is filial piety."[32] He also held: "The virtue of filial piety can be applied to everything in the world. The ways of brothers, married couples, and friends are included [in the virtue of filial piety]. This also explains the meaning of applying filial piety to serve the ruler at the end of the *Xiaojing*."[33] In addition, he interpreted the Confucian notion of *zhiming* (accepting fate) in terms of filial piety:

> The *Xiaojing* reads: "Filial piety is the heavenly principle, the earthly way, and human behavior." The three are subject to one principle, showing the substance of filial piety. Following it, one can settle down and know destiny. Although one might not be perfect, one can become a gentleman. Going against it, one will fall into heresy and strange territory. Even though one might have the ability of the Duke of Zhou, one cannot become a gentleman without knowing one's destiny. The *Lunyu* [Analects of Confucius] mentions this in the end, explaining this profound message in detail. Confucius loved to follow the orders of his mother. He loved his mother without going to extremes. This is the meaning of *zhiming*.[34]

Rhetoric preferences indicate the attitudes of Tokugawa Confucians toward the loyalty-filial piety relationship. Tokugawa Confucians were divided over the issue regarding the order of filial piety and loyalty in terminology. The *bakufu*'s documents and writings of the Zhu Xi school scholars usually used *chūkō* and not *kōchū*. For example, the *Shoshihatto* (Regulations for Retainers) of 1636 mentions loyalty and filial piety in its first rule.[35] Likewise, scholars of the Hayashi school and Kimon school placed loyalty before filial piety. For example, Hayashi Razan and Matsunaga Sekigo (1592–1657) stated that loyalty to the ruler was a natural principle that every subject must obey.[36] Whenever discussing filial piety and loyalty together, Tōju always put filial piety ahead of loyalty. For instance, he used the term *kōchū* (孝忠 filial piety and loyalty) instead of the more popular term, *chūkō* (忠孝 loyalty and filial piety), in his writings, discussing things like *kōchū no kokoro* (heart of filial piety and loyalty), *kōchū no ichiiro* (harmony of filial piety and loyalty), *kōchū jingi* (filial piety, loyalty, benevolence, and righteousness), and *kōkō chūsetsu* (filial acts and loyal manners).[37] Tōju's use of *kōchū* did not represent a mainstream practice, but it was used by not a few Tokugawa intellectuals, including Fujita Tōko (1806–55).

Tōju's faith in filial piety can also be seen from his view of *wulun* or *wujiao* (the five relations, i.e., those between father and son, ruler and subjects, husband and wife, elder and younger brothers, and friends). The *Mengzi* reads: "These are the human relations to be taught: father and son should be affectionate, emperor and minister should be righteous, husband and wife should have different roles, elder and younger brothers should be in the right order, and there should be mutual trust among friends." Hence, father-son relations were placed above emperor-minister relations.[38] However, in Tokugawa Japan, many Zhu Xi school scholars (such as Hayashi Razan, Yamaga Sokō, Kaibara Ekken, Miyake Shōsai, and Asami Keisai), as well as Mito school scholars (such as Aizawa Seishisai,), put the ruler-subject relation prior to that of the father-son relation.[39] However, there were a substantial number of Tokugawa Confucian scholars (such as Muro Kyūsō) who regarded the relationship between father and son as the first among all social relations, following the common Chinese practice. Tōju unambiguously made father and son the number one tie: "Filial piety is the source of all human virtues and the most important principle in human relations. In the five relations created by the sages, the filial love between father and son is the number one teaching."[40] According to Tōju, the main difference between father-son and ruler-subject relations is that the former is a natural blood relationship, whereas the latter is an artificial bond.[41]

Tōju frequently cited Chinese classics to suggest that filial piety can become loyalty and that loyal subjects can only be found among filial sons.[42] This was supposedly a saying of Confucius, cited in the *Hou Hanshu* (History of the Later Han). The original text reads: "Filial piety to parents can be transferred as loyalty to serve the emperor, and thus loyal subjects can only be found among filial sons." Tōju saw loyalty as an extension of filial piety, because filial sons serve the ruler in order to bring comfort and glory to their parents. He wrote: "My parents and I originally belong to the same source. Hence, if I do good deeds, my parents and the spirits will benefit. If I earn my reputation, my parents' names will also be glorified."[43] In other words, loyalty became a means of fulfilling filial piety. This view adds a utilitarian dimension to this discussion. As he explained:

> With regard to filial piety, we must know that not to harm one's body is the beginning of the teaching. The purpose of making our career and pursuing the truth is to bring glory to our parents. This is why the *Xiaojing* reads: "In the beginning, we serve our parents, and then we serve the ruler." Here "the beginning" and "then" show the priority in carrying out the Way.[44]

With regard to the loyalty–filial piety relationship, Tōju's position was opposite to that of *bushidō* advocates, who included filial piety within loyalty.[45] Unlike *fajia* (legalists) in China, Tōju did not see filial piety and loyalty as two conflicting virtues, and he tried to include loyalty within filial piety. To him, "loyalty is the application of filial piety to serve the ruler."[46] He said:

> Loyalty is originally one aspect of filial piety. A retainer can apply the reverence that people hold for family and father to serve his ruler. The *Xiaojing* reads: "Applying filial piety to serve the ruler is loyalty."[47]

Tōju believed that the ruler could rule the nation by means of filial piety, or *xiaoji*, whereas the subjects could apply the same principle of filial piety to serve their ruler. He suggested that the ruler should set an example of filiality by worshipping heaven and should build an environment for the people in which they could practice filial piety.[48] He added that courtiers, officials, and samurai should also apply the principle of filial piety to carry out their political duties.

Tōju attempted to harmonize filial piety and loyalty whenever possible. Asked whether a man should go to battle for the nation or stay home to preserve his body as a gift of his parents, he replied that preserving virtue was more important than the body, and that the man should go to battle in order to achieve true filial piety.[49] Some ambiguity remains, but his attempt to narrow the difference between these two virtues is obvious. The important thing here is not the action itself, but the reasons behind it. According to Tōju, the ultimate concern of a filial son is always his parents or family rather than the emperor or state. Hence, both going to war and staying at home are two different ways of achieving the same goal of fulfilling filial piety.

Tōju had a preference for the *jinwen* (new-script edition) of the *Xiaojing*, showing that his view of filial piety and loyalty was more liberal than many of his contemporaries. The *guwen* (old-script edition) of the *Xiaojing* was more popular than the new-script edition in the Tokugawa period. The *bakufu* promoted the old-script edition, which put emphasis on the political implications of filial piety and the absolute authority of the ruler.[50] The preface of the old-script edition underscores the absolute authority of the ruler and father over the subject and son. Hence, it is by no means coincidental that Tōju was critical of the old-script edition of the *Xiaojing* and that he preferred the new-script edition, especially the Ming commentaries on it. In particular, he was indebted to Jiang Yuanzuo's *Xiaojing daquan* (The Complete Annotated Editions of the *Xiaojing*; 1633), which he believed was closer to the original text. He criticized the old-script edition for containing many ideas added by later generations. For instance, in his *Kōkyō keimō*, Tōju deleted the famous saying written in the preface of the old-script edition by Kong Anguo of the Western Han Dynasty: "Even if the emperor does not behave like an emperor, his minister cannot be disloyal. Even if the father does not behave like a father, his son cannot be unfilial." Tōju's position was altogether different from that of Hayashi Razan, who promoted the old-script edition in his *Kobun kōkyō genkai* (Colloquial Explanation of the *Xiaojing* in the old-script text). Tōju did not uphold the idea of absolute loyalty and filial piety that many neo-Confucian scholars in China and Japan advocated, stressing that parents should show mercy to their children, while rulers should hold their subjects in high esteem. He wrote: "The subjects serve the emperor with loyalty, while the emperor treats his subjects with respect. They can communicate on friendly terms and unite."[51] He argued that filial sons and loyal retainers should not endorse or follow the wrongdoings of their parents and rulers, and should try everything possible to reason with and warn them.[52] Tōju himself set an example as a filial yet self-conscious son. He married Takahashi Hisa at the age of thirty. When his mother asked him to divorce his wife simply because she was ugly, Tōju did not obey, and tried to reason with his mother, saying that inner beauty was more important than physical appearance.[53] In addition, he argued that his disciple Morimura Chō made the right decision to study under him, even though it went against his father's opinion. He explained that pursuing knowledge is an act of filial piety and is in agreement with the idea of *yanfu peitian* (in revering the father, nothing is greater than associating him with heaven) expounded in the *Xiaojing*. He commented on this case:

Although the son came without following his father's opinion, he had a heart for his father. Although he did not obey his father, he did it to associate his father with heaven. This knowledge cannot be acquired without learning. This is the so-called *liangzhi* [innate moral knowledge].... Although he did not obey his parents, he was filial to his parents. If he followed his parents to make a wrong decision, he would be an unfilial son.[54]

Concerning filial piety as a prerequisite for loyalty, Tōju condemned people who served the ruler wholeheartedly and forgot their parents:

[The *Xiaojing* reads:] "To love others and not one's own parents is against morality; to respect others and not one's own parents is against proprieties." Not to love and respect parents here refers to a person who does not use *shinpō* [the method of mind] to regard their father with reverence by associating him with heaven. Other people refer to ruler and subjects, husband and wife, brothers, children, and grandchildren, as well as friends.[55]

In this respect, Tōju criticized two of Fujiwara Seika's disciples, Suga Gendō (?–1628) and Hayashi Razan, for receiving the Buddhist tonsure. The early Edo *bakufu* granted Buddhist honorific titles to Confucians as a recognition of their services. Tōju criticized tonsured Confucians for breaking the fundamental teachings in the *Xiaojing*: "Body, hair, and skin are all from our parents and should not be damaged. This is the beginning of filial piety. Building one's reputation and leaving an impact on later generations are the ways to glorify one's parents. This is the goal of filial piety."[56] Tōju's position was that disrespecting parents was a more serious offense than disobeying the ruler.

Tōju's view of filial piety and loyalty had a strong impact on Wang Yangming school scholars in the Tokugawa period such as Kumazawa Banzan (1619–91) and Ōshio Heihachirō (1793–1837). Like Tōju, Banzan privileged filial piety over loyalty, stressing that loyalty should be based on filial piety. Banzan criticized the idea of upholding loyalty at the expense of filial piety in his *Kōkyō shokai* (A Simple Explanation of the *Xiaojing*) and *Kōkyō gaiden wakumon* (Questions about the Commentary on the *Xiaojing*). He said:

[Rulers] admonish their ministers to be loyal to themselves and to render good service, and neglect the teachings of filial piety and fraternal respect in the districts and villages. Therefore, loyal ministers are scarce. Those who serve do so only out of interest in their own promotion and for profit.[57]

Banzan reprinted Tōju's *Kōkyō keimō* and lectured on it.[58] Likewise, Heihachirō, in his *Zōho Kōkyō kaichū* (Additional Annotation of the *Xiaojing*) and *Kōkyō kōgi* (Lectures on the *Xiaojing*), attributed loyalty and all virtues to filial piety, and disagreed with people who advocated loyalty at the expense of filial piety. He associated filial piety with *zhi liangzhi* (the expansion of innate moral knowledge), which served as ideological grounds for his uprising in 1837.[59] In the *Tōju-sensei chiryōchi sandaiji shinseki* (The Three Big Characters *Zhi Liangzhi* by Master Tōju), he praised Tōju: "The teaching of my master is to spread filial piety to the nation and the world."[60] He explained the acquisition of innate moral knowledge in terms of the fulfillment of filial piety:

> In benevolence, righteousness, propriety, and wisdom, benevolence and righteousness are more important. Benevolence and righteousness depend on filial piety and fraternal duty. Between filial piety and fraternal duty, filial piety is more important. Filial piety does not come from outside. Even without learning or thinking, one can acquire it. A child has the innate moral knowledge of loving its parents.[61]

It is salient that even in the mid-Tokugawa period, filial piety remained a very strong morality and was never completely swallowed by the expanding discourse of loyalty.

LIMITATIONS OF LOCALIZATION OF CONFUCIAN ETHICS

Using Nakae Tōju's perception of filial piety as a point of departure, this chapter examines the debate over the relationship between loyalty and filial piety in Tokugawa Confucianism. It has shown that Confucian virtues were localized in Tokugawa Japan, where imported ideas and indigenous values competed and fused with each other. Chinese Confucian ethics were not always in agreement with the samurai-ruled society, and thus how to accommodate Chinese ethics within the Tokugawa system was a common concern among Tokugawa Confucians. It seems that many (Zhu Xi school scholars, particularly) added Japanese elements into Chinese Confucian ethics, whereas others (such as Wang Yangming school scholars) preserved more Chinese elements in the adoption of Chinese Confucianism. This tug-of-war can be seen in the Tokugawa debate over the relationship between filial piety and loyalty.

Through the case of Tōju, we can understand that the existence of a voice for filial piety in Tokugawa Confucianism is undeniable, and the myth that Japanese Confucianism has a preference for loyalty over filial piety is problematic and simplistic, at least in the historical context of Tokugawa thought and culture. Although Tōju's actions and thoughts were not always in agreement with samurai ethics or nativist discourse, they were not banned or censored, and indeed they were appreciated by Tokugawa officials and scholars. This demonstrates that the *bakufu* did not have a powerful and rigid state ideology, and the naturalization of Chinese Confucian ethics was not complete. Tokugawa intellectual space was large enough for different schools of thought and culture to flourish and express their views. On the issue of the relationship between filial piety and loyalty, Tōju's position was close to the majority of Chinese Confucians, and differed from many of his countrymen. The coexistence of various views of the relationship between loyalty and filial piety in Tokugawa thought serves as a footnote to the tensions and disharmony between Chinese learning and Japanese reality and the limitations of localization of Chinese Confucianism. The idea that the Japanese prefer loyalty to filial piety as suggested by *bushidō* and *tennōsei* ideologies never truly characterized Tokugawa Confucianism.

6

THE *YIJING* AND SHINTO

Dᴵꜰꜰᴇʀᴇɴᴛ ꜱᴄʜᴏᴏʟꜱ ᴏꜰ ᴄᴜʟᴛᴜʀᴇ ᴀɴᴅ ᴛʜᴏᴜɢʜᴛ, ꜱᴜᴄʜ ᴀꜱ *KANGAKU* (Chinese learning), *kokugaku*, and *rangaku* (Dutch learning), reached their apex during the Tokugawa period as they competed with and influenced one another. *Kokugaku* was a nativist discourse that underscored traditional or indigenous beliefs, values, and aesthetics. In the *kokugaku* order of knowledge, Chinese culture played the role of "the Other," often marginalized and demonized in cross-cultural comparison.[1] Although *kokugaku* and Chinese learning seemed to stand on opposite sides, they actually had a much more complicated relationship.[2] Many Tokugawa Confucians also engaged in the study of ancient Japanese classics, historical records, and religious texts, and some even advocated the doctrine of *shinju gōitsu* (unity of Shinto and Confucianism).[3] Likewise, *kokugaku* scholars also read Chinese texts and Confucian classics, using them either as useful references or negative examples. The *Yijing* (Book of Changes) was a text of particular interest to *kokugaku* scholars.[4] Using the *kokugaku* thinker Hirata Atsutane (1776–1843) and his school as its main references, this chapter examines how *kokugaku* scholars transformed the *Yijing* from a Chinese Confucian classic into a Japanese Shinto text. Through an investigation of the uses and appropriation of the *Yijing* among *kokugaku* scholars, this study aims to analyze the nature of *kokugaku*, the relationship between Confucianism and *kokugaku*, and the localization of Chinese learning in the Tokugawa period.

THE *YIJING* IN EARLY *KOKUGAKU*

The Hirata school of *kokuagaku* was a strong intellectual current in late Tokugawa Japan. Studying and localizing the *Yijing* was one of its features. The localization of the *Yijing* in Japan started in the medieval and early

Tokugawa periods, and the Hirata school continued the trend and made break-throughs. *Yijing* studies in medieval Japan incorporated elements from Shinto, Buddhism, *onmyōdō* (way of *yin-yang*), and *shūkendō* (mountain asceticism). For instance, the Zen monk scholar Tōgen Zuisen (1403–89) and rectors of the Zen monk academy Ashikaga gakkō prayed to Chinese and Japanese deities for help before using the *Yijing* for divination.[5] Medieval Shintoists applied the principles in the *Yijing* to explain the Age of the Gods.[6]

Early and mid-Tokugawa *kokugaku* scholars tended to see the *Yijing* in a negative light, either ignoring or criticizing it. This attitude can be found in the works of Kada Azumamaro (1669–1736) and Kamo Mabuchi (1697–1769), who focused on Japanese history, literature, and religion, and were not par-ticularly interested in Confucianism and Chinese culture.[7] However, the div-inational and metaphysical values of the *Yijing* were recognized by such early *kokugaku* scholars as Amano Sadakage (1663–1733) and Yoshimi Yukikazu (1672–1761). Sadakage, a retainer of the Owari domain, studied Japanese texts under the Shintoist Watarai Nobuyoshi (1615–90), but also read Chinese books and Confucian writings. He wrote the *Kokin ekikai* (Explanations of the *Yijing*, Past and Present), *Sōeki engi* (An Explanation of Song Commentaries on the *Yijing*), and *Shūeki medogi zukai* (An Illustrative Explanation of the Yarrow Stalks Used in the *Zhouyi*). Yukikazu was a Shinto priest in the Owari domain. He was influenced by Suika Shinto and the Zhu Xi school of Confucianism. He was interested in the oracles of the *Yijing* and wrote the *Shūeki zeigi kuden* (The Oral Transmission of Divination of the *Zhouyi*).

Compared with early Tokugawa *kokugaku* scholars, Motoori Norinaga (1730–1801) was more critical of Confucian values. Like the naturalism in Lao-Zhuang Daoism, Norinaga criticized the so-called ancient Chinese sages for making such artificial constructs as morality, law, and institutions to rule. To Norinaga, there was no fundamental difference between the *Yijing* and other Confucian classics, and he regarded it as a tool created and used by Chinese sages to deceive the people. He remarked: "Confucians believe that they have grasped the meaning of the universe through the creation of the *Yijing* and its very pro-found words. But all of that is only a deception to win people over and become masters over them."[8] At the age of twenty-three, he studied Confucianism under Hori Keizan (1688–1757), a Confucian physician who combined the Zhu Xi school with the Sorai school in his interpretation of Chinese classics.[9] During this period, Norinaga read Zhu Xi's (1130–1200) *Yixue qimeng* (Enlightenment

on the Study of the *Yijing*), but it did not leave a deep impression.[10] He looked
down upon the *Yijing* as a profound-looking "white elephant" (*muyō no chōbutsu*)
and its *yin-yang wu-xing* (*yin-yang* and five phases) doctrine as a foolish specu-
lation that could not explain the mysteries of the universe.

> The *yin-yang wu-xing* theory in Shina [China] was not the way founded
> by the deities in the beginning [of creation]. The [Chinese] sages used
> their wits, believing that the theory could be used to explain every-
> thing. However, we should know that their knowledge was limited and
> they could not match the way of the deities.[11]

Hence, Norinaga disapproved of Hayashi Razan and Watarai Nobuyoshi using
such *Yijing*-related concepts as *taiji* (the Supreme Ultimate), *yin-yang wu-xing*,
sancai (three powers), and hexagrams to explain the Age of the Gods and Shinto
teachings.[12] In reconstructing the Age of the Gods, he preferred the *Kojiki* to
the Chinese-influenced *Nihon shoki*.[13] The *Nihon shoki* identifies Izanagi and
Izanami, the two central deities in the Japanese creation myth, with *yin-yang*
and *qiankun* (the first two hexagrams), respectively. Razan and Nobuyoshi
were the champions of this theory in the early Tokugawa period, and thus were
under a severe attack by Norinaga. With regard to some Tokugawa Confucians
and Shintoists who used the *Yijing*-related concepts to elucidate the gender of
Amaterasu-Ōmikami, the Sun Goddess and divine ancestor of the Japanese
imperial family according to Shinto myth, he remarked:

> We can conclude that using the concepts from the *Yijing* to explain why
> the Sun Goddess was a female and making things in accordance with
> the principle of *yin-yang* are foolish thoughts. Early scholars cited the
> principle of the hexagrams of the *Yijing*, and present-day people fol-
> lowed. The *Yijing* and the principle of *yin-yang* are fallacies.[14]

Many early Tokugawa Confucians, including Hayashi Razan, Yamaga Sokō,
and Ogyū Sorai, cited the passage "The sages, in accordance with *shintō* [spir-
it-like way], laid down their instructions, and all under heaven yield submission
to them" from the hexagram *guan* (contemplation) to suggest that Shinto was
also a way of the Chinese sages and both Shinto and Confucianism shared
the same natural principle. Norinaga stressed that the term *shintō* came from
the *Nihon shoki* and not the *Yijing*, and that Japanese Shinto and the way of
the Chinese sages were fundamentally different:

However, a Chinese book [the *Yijing*] reads: "The sages, in accordance with *shendao* [way of the gods, the same Chinese character as *shintō*], laid down their instructions." Hence, some people believed that Shinto in my nation borrowed its name from it. These people do not have a mind to understand things. From the beginning, the meanings of gods in Japan have been different from those used by the Chinese. In that nation [China], they explain gods and the universe in terms of the *yin-yang* of heaven and earth. Their discussion is only empty theory without substance. The deities of our imperial nation were the ancestors of the current emperor and thus our discussion is by no means empty theory. The spirit-like way in the Chinese book is an unpredictable, strange idea. Shinto in Japan has been passed on from our ancestral deities and thus is different.[15]

All in all, in Norinaga's thinking, China served as a negative model or "the Other" to highlight the superiority of Japan from a comparative perspective. For instance, in his mind, China was a land of non-stop revolution, whereas Japan enjoyed an unbroken line of imperial succession. *Karagokoro* (the Chinese heart) was artificial and empty, but *Yamatogokoro* (the Japanese heart) was natural and true. The Japanese language was elegant, while the Chinese was decorative.[16]

While Norinaga's view of China represented the mainstream voice in *kokugaku* circles, there were also *kokugaku* scholars who were more accommodating of the *Yijing* and other Chinese classics. Izumi Makuni (1765–1805), a disciple of Norinaga and book dealer in Edo, was familiar with Confucian classics and Chinese books, and particularly liked to use the *Yijing* and *Zhongyong* (Doctrine of the Mean) to explain the nature of Shinto, asserting that some of the ideas in those two texts were in agreement with Shinto.[17] As a *kokugaku* scholar, he underscored the superiority of Japan over China in terms of morality and longevity, and denied any Confucian or Chinese impact on Shinto. Taking sincerity (*cheng* in Chinese, *makoto* in Japanese) as an example, Makuni pointed out that both Japan and China put emphasis on this virtue, but *cheng* in Confucianism was an empty theory, while *makoto* in Shinto was a feasible lifestyle:

> The *Zhouyi* and *Zhongyong* are fine books with many right words. However, the so-called way of sincerity has been an impractical and unprofitable armchair theory since the founding of China. Our

imperial nation did not have a name for the Way or books to teach it. The Way has been carried out for ten thousand generations from the Age of the Gods. Its benefits can be seen even now.[18]

Ban Nobutomo (1773–1846), a student of Norinaga's adopted son Motoori Ōhira (1756–1833), was interested in the oracles of the *Yijing*. He compared methods of divination in Japan and China in the *Shūeki shiron* (My Personal Views of the *Zhouyi*, also entitled *Ekisenben* [Debating the *Yijing* Oracles; 1834].[19] Norinaga denied the value of the divination of the *Yijing* in his *Naobi no mitama* because it was invented by Chinese sages and did not originate from the gods. Nobutomo was more flexible in choosing ways to divine. According to his study, the Japanese used deer bones to divine in antiquity, but turned to consulting the *Yijing* in the Tokugawa period. Although the *Yijing* was a divinational manual of foreign origin, he believed that, if the users were sincere, the oracles would be accurate. In regard to the divination of the *Yijing*, he remarked: "Introduced to my nation, its divination has been used for a long time. If the people use its oracles to communicate with the deities, we cannot deny that its oracles can be accurate."[20] While acknowledging the divinational value of the *Yijing*, he was mindful of the opinion that people should not consult the oracles too often.

HIRATA ATSUTANE'S APPROPRIATION OF THE *YIJING*

Hirata Atsutane and his school changed the direction of the study and uses of the *Yijing* in *kokugaku*. Seeing Norinaga as his spiritual mentor, Atsutane at first adopted the views of the *Yijing* from Norinaga and therefore opposed the use of *yin-yang wu-xing* and Confucian concepts to explicate Shinto. Like Norinaga, he divided Shinto into Chinese Shinto and Japanese Shinto. He maintained that the Chinese Shinto associated with the *Yijing* was an empty theory, because the notion of gods did not really exist in either Chinese history or Confucian thought. In contrast, Japanese Shinto was a living principle manifested and implemented uninterruptedly in Japanese history from Amaterasu to the current emperor.[21]

Atsutane seldom studied Confucian classics in his early years. At the age of eighteen, he was scolded by his father for failing to read the *Yijing* and *Lunyu*. As a punishment, he was not allowed to wear a sword. At the age of twenty, he began to study Chinese books seriously. Having read many Confucian classics and Chinese historical writings, he was able to cite Chinese sources extensively and compose in Chinese in his own writings. In his later years, he became absorbed in the study of the *Yijing* and developed his own views that changed the direction of discussions of the text among *kokugaku* circles. In his reading of the *Yijing*, he found that many of its ideas were in agreement with Shinto and could be used to explicate and enrich Shinto. Atsutane fully understood that praising a Chinese text could create problems in terms of cultural identity, and put himself in the position of endorsing the Confucian Shinto that Norinaga so severely criticized. In order to solve this dilemma, he advocated a very innovative view of the history of the *Yijing* by reinterpreting the theory of *sanyishuo* (the three versions of the *Yijing*).

According to Chinese tradition, the Xia, Shang, and Zhou dynasties each had its own version of the *Yijing*; they were the *Lianshan* by Fu Xi, the *Guicang* by Shennong and Huang Di, and the *Zhouyi* by King Wen, respectively.[22] Most Chinese Confucians regarded the *Zhouyi* as the best edition, but Atsutane disagreed. He praised the *Lianshan* and *Guicang* as works of wisdom transmitted orally in the Xia and Shang eras, and condemned King Wen for compiling the *Zhouyi* based on distortion and corruption of the *Lianshan* and *Guicang*. Of the three versions of the *Yijing*, only the *Zhouyi* survived and thus the real meaning of the *Yijing* was lost in transmission. Atsutane offered his own interpretation of the theory of the three versions of the *Yijing* in the *Saneki yuraiki* (The Origins of the Three Versions of the *Yijing*; 1835) and *Taiko koekiden* (The Old Edition of the *Yijing* by Tai Hao [Fu Xi]; 1836). In the *Kōshi seisetsukō* (An Investigation of the Theory about Confucius as Sage) and *Sango hongokukō* (An Investigation of the Japanese Origins of the Three Sovereigns and the Five Emperors), he alleged that the sage-kings of ancient China were manifestations of Japanese Shinto deities and that Fu Xi, Shennong, and Huang Di, the three alleged authors of the *Yijing*, were no exceptions.[23] The beginning of the *Sango hongokukō* reads:

> The three and five refer to the Three Sovereigns and the Five Emperors. They were not born in that country [China], but were indeed the deities of my country. Having seen the foolishness of the people in China, they went across the ocean to cultivate them.[24]

In the *Taiko koekiden*, Atsutane maintained that Fu Xi was the manifestation of Ōmononushi-no-Kami:

Later, our deity, Ōmononushi-no-Kami, also known as Taikō-
fukki-shi, granted the *He Tu* [Yellow River Chart] and *Luo shu*
[Luo River Writing] and created the wonderful trigrams. Mastering
the numerology of the universe, he communicated with gods
and spirits. Based on the images of the oracle bones, he invented
Chinese characters. The so-called *Yijing* was exclusively used for
cultivation.[25]

Ōmononushi-no-Kami is an important Shinto deity, also called Miwa-myōjin
(deity of Mount Miwa) and Ōkuninushi-no-Kami. He is the serpent god,
thunder god, and rain god, and his daughter was said to be the queen of the
legendary Emperor Jimmu. Atsutane attributed his idea to Norinaga in the
Tama no mihashira (The True Pillar of Spirit; 1812):

> [Motoori Norinaga said]: "Later, Sukunabikona-no-Kami [the god of
> healing and wine] descended from heaven to manage foreign nations."
> Atsutane added: "Moreover, Sukunabikona-no-Kami and Ōkuninushi-
> no-Kami also went to manage foreign nations."[26]

He listed the names for Fu Xi in China and Japan as follows:

> Taiho Fu Xi shi [Taikō-fukki-shi] is also called Taiho paoxi shi, Cangdi,
> Chunhuang, Taihao shi, Muhuang, Taizhen dongwangfu, Mugong,
> Qingdi, and Fusang dadi. Our Shinto text suggests that he was the
> manifestation of Ōkuninushi-no-Kami. Taiyi xiaozi, Donghaihuang
> qinghua xiaotongjun, Donghua dashen qingtongjun, Fangzhu qin-
> gtongjun, and Qingzhen xiaotongjun are all manifestations of
> Sukunabikona-no-Kami. I have investigated this issue in the *Sekiken
> taikoden* [The Legend of Ancient China], *Sango hongokukō*, *Kōkoku
> ishō kō* [An Investigation of Different Names for Japan], and *Shunjū
> meirekijo kō* [A Study of the *Chunqiu minglixu kō*]. Read them and
> you will understand.[27]

Fu Xi was the first of the *sanhuang* (Three Sovereigns), also named Taihao
and Mixi. According to tradition, Fu Xi created the trigrams, Chinese characters, and music, and also taught people how to fish and hunt. Atsutane did
not explain why he associated Fu Xi with Ōmononushi-no-Kami. These two
figures have little in common, except that both are serpent gods.

Why did Atsutane believe that Fu Xi was indeed a Japanese deity? First, by citing Han Chinese texts such as the *Huainanzi* (The Master of Huainan) and *Yiwei ganzaodu* (Chiseling Open the Regularity of Heaven in the Apocrypha of the *Yijing*) that associated Fu Xi with the elements of wood, he employed the *wu-xing* (five phases) theory to argue that Fu Xi came from Japan, as the element of wood represents the East:

> Fu Xi lived in the East, and he came to cultivate the foolish people with the virtue of wood. Hence, he was also called *chunhuang* [King of Spring] and *muhuang* [King of Wood].[28]

In another text, he added:

> Baihunagshi and Fu Xi belonged to the virtue of wood. They came from the East, showing the image of the rising sun. This can be seen in the [*Dai*] *fusō kokukō* [An Investigation of the Nation of Fusō].[29]

Second, he cited Chinese texts to show that Fu Xi was also named Fusang dadi (Great Emperor of Fusō). In the *Daifusō kokukō*, he was fully convinced that Fusō was Japan and thus Fu Xi was a Japanese deity:

> Taiho Fu Xi shi is called Taidi 太帝 in such texts as the *Huainanzi* and *Fengshanshu* [Book of the Ceremony of Heaven Worship] in the *Shiji*. It is also written as Taidi 泰帝. The *Shiji zhengyi* [Correct Meanings of the *Shiji*] and [*Shiji*] *Suoyin* [Seeking Hidden Meanings of the *Shiji*] also call Taiho Fu Xi shi Taidi. Daoist texts refer to him as Fusang dadi or Taizhen dongwangfu [Father of the Eastern Emperor]. I have discussed this in my *Sango hongokukō*.[30]

Likewise, Fu Xi's other names, including Donghua dashen (Great God of the Eastern Land) and Donghai xiaotong (Child of the Eastern Sea), were also used by Atsutane to uphold his assertion.[31]

Third, Atsutane cited Chinese sources such as the *Shanhaijing*, *Liezi* (Book of Master Lie), and *Huainanzi* to maintain that the Nation of Giants existed in the Eastern Sea. He explained that Fu Xi and other ancient kings were all giants because they came from Japan. The rulers and the ministers of the Nation of Giants were their descendants.[32]

In regards to the question, "Why did a Japanese deity have to go to China in the times of antiquity?" he explained:

[Fu Xi] was actually Ōmononushi-no-Kami, a deity of our divine nation of Fusō. He exploited that land [China] and taught its foolish people the way of human relations. He went [to China] for a short period and thus acquired a Chinese name.[33]

He elaborated this point further in the *Saneki yuraiki*:

Paoxishi is also called Taiho Fu Xi shi. He was actually Ōmononushi-no-Kami, a deity of our divine nation of Fusō. He went to ancient China to exploit its land and became the emperor. He taught its foolish people the ways of heaven, earth, and humanity. By observing the changes of the universe and everything, he created the trigrams. The *Sekiken taikoden* and this work have explained this idea implicitly.[34]

According to the *Kojiki*, Ōkuninushi-no-Kami had one hundred and eighty children. Atsutane claimed that "Ōkuninushi-no-Kami traveled to foreign lands, and his children went to foreign nations in the four corners."[35] Legendary emperors of the Xia dynasty were considered descendants of Ōmononushi-no-Kami:

Taiho Fu Xi shi was actually our Ōmononushi-no-Kami who went to that country to rule and educate its people. I have heard that Yandi Shennongshi and Huang Di Youxiongshi were descendants of Fu Xi. Shaohao Jintianshi and Zhuanxu Gaoyangshi were also his descendants. Owing to his great feats, his descendants flourished for many generations.[36]

In the *Daifusō kokukō*, he added that founding gods (such as Nuwa), great emperors (such as Fu Xi), and representative ministers (such as Yi Yin) of ancient China were mostly Japanese deities. Regarding the real identity of Fu Xi, it reads:

Fu Xi lived during the reign of Emperor Yan. In the early stage of civilization in that country [China], our Japanese deity descended from heaven to create a governance system and educate its people.... He sojourned there for a while. Wise men all came from Japan.[37]

In the *Shunjū meirekijo kō*, Atsutane, based on his own calculations, came to the conclusion that from the birth of Fu Xi to the second year of the Tenpō era (1831) when the book was written, 4,892 years had passed.

Atsutane did not rate the *Zhouyi* highly, since he saw it as a corrupt edition of the *Yijing*. He blamed King Wen for changing the order of the sixty-four hexagrams and the number of yarrow stalks used in oracles, and for adding the *Tuanci* (Commentary on the Hexagram Statements) and *Yaoci* (Commentary on the Line Statements) in order to justify the revolution that overthrew the Shang dynasty:

> Only the ancient charts of the sixty-four hexagrams and the names
> of the hexagrams are correctly transmitted in the *Zhouyi*. The *Tuanci*
> and *Yaoci* were written by King Wen and his son to advocate their
> views. Although its wordings sound auspicious, they carry the rebel-
> lious idea of overthrowing the Yin regime in the hexagram and line
> statements implicitly.[38]

In particular, Atsutane condemned King Wen for writing in the *Tuanci* the line "Tang and Wu made revolution. They followed heaven and responded to the people" As he explained:

> It [the *Tuanci*] reads: "Heaven and earth revolve and the four seasons
> take shape. Tang and Wu made revolution. They followed heaven and
> responded to the people. The season of revolution is great indeed."
> Claiming heaven's mandate to uphold the idea that the revolts launched
> by King Tang and King Wu followed heaven's will and the people's
> wishes was indeed an act of disrespect to heaven and disloyalty to the
> emperor. Both the "Tangshi" [The Oath of King Tang] and "Taishi"
> [The Oath of King Wu in the *Shangshu*] contain perfidious words.[39]

In order to compare the three different editions of the *Yijing* in ancient China, Atsutane cited extensively from the *Yuhai* (Jade Ocean), an encyclopedia written by Wang Yinglin (1223–96), among other Chinese sources in his writings on the *Yijing*. He came to realize that the order of the sixty-four hexagrams, the names of the hexagrams, the divinational method, and the number of yarrow stalks were not the same. As an example, the first hexagram was *gen*, *kun*, and *gian* in the *Lianshan*, *Guicang*, and *Zhouyi*, respectively. According to the *Zhouli* (The Rites of Zhou), the *taibo* (imperial diviner) mastered the three early editions of the *Yijing* and used all of their methods to divine. He added that the *Zhouyi* was promoted, but further distorted in the hands of the Duke of Zhou and Confucius. The *Lianshan* and *Guicang* had lost their popularity and did not survive into the Han period. The so-called *Lianshan* and *Guicang* that reappeared in the Tang period were fakes.[40] By writing the *Koeki taishōkyō* (Commentary on the Great Image in the Ancient *Yijing*) and *Tanekiron* (Discourse on the Commentary on the Hexagram Text in the *Yijing*), Atsutane strove to restore the original *Yijing* through an examination of the *Daxiang* (Commentary on the Great Image) and *Tuan Chuan* (Commentary on the Hexagram Text), the two old commentaries on the *Yijing* that Atsutane believed to contain fragments of the lost *Lianshan* and *Guicang*. He alleged that the *Daxiang* was originally a commentary on the *Guicang*, and thus preserved elements of the ancient *Yijing*.[41] Using some Chinese commentaries and apocrypha on the *Yijing* as references, he reorganized the order of the sixty-four hexagrams and reduced the number of yarrow stalks from forty-nine to forty-five.[42] Many of his ideas were borrowed from Wang Yinglin's *Yuhai*. For instance, Wang Yinglin held that they were only forty-five yarrow stalks used in the *Guicang*. Atsutane referred to his own divination of the *Yijing* as *fukkoeki* (restoration of the ancient *Yijing*), a term adopted widely by his students and many late Tokugawa diviners.[43]

Atsutane called the *Lianshan* and *Guicang shineki* (authentic *Yijing*), *koeki* (ancient *Yijing*), and *shineki* (divine *Yijing*), but discredited the *Zhouyi* as a *gieki* (fake *Yijing*). Applying the same logic to evaluate ancient Chinese sages, he praised the Three Sovereigns and the Five Emperors of the Xia and Shang periods as *shinsei* (real sages), but condemned King Wen, King Wu, the Duke of Zhou, and Confucius of the Zhou period as *gisei* (fake sages).[44] Hence, he did not rate Confucius and Zhu Xi highly and paid less attention to their *Yijing* studies. Among the works of Confucius, he preferred the *Lunyu*, because he believed that it contained elements of the ancient *Yijing*: "Many dialogues of Confucius in the *Lunyu* were derived from the wording of the *Daxiang*."[45] It is obvious that his perception of Confucianism was influenced by his theory of Japanese origins of Chinese sages.

THE SHINTOIZATION OF THE *YIJING* AFTER ATSUTANE

The *Yijing* scholarship of Hirata Atsutane was succeeded by a number of disciples, making the *Yijing* one of the areas of specialization in the Hirata school.[46] Ikuta Yorozu (1801–37) and Ōkuni Takamasa (1791–1871) were the two major successors who made a significant contribution to the intellectual discussion of the *Yijing*. Other students of Atsutane who studied the *Yijing* included Arai Morimura (1808–93), Aratame Michishige (1800–56), Izumi Ietane (1819–75), Hirata Kanetane (1799–1880), and Midorikawa Yoshihisa (1807–?).[47] Konishi Atsuyoshi (1767–1837) and Tamura Yoshishige (1790–1877) applied the theories of the *Yijing* to agriculture.[48]

Ikuta Yorozu was a faithful disciple of Atsutane, following his teachings about the *Yijing* closely. He was also influenced by the Kimon school, founded by Yamazaki Ansai, and the *Yōmeigaku* (Wang Yangming) school in Confucianism, and thus was familiar with Confucian classics. His *Koeki taishōkyō den* (Commentary on the *Koeki taishōkyō*) and *Taneki seigi* (The Correct Meanings of the *Tanekiron*) were commentaries on Atsutane's *Koeki taishōkyō* and *Tanekiron*, respectively. Endorsed and proofread by Atsutane, these two commentaries promoted and elaborated upon Atsutane's views of the ancient *Yijing*. For instance, he agreed that the *Yijing* was written by Ōkuninushi-no-Kami, who travelled to China in the ancient past to cultivate the Chinese:

> How wonderful! What is the so-called divine *Yijing*? In the time before the establishment of human relations and borders, our deity, Ōkuninushi-no-Kami, also known as Fu Xi, went across the ocean to China and taught its foolish people about morality. The *Yijing* was written for this purpose. This happened four thousand and eighty some years ago.[49]

Yorozu's commentaries focus on divination based on the images of the hexagrams. He claimed: "The fortune based on the images of the hexagrams can be told from the [*Koeki*] *taishōkyō den* and the *Taneki seigi*."[50] The *Koeki taishōkyō den* became the divination manual of the Hirata school. In the preface to the *Koeki taishōkyō den*, Atsutane openly acknowledged Yorozu as the successor of his *Yijing* scholarship:

> We can know it from the *Taiko koekiden*, *Saneki yuraiki*, *Kinmei roku* [also known as *Koeki taishōkyō*], and *Taneki hen* [also called *Tanekiron*]. There are many people who have studied under me. When I taught these books and shared my views, only Sugawara [Yorozu] could know all after hearing one point and accumulate knowledge little by little.... I believed that he could make his career; I asked him to comment on the *Koeki taishōkyō*.... He stated what I taught and elaborated upon things that I did not teach.[51]

Yorozu developed Atsutane's historical views in the *Koeki taishōkyō den* in his explanation of the sixty-four hexagrams. For example, the hexagram *bi* (holding together) in *The Great Image* reads: "Water on the earth is [the image of] *bi*. Ancient kings, based on this principle, established thousands of states and maintained a close relationship with the nobles." Atsutane praised the feudalism of the Xia dynasty as a divine system created by Japanese deities:

> Early emperors of the Xia dynasty established thousands of states and maintained a close relationship with the nobles. From the *Yugong* [The Tribute of King Yu], we can understand this system. Feudalism was the system adopted in the Three Dynasties. In antiquity, our deities taught [the Chinese] this system. Having destroyed the six nations, the Qin regarded the entire territory as its own and thus launched the system of prefectures and counties.[52]

Like Atsutane, Yorozu criticized King Wen, the Duke of Zhou, and Confucius for distorting the meanings of the *Yijing*, stressing that the only way to restore the original *Yijing* was to study *The Great Image*. He was confident that the Hirata school was making a major breakthrough in *Yijing* studies:

> When people talk about the *Yijing*, they all refer to King Wen, the Duke of Zhou, and Confucius. Diviners and the like often only read books written by a few scholars, including Hirasawa [Zuitei, 1697–1780], Baba [Nobutake, ?–1715], Arai [Hakuga, 1715–92], and Mase [Chūshū, 1754–1817]. Only two or three of us strive to study the ancient *Yijing* by Fu Xi. How great our endeavors are![53]

Like the *Koeki taishōkyō den*, the *Taneki seigi* was another commentary that Atsutane asked Yorozu to write. Its aim was to restore the divination of the *Guicang*. Arakawa Hidetaka, another of Atsutane's students from the Akita domain, wrote in the preface: "[My master] asked his student Sugawara Dōman [Ikuta Yorozu] to write a commentary on the [*Koeki*] *taishōkyō*. Having finished this assignment, my master then asked Dōman to comment on his *Tanekiron*."[54] This commentary uses the theories of the *Yijing* to explain the Age of the Gods and introduces this allegedly ancient method of divination. Yorozu maintained that the *Yijing* oracles are applicable to all nations because they are based on the universal principle of nature:

Ōkuninushi-no-Kami, also called Taiho Fu Xi shi, went to that country and became its emperor for a short period of time. Based on our Shinto, he created the eight trigrams.... The eight trigrams of the *Yijing* follow the natural principle of change. Out of the fifty yarrow stalks, only forty-five are used. The practice that repeats between six to twelve times to acquire *benqua* (the original hexagram) and *bianqua* (the changed hexagram) also follows the numerology of the universe.[55]

Ōkuni Takamasa provided original ideas regarding the origins of the *Yijing* in his writings, although he did not leave behind any specific works on the *Yijing*. Takamasa was a broad-based scholar influenced by *kokugaku*, Confucianism, *rangaku*, and *bongaku* (Sanskrit learning). His knowledge of Confucian and Chinese studies was superior in the Hirata school, and his representative work, *Koden tsūkai* (An Explanation of the *Kojikiden*), cites extensively from Chinese and Japanese sources to discuss ancient Japanese history.[56] Compared with Yorozu, Takamasa offered more new ideas based on Atsutane's teachings. Among Atsutane's writings on the *Yijing*, he preferred the *Taiko koekiden* for outlining the history of the transmission of the *Yijing* in antiquity, listing it as one of the four greatest works of Atsutane.[57] He himself also added something new in this regard. Although he accepted Atsutane's view that Fu Xi and other ancient Chinese sage-kings were Japanese deities, he changed their names. Fu Xi was no longer Ōkuninushi-no-Kami, but rather Yashima-jinumi-no-Kami; Huang Di was the manifestation of Ōkuninushi-no-Kami.[58] Takamasa further alleged that the great ministers of the Chinese sage-kings were also Japanese deities:

> Our fourth-generation master, Hirata [Atsutane], associated Fu Xi with Ōkuninushi-no-Kami. I have made the following changes: Yashima-jinumi-no-Kami was Fu Xi, Ukanomitama-no-Kami was Shennong, and Ōkuninushi-no-Kami was Huang Di. These three emperors were manifestations of our deities in that country. Later, having read the ancient texts of that country, I came to realize that the assistants of Huang Di were also our Shinto deities. Manifested in human form, they helped Huang Di cultivate the Chinese. Qibo was the temporary manifestation of Funado-no-Kami.[59]

In addition to his opinions on the history of the transmission of the *Yijing*, Takamasa's view of the writing system was equally significant and stimulating. Hirata Atsutane believed that Japan possessed its own writing system in the Age of the Gods that he called *jindai moji* (scripts of the Age of the Gods). Scholars of the Hirata school basically accepted this view, and Takamasa was no exception. Takamasa further alleged that *jindai moji* were developed from divinational images in the Age of the Gods that became the origin of all languages in this world, including the trigrams and hexagrams of the *Yijing*, Chinese, Sanskrit, and Dutch. He used the characters for heaven, earth, water, and fire as examples to demonstrate how the hexagrams and Chinese characters derived from the divination images in the Age of the Gods.[60] To a certain extent, Takamasa's idea was inspired by Atsutane, who alleged that all languages were gifts from the Shinto deities as follows: "Languages of all nations were granted by Ōnamochi-no-Kami and Sukunami-no-Kami, Sukunabikona-no-Kami of Tokoyo-no-kuni (Land of Immortality)."[61] Takamasa even acknowledged different Japanese deities for inventing various Chinese scripts.[62]

Seeing the *Yijing* as a Shinto text, Takamasa could thus comfortably employ the *wu-xing* theory in his writings. He cited some Japanese sources to claim that this theory existed in ancient Japan before the importation of Chinese texts. While condemning the Chinese Confucians for turning *wu-xing* into an armchair theory, he praised Atsutane for restoring its original meaning.[63] In order to argue that Japanese was the most elegant language in the world, he applied the *wu-xing* (in the order of wood, fire, earth, metal, and water) to match the five basic vowels of the Japanese language (in the order of a, i, u, e, o: あ、い、う、え、お). Moreover, he used *Yijing* divination and *yin-yang wu-xing* to explain the Age of the Gods.

THE *YIJING* AS A BUILDING BLOCK OF SHINTO

Yijing scholarship in *kokugaku* was significant in Japanese intellectual history and in the history of Sino-Japanese cultural exchange. It deepens our understanding of the nature and transformation of *kokugaku*, the relationship between *kokugaku* and Confucianism, and the cultural appropriation of the *Yijing* in the Tokugawa period.

Kokugaku was an intellectual discourse that advocated nativist ideologies through the study of early Japanese literature and history. Early *kokugaku* scholars focused on the Japanese classics and thus paid less attention to foreign texts. In the time of Hirata Atsutane, the worldview of the Japanese had undergone a dramatic change. Mid- and late *kokugaku* scholars could not ignore the fact that Japan was only a tiny piece of land in the world, and they felt the need to give *kokugaku* and Japan a place in the new world order.[64] Scholars of the Hirata school no longer limited the scope of their scholarship to the Japanese classics, but strove to examine Japan from a more global perspective. Hence, they also incorporated knowledge from China, India, and the Western world.[65] Hirata Atsutane's academic interest included Japanese and Chinese ancient history, *Yijing*, Confucianism, Dutch learning, Sanskrit studies, Western medicine, Chinese calendric studies, Christianity, and Daoism. The transformation of *kokugaku* in the mid- to late Tokugawa period provided conditions favorable to the growth of *Yijing* studies.

Kokugaku contained an anti-Confucian and anti-Chinese ideology. Early *kokugaku* scholars either looked down upon (like Motoori Norinaga) or ignored (like Kada Azumamaro and Kamo Mabuchi) Confucian and Chinese studies. Nevertheless, the Confucian classics and Chinese proficiency were included in Tokugawa basic education for intellectuals and samurai, and thus *kokugaku* scholars were not unfamiliar with things Confucian and Chinese. The relationship between *kokugaku* and Confucianism was complicated, and thus they should not be defined as two irreconcilable intellectual forces. Some early *kokugaku* scholars did not reject Confucianism. Mid- to late Tokugawa scholars of the Hirata school were well versed in the Confucian classics and in classical Chinese. They were particularly interested in the *Yijing* and tried to include it in the *kokugaku* system. Likewise, Tokugawa Confucians demonstrated national sentiments and cultural pride in the study of the classics of Chinese thought. Many also studied Japanese history and literature and believed in Shinto, and thus they were tolerant of nativist currents.

The *Yijing* scholarship of the Hirata school showed a high level of localization. The *Yijing* was modified, naturalized, and appropriated to advocate nativist ideas. In order to justify the uses of the concepts and divination of the *Yijing*, scholars of the Hirata school identified ancient Chinese sage-kings as the manifestations of Shinto deities. In the history of the *Yiying* in East Asia, the scholarship of the Hirata school was bizarre and far-fetched, but unique and creative at the same time. Seeing the Xia and Shang editions of the *Yijing* as the authentic text and the *Zhouyi* as a corrupt revision was a very breathtaking idea. The same logic was applied to the evaluation of medical and calendrical studies in ancient China. The *Yijing* scholarship of the Hirata school should be deeply investigated and fairly evaluated within the context of the localization of Chinese learning.

Part III

REDEFINITION OF
HISTORICAL TERMS

NAMES FOR CHINA

As political and historical terms contain ideologies, the ways in which the Tokugawa Japanese referred to China reflected their national consciousness and cultural identity. Names for China in Tokugawa writings were usually carefully chosen, and some Tokugawa scholars even wrote books or theses to discuss the proper ways to refer to China. In general, Confucians and Sinologists tended to apply honorific terms borrowed from Chinese classics to refer to China, whereas nativist scholars, including those from *kokugaku*, Shinto, and the Mito school, used neutral or negative terms. In the Sino-Japanese comparison among nativist scholars, China was often used as "the Other" to underline the superiority and uniqueness of Japan's nationality. More significantly, some Tokugawa Japanese even borrowed names that were originally applied to China to refer to Japan, following the rise of the theory of *kai hentai* (the transformation from civilized to barbarian) and the Japanese version of the Sinocentric world order. This kind of semantic appropriation deserves academic investigation within the context of Sino-Japanese cultural exchange and Japanese intellectual history. Based on textual analysis of Tokugawa writings, this chapter examines the rhetorical strategies used by Tokugawa scholars from different schools of thought and religion to name China. It deepens the understanding of the tug-of-war between Japan-centrism and Sinophilia in Tokugawa thinking and the appropriation of Chinese names to express Japanese ideas.

NAMES FOR CHINA IN TOKUGAWA WRITINGS

Zhongguo (Central Kingdom) and *Zhonghua* (Central Civilization) are now the common names for China, but they were not frequently used in premodern texts. First appearing in pre-Qin texts such as the *Shijing* (Classic of Poetry), *Shangshu* (Classic of History), and *Chunqiu* (Spring and Autumn Annals), *Zhongguo* carried different meanings, including the region under the Han race, the Central Plain of China, the capital city, and the upland region.[1] Other names for China in pre-Qin texts were *Zhongyuan* (Central Plain), *Zhongxia* (Central Civilization), *Zhongzhou* (Central Province), *Huaxia* (Central Civilization), and *Shenzhou* (Land of the Deities). *Zhonghua* was only coined in the Eastern Jin period (317–420), and was rarely used until the modern period. Instead of *Zhongguo* or *Zhonghua*, dynastic names, such as Han, Tang, Song, Ming, and Qing, were used by the regimes and their people from Qin to Qing to represent China. *Da* (great) was often added to show respect to the dynasties under which they lived.

Like the Chinese, the pre-Tokugawa Japanese applied Chinese dynastic names to refer to China. *Zhongguo* and *Zhonghua* were rarely used.[2] In the Heian period, many Japanese called China *Dai-Tō* (Great Tang) out of respect.[3] Other names for China were *Karakuni* (the Tang Nation), *Morokoshi* (Land of Tang 唐土), *Kan* or *Shintan* (ancient China, originally from the Sanskrit *cīna-sthāna*), and *Seido* (Western Land). In the medieval period, *Tō* and *Dai-Tō* could be used as general terms to refer to China rather than a specific dynasty. For instance, Japanese imperial missions to Ming China in the Muromachi period were called *kentō* (envoys to Tang) and not *kenmin* (envoys to Ming).[4] Later, in *kangō bōeki* (the tally trade), Japanese regional leaders and merchants referred to China as *Dai-Min* (Great Ming) or *Dai-Minkoku* (Great Ming Empire).

The worldview of the Japanese prior to the arrival of the Europeans in the late sixteenth century was somewhat narrow. Influenced by Buddhist writings, many Heian and medieval Japanese saw India, China, and Japan, the three major Buddhist nations, as the *sangoku* (three nations), whereas Korea, the Ryūkyū Kingdom, and other nations were the periphery. For instance, the early Heian monk Saichō (767–822) regarded *Tenjiku* (India), *Shintan* (China), and *Nihon* (Japan) as the three nations. The late Heian storybook *Konjaku monogatarishū* (Anthology of Tales from the Past) was divided into three parts: *Tenjiku*, *Shintan*, and *Honchō* (our dynasty, i.e., Japan). The Buddhist three-nation worldview became prevalent in the medieval period. An early Kamakura history book, *Gukanshō* (Jottings of a Fool), cited *Yamato-no-kuni* (Japan), *Morokoshi*, and *Tenjiku* as the three nations. Toyotomi Hideyoshi

(1537–98), in a letter to the Portuguese viceroy in Asia, advocated the doctrine of the unity of the three teachings as follows: "Japan is a nation of *kami* (deity). *Kami* is mind and everything is derived from mind. Without *kami*, there is no life. Without *kami*, there is no Way.... What is immeasurable in *yin* and *yang* is called *kami*. *Kami* is the origin of everything. Our religion is called Buddhism in India, Confucianism in China, and Shinto in Japan. If you understand Shinto, you will also understand Buddhism and Confucianism."[5]

Names for China became more diversified in the Tokugawa period, when different schools of thought and religion competed with and influenced one another.[6] The introduction of Western astronomy and geography challenged the Buddhist worldview.[7] According to the *Wakan sansai zue* (Illustrated Encyclopedia of Japan and China; 1712) compiled by the mid-Tokugawa scholar Terajima Ryōan, the most widely used names for China among Tokugawa Japanese were *Chūgoku* (Central Kingdom), *Kan, Shintan, Chūka* (Central Civilization), and *Shina*.[8] Based on Tokugawa texts, I classify the names for China into the following six categories: imported honorific names, dynastic names, translated Buddhist names, discriminatory names, geographical names, and newly coined names.

First, the imported honorific names were *Chūgoku* (used by Fujiwara Seika, Asami Keisai, Itō Jinsai, Ogyū Sorai, Nishikawa Joken, Amenomori Hōshū, and Satō Issai) and *Chūka* (used by Fujiwara Seika, Hayashi Razan, Hayashi Gahō, Yamaga Sokō, Kumazawa Banzan, Ogyū Sorai, Dazai Shundai, and Hori Keizan). Tokugawa Confucians liked to use these names to show respect for their cultural homeland. However, they were used to refer to the cultural strength of China and were unrelated to any political or diplomatic order. For example, Fujiwara Seika expressed his nostalgia for ancient China as follows: "I always admire the ancient Chinese civilization and long to see its cultural relics."[9] Kumazawa Banzan compared the three nations as follows: "*Chūka* and *Tenjiku* are big nations. They are fifty or even one hundred times bigger than Japan."[10]

Second, Chinese dynasty-related names that were used included *Kando* (literally, the Land of the Han; used by Goi Ranshū, Ueda Akinari, Sakuma Taika, Tani Shinzan, Fujita Tōko, Aizawa Seishisai, and Yoshida Shōin), *Kangoku* (literally, the Han Nation; used by Motoori Nobunaga, Ikuta Yorozu, and Izumi Makuni), *Kan* (used by Kaibara Ekken and Bitō Jishū), *Kara* or *Morokoshi* (唐; used by Asami Keisai, Kumazawa Banzan, Tokugawa

Mitsukuni, Keichū, and Amenomori Hōshū), *morokoshi* (唐土; used by Asami Keisai, Satō Naotaka, Tokugawa Mitsukuni, Amenomori Hōshū, and Tani Shinzan), *Tōzan* (literally, Mountain of the Tang; used by Hayashi Shihei and Watanabe Kazan), *Tōkoku* (literally, the Tang Nation; used by Motoori Nobunaga, Izumi Makuni, and Kamo Mabuchi), and *Shinkoku* (literally, the Qing Nation; used by Amenomori Hōshū and Moriyama Teijirō). Although the Han and the Tang were long gone, many Tokugawa Japanese used their names to represent China.[11] They called Qing Chinese *Tōjin*, Chinese merchant ships *Tōsen*, and Chinese interpreters in Nagasaki *Tōtsūji*. Han and Tang were used because they were the golden eras of Chinese history and the apex of Sino-Japanese interaction. Users came from different backgrounds, and included *bakufu* officials, Confucians, Mito scholars, and *kokugaku* scholars. Following the rise of the seclusion policy and the new worldview, Tokugawa Japanese no longer added *dai* (great) as a prefix for Chinese dynastic names. Amano Sadakage explained: "Our people referred to China as Great Tang, Great Song, Great Yuan, Great Ming, and Great Qing in their Chinese writings. This is not the right thing to do. *Dai* [great] is an honorific term used by subordinates. We should simply use Tang, Ming, or Qing."[12]

Third, Buddhist terms translated from Sanskrit were *Shina* (used by Arai Hakuseki, Motoori Norinaga, Sugita Genpaku, Tominaga Nakamoto, Kaiho Seiryō, Satō Nobuhiro, Takano Chōei, and Watanabe Kazan) and *Shintan* (used by Terajima Ryōan and Nishikawa Joken). *Shina* usually had no negative implications in the Tokugawa period. It was indeed a neutral term to replace both Sinocentric and Japan-centric terms.[13] *Shinakoku* (Nation of *Shina*) was a derivative term, used by Tachibana Moribe and Satō Nobuhiro. The use of *Shina* and *Shintan* instead of honorific terms was a gesture indicating that Japan was on equal footing with China.[14]

Fourth, discriminatory names that posed China as "the Other" were used by scholars with strong national sentiments such as *kokugaku* and Shinto scholars. *Ichō* (alien dynasty; used by Yamazaki Ansai, Watarai Nobuyoshi, Yamaga Sokō, Arai Hakuseki, and Tokugawa Mitsukuni) and *ikoku* (alien nation; used by Ogyū Sorai, Motoori Norinaga, Ise Sadatake, and Hayashi Shihei) were the most common in this category. Other terms included *iiki* (alien land; used by Yamaga Sokō), *gaichō* (foreign dynasty; used by Yamaga Sokō), *gaihō* (foreign nation; used by Yamaga Sokō), *ihō* (alien nation; used by Fujita Yūkoku), *gaikoku* (foreign nation; used by Yamaga Sokō and Goi Ranshū), *Kanjū* (漢戎, barbaric Han; used by Kamo Mabuchi), and *Kani* (漢夷, Han barbarians; used by Kamo Mabuchi).

Fifth, geographical terms from Chinese classics were used, including *Sekiken* (Red Province; used by Hirata Atsutane and Suzuki Shigetane), *Chūgen* (Central Plain; used by Hayashi Gahō), and *Saishū* (the Province of Qi; used by Goi Ranshū). These names were not very popular, and were employed by some Confucians and Shintoists to refer to China without emotional attachment. For example, *Sekiken* (or *Chixian* in Chinese) was quoted from the passage "China is called *Chixian Shenzhou* [Red Province and Divine Land]" in the *Shiji*. Hirata Atsutane and his disciples deleted *Shenzhou* (Divine Land) to avoid ideological confusion.

Sixth, names created by the Japanese were *Seido* (Western Land; used by Rai Sanyō, Tani Shinzan, Fujita Tōko, Aizawa Seishisai, Izumi Makuni, and Yoshida Shōin), *kanokuni* (彼邦, that nation; used by Yamazaki Ansai), *kanokuni* (彼国, that nation; used by Motoori Norinaga and Watarai Jōshō), and *Kaiki* (Chinese territory; coined by Nakai Chikuzan). The use of *Seido* can be dated back to the medieval period, and it was one of the most popular names for China among Tokugawa Japanese.

Different intellectual schools had their own naming preferences to show their attitudes toward China. On an individual level, naming China was a complicated and, at times, ambiguous matter. First, the same person would sometimes use various names for China in different capacities. For instance, Ogyū Sorai, in his private writings, referred to China as both *Chūka* and *Chūgoku*. Admiring the ways of the Chinese sages, he called himself a *tōi no hito* (eastern barbarian) and *Nihonkoku ijin* (barbarian of the nation of Japan) and was upset that he was not born in the land of the sages and could not speak Chinese fluently. However, in the *Seiron* (Discourse on Politics), a proposal to the *bakufu*, Sorai called China *ikoku* (alien nation). This kind of split personality was common among Tokugawa thinkers. Second, the same person would name China differently at various stages of his life. Yamaga Sokō, called China *Chūka* in his early years. He became more nationalistic in his later years, labeling China as *gaichō*, *gaikoku*, *ichō*, and *iiki*. Third, the same person would use different names for China in one and the same text as a matter of writing style.[15]

CHINA AS "THE OTHER" FOR JAPAN

China had unique functions in Tokugawa thinking. On the one side, it served as a model, or a kind of cultural homeland. On the other side, it was used to boost Japan's own identity.[16] From the perspective of a Sinophile, China was Japan's tutor. Kumazawa Banzan was thankful to China for introducing advanced civilization to Japan as follows:

> *Chūka* is the teacher for the four seas and has contributed tremendously to Japan. Rites, music, books, mathematics, architecture, costume, transportation, agricultural tools, weapons, medicine, acupuncture, officialdom, ranking, military codes, the way of archery and riding, and miscellaneous skills and technologies were all imported from *Chūka*.[17]

However, in Sino-Japanese comparison, China often played the role of "the Other" to make Japan look superior. The notion of Divine Nation (*Shinkoku*) can be traced to Kitabatake Chikafusa. The opening sentence of the *Jinnō shōtōki* (Chronicles of the Authentic Lineages of the Divine Emperors) reads:

> Great Japan is the Divine Nation. The heavenly progenitor founded it, and the Sun Goddess bequeathed it to her descendants to rule eternally. Only in our country is this true; there are no similar examples in other countries. This is why our country is called the Divine Nation.[18]

In Tokugawa political discourse, the otherness of China was manifested in various strata of Sino-Japanese comparisons.

The first form was the difference between Divine Province (*Shinshū*) and Western Land (*Seido*). These two names were used extensively by Mito scholars. For example, Fujita Yūkoku (1774–1826) criticized China for having many bad customs: "The civilized nation in the Western Land has these problems. Only my Divine Province does not have them."[19] The calligrapher Iwaya Osamu (1834–1905) praised the unique nationality of Japan in the preface to the *Kōdōkan kijutsugi* (Manifesto of Kōdōkan) as follows: "Following the way of the Divine Province and learning from the ways of the Western Land, our loyalty and filial piety are beyond comparison. We respect both literature and martial arts. We promote learning. We revere deities and respect Confucianism."[20] Yūkoku's son, Fujita Tōko, clearly stated that "the Divine Province is the Divine Province; the Western Land is the Western Land. They call us alien; we rate them as inferior."[21] While emphasizing the national identity of Japan, Mito scholars gave due respect to China. Tōko maintained:

> The quality of our Divine Province is the best among ten thousand nations in the world. We have the quality, but not the literature. We have the substance, but not the name. The Western Land, as a nation, is wise and open and its system and literature are magnificent. Using its good qualities to rectify our shortcomings is natural.[22]

In Japan-China comparisons, China served as "the Other." However, in the order of world civilization, China maintained a respectable place in the eyes of the Mito scholars.

The second form was the distinction between *honcho* (our dynasty) and *ichō* or *gaichō* (alien dynasty). Yamaga Sokō called China *ichō* and *gaichō*, and referred to Japan as *honchō* and *Chūchō* (Central Dynasty). He held: "Someone has said, 'Japan is a small nation and everything is inferior to China. The sages only lived in China.' Contemporary scholars accept this view. They admire the alien dynasty to such an extent."[23] The Shintoist Watarai Nobuyoshi (1615–90) stressed that Shinto was an indigenous religion and had nothing to do with China. He wrote: "Shinto is not derived from the *Yijing*. Some people speculate that Shinto is derived from the *Zhouyi* based on the books of the alien dynasty. Born in our dynasty, but having this thinking, they live amongst us but do not know the grace of our dynasty."[24] Likewise, Goi Ranshū (1697–1762), a scholar of the Kaitokudō merchant academy, asked: "Born and raised in our dynasty, why do you follow the teachings of the Duke of Zhou and not believe in Shinto?"[25] The above-quoted passages show the emergence of an identity crisis and anxiety in accepting imported Chinese Confucian ideas among Tokugawa Japanese.

The third form was the contrast between *kōkoku* (imperial nation) and *Tōkoku* (Tang Nation). With the rise of loyalism in the late Tokugawa period, *kōkoku* became a popular term in *kokugaku* and Mito school circles. In their Sino-Japanese comparison, the role of China as "the Other" was salient. Motoori Norinaga commented on the difference between the Chinese way of the gods (*shentao*) and Japanese Shinto in this way:

> However, a Chinese book [the *Yijing*] reads: "The sages, in accordance with *shendao* ["way of the gods," the same Chinese character

as *shintō*], laid down their instructions." Hence, some people believed
that Shinto in my nation borrowed its name from it. These people
do not have a mind to understand things. From the beginning, the
meanings of gods in Japan have been different from those used by the
Chinese. In that nation [China], they explain gods and the universe
in terms of the *yin-yang* of heaven and earth. Their discussion is only
empty theory without substance. The deities of our *kōkoku* were the
ancestors of the current emperor and thus [Japanese Shinto] is by no
means empty theory.[26]

He praised Japan as a *jōkoku* (上国, advanced nation) and saw China, India, and
Western nations as *kakoku* (下国, inferior nations). He explained that Japan was
the finest nation in the world because it was blessed by the Sun Goddess. He
made the comparison as follows: "The heaven and earth of China and India are
different from the heaven and earth of our *kōkoku* . . . and so on and so forth.
If you read the *Jindaiki* ["Records of the Deities," the first two chapters of the
Nihon shoki], you will understand. Undoubtedly, the Sun and Moon of China
and India are also different from the Sun and Moon of our imperial nation."[27]
Norinaga's disciple, Izumi Makuni (1765–1805), shared similar views with his
teacher regarding the superiority of Japan. He compared Japanese Shinto and
Chinese Confucianism:

> The *Zhouyi* and *Zhongyong* are fine books with many right words.
> However, the so-called way of sincerity has been an impractical and
> unprofitable armchair theory since the founding of China. Our *kōkoku*
> [imperial nation] did not have a name for the Way or books to teach it.
> The Way has been carried out for ten thousand generations from the
> Age of the Gods. Its benefits can be seen even now.[28]

In the three abovementioned forms of Sino-Japanese comparison, China was
treated as "the Other" by Tokugawa scholars to underline the superiority of
Japan on religious, political, and moral grounds.

JAPAN AS THE CULTURAL CENTER

The Chinese concept of distinguishing between civilized and barbarous people
was challenged by many Tokugawa Japanese. This intellectual change was

caused by the rise of the Manchu dynasty and the introduction of knowledge of the sphericity of the Earth from the Dutch.[29]

Even some Confucian scholars at the Edo Confucian academy Shōheiko questioned whether Japanese should call China *Chūgoku* and *Chūka*. Bitō Nichū (1747–1813) and Satō Issai (1772–1859) were examples. Nichū stressed that the Japanese should not call China *Chūgoku* and *Chūka* because Japan was not a tributary state of China:

> The nation of the Han is huge, populous, and civilized. No other nations can compare. It is proper for the Chinese to call their nation *Chūgoku* or *Chūka*. The Chinese are not arrogant to use these names. Our nation is not as large and rich as China, but we survive in the great sea without paying tribute to China. We are populous, wealthy, and self-sufficient. We do not rely on other nations. Other barbarians call China the Central Kingdom and themselves aliens. We do not follow this.[30]

Issai added that the distinction between civilized and barbarian followed subjective standards, because from heaven's perspective all nations should be subject to the same natural principle. He explained: "In this vast universe, one principle prevails. From a human's point of view, there is a central kingdom and barbarians. From heaven's point of view, there is no distinction between the central kingdom and the barbarians."[31]

Similarly, the Osaka merchant scholar Goi Ranshū stressed that the ways of naming China were controversial:

> In the Land of the Han, rulers establish new dynasties through revolution, and therefore there are many names for the nation. *Chūgoku* and *Chūka* are the names used by the Han in front of the four barbarians. They are not common names. Western people call it *Shintan*. The people of our nation refer to it as Han, as we began to communicate with each other during the Han period. We also named it Tang because we had official exchanges in the Tang period. Scholars of today call it *Chūgoku* and *Chūka*, willingly putting themselves in the position of the barbarians.[32]

Japan-centric ideologues criticized Sinophiles more severely for calling China *Chūgoku* or *Chūka*. Motoori Norinaga strongly opposed the use of these two terms to refer to China:

The Nation of Tang can be pronounced *Morokoshi* or *Kara*. In Chinese, it can be written as *Han* or *Tang*. People of our imperial nation are not proper when they use *Chūka* and *Chūgoku*. I have discussed this in the *Gyojū gaigen* [Comments on How to Subdue Barbarians; 1778] and thus do not write in length here. . . . Some people use *Shintan* and *Shina*. They should be given credit for not using *Chūka* and *Chūgoku*. However, *Shintan* and *Shina* were names given by Western nations. Using such foreign terms is as strange as using *Morokoshi* or *Kara*.[33]

Influenced by the concept of *kai hentai*, many Tokugawa Japanese believed that China had degenerated into a barbaric nation under the Manchu, and Japan had thus replaced China as the center of Confucianism. Tokugawa Confucians valued traditional China more than Ming-Qing China, whereas Shintoists and *kokugaku* scholars did not rate the Chinese tradition highly at all. The Shintoist Tani Shinzan (1663–1718) called the Chinese "barbarians" because Chinese history was full of rebellions and chaos. He argued that Japan had been the central kingdom in Asia for more than a thousand years, and thus it was more legitimate than China to bear the name *Chūgoku*. Another Shintoist, Izawa Banryō (1668–1731), stressed that Japan had established its own distinction between the civilized world and barbarians a long time ago:

> The *Nihon shoki* [Chronicles of Japan] calls Japan *Chūgoku* and refers to those in the three kingdoms in Korea and Xiqiang as *i* [barbarians]. To foreigners, our envoys were called the envoys of *Ōka* [皇華, the Imperial Central Kingdom] and our countrymen people of the imperial nation. Foreign nations were called *shoban* [miscellaneous barbarians]. . . . Nowadays, Confucians call those of our nation the eastern barbarians and the Land of Tang *Chūgoku*. Following the law of the Land of Tang, they put Japan in a subordinate position. If the Battles of Bun'ei and Kōan would be restaged, these people would betray their principles and our nation would be weakened further.[34]

Likewise, *bakufu* official Ise Sadatake rebuked his countrymen for failing to understand the principle of *kai hentai*: "Recently some Japanese Confucians have been looking down on Japan, calling it the *bani* [barbaric nation]. However, they call China *Chūka*. They are indeed disloyal traitors of Japan."[35]

The Japanese version of the concept that implied a distinction between "civilized" and "barbarian" emerged in the Nara period, when some Japanese referred to Japan as *Chūgoku* or *Waka* (華夏, Civilized Nation), and classified the three kingdoms in Korea as barbaric states.[36] In official documents, *Chūka* and *Tenka* ("all under heaven") referred to Japan.[37] Some Tokugawa Japanese continued this practice. Yamaga Sokō, in the *Chūchō jijitsu* (True Facts Concerning the Middle Kingdom; 1699), recorded the move of the capital during the reign of the Emperor Jimmu as follows: "*Honchō* [Japan], from this time onward, carried the names *Nakabashira* [Central Pillar] and *Chūgoku*."[38] Arai Hakuseki also mentioned that, according to the *Kojiki* (Record of Ancient Matters), the Emperor Jimmu advanced toward the East and then arrived at *Chūhō* (中邦, Central State) and *Ashihara Nakatsukuni* (葦原中国, Central Kingdom in the Plain of Reeds).[39] The Confucian scholar Amemori Hōshū (1668–1755) remarked that Korea and Vietnam also each considered themselves the Central Kingdom:

> Someone said: "The Land of Tang is the origin of morality in this world. It is the nation of the sages and thus is named *Chūgoku*." Others argued: "From their own perspective, people call their own nation *Chūgoku*." Out of respect for their country, the Koreans do not consider themselves barbarians, calling Korea *Tōka* [Nation of Eastern Civilization].[40]

The Kimon school had a strong impact on Japan's perception of the dichotomy between "civilized" and "barbarian." Yamazaki Ansai held that both of these elements had a relative status: "Every nation calls itself *Chūgoku*, believing that it [rests in] the middle, while its neighbors are [all] barbarians."[41] He himself called Japan *Ashihara Nakatsukuni*: "Like heaven and earth, as well as the Sun and Moon, the nation that lasts forever is my *Ashihara Nakatsukuni*. Our emperors are descendants of the Sun Goddess, whereas our ministers are children of Kogoto-musubi. A billion years are like one day. How great we are!"[42] His disciple Asami Keisai stressed that the distinction between the civilized and the barbarians should be judged by the level of civilization. If China degenerates, it should be labeled as a "barbaric nation." If the barbarians turn to morals and become civilized, they deserve to be named *Chūgoku*.[43] Hence, he agreed with his countrymen who called Japan *Chūgoku*, but strongly disagreed with those who regarded themselves as barbarians. He held:

Confucian books have used *Chūgoku* and *iteki* [barbaric nations] for a long time. Confucian books are popular in our nation. Having read Confucian books, our people call Tang *Chūgoku* and Japan *iteki*. Worse than that, some cried for being born as a barbarian. How ridiculous! People who read Confucian books do not understand their duties to our nation. How pathetic![44]

Another of Ansai's disciples, Satō Naokata (1650–1719), cited the teachings of his master: "According to the Shinto advocated by my master Suika [Ansai], Japan can be called *Chūgoku*. [This] is supported by [the ideas of] Chengzi [or Cheng Yi] who held that there is no location in this world that one may not call 'central.' "[45] Sasaki Takanari, a student of Naokata, took a more radical stance, calling China a *kakoku* (inferior nation) as follows: "The customs of the *Seido* are radical and dirty. It has been a land of beasts since its foundation. Our nation is a land of deities and thus it has moral standards and a good balance between *yin* and *yang*."[46]

Similar voices could also be heard from other intellectual schools. Watarai Jōshō (1675–1752), a Shinto priest of the Outer Shrine of the Ise Shrine, maintained that every nation placed itself in a central position, and therefore his countrymen should not apply that term to China and call themselves eastern barbarians:

> Our scholars were born in Japan, drinking the spring water and eating the crops of [their native land]. However, many do not make [a clear] distinction between [what is] within and [what rests] without, [nor between] close and distant relationships, [thereby] ignoring our advantages and highlighting our weaknesses, calling themselves "eastern barbarians." They call that nation [i.e., China] *Chūka*, *Chūgoku*, *Chūgen*, and *Chūdo* [Central Land], ignoring its weaknesses and highlighting its advantages. This is a common mistake.[47]

Another Shinto priest, Fukagawa Yūei (1695–1768), insisted that only Japan was entitled to the name *Chūgoku* or *Chūka*, and that China was nothing but *Kani* (漢夷, Chinese barbarians):

> That nation calls itself *Chūka* and our *sumera mikuni* [imperial nation] a barbarian [nation]. Indeed, our name should be called *Chūka* or

Chūgoku. That nation is nothing but barbaric. . . . We should uphold the dignity of our imperial nation. However, many Confucians nowadays call the nation of the *Kani* [Han barbarians] *Chūka, Chūgoku*, or a nation of sages and gentlemen, but refer to our imperial nation as a nation of barbarians without manners and principles.[48]

Tokugawa Mitsukuni, the second *daimyō* of the Mito domain, also opposed the use of *Chūka* for China: "According to *Morokoshi* [China], the Chinese call their nation *Chūka*. We Japanese should not follow that. We should call the capital of Japan *Chūka*. Why do we call the foreign nation *Chūka*?"[49]

The rise of Western learning also dealt the Sinocentric view a considerable blow. Sugita Genpaku (1733–1817), a scholar of Dutch learning, asked:

> Stubborn Confucians and quacks read Chinese books and call China the Central Land. The Earth is a sphere and thousands of nations are inside of it. They are all in a central position. Which nation is not a central land? China is only a tiny nation in the Eastern Sea.[50]

His disciple, Ōtsuki Gentaku (1757–1827), expressed a similar view:

> Stubborn Confucians and quacks do not know the world and are confused by Chinese ideas. They call China the "Central Kingdom" and use the term "the way of the Central Kingdom." The Earth is a sphere that contains thousands of nations. They only live in one region. *Shina* calls itself the Central Land, Central Plain, Central Civilization, Capital of Civilization, the Land of Gods, and so on.[51]

Both the nativist consciousness and Western learning caused the decline of the Confucian world order in the latter half of the Tokugawa period. In the mind of many Tokugawa scholars, the cultural status of Japan shifted from periphery to center.

THE APPROPRIATION OF NAMES

Not a few Tokugawa Japanese applied honorific names originally reserved for China to Japan.[52] Yamaga Sokō is one such example. In the *Chūchō jijitsu*, he reiterated that only Japan was entitled to be named *Chūka, Chūgoku, Chūchō,* and *Chūshu* due to geographical and moral reasons, and that China should be called *gaichō*, *gaikoku*, *ichō*, and *iiki*.[53] He explained:

> Regarding the movement of heaven and earth and the four seasons, if these reach a balance, wind and rain and cold and heat will not disappear. The soil will turn fertile and the people will become clever. One may then speak of *Chūgoku*. In the whole world, only *honchō* and *gaichō* have achieved this balance. In the Age of the Gods, Ame-no-Minaka-Nushi-no-Kami [the God of Creation] and the two divinities of creation [Izanami and Izanagi] shaped our nation in the [area of the] central pillar. Hence, it is natural to call our nation *Chūgoku*.[54]

Sokō felt remorseful for failing to understand the excellence of Japan in his early years: "How foolish I was! Born in *Chūka* [Japan], but failing to understand its beauty, I was absorbed in the classics of *gaichō* [China] and admired its people. How absent-minded I was! How lost I was!"[55] In his study of the Age of the Gods, he found evidence that Japan bore the name *Chūgoku* in antiquity: "Our nation is *Chūgoku*. The Sun Goddess heard that Ukemochi-no-kami [the goddess of farming] lived in *Ashihara Nakatsukuni*. This shows that *Chūgoku* has been used since the ancient past."[56]

The astronomer Nishikawa Joken (1648–1724) discussed the distinction between the civilized and the barbaric from cultural and politico-economic perspectives. In the *Kai tsūshōkō* (An Investigation of the Trade between China and the Barbarians; 1708), he asserted that both China and Japan could be named *Chūka*. He measured the civilization of a nation by looking at their ties with China and Japan. *Gaii* (barbarians) were from nations immune to Chinese and Japanese influences. The historian Rai Sanyō (1781–1832) called Japan *Chūgoku* and *Chūchō* in the *Shinsaku* (New Thesis). For instance, he wrote: "Our *Chūchō* followed the Tang system," and "our *Chūgoku* was a self-sufficient nation in antiquity. The Silla, Goguryeo, and other barbarians borrowed ten thousand bales of seeds from us to sow in their lands."[57]

The Mito scholar Fujita Tōko used *Chūgoku* to refer to Japan in his explanation of the Age of the Gods in the *Kōdōkanki jutsugi*:

> In the times of early civilization, evil gods were everywhere in *Chūgoku* [i.e., Japan], Ōkuninushi-no-kami was particularly powerful. Our imperial ancestor sent Ameno-hohi and Ameno-wakahiko to pacify

him. They were defeated by Ōkuninushi-no-kami and never returned. Takemikazuchi was ordered to appease him. Ōkuninushi-no-kami dared not resist, surrendering his territory and fleeing far away. All other evil gods were expelled. *Chūgoku* was finally pacified.[58]

In the same text, he added: "Thanks to Takemikazuchi, there are no more evil gods and spirits in the land of *Chūgoku* [i.e., Japan] today. We are blessed by the grace of the imperial family."[59] He criticized Sinophiles as follows:

> Confucians said: "The Land of the Han is *Chūgoku* and its neighbors on four sides are barbarians. All rites, music, legal systems, and institutions were created by the Chinese. The three principles and five virtues do not belong to the barbarians." Scholars frequently get to hear this view, but they do not realize the problem. Some are self-confessed barbarians.[60]

Another Mito scholar, Aizawa Seishisai, referred to Japan as *Chūgoku*, *Shinshū*, and *Chūdo* in his *Shinron* (New Thesis; 1825).[61] For instance, he commented on the introduction of Buddhism to Japan as follows: "When Buddhism was introduced to *Chūgoku* [Japan], some ministers argued that Japan had its own religious ceremonies, and that it was wrong to worship foreign deities. However, the traitor [Sogano] Umako believed in Buddhism secretly."[62] With regard to the banning of Christianity in the early Tokugawa period, Seishisai praised it, saying: "In *Chūdo*, we have carried this policy for about two hundred years, and thus our people will not be influenced by the aliens. How great is this policy to benefit the people!"[63] When comparing China and Japan, Seishisai rated Japan higher because it had a better geographical location, an unbroken imperial line, and had never suffered conquest. Hence, Japan, in lieu of China, was *Chūgoku*. Nevertheless, he treated China with due respect, because both China and Japan had similar customs and human relationships, saying: "Adjacent to *Shinshū*, China shares similar customs with Japan and its teaching is based on the mandate of heaven and human mind."[64] He called China *Kando* (Land of the Han) and the current regime, *Manshin* (Manchurian Qing). Seeing Russia as the biggest threat to Asia, he believed that Japan and China should form an anti-Russian alliance.

The foregoing quotations show that Tokugawa scholars from different schools of thought reinterpreted the distinction between civilized and barbarian from their own vantage points. Seeing China as a sister nation (like Aizawa Seishisai) or an uncivilized foreign country (like Fukagawa Yūei), these men of letters located Japan in the center of human civilization, thereby relegating China to an inferior position along the semi-periphery or even periphery of a world order that was centered on Japan.

BEHIND THE NAMES FOR CHINA

In Tokugawa discourse, China was an imagined community and fluid concept based on cultural and psychological perceptions. In other words, it was a "cultural China."[65] Both Sinophiles and Sinophobes discussed China from a cultural rather than political perspective.

A textual examination of the names used for China in Tokugawa writings clearly demonstrates the rise of national consciousness and cultural identity in Tokugawa Japan. Even Japanese Confucians who believed in the Way of the Chinese sages kept a distance from China, and refrained from using exceedingly dignified names such as *jōkoku* (advanced nation), *Chūchō* (central dynasty), *Dai-Kan* (Great Han), and *Dai-Tō* (Great Tang) for China. By maintaining the political and cultural autonomy of Japan, they could release some of the tension involved in accommodating Chinese culture.[66]

The use of different names for China demonstrates the rise of a Japan-centered ideology in which Japan was presented as the new cultural center in Asia. Tokugawa Japanese scholars were fully aware of their national identity and thus were very cautious in naming China. In order to underline the independence of Japan in the East Asian political and cultural order, they adopted the following rhetorical strategies: First, they coined new terms to avoid using imported Chinese names associated with the Sinocentric world order. These Japanese-coined terms could be relatively neutral (e.g., *Seido*, *Morokoshi*, *Sekiken*, *gaichō*, *ikoku*, and *kanokuni*) or negative (e.g, *Kani* and *Kanjū*). Second, they chose neutral (e.g., *Shina* and *Shintan*) or relatively negative names (e.g., *ichō*, *iiki*, and *kakoku*) for China in Sino-Japanese comparisons to demonstrate the superiority and uniqueness of Japan. Third, they borrowed honorific names originally for China (e.g., *Chūka*, *Chūgoku*, *Chūchō*, and *Shinshū*) to refer to Japan, showing the rise of a Japan-centric nationalism and worldview.

An investigation of the names for China in Tokugawa political discourse indicates that national sentiments penetrated deeply into all walks of life. From the relatively pro-Chinese Zhu Xi school and *kogaku* (ancient learning) to the middle-of-the-road Mito school and the relatively anti-Chinese *kokugaku* and Shinto, Tokugawa people sought their own national and cultural identity in different directions. Treated either as a role model or "the Other," China was an indicator of Japanese nativism, and names borrowed from China were often used to express Japanese ideas and nativist sentiments.

8

BAKUFU AND *SHŌGUN*

POLITICAL TERMS IN JAPANESE HISTORICAL WRITINGS LARGELY ORIGI-
nated in China. While some kept their original meanings, most underwent
processes of localization. *Bakufu* (military government, or, literally, tent government) is one such example. What does the word *bakufu* mean? A popular
Japanese history textbook provides the following definition: "*Bakufu*—originally a term meaning military government, it came to designate the central
administration of the country, headed by the *shogun* [military dictator]."[1]
This also represents the general understanding of the term among students
of Japanese history. Nowadays, *bakufu* is widely used as a historical term
to describe the military governments established by the *shōgun* during the
medieval and early modern (or Tokugawa) periods. Related terms, such as
bakufu seiji (*bakufu* politics), *bakuhan taisei* (*bakufu*-domain system), *bakumatsu* (late Tokugawa), *tōbaku undō* (campaign to overthrow the *bakufu*),
Kamakura *bakufu*, Muromachi *bakufu*, and Edo *bakufu*, have become standardized in modern historiography. Coined by modern scholars and textbook
writers, these terms were not used in the Tokugawa period.

Whether we should be more cautious in using *bakufu* and other anach-
ronistic terms, such as *shōgun*, *tennō* (emperor), and *han* (domain), in our
research and teaching has been a topic of hot debate among scholars of early
modern Japan. The debate over the use of historical terms was triggered by the
historian of Tokugawa political thought Watanabe Hiroshi, who challenged
the application of "modern" terms in writing Tokugawa history.[2] Historically
speaking, *bakufu* was never originally a term meaning the government of the
warrior class headed by a *shōgun*. In premodern Japan, it was not a common
term, being used rarely and only in private writings, and never in official documents. The Kamakura *bakufu*, Muromachi *bakufu*, and Edo *bakufu* never

41

used the term to refer to themselves or their politics. The meaning of *bakufu* was never settled in the medieval and early modern periods. Up until close to the end of the Tokugawa period, the word was not used by either officials or the people to refer to the military government in Edo. The modern definition of *bakufu*—*bakufu* as the "central government" headed by the *shōgun*—only gained currency during the last decades of the Tokugawa period and in the Meiji period (1868–1912).[3] Likewise, the political term *shōgun* had various meanings and related terms in different ages. By documenting the semantic changes of the terms *bakufu* and *shōgun* over the ages in Japan since their importation from China and examining how Tokugawa officials and intellectuals referred to what we now call the *bakufu* and the *shōgun*, this chapter attempts to deepen our understanding of the localization of Chinese political terminology, the tug-of-war between the court and the *bakufu* over legitimacy, and the Confucian influence in Tokugawa politics and the Meiji Restoration.

THE SEMANTIC CHANGE OF *BAKUFU*

Bakufu is the Japanese reading of the Chinese term *mufu*. Although originating in China, it was not a common term in Chinese history and was only used occasionally to describe certain military-related matters. It meant different things in different periods. *Mufu* had three meanings in Chinese history. It first appeared in the Han period (206 BCE–220 CE), when it referred to the temporary residence of a general on the battlefield.[4] In the Tang period (618–907), it was used to refer to a military unit in the *jinjun* (inner palace guard) or the office of the *jiedushi* (military governor).[5] In Ming (1368–1644) and Qing (1644–1911) times, it meant the governor's office in the regions. Some related terms (such as *muliao* [secretaries of the governor's office]) were also derived from it.

The term *bakufu* was imported to Japan during the Heian period and used to refer either to the headquarters of the inner palace guard (the official name was *konoefu*) in Kyoto or the inner palace guard itself. However, *bakufu* was not an official name and was rarely used.[6] When Minamoto Yoritomo (1147–99) was appointed the commander of the inner palace guard in 1190, his residence was called the *bakufu*.[7] Two new meanings were given to the term in 1192, when Yoritomo was appointed *shōgun*.[8] From that time on, *bakufu* referred to the residence of the *shōgun* or to the *shōgun* himself. Nevertheless, it was not frequently used by civilians and was never applied to the military headquarters itself. As far as I have been able to determine, the term appeared only seldom in medieval documents. It carried the following five meanings:

1. *Bakufu* as the *shōgun* or *taishō* (commander) of the inner palace guard: The *Shūkaishō* ("Collection of Sources like Picking Small Grass"), a Kamakura encyclopedia, lists *bakufu* as the Chinese name for the commander of the inner palace guard. The *Shokugenshō* (The Record of Government Posts; 1340) by Kitabatake Chikafusa (1293–1354), remarks: "A *taishō* of junior third rank was called *Urin tai-shōgun* by the Tang Chinese. The position was commonly referred to as *bakufu*, *bakka* [幕下, literally, under the tent], *taiju* [大樹, literally, big tree], or *ryūei* [柳營, temporary military camp]. They all represented the commander."[9] In the *Muromachike ona-ishoan* (Documents of the Muromachi House), Ashikaga Takauji (1305–58) was referred to as "Takauji, the left commander of the *bakufu* [inner palace guard]."

2. *Bakufu* as the residence of the commander of the inner palace guard: In the *Honchō bunzui* (The Best of Chinese Literature in Japan), compiled by Fujiwara Akihira (989–1066), it is recorded that someone asked the commander "How could you sleep well in the *bakufu*?"[10] An 1195 entry in the *Sanchōki* (The Diary of Fujiwara Nagakane) reads: "I was allowed to enter the *bakufu* and lectured for him [the commander] about two poems."[11]

3. *Bakufu* as the *shōgun*: The *Shogen jikō setsuyō shū* (A Collection of Words and Their Usage), a medieval dictionary, defines *bakufu* as follows: "*Bakufu*, pronounced as *ba-ku-fu*, is the title for *shōgun*."[12] A Zen monk named Gidō Shūshin (1324–88) wrote in his diary, *Kūwa nichiyō kufūshū* (The Diary of Monk Kūwa on His Training): "The *bakufu* [*shōgun*] declared new decrees, manifesting the light of the virtue of frugality."[13]

4. *Bakufu* as the residence of the *shōgun*: A record of the year 1260 found in the *Azuma kagami* (The History of Eastern Government), the official history of the Kamakura *bakufu*, reads: "The residence of the *shōgun*'s family is called the *bakufu*." In another place, it

records: "The *bakufu* [the *shōgun*'s residence] is located at the evil gate [the worst location in geomancy]."[14]

5. *Bakufu* as the military government headed by the *shōgun*: The *Taiheiki* (Record of the Great Peace; c. 1372) reads: "There were senior generals in the *bakufu* who could pacify the nation."[15]

The term *bakufu* also appeared in several other medieval records, but usually no more than a few times in a single work. The military headquarters at Kamakura and Muromachi never used it in their official documents or decrees to refer to their administration, because *bakufu* implied something military, rude, and temporary and was by no means an honorific or auspicious title.

Likewise, *shōgun* was also rarely used to refer to the head of the warrior class in medieval and early modern documents. *Shōgun* (*jiangjun* in Chinese) was the title for a commander or general in China. Nara and Heian Japan adopted this definition. The title was occasionally granted to generals who were assigned temporary duty to fight in the frontier north. From the establishment of the Kamakura *bakufu* in the late twelfth century, *shōgun* acquired a new meaning—the leader of the warrior class who was also the de facto ruler of the nation.

KŌGI AND KUBŌ

The prestige of the military houses reached its apex in the Tokugawa period.[16] As could be expected, *bakufu* was not used in Tokugawa official documents. Indeed, even private writings shunned its use until the final decades of the period.[17] Today, however, very few people acknowledge this fact. This is true partly because a large number of remaining Tokugawa official documents carry the term *bakufu* in their titles, giving rise to the misconception that *bakufu* was commonly used in the Tokugawa period, whereas in fact these titles were actually given after the Tokugawa.[18] In the texts themselves, *bakufu* was never used.

Tokugawa official documents commonly refer to the *bakufu* as *kōgi* (公儀). Coined by the Japanese, *kōgi* has two literal meanings: the highest public authority of a territory and the regime itself. It was an honorific term first applied to the imperial court and the imperial family in Kyoto during the Kamakura period. For instance, Kitabatake Chikafusa (1293–1354) used this term to refer to the Southern Court in Yoshino in the *Sekigensho* (A Review of Government Posts). By the time of the Muromachi period, this term became the name for the *bakufu* and the shogunal family. The *Taiheiki*, an early Muromachi history book, already adopted this new interpretation, referring to the *shōgun* as *kōgi*. In the *Sengoku* period (Warring States period, 1467–1600), when the *shōgun*'s authority declined, *Sengoku daimyō* used *kōgi* to refer to their domains.[19] *Kōgi* was, however, a relative term in the Tokugawa period. Sometimes, the retainers referred to their *daimyō* as *kōgi*. The *daimyō* sometimes also used *kōgi* to define their polity. Thus, whether *kōgi* referred to the *shōgun* or a *daimyō* depended on the context and the relationship between the speaker and subject. To avoid this confusion, after the Kanei era (1624–45), people referred to the Edo *bakufu* as *dai-kōgi*.

Regarding the naming of the Edo *shōgun*, Tokugawa official documents often used *kubō* (公方, literally, the public realm or the holder of public authority). Like the semantic changes in the use of *kōgi*, *kubō* was coined by the Japanese and was identified with the emperor and his court in the Heian and early Kamakura periods, and then with the *shōgun* and his deputies during the late Kamakura and Muromachi periods. The land under the direct control of the Muromachi *shōgun* was named *kubō ryōsho*. The officials of the Muromachi *bakufu* were called *kubō mono*. From Ashikaga Yoshimitsu (1358–1408) onwards, Muromachi *shōgun* called themselves *kubō* in official documents. The Muromachi *bakufu* had the post of *kubō okura* (finance minister of the *bakufu*) to take charge of financial matters. In the Tokugawa period, *kubō* (or *kubō-sama*) was used exclusively for the *shōgun*. The use of *kōgi* and *kubō* in Tokugawa official documents to refer to the *bakufu* and the *shōgun* was a continuation of late medieval practice.

Although *kōgi* and *kubō* were standard terms for the *bakufu* and *shōgun*, respectively, in Tokugawa official records, private writings were not obliged to follow this practice. Such writings used various names for the *bakufu* and *shōgun* in different eras. To a certain extent, naming indicates the rise and fall of the authority and popularity of the Tokugawa administration. The ways in which Tokugawa intellectuals referred to the *bakufu* and the *shōgun* were largely a personal matter, and it is very difficult to generalize. Nevertheless, there were three major factors influencing their choices: The first of these was intellectual orientation and political ideology. Zhuxi scholars tended to adopt more respectful names than scholars from other schools, such as those from the *Yōmeigaku* (Wang Yangming) school, *kogaku*, *rangaku* (Dutch learning), and *kokugaku*. The second factor was their social status and the nature of their personal relationships with the *bakufu*, such as whether they worked for the *bakufu* or a domain, and whether their intellectual lineages or academies were sponsored by the *bakufu*. Samurai and Confucians who were in the public service respected the *bakufu* more than merchants, peasants, courtiers, and *rōnin* (masterless samurai). The political and intellectual atmosphere of the times in which they lived constituted the third factor. The early Tokugawa was an age of "Tokugawa peace," and thus early Tokugawa intellectuals generally showed more respect to the *bakufu* and the *shōgun* than their late Tokugawa counterparts.

NAMES FOR THE TOKUGAWA *BAKUFU*

How did Tokugawa intellectuals refer to the *bakufu*? Most Tokugawa intellectuals respected the Edo *bakufu*. Critics were few and soon silenced by the *bakufu*'s censorship and cultural policy. Hence, names for the Edo *bakufu* were, in general, respectful and courtly.[20] Following the *bakufu*'s practice, many intellectuals, such as Ogyū Sorai (*kogaku* scholar), Ishida Baigen (1685–1744, *shingaku* [mind learning] scholar), Kaiho Seiryō (1755–1817, economist), and Sakuma Shōzan (1811–64, *yōgaku* [Western learning] scholar) referred to the *bakufu* as *kōgi*. In addition to *kōgi*, there were three groups of names used frequently by Tokugawa intellectuals throughout the entire period.

The first of these stressed the geographical location of the Edo *bakufu*. Many people simply used "Edo" to represent the *bakufu*. They did so to avoid directly referring to the Tokugawa regime either out of respect or fear. This practice was widely followed by scholars such as Kaiho Seiryō and Sakuma Shōzan. Other terms in this group were *tōto* (東都, eastern capital), used by Dazai Shundai (*kogaku* scholar) and Takano Chōei (1804–50, *rangaku* scholar); *Edo omote* (江戸表, Edo Castle), used by Ōhashi Totsuan (1816–1862, Zhuxi scholar), Fujita Tōko Mito school scholar), Sakuma Shōzan, and Tokugawa Yoshinobu (1837–1913, fifteenth *shōgun*); *Kantō*, used by Emperor Kōmei (1831–66) and Nakai Chikuzan (1730–1804, eclectic school scholar), Katsu Kaishū (1823–99, *bakufu* naval officer), Iwakura Tomomi (1825–83, courtier), Saigo Takamori (1821–77, Satsuma samurai), Yamagata Daini (1725–67, loyalist thinker); *kōfu* (江府, Edo *bakufu*), used by Yokoi Shōnan (1809–69, political reformer) and Mōri Takachika (1819–71, *daimyō* of Chōshū); and *tōbu* (東武, East of Musashi), used by Asami Keisai (Zhuxi scholar), Muro Kyūsō (Zhuxi scholar), and Yoshida Shōin (Chōshū imperial loyalist).

The second group emphasized the legitimacy of the *bakufu* as the administrative center. The most popular name used by this group was *chōtei* (朝廷, central court government). The term first appeared in the *Lunyu* (Analects of Confucius), referring to the venue where the emperor discussed politics with his ministers. The *Kojiki* (Records of Ancient Matters) and *Nihon shoki* (Chronicles of Japan) used this term in the Chinese fashion. Like *kōgi* and *kubō*, *chōtei* referred to the Kyoto court government in the medieval period, and during the Tokugawa period referred almost exclusively to the Edo *bakufu*. Users included Yamaga Sokō (forerunner of *kogaku*), Muro Kyūsō, Ogyū Sorai, Yuasa Jōzan (1708–81, *kogaku* scholar), Matsura Seizan (1760–1841, military strategist), Dazai Shundai, Takano Chōei, and Sakuma Shōzan. A similar term was *kōhen* (公辺), a term created in Tokugawa Japan to refer to the public realm and used by Fujita Tōko, Tokugawa Nariaki (1800–60, *daimyō* of Mito), and Maeda Harunaga (1740–1810, *daimyō* of Kaga).

The third group underscored the military nature of the regime and carried negative tones. These terms were used mostly by courtiers and imperial loyalists. Iwakura Tomomi referred to the *bakufu* as *Kantō no haken* (関東の覇権, Hegemonic Regime in the Kanto Plain). Other names in this group included *buke* (武家, military house), used by Honda Toshiaki (1743–1820, economist) and Kaiho Seiryō, and *ryūei*, favored by Mōri Takachika and Emperor Kōmei. *Ryūei*, a term from the *Han shu* (Book of Han) that referred to a military camp, was used to represent the commander of the imperial guard and his residence in the medieval period. It became a name for the Edo administration during the Tokugawa period.

In the final decades of the Tokugawa period, following the decline of Edo authority and the rise of loyalism, people began to use *bakufu* to refer to the Edo administration. Most *shishi* (imperial loyalists), including Yoshida Shōin, Hashimoto Sanai (1834–59), Takasugi Shinsaku (1837–67), Ōhashi Totsuan, Inoue Kaoru (1835–1915, Chōshū loyalist), Itō Hirobumi (1841–1909, Chōshū loyalist), and Ōkubo Toshimichi (1830–78, Satsuma loyalist), used this term to show their disdain for the Edo government. Other users were Mito scholars, such as Fujita Yūkoku, Fujita Tōko, and Aizawa Seishisai; *daimyō*, such as Shimazu Hisamitsu (1817–87, *daimyō* of Satsuma), Matsudaira

Yoshinaga (1828–90, *daimyō* of Fukui), and Ikeda Yoshinori (1837–77, *daimyō* of Tottori); emperors, such as Emperor Kōkaku (1771–1840) and Emperor Kōmei; reform-minded scholars, such as Sakuma Shōzan and Yokoi Shōnan; and peasant leaders, such as Kanno Hachirō (1810–88). Interestingly enough, even the fourteenth Edo *shōgun* Tokugawa Iemochi (1846–66) referred to his government as *bakufu* to humble himself in his memorial of Emperor Kōmei.[21]

Relevant terms were also derived from *bakufu*. Bitō Nishū (1745–1813, Zhuxi scholar), Yoshida Shōin, and Emperor Kōmei sometimes called the Tokugawa government *sei-i-fu* (征夷府, the military government subduing the barbarians). *Sei-i* was the abbreviation for *Sej-i Taishōgun* (Commander-in-Chief of the Expeditionary Force against the Barbarians), the official title of the *shōgun*. The Edo *bakufu* liked to appoint Confucian scholars to serve as *sei-i-fu taimon* (advisors to the *bakufu*). Imperial loyalists used this term to remind the *bakufu* of the importance of *sonnō jōi* (revere the emperor and expel the barbarians). Emperor Kōmei told Tokugawa Iemochi: "You have tried your best to fulfill your duty in *sei-i-fu* and thus should be able to answer the hopes of the people."[22] Emperor Kōmei and Iwakura Tomomi called the *bakufu* officials *bakuri* (*bakufu* bureaucrats) or *bakushin* (*bakufu* ministers). Iwakura Tomomi referred to the decrees of the *bakufu* as *bakui* (幕意, *bakufu*'s opinions), and to the authority of the *bakufu* as *bakui* (幕威) as well. Ōkubo Toshimichi used *fubaku* (pro-*bakufu*) to describe the movement to support the *bakufu*. Matsudaira Yoshinaga condemned the *bakufu* as *hafu* (覇府, hegemonic government).[23]

Another term popular for the *bakufu* in the late Tokugawa period was *byōdō* (廟堂, central government). It appeared in the *Zhuangzi* (Master Zhuang) and *Chu Ci* (Poetry of the State of Chu), meaning the ancestral temple and the central government, respectively. This term referred to the ancestral temple before the Tokugawa and to the *bakufu* during the last decades of the Tokugawa period, and was used by Ōtsuki Bankei (1801–78, *yōgaku* scholar), Matsudaira Yoshinaga, Ōhashi Totsuan, Fujita Yūkoku, Aizawa Seishisai, Yokoi Shōnan, Sakuma Shōzan, Iwakura Tomomi, and Yoshida Shōin.

More significantly, Yoshida Shōin, Iwakura Tomomi, Ōhashi Totsuan, Mōri Yoshichika, Shimizu Hisamitsu, Ōkubo Toshimichi, Sakamoto Ryūma (1835–67, Tosa loyalist), and many late Tokugawa imperial loyalists restored the original meaning of *chōtei*, applying it to the imperial court in Kyoto. For instance, Ōhashi Totsuan remarked in his *Seiken kafuku hisaku* (Secret

Policy to Restore the Imperial Rule; 1861): "Nowadays, the *chōtei* [imperial court] looks weak, but it is indeed strong. The *bakufu* in the Kanto area looks strong on the surface, but it is not popular among the people and thus indeed it is reality weak."[24] An 1865 letter by Iwakura Tomomi asking the nation to overthrow the *bakufu*, fully indicates the changing perceptions of many terms. Iwakura wrote:

> The *byōdō* [*bakufu*] expends its efforts on trivial things and forgets the most important matters. As a result, many deplorable things have occurred. Nowadays, in the *chōtei* [imperial court], if the courtiers and officials cooperate, and if the sixty-some provinces unite, we can expel the barbarians. Recently, the entire nation has paid no attention to the moves of the *byōdō*, and only kept a close eye on the developments in the *chōtei*.[25]

Even the *bakufu* official Katsu Kaishū used *chōtei* to refer to the court in his diary during the last days of the Tokugawa regime.[26]

NAMES FOR THE TOKUGAWA *SHŌGUN*

How did Tokugawa intellectuals refer to the *shōgun*? With regard to a deceased individual *shōgun*, there were two major ways to refer to him—*byō* (廟) and *in* (院)—originally both used as posthumous titles for the retired or late emperor. For instance, after their deaths, the third *shōgun*, Tokugawa Iemitsu (1604–51), was honored as Taiyūin, and the fifth *shōgun*, Tokugawa Tsunayoshi (1646–1709), was remembered as as *Kenbyō* or *Jōkenin*. Retired generals were named *ōgosho* (大御所), a term originally applied to retired emperors.

As for the reigning *shōgun* in general, there were a number of ways to refer to him. Most of the terms were honorable and elegant. The names by which the *shōgun* were called can be divided into three categories:

The first category was most respectful, being adapted from imperial titles. There were five names in this category:

6. *Kubō*: This was the official and the commonest name for the Tokugawa *shōgun*, adopted by both officials and non-officials. A letter from the Edo *bakufu* to the Kyoto court usually used *Kubō-sama kara kinri he* (公方様より禁裏へ) as a salutation.[27] Interestingly, Tokugawa Tsunayoshi acquired the nickname

inukubō (dog *shōgun*) for his obsessive passion for dogs. Due to the fluctuation*s* of rice price during the reign of Tokugawa Yoshimune (1684–1751), he bore the nickname *komekubō* (rice *shōgun*).

7. *Taikun* (大君, literally, great ruler): This term was quoted from the *Yijing*. It reads: "The great ruler (*dajun*) delivered his charges, appointing some to be rulers of states, and others to undertake the headship of clans." *Taikun* refers to the emperor of the Zhou dynasty. In ancient Japan before the Asuka period (538–710), emperors were called *Ōkimi* (大君). In the early Tokugawa period, *taikun* was used in diplomatic correspondence with Korea, and later became a general name for the *shōgun* used by intellectuals like Kumazawa Banzan (*Yōmeigaku* scholar). Both Hakuseki Arai (*bakufu* statesman) and Yoshida Shōin disapproved of its use, but their reasons were opposite. Hakuseki suggested using *Nihonkokuō* (King of Japan) to underscore the legitimacy of the *shōgun*, while Yoshida stressed that only the emperor should be called *taikun*.[28]

8. *Kami* (上, literally, the ruler, also called *kami-sama* [上様] and *kunjō* [君上]): Originally referring to the emperor, this term became an honorific name for the *shōgun* in the Tokugawa period, used by Satō Naokata (Zhuxi scholar), Asami Keisai, Arai Hakuseki, Ogyū Sorai, Satō Nobuhiro (1769–1850, economist), and Sakuma Shōzan. However, regional retainers also called their lords *kami-sama*.

9. *Kinchū* (禁中, literally, the person inside the forbidden quarter, a term first used in the *Shiji* [Records of the Grand Historian]): A term taken from the imperial family, this term originally referred to the residence of the emperor or to the emperor. In 1615, the *bakufu* issued the *Kinchū narabini kuge shohatto* (Regulations for the Emperor and the Court), showing that *Kinchū* remained a term for the imperial family in the early Tokugawa period. Later, this term became a title for the *shōgun* and was used by a number of Tokugawa officials and intellectuals such as Kaibara Ekken (Zhuxi scholar) and Suharaya Mohei (publisher and editor). However, the usage of this term was not settled. Some Tokugawa intellectuals still used it to refer to the emperor throughout the entire period.[29]

10. *Denka* (殿下, literally, the one under the imperial palace): This was a term originally used to describe the emperor-designate, princes, or queens. In ancient Japan, it was applied to the queens (current queen, former queen, and empress dowager) and to *shōgun*, and regents (*sesshō* and *kampaku*) in the Muromachi period. In the Tokugawa period, it was a title for the *shōgun*. Korean official documents sent to the *shōgun* usually used *Nihonkoku taikun denka* (日本国大君殿下) in the beginning as a greeting. In an official letter to the *shōgun* in 1844, King Willem II of the Netherlands called the *shōgun Nihonkokutei denka* (日本国帝殿下).

The second category was a collection of honorific titles for the general. There were three names in this category:

1. *Go-tōke* 御當家 (literally, the people in charge): A term seldom used before the Tokugawa, it was applied by Asami Keisai, Arai Hakuseki, Ogyū Sorai, Hayashi Jussai (1768–1841), and Yoshida Shoin to refer to the *shōgun*. Hayashi Jussai used it to refer to Tokugawa Ieyasu.[30] Yoshida Shoin, in his *Jimu oboegaki* (Notes on Current Affairs), questioned the *shōgun* as follows: "How will you deal with the things about the imperial court and the *bakufu*? How can you save the dignity of *go-tōke*?"[31] Domain retainers also called their *daimyō go-tōke*.

2. *Taiju*: A Chinese term referring to a general, this word was never frequently used in China.[32] Terajima Ryōan (physician), in his *Wakan sansai zue* (Illustrative Encyclopedia of Japan and China; 1713) remarked that the *shōgun* was also called *kubō* or *taiju*. Ashikaga Takauji, the first Muromachi *shōgun*, was called *taiju*. Ashikaga Yoshimitsu also bore this title. Referring to *shōgun* since the Muromachi period, *taiju* was adopted by Kumazawa Banzan, Tsuchimikado Yasunaga (1757–1805, head of *onmyōdō* [Bureau of *Yin-yang*]), Mōri Takachika, Shimizu Hisamitsu, Matsudaira Yoshinaga, Ikeda Yoshinori, Hashimoto Sanai, Emperor Kōmei, and Ōkubo Toshimichi. The term *taijukō* (大樹公) also became particularly popular in the late Tokugawa period. The family temple of the Matsudaira (Tokugawa) in Mikawa was the Taiju

Temple (established in 1535) where the tablets of Edo *shogun* were enshrined. At the same time, domain retainers also called their lords *taiju*.

3. *Bakka*: A Chinese term first used in the *Zhanguo ce* (Strategies of the Warring States) to refer to the military camp, it had been used in Japan since the Muromachi period to represent the *konoefu taishō* (general of the imperial guard unit) and *shogun*. For instance, *u-konoe taishō* (general of the imperial guard unit of the right) was *u-bakka* and *shogun* was *bakka shogun* (幕下將軍). Muro Kyūsō was of those who used this term in the Tokugawa period.

The third category consisted of four informal or impolite ways to refer to the *shogun*.

1. *Shōgun*: This was an abbreviation for *Sei-i Taishōgun*. Originally a title bestowed upon the general who led campaigns against the Ainu in the Nara and Heian periods, from the medieval period onward it became the title for the head of the military class. Referring to the *shogun* directly as *shogun*, depending on the context, could be considered rude. This term was used throughout the Tokugawa period and was particularly popular in its last decades. The late Mito school popularized its usage. Muro Kyūsō, Matsudaira Sadanobu (1758–1829, statesman), Rai Sanyō, Emperor Kōmei, Mōri Takachika, Matsudaira Yoshinaga, Hashimoto Sanai, Yoshida Shōin, and Sakuma Shōzan also referred to the *shogun* in this way.

2. *Tokugawa-shi* (德川氏, Tokugawa) or *Tokugawa-ke* (德川家, Tokugawa house): These terms were used by imperial loyalists like Yoshida Shōin, Yokoi Shōnan, Ōhashi Totsuan, and Ōkubo Toshimichi. Rai Sanyō and Katsu Kashū also used this term.

3. *Kenjin* (権臣, authoritarian official): Ogasawara Keisai (1828–63, loyalist) used this term to condemn the *shogun*. He wrote: "I have severely criticized the shortcomings of the *bakufu* and condemned the evils of the *kenjin* [*shogun*]. Sometimes my assertions might be too radical, but if I am prosecuted for doing this, I am willing to take responsibility."[33]

RECTIFICATION OF NAMES

Investigating the aforementioned political terms in Japan from philological and historical perspectives, it can be understood that the names for the *bakufu* and *shōgun* were not standardized in the Tokugawa period. Depending on the context, even a single individual might refer to them in a number of ways. For example, Sakuma Shōzan used *kōgi* and *kami* in his letters to the *bakufu*, but *bakufu* and *shōgun* in his private writings. In ancient and medieval Japan, most of these titles (such as *kōgi, kubō, chōtei, kōtei, in, byō, taikun, denka, kami, kinri,* and *kinchū*) referred to the court. The transformation of their uses in the Tokugawa period indicates that the Edo *bakufu* attempted to establish its own legitimacy and authority at the expense of the imperial court. This misuse of names went against the Confucian principle of *seimei* (rectification of names), which emphasized that *mei* (names) and *bun* (functions) must be consistent. For instance, an emperor should behave like an emperor and an official should behave like an official.[34]

Most early and mid-Tokugawa intellectuals either condemned, ignored, downplayed, or distorted the meaning of *seimei*, just the way they did for the ideas of *sonnō* (reverence for the emperor) and *ekisei kakumei* (the change of imperial house following a dynastic revolution), which were considered incompatible with Tokugawa ideology. The principle of *seimei* was sometimes reinterpreted and used by early Tokugawa officials and scholars (such as Arai Hakuseki and Dazai Shundai) to legitimize the *bakufu*. For instance, Dazai Shundai, an ardent supporter of the *bakufu*, saw the Kyoto court as a decoration. In his *Keizaikoku* (Discourse on Politics; 1729), he argued that the *shōgun* was indeed the legitimate ruler of Tokugawa Japan, justifying *bakufu's* behavior in using the title *Nihonkokuō* (King of Japan):

> Nowadays, the *shōgun* is the *Nihonkokuō* in both domestic and foreign affairs. During the Muromachi period, the Ming Yongle Emperor endowed Ashikaga Yoshimitsu with the title of the King of Japan in his credentials. In our [Tokugawa] period, Tōshōgū [Tokugawa Ieyasu], out of respect for Emperor Yamashiro, did not use the title of king. Although Tōshōgū perfected the virtue of modesty, inappropriate names for the nation were used in books. All of the titles [for the *shōgun*] are not good. Some people use *taikun*. I think this is

a misuse of the imperial title. *Taikun* only means the emperor, and it should not be an honorific title for the *shōgun*. Some people refer to the *shōgun* as *taiju*, which is another name for a general. *Kubō* has been used since the Muromachi period, but it is a term without substance. Having examined the rites and institutions of Japan and China, I am convinced that King [of Japan] is the only appropriate title for the *shōgun*. . . . Confucius said: "If the name and the thing do not match, we cannot express ourselves in language smoothly." I think this is particularly true in our times. Tokugawa Ienobu [the sixth *shōgun*] used *Nihonkokuō* in his correspondence with the King of Korea. This was a wise and justifiable decision. This was not a misuse of imperial titles.[35]

In the late Tokugawa period, however, the Confucian notion of *seimei* became a powerful political notion. It was developed into the concept of *taigi meibun* (the absolute truth of the unity of names and functions) by scholars of the Mito school and *shishi*, who discussed *seimei* within the political context of Tokugawa Japan—the return of political authority from the *bakufu* to the emperor. For instance, Yamagata Daini used *seimei* to advocate the restoration of power from the *shōgun* to the emperor.[36] In his *Ryūshi shinron* (Master Ryū's New Thesis; 1759), he wrote:

Confucius deplored the condition in Wei, saying: "Name and actuality must conform. If not, officials will speak inaccurately, their work will go undone, state ritual and music will not flourish, punishments will not fit crimes, and commoners will be unsure of what they may and may not do." What would he say about us? Imperial rule lasted over two thousand years. . . . Restored to power by one or two loyal subjects, he [Emperor Godaigo] ruled only a small provincial state, but still he maintained his ancestral tombs. The imperial line remains eternal; it has survived over four hundred years to the present. Though power has fallen to underlings, the Way remains intact above and the canons of former sage-emperors are in the imperial law codes for all to see. If someone but fostered love for the people, he could make name and actuality conform, make ritual and music flourish, and end the need for punishments. How sad that no such man exists in the realm.[37]

Two Confucian scholars from an eclectic background, Nakai Chikuzan and Yamagata Taika (1781–1866) also underscored the importance of *seimei*. Both of them opposed the application of *in* and *byō*, the court titles used for former emperors, to refer to former *shōgun*.

daimyo

Seimei was a key concept in the Mito school and in late Tokugawa political ideology. Fujita Yūkoku wrote the *Seimeiron* (Discourse on the Rectification of Names; 1791) to criticize the abuse of power by the Fujiwara, the Kamakura *bakufu*, and the Muromachi *bakufu* in the past and remind the Tokugawa *bakufu* that it must fulfill its duty as the retainer of the emperor, lest it lose its prestige and throw the nation into disorder. He wrote:

> If the *bakufu* respects the court, then the lords of the domains will respect the *bakufu*. If the lords of the domains respect the *bakufu*, ministers, officials, and noblemen will respect the lords of the domains. As a result, the upper and the lower will support each other and all domains will be in harmony. Hence, names and functions must be strictly consistent.... Our country already has a real emperor, and thus the *bakufu* should not claim to be the king. Without the title of the king, it can manage the nation in a kingly way. In the capacity of a duke and not king, [Zhou] Wen Wan was ultimately virtuous. A king using the hegemonic way is not as good as a hegemon using the kingly way.[38]

Fujita Tōko, the son of Fujita Yūkaku, further developed the idea of *seimei* in his *Kōdōkankiju tsugi* (A Brief Explanation of *Kōdōkanki*; 1847). He criticized people for using court titles to refer to the *bakufu*: "Therefore, the innocent people refer to the *bakufu* as the *chōtei*, and some even as the *ō*."[39] He believed that these two terms were only applicable to the Kyoto court and the emperor, respectively.

BAKUFU AND *SHŌGUN* AS BUILDING BLOCKS

From the appropriation of Chinese political terminology to the rise of *seimei*, the naming of the *bakufu* and *shōgun* demonstrates the localization of Confucian values and the tug-of-war between the Edo *bakufu* and Kyoto court for legitimation.

Political terms used by the Tokugawa Japanese can be classified into the following four groups: first, imported Chinese terms that retained their original meanings with little change, such as *tenshi* (son of heaven) and *shujō* (supreme lord); second, Chinese terms, such as *bakufu, shōgun, chōtei, taikun, bakka, ryūei, denka,* and *kinchū,* that had their meanings and usages changed; third, terms such as *kōtei* and *byōdō* created by reorganizing existing Chinese terms; and, fourth, terms coined by the Japanese, such as *kinri, kubō, kōhen, kōgi, kami-sama,* and *gosho.* The first three groups were directly or indirectly related to China. In particular, the number of terms in the second group was large, showing a high level of localization in the uses of Chinese political terminology.

The meanings of *bakufu* and *shōgun* changed throughout the history of Japan. In the first half of the Tokugawa period, Chinese political terms were modified and appropriated to legitimize the Edo administration. Titles for the Kyoto court and emperor went to the *bakufu* and *shōgun.* In the late Tokugawa period, the Confucian concept of *seimei,* or rectification of names, became a powerful political discourse, playing an important role in the ideology of the Meiji Restoration. The *Sei-i Taishōgun* was asked by the emperor, the *daimyō,* and the people to fulfill his duty of *sonnō jōi.* When the *shōgun* failed to honor his duty, late Tokugawa Japanese asked for the restoration of political power from the *bakufu* to the court. In this changing political climate, more and more people no longer felt the need to use honorific titles, using instead *bakufu, shōgun,* and other terms to refer to the Edo administration. Many titles that the *bakufu* had acquired from the court were then restored to their original meanings and usage, serving as the writing on the wall for the restoration to come.

9

REDEFINING LEGITIMACY

Both the Chinese and the Japanese have a tradition of compiling
and using history. From the *Kojiki* and *Nihon shoki* to the *Dai Nihonshi*,
Japanese historical writings absorbed Chinese political philosophy and terminology in various degrees. Chinese historical writings, particularly the
format of *Shiji* (Records of the Grand Historian) by Sima Qian, and the historical critique of the *Chunqiu* (Spring and Autumn Annals), *Zizhi tongjian*
(Comprehensive Mirror for Aid in Government; 1084) by Sima Guang (1019–
86), and *Tongjian gangmu* (Summary of the *Comprehensive Mirror*; 1172) by
Zhu Xi, provided important references for Japanese historians.

Political legitimacy (*zhengtong* in Chinese, *seitō* in Japanese) is a key concept
in East Asian historiography. Legitimizing the current regime was a hidden
political agenda of many Chinese and Japanese historical writings in which the
discussion of political legitimacy was passionately engaged. At a glance, the discourse on political legitimacy looks similar in Chinese and Japanese historical
writings, as both laid emphasis on blood lineage and morality in the fashion of
the *Chunqiu* and the Zhu Xi School. A virtuous ruler descending from the royal
bloodline would be in a good position to contest legitimacy. A closer investigation reveals that Japanese historians modified Chinese concepts and added
indigenous elements in writing their own histories.[1] In the Tokugawa period,
Japanese historians redefined and indigenized Chinese concepts of legitimacy
to rationalize political realities in Tokugawa Japan, such as the *bakuhan* system
(the Tokugawa political structure that defined the relationship between the shogunate and the domains), the authority of the Edo *bakufu*, the coexistence of
two central governments, and the political implications of Shinto.

The writing of history in Japan reached its peak in the Tokugawa period.
The *bakufu* cultivated Tokugawa Ieyasu's cult through the compilation of

official histories and establishment of the *Tōshōgū*, a shrine dedicated to Ieyasu.[2] The first Edo *shōgun*, Tokugawa Ieyasu was presented as a sage ruler and a deity. In the seventeenth century, Japanese historians were preoccupied with the idea of legitimizing the newly founded regime.[3] The three representative Tokugawa historical writings—the *Honchō tsugan* (Comprehensive Mirror of Japan; 1670), written by Hayashi Razan and his son Gahō; the *Dai Nihonshi*, compiled by Tokugawa Mitsukuni; and the *Tokushi yoron* (A Reading of History; 1712), written by Arai Hakuseki—all agreed that Emperor Go-Daigo (1288–1339) split the nation in two and thus lost legitimacy to rule, and that Tokugawa Ieyasu received the *tenmei* (heaven's mandate) to rule by virtue of his high moral standard and military abilities. In these writings, Japanese historians developed their own definition of political legitimacy. Using major Tokugawa historical writings as the main references and highlighting the legitimacy of the Southern and Northern Courts and the legitimacy of the Edo *bakufu*, this chapter examines the making of Japanized concepts of legitimacy in Tokugawa historiography. It sheds light on how Tokugawa historians creatively modified and appropriated Chinese historical ideas and terms to accommodate Japanese tradition and the Tokugawa political system.

THE LIMITATION OF CHINESE CONCEPTS OF LEGITIMACY

Political legitimacy in Chinese historiography was a complicated concept intricately intertwined with morality, unification, *huayi zhi bian* (the distinction between the Han and barbarians), blood lineage, transmission of the *daotung* (sagely way), the *wuyun* (five circulatory phases), and heaven's mandate.[4] Unlike their Chinese counterparts, Japanese historical writings did not use the distinction between the Han and barbarians, the five circulatory phases, or the transmission of the sagely way. In order to legitimize the Tokugawa system, Japanese historians created their own theories of legitimacy (such as the imperial regalia theory) and modified Chinese concepts (such as heaven's mandate).

The distinction between the Han and barbarians was applied to discuss the legitimacy of regimes founded by non-Han peoples. When there was a coexistence of a Han regime and non-Han regime in China, the former had a better chance of being regarded as legitimate. Non-Han regimes, unless they could unify the nation, such as the Mongol Yuan Dynasty and the

Manchu Qing Dynasty, were seldom considered legitimate.[5] This doctrine
was not applicable to premodern Japan, which had never been conquered
by foreign nations. The Koreans, Chinese, Ryūkyūans, and the Ainu people
were largely assimilated into the Yamato race-dominated Japan. A sense of
racial superiority did exist in Tokugawa historical writings. For instance, the
Dai Nihonshi put China, Korea, Ezo, the Bohai Kingdom, and Southeast
Asia under the category of *shohan retsuden* (Biographies of Alien Nations).
This was only a nationalist expression and was not used to discuss legitimacy
in Japanese history.

The theory of five circulatory phases had been influential in the discussion
of political legitimacy in China from the Qin-Han era through the Tang-Song,
using the doctrines of *wude zhongshi* (the rotation of the five virtues) and *wu-
xing xiangsheng xiangke* (mutual creation and destruction of the five agents) to
argue that dynastic change was historically inevitable.[6] Introduced to Japan
in ancient times, this theory was mainly applied to astronomy, geography,
medicine, the military, and divination. In politics, it only exerted influence
on matters of secondary importance, such as revising the calendar according
to the *jiazi* (sixty-year cycle), and was not applied to political legitimacy.[7]
Although many Tokugawa historical writings contained the idea of historical
trends or inevitability, they did not adopt the theory of five circulatory phases.

The transmission of the sagely way was an important idea in neo-
Confucianism. According to this theory, when China was not unified, the
regime that transmitted Confucian orthodoxy was legitimate. Hence, many
scholars of the Zhu Xi School claimed legitimacy for Shu and Southern Song
on the basis of morality. Some Tokugawa Confucian scholars suggested that
the transmission of the sagely way shifted from China to Japan.[8] Yamaga
Sokō, in his *Chūchō jijitsu* (The True Facts Concerning the Central Dynasty;
1669), referred to China as *Shina*, *gaichō* (foreign dynasty), and *ichō* (alien
dynasty). He maintained that China lost the transmission of the sagely way
to Japan due to dynastic change and foreign invasion, and thus only Japan,
the land of absolute loyalty, was entitled to use *Chūchō* (Central Dynasty),
Chūshū" (Central Province), and "*Chūka*" (Central Civilization). Mito scholars
Tokugawa Mitsukuni, Kuriyama Senbō (1671–1706) and Aizawa Seishisai
expressed similar views. Sokō, Mitsukuni, Senbō, and Seishisai discussed the
transmission of the sagely way from a cross-cultural perspective; none of them
applied it to political legitimacy in Japanese history.

Blood lineage was a useful means to claim legitimacy in China. Insurrectionists and new emperors liked to claim that they carried noble blood and to emphasize their Han identity (in the case that the overthrown regime was non-Han). In Japan, blood lineage was applied to legitimize the authority to govern, not sovereignty itself. De facto rulers of Japan, including courtiers, imperial relatives, and warriors, gained prestige and authority from their alleged noble origins. Like their Chinese counterparts, for the sake of political justification, the Japanese forged a large number of family histories and historical sources. The early Tokugawa period was the heyday of forgery, when the *bakufu* and domains strove to establish their legitimacy through problematic genealogies.[9] Matsudaira (later renamed Tokugawa), a military clan of Mikawa Province in the Kantō region, claimed descent from the Seiwa Genji, one of the most powerful branches of the Minamoto clan. Seiwa Genji was the most prestigious family among the warriors. The founder of the three military regimes—Minamoto no Yoritomo (1147–99), Ashikaga Takauji (1305–58), and Tokugawa Ieyasu—all claimed descent from this lineage. There was even a saying that "non-Seiwa Genji cannot be appointed *shōgun*." There were exceptions in Japanese history, but the influence of Seiwa Genji in the medieval and early modern periods was undoubtedly strong. Tokugawa Ieyasu had already called himself "Minamoto Ason" prior to the founding of the Edo *bakufu*. Throughout the Tokugawa period, disputable blood ties between the Tokugawa and the Seiwa Genji became widely accepted. For instance, Rai Sanyō (1781–1832), in his *Nihon gaishi* (An Unofficial Japanese History; 1829), introduced the origins of the Tokugawa house as follows: "My Tokugawa clan was descended from Nitta Yoshishige. Yoshishige was the eighth-generation descendant of Emperor Seiwa. Tsunemoto, the grandson of Emperor Seiwa, was granted the surname Minamoto and downgraded to a military house."[10]

JAPANESE INTERPRETATION OF HEAVEN'S MANDATE

Heaven's mandate was a key concept in Chinese historical writings. Based on Confucian classics such as the *Shujing* (Book of Documents), *Shijing* (Book of Poetry), *Mengzi* (Sayings of Mencius), and *Yijing* (Book of Changes), this concept constituted a political philosophy that fused morality, heaven's will, people-oriented politics, and revolution. In the Chinese political tradition, the throne held sovereignty and carried out governance. When the incumbent emperor was morally compromised, his heaven's mandate would be taken away and given to another person to found a new dynasty by means of revolution. The doctrine of heaven's mandate was a powerful ideology to justify dynastic change and legitimize new regimes.

Japanese historical writings used the concept of heaven's mandate in a different manner. In Japanese history, the separation of sovereignty and governance was the norm. The imperial family reigned in unbroken succession, but did not usually rule. Heaven's mandate in Japanese historical writings, except in a few cases, referred to the right to govern.[11] Tokugawa scholars, perhaps with a few exceptions like Arai Hakuseki and Daizai Shundai, discussed the political legitimacy of the Edo *bakufu* within the traditional political framework.[12]

The earlier form of the heaven's mandate theory in Japan was *tendō* (heaven's way).[13] Historical writings of the medieval and *Sengoku* (Warring States) periods, such as the *Taiheiki* (Record of the Great Peace), *Genpei sei-suiki* (An Account of the Genpei Wars), *Heike monogatari* (Tale of Heike), and *Shinchō kōki* (Chronicle of Lord Nobunaga), contained the idea of heaven's way, showing that warrior families used heaven's way to justify their ever-increasing powers. According to the heaven's way doctrine, heaven's way was higher than secular powers, including the imperial house. Warrior leaders claimed that their powers came from heaven and not the imperial house. Hence, the heaven's way doctrine undermined the authority of the imperial house.[14] In the *Sengoku* period, warrior leaders began to use both heaven's way and heaven's mandate in their writings, claiming that they had received heaven's mandate to carry out heaven's way.

In the Tokugawa period, the theory of heaven's mandate was frequently used in historical writings to legitimize the *bakufu* as the de facto central government. Both official and unofficial histories agreed that Tokugawa Ieyasu received heaven's mandate to govern the nation. The *Honchō tsugan*, *Tokushi yoron*, and *Dai Nihonshi* all pointed out that Emperor Go-Daigo lost heaven's mandate to the warrior house due to his ethical failures. For instance, although the *Dai Nihonshi* appreciated Emperor Go-Daigo's efforts in the Kenmu Restoration (1333–36), it blamed him for making politics chaotic and for losing heaven's mandate. It reads: "[Ashikaga] Takauji was full of disloyal acts, but they were caused by the collapse of imperial rule."[15] The three representative Tokugawa historical writings, based on Ieyasu's morality, ability, bloodline, and achievement of unification, confirmed that he had received heaven's mandate. The Hayashi family compared the Battle of Sekigahara to "the righteous uprisings of King Tang of Shang and King Wu of Zhou." Arai Hakuseki, in his *Hankanpu* (Genealogies of *Daimyō*; 1702), used *tenmei ikkai* (a change in heaven's mandate) to refer to Ieyasu's victory at the Battle of Sekigahara. In the *Tokushi yoron*, Hakuseki divided Japanese history into fourteen epochs, representing the frequent changes in heaven's mandate. Ironically, the same theory of heaven's mandate took an opposite turn in the *bakumatsu* period, and was used by imperial loyalists (*shishi*) to express anti-*bakufu* views. For instance, Yoshida Shōin believed that the *bakufu* had lost heaven's mandate for failing to carry out the policy of *sonnō jōi* (revere the emperor and repel the barbarians). He said:

> King Tang and King Wu received the mandate of heaven to fight against the evils. Our nation is different. The descendants of the Sun Goddess in our heavenly dynasty shine on the universe. If the *bakufu* does not follow the order of the heavenly dynasty and does not carry out his duty to repel the barbarians, this is called "using the state of Yan to fight against the state of Yan."[16]

THE SOUTHERN AND NORTHERN COURTS CONTROVERSY

Japanese historiography reached its apex in the Tokugawa period, when the *bakufu*, domains, and independent scholars were enthusiastic about historical writings and critiques. There were two major issues concerning legitimacy in Tokugawa historical writings: the Southern and Northern courts controversy and the legitimacy of the Edo *bakufu*, addressing questions of sovereignty and governance, respectively.

The era of *Nanbokuchō* (Southern and Northern Courts; 1336–92) was the only period in Japanese history that had two rivaling dynasties; each had its own imperial house, central government, army, land, and people. It was not easy for the *bakufu* to handle this issue. From the perspective of the regime's unification and the current imperial bloodline, the Northern Court should have been legitimate. Judging from morality and blood ties with the Tokugawa house, it was the Southern Court that should have been legitimate. The *bakufu* declared the Northern Court the legitimate regime, and official writings, ceremonies, and rituals basically followed this position. Nevertheless, a certain level of ambiguity remained. The *bakufu* never imposed this official stance on the Tokugawa intellectual world. Tokugawa historians, particularly those from outside the *bakufu* circle, were thus free to express their views. There was no consensus whatsoever among historians and scholars on this issue.

As an official history, the *Honchō tsugan* had to follow the *bakufu*'s position to claim legitimacy for the Northern Court out of respect for the current imperial house. In the Tokugawa period, the throne went to the bloodline of the Northern Court. Recognizing the Northern Court meant maintaining the status quo and avoiding unnecessary controversy or a sovereignty crisis. The Hayashi family presented their arguments in two aspects: First, the reigning emperor came from the bloodline of the Northern Court, and thus the Northern Court was the direct line of decent. The Southern Court was only a collateral branch of the imperial family, and its bloodline had not been enthroned since 1458. Second, the Northern Court was geographically located in Kyoto, the imperial capital for more than a thousand years, whereas the Southern Court built its capital in Yoshino, a remote countryside area in Nara. The *Honchō tsugan* reads:

> In the first year of Engen, Emperor Go-Daigo moved the capital to Yoshino, marking the beginning of the imperial line of the Southern Dynasty. Emperor Go-Daigo did not formally pass on the throne. Emperor Kōmyō was appointed by Takauiji. In the reign of Emperor Go-Daigo, he represented the legitimate succession of the imperial line. However, from Emperor Go-Murakami in Yoshino, we cannot ignore the distinction between the capital and countryside. Besides, the imperial line of the Northern Court has survived into the present day. These are the reasons why we take this position.[17]

This kind of geopolitical legitimacy can also be found in Chinese historiography. In discussing legitimacy, whether the dynasty was located in the Central Provinces of the North was sometimes taken into consideration.[18] Although the *Honchō tsugan* adopted the official position, it was very prudent and subtle when narrating this period. In the preface to the *Honchō tsugan*, Hayashi Gahō revealed his principle as follows:

> From the Ryakuō to the Meitoku [reign periods], both the Southern Court and the Northern Court had emperors. It was a period of great

change in my country. We should not make judgments on legitimacy lightly, and thus I have only added subtle comments on individual chapters once in a while.[19]

Historical compilations by domains and independent scholars had more freedom and did not have to be in accord with the official position. Influenced by neo-Confucian ethics, just as the *Tongjian gangmu* had supported the legitimacy of the state of Shu, the *Dai Nihonshi* claimed legitimacy for the Southern Court on moral grounds. It saw the Northern Court as merely a puppet regime controlled by Ashikaga Takauji. More interestingly, the *Dai Nihonshi* also argued its case on religious grounds, using the three imperial regalia (sword, jewel, and mirror) as evidence. The regalia holder was considered the legitimate ruler. The regalia theory had a very strong impact on the Mito school. Asaka Tanpaku (1656–1738), a chief historian of the *Dai Nihonshi* project and a disciple of the late Ming refugee scholar Zhu Shunshui (1600–82), explained: "The place that holds the regalia can use them to unite the people.... The importance of the regalia rests in their ability to unite the people. If the people support them, the regalia are important. If the people do not support them, the regalia are unimportant. As heaven and man are united, the Way and the regalia are not two different things."[20] Tanpaku's idea of the moralistic aspect of the regalia might have been inspired by Kitabatake Chikafusa's *Jinnō shōtōki* (Chronicles of the Authentic Lineages of the Divine Emperors; 1339) and Hayashi Razan's *Jimmu tennō ron* (On Emperor Jimmu).[21] Chikafusa associated the three imperial regalia with determination, graciousness, and sincerity, whereas Razan associated them with the three Confucian virtues (wisdom, benevolence, and courage).[22] How could one be sure that the regalia would not fall into the wrong hands? Tanpaku replied that the regalia had spiritual power, and thus they would only go to the righteous side. He rated Emperor Go-Daigo highly:

> He was better than other emperors of the medieval era. He firmly believed in the restoration of power against all odds. When he was dying, he held the sword with no fear. In times of difficulty, he kept the regalia, laying the foundation for more than fifty years. Having gained legitimacy, his regime was as bright as the Sun and the Moon. How great he was![23]

Since the regalia went to the Southern Court and were kept there until 1392, Tanpaku claimed legitimacy for the Southern Court as follows:

> Imperial lines descended from Emperor Go-Saga have the same impor-
> tance, and thus holding the regalia was crucial. Emperor Kōgon and
> Emperor Kōmyō succeeded to the throne with the help of traitors.
> Although [the Northern Court] had the regalia, what it owned was
> fake. Hence, we cannot say that they acquired the regalia.[24]

Kuriyama Senpō, another historian on the *Dai Nihonshi* project and a student of the Kimon school, in his *Hōken taiki* (Records of the Hōgen and Kenkyū Eras; 1689), expressed similar views to those of Tanpaku. Senpō believed in the absolute authority of the regalia, and his historical narrative focused on the possession and transmission of the regalia. For example, in his discussion of the fight between former emperor Sutoku (1119–64) and Emperor Konoe (1139–55), he explained the victory of the latter in terms of possession of the regalia as follows:

> The regalia give protection to and authority over everything in the
> world. We do not allow illegitimate rulers to use fake regalia to confuse
> the true transmission of the imperial line. Although the world becomes
> uncivilized and the influence of the imperial court declines, the
> authority of the imperial seal remains intact, and he who owns the
> three imperial regalia is the true ruler of my nation.[25]

Tokugawa Harutoshi (1773–1816), the seventh *daimyō* of the Mito domain, saw the regalia as the criteria for legitimacy in his *Shin Dai Nihonshi hyō* (Memorial on the *Dai Nihonshi*):

> The regalia granted to the emperors represent the divine instructions.
> The regime will last forever. The regalia can unify the nation and
> undermine any ambition to overthrow the throne.... The conflict
> between the East and West, the civil war between the North and South,
> and the legitimacy of the imperial line can all be settled by the regalia.[26]

In addition to the Mito school, the Kimon school under the tutelage of Yamazaki Ansai also supported the regalia theory. Ansai himself used the regalia to legitimize the Southern Court in his *Yamato kagami* (Mirror of Japan), criticizing the Hayashi family for recognizing the Northern Court.[27]

His disciples basically followed Ansai's position. For instance, Atobe Yoshiaki (1656–1729) cited the *Nihon shoki* to support the regalia theory in the *Nanzan hennenroku* (The Annals of the Southern Court; 1713):

> In a scroll on Emperor Jimmu of the Age of the Gods in the *Nihon shoki*, Amaterasu-Ōmikami (the Sun Goddess) gave the Yasakani-no-magatama (eight-*shaku* curved jewel), Yata-no-kagami (eight-span mirror), and Kusanagi-no-tsurugi (grass-cutting sword) to the grandson Ninigi-no-Mikoto, abdicating the throne in favor of Ninigi-no-Mikoto, not Nigihayahi-no-Mikoto. The ten auspicious treasures indicate the legitimacy.[28]

Like Ansai, he also criticized the historiography of the Hayashi family and supported the stance of the Mito school on the legitimacy of the Southern Court.

The regalia theory had large followings in different schools of thought and culture. As a matter of fact, Hayashi Gahō, the chief compiler of the *Honchō tsugan*, accepted the theory of the regalia and regarded the Southern Court as the legitimate dynasty in his own private capacity. In the *Honchō keikohen* (Chapter on the Investigation of Ancient Matters of Japan; 1660), he condemned Ashikaga Takauji for kidnapping the emperor and using fake regalia to build an illegitimate regime as follows:

> The prince succeeded to the throne with the three regalia. However, he did not have the true ones. The weak one became the illegitimate emperor. Who can understand the hidden views in history? This is the standard to evaluate my nation. Even now, no one really understands legitimacy.[29]

However, due to his official assignment, he could not express his personal views in the *Honchō tsugan*. He explained: "If I claim legitimacy for the Southern Court, then the ancestors of the current emperor would become traitors. I am concerned about the feelings of the imperial family."[30] Even Arai Hakuseki admitted the value of the regalia as symbols of legitimacy, although he did not believe that they had any magical power.

Rai Sanyō supported the Southern Court in his *Nihon gaishi*, based on neo-Confucian ethics. Between the Southern Court and the Northern Court, he stressed that the one that represented righteousness, followed the ancestors, and won the heart of the people was legitimate. He claimed that if the Northern

Court was accepted as the legitimate regime, then Nitta Yoshisada (1301–38) and Kusunoki Masahide (1294–1336) would become traitors. This went against his moral principles. Regarding the three regalia, he did not deny their importance, but maintained that morality was the decisive factor in legitimation. To him, with or without the regalia, the Southern Court was the legitimate regime. He explained in the *Nihon seiki* (Political Records of Japan; 1832):

> The wonder of the regalia can be seen from the fact that they were not in the North, but the South. The imperial ancestors made this happen. This was the heavenly way. The North used unreasonable means to gain the upper hand. It had the sword of [Ashikaga] Takauji and the seal of [Nijō] Yoshimoto. It should have been fine with the sword and seal. Why did it use the sword of the thief and the seal of the unfaithful minister? This self-proclaimed central court was not supported by the faithful ministers and righteous samurai. They did not support the North even though it held the sword and seal. They support the South that did not have the sword and seal.... Hence, I would suggest that the person who can win the heart of the people can claim legitimacy, and then the regalia will go to his side. It is wrong to think that legitimacy will go with the regalia.[31]

Independent historians did not reach a consensus regarding the legitimacy of the Southern Court or the Northern Court. Some, such as the Confucian scholar Ugai Sekisai (1615–64) and the Kyoto courtier-scholar Yanagi Toshimitsu (1746–1800), regarded the Northern Court as legitimate; whereas others, such as Yamazaki Ansai and the *kokugaku* (national learning) scholar Hirata Atsutane, preferred the Southern Court. There were people who considered both legitimate, such as the Confucian scholar Narushima Motonao (1778–1862) and the *kokugaku* scholar Shikamochi Masazumi (1791–1858), or thought of both as illegitimate like Arai Hakuseki.[32] In general, the pro–Northern Court voice was stronger in the early Tokugawa period, whereas support for the Southern Court gained momentum in the late Tokugawa period, culminating in the rise of loyalism and the fall of the *bakufu*. Until the *bakumatsu* period, the majority of Tokugawa historians, regardless of their stance on *nanbokuchō*, had no intention of challenging either the imperial house's right to reign or the *bakufu*'s right to govern. The existence of different views indicates that there was plenty of space for opinions in Tokugawa thought.

THE LEGITIMACY OF THE EDO *BAKUFU*

The legitimacy of the Edo *bakufu* was upheld by Tokugawa historical writings until the *bakumatsu* era when individuals challenged the *bakufu* from historical and rhetorical perspectives.[33] In the decades after the establishment of the Edo *bakufu* in 1603, there was a movement to glorify Tokugawa Ieyasu and his ancestors. The *Mikawa monogatari* (Tale of Mikawa; 1622) by Ōkubo Tadataka (1560–1639), *Mikawa ki* (Record of Mikawa; 1622) by Hori Kyōan (1585–1643), and *Tōshōgū gonenpu* (Annals of Tokugawa Ieyasu; 1631) by Tokugawa Yoshinao (1600–1650) were products of this movement.

The *Honchō tsugan* was the *bakufu*'s first official history project. Commissioned by the third *shōgun* Tokugawa Iemistu in 1644, Hayashi Razan compiled the annals of Japanese history from Emperor Jimmu to Emperor Go-Yōzei (1572–1617) in the fashion of Sima Guang's *Zizhi tongjian* and Zhu Xi's *Tongjian gangmu*. After Razan's demise in 1657, his son Hayashi Gahō succeeded to his father's project and finished it in 1670. Highlighting Ieyasu's role in unifying the nation, the *Honchō tsugan* referred to Ieyasu as *jinkun* (divine ruler) or *dai-jinkun* (great divine ruler). The end of the *Honchō tsugan* puts Ieyasu at the pinnacle of Japanese political development, praising him for laying the foundations for the first four Edo *shōgun* and achieving an unprecedented feat in Japanese history. It reads:

> Over the first four generations, from the great victory at the Battle of Sekigahara in the fifth year of Keichō to the tenth year of Kanbun, more than seventy years have passed and the nation is unified. He could look down upon the right great general of the Kamakura [i.e., Minamoto Yoritomo], surpassing Rokuon [i.e., Ashikaga Yoshimitsu]. His victory brought stability for two generations. Alas! With his military might and moral power, he protected the imperial court and pacified the nation and the sea. His regime will last for thousands of generations, like heaven and earth.[34]

The Hayashi family was ambivalent about the nature of the legitimacy of the Edo *bakufu*. While recognizing the coexistence of the Kyoto court and the Edo *bakufu*, they implicitly suggested that the *bakufu* was the legitimate regime in terms of both sovereignty and governance.[35]

The *Tokushi yoron* was a historical analysis of Japanese history from the past to the founding of the Edo *bakufu*. Its conceptualization of Japanese history as a history of warriors was a departure from the Japanese historiographical tradition.[36] Written as a history textbook to teach the sixth *shōgun* Tokugawa Ienobu (1662–1712), Arai Hakuseki expressed his own philosophy of history and justification of the dominance of the military house. To Hakuseki, the rise of the military regime was inevitable, as the imperial house had lost the mandate of heaven due to moral corruption. He praised the military government for bringing stability and order to the nation. In order to legitimize the Edo *bakufu*, Hakuseki placed Ieyasu at the apex of Japanese history in his interpretation of the hexagram *qian* from the *Yijing*. He summarized Japanese history as follows: "Regarding the historical trends in Japan, the government of the realm fell to the military house after nine epochal changes. The military government fell to the rule of the present house after five epochal changes."[37] According to the hexagram *qian*, nine in the fifth place was the position of the ruler. His philosophy of history aimed to demonstrate that the Edo shogunate was in the legitimate position of nine in the fifth place.[38] In his *Hankanpu*, Hakuseki compared Ieyasu's victory at the Battle of Sekigahara to the revolution led by the King of Zhou to overthrow the Shang Dynasty. He also praised Ieyasu for implementing feudalism in Japan in the manner of the ancient Chinese sage-king. To Hakuseki, the Edo *bakufu* was the legitimate dynasty in place of the Kyoto court. In the *Tokushi yoron*, he called the emperor in Kyoto *kyōshu* (common lord), a term used to describe a monarch without real power. Hakuseki's historical views represented a departure from concepts of the separation of sovereignty and governance, as well as the distinction between the kingly *way* and the hegemonic *way*.

The *Dai Nihonshi* was a general history of Japan compiled by scholars in the Mito domain. Following the annals and biographical style of the *Shiji* and the principle of *sonnō senba* (revere the Emperor, condemn the hegemon) expounded in the *Chunqiu*, the *Dai Nihonshi* focused on the history of the imperial court, imbued with loyalist ideas and moral judgments.[39] Tokugawa Mitsukuni was not pleased with the Hayashi family, who refrained from making moral judgments on historical figures and regarded Wu Taibo, a prince of the Zhou dynasty, as the founder of the Japanese imperial house. He decided to compile a national history on his own in the style of the *Chunqiu*. He wrote:

I wanted to compile a history since childhood. I tried my best to search for rare books and to buy them. I selected unofficial histories, finding out which were true and which were suspicious. In order to clarify the legitimacy of the imperial house and the distinction between the ruler and the ruled, I compiled this history to form my personal view.[40]

As a champion of *taigi meibun* (literally, great cause and supreme duty, the moral obligation of the subject to the lord), Mitsukuni always reminded himself, "my lord is the emperor. The present *shōgun* is the head of my family."[41]

The *Dai Nihonshi* was harsh on military regimes and warrior leaders. Asaka Tanpaku looked down upon the Kamakura and Muromachi *bakufu*, referring to them as *hafu* (hegemonic governments) and *hagyō* (hegemonic careers). He criticized Ashikaga Yoshimitsu (1358–1408) severely for accepting the title of "King of Japan" (*Nihonkokuō*) from the Ming emperor. He did not raise any criticism against the Edo *bakufu*, however, and gave the Edo *bakufu* support by praising Nitta Yoshisada's loyalism. He wrote: "He [Nitta] had high moral standards. Although he failed in his times, his offspring [the Tokugawa] succeeded. Heaven blesses loyal people."[42] In the late Tokugawa period, the Mito school turned increasingly emperor-centered and loyalist. The attitude toward the *bakufu* among Mito historians became less supportive. Fujita Yūkoku (1774–1826), a Mito historian who participated in the *Dai Nihonshi* project, praised the unbroken lineage of the imperial line and the absolute loyalty to the emperor as Japan's unique national polity (*kokutai*) in his *Seimeiron* (Rectification of Names; 1791):

> From antiquity to the present, ordinary people never dared to over-throw the throne. The differences between the emperor and his subjects and high and low are very strict. Like heaven and earth, this rela-tionship cannot be changed. In terms of the longevity of the imperial line in my nation, wherever you go, we cannot find its parallel in the whole wide world. How great we are![43]

Under the principle of the distinction between the kingly way and hegemonic way, Yūkoku referred to the Edo *bakufu* as *hashu no gyō* (hegemonic career).[44] He reminded the *bakufu* that, "if the *bakufu* respects the imperial family, then the *daimyō* will respect the *bakufu*."[45]

The *Dai Nihonshi* adopted the traditional view of the separation of sovereignty and governance. Mito historians agreed that, while the imperial house continued to reign, the Edo *bakufu* received heaven's mandate to govern. In the *Dai Nihonshi*, following the Chinese historiographical style, the emperors were listed in *honki* (imperial annals), whereas the ministers were placed in *rekiden* (collection of biographies). How to position the Tokugawa *shōgun* was a thorny issue, as he was neither the emperor nor an ordinary minister. To address this dilemma, the *Dai Nihonshi* created a new category, *shōgunden* (biographies of the *shōgun*).[46] Since the *bakufu* was the de facto central government, it also added *shōgun kazoku rekiden* (biographies of the family of the *shōgun*) and *shōgun kashin rekiden* (biographies of the retainers of the *shōgun*) to accommodate the political reality.

The *Nihon gaishi* outlined the history of warrior families from the Genpei War to the late Tokugawa period. Rai Sanyō rated the warrior families based on their ability to implement feudalism. He considered feudalism the best system created by the ancient sage-kings in China, and it was finally successfully established in Japan under the Edo *bakufu*. He remarked:

> Feudalism originated in the time of the Minamoto family and was completed under the Ashikaga shogunate. The Ashikaga shogunate suffered before enjoying any benefit. The Oda and Toyotomi families continued to encounter its drawbacks and did not find a solution. Finally, our Tokugawa family came.... Having learned from the lessons of the two families, the Tokugawa shogunate adopted a middle-of-the-road approach and improved the situation gradually. Making a balance between internal and external forces, [the *bakuhan* system] could last for ten thousand years. Feudalism has been firmly established and can never be destroyed.[47]

He preferred feudalism over the system of prefectures and counties, because the former would unify the nation by fulfilling the wishes of the powerful people, whereas the latter created evil local administrators and rebellious villagers.

Sanyō believed that Chinese-style "revolution" and dynastic change did not fit in Japan because it had the unbroken line of the reigning imperial family. He rated Tokugawa Ieyasu highly for showing due respect to the imperial family and providing protection. He remarked:

Lord Tōshō [Tokugawa Ieyasu] was patient and extremely clever. He had incredible military ability and a passion for knowledge. He loved people and treated his guests kindly. He made decisions that had a far-reaching impact over a hundred generations. He served the imperial court with extreme humbleness and reverence, regarding the protection of the emperor as his own duty.[48]

Regarding the long Tokugawa peace, Sanyō's comments were ambiguous and ambivalent. In the preface, he lamented the decline of the imperial family in national politics as follows: "In the *Nihon gaishi*, I wrote that it first introduced the Minamoto and Taira families. I could not help lamenting the loss of power of the imperial house. The change of the times was beyond the control of human beings."[49] In the end of the *Nihon gaishi*, he wrote the following remarks on the eleventh *shōgun* Tokugawa Ienari (1773–1841): "Since Minamoto and Ashikaga, he was the only warrior to be appointed *daijōkan* (great minister). The military house has brought peace to the nation and reached its peak."[50] This wording might have been a subtle way of expressing loyalism.[51]

Tokugawa historical writings treated the imperial family in a different manner, ranging from the imperial loyalist *Dai Nihonshi*, *Nihon gaishi*, and *Chūchō jijitsu* to the ambiguous and fence-sitting *Honchō tsugan* and the pro-*bakufu Tokushi yoron*.[52] The *Dai Nihonshi* was one extreme. By stressing the unbroken lineage of the imperial family, the importance of *taigi meibun*, and the distinction between the kingly way and the hegemonic way, Mito school historians expressed imperial loyalism explicitly.

The loyalist bent of the *Nihon gaishi* was not as explicit as that of the *Dai Nihonshi*. While praising the military warriors for bringing stability and feudalism to Japan, Rai Sanyō was saddened to see the fall of the imperial house. His support for the Southern Court and the idea of the distinction between the kingly way and the hegemonic way also indicated his loyalist sentiments. Both the *Dai Nihonshi* and *Nihon gaishi* had an impact on loyalists in the *bakumatsu* period.

The *Honchō tsugan* represented the middle of the road. Hayashi Gahō admitted the coexistence of Edo *bakufu* and Kyoto court as two central governments and paid respect to the imperial family and the Southern Court. Regarding the unbroken line of imperial succession, he made the following cogent comment:

Between Jimmu and Go-Yōsei, Japan had one hundred and eight emperors. During this period, the line of imperial succession experienced termination and revision, as well as alternative succession of the two branches. This happened within the imperial family, and therefore the Chinese way of dynastic change should not be applied [53]

The *Tokushi yoron* was on the other side of the political spectrum. Written as a history to glorify the military house, it effectively sidelined the imperial house. Arai Hakuseki also demystified the legendary emperors and the imperial regalia in his *Koshitsū* (Understanding Ancient History; 1716). In the *Tokushi yoron*, Arai Hakuseki went so far as to endorse Ashikaga Yoshimitsu's acceptance of the title of "King of Japan" from the Ming dynasty. He wrote: "He made himself known outside of Japan. Appointed by the emperor of the Great Ming dynasty, he earned his reputation overseas."[54] From the perspective of the Confucian concept of *zhengming* (rectification of names), Yoshimitsu did something highly inappropriate and even treasonable. Rai Sanyō condemned him without reservation in this matter. Fujita Yūkoku reminded the Edo *bakufu* not to challenge the sovereignty of the imperial family in his *Seimeiron*. He wrote: "The sky cannot have two suns. A nation cannot have two kings. Our nation has the real emperor, and thus the *shōgun* should not claim to be the king. His governance is not the kingly way."[55] Interestingly enough, Hakuseki twisted the meaning of *zhengming* to the exact opposite position. Instead of the traditional interpretation of *junjun chenchen* (a king should behave like a king; a minister should behave like a minister) as expounded in the *Lunyu*, Hakuseki insisted that the *shōgun* was the de facto ruler and thus it was proper for him to use the title of king as commensurate with his authority.[56] He endorsed Yoshimitsu for accepting the title of "King of Japan" because "although he was a minister by title, he was actually the opposite."[57] This kind of rhetorical appropriation turned the meaning of the Chinese term upside down, showing a high level of localization of Confucianism in Tokugawa Japan.

THE MAKING OF JAPANESE CONCEPTS OF LEGITIMACY

Due to different historical developments and political traditions in China and Japan, Chinese concepts of legitimacy could not be applied to Japan without major modifications. Tokugawa historians demonstrated a high level of flexibility and creativity in their discussions of political legitimacy. They held three different attitudes toward imported Chinese concepts of legitimacy, namely, acceptance, refusal, and revision. Ideas such as blood lineage and morality that did not go against the political ethics of Japan were accepted. Others, such as the distinction between the Han and barbarians, the five circulatory phases, and transmission of the sagely way were flatly refused admission because they were considered irrelevant, far-fetched, or inapplicable. Some Chinese concepts were reinterpreted to fit into the Tokugawa system. For instance, heaven's mandate was used primarily to discuss the right to govern and denied a Chinese-style concept of "revolution" and dynastic change. Rectification of names became a means to justify the authority of the *shōgun*. Perhaps more significantly, Tokugawa historians created their own concepts of legitimacy, such as theories about the imperial regalia, reverence for the emperor, historical trends, and feudalism. These Japanese interpretations of legitimacy were created in Japan and could not be found in China.

This study has demonstrated two important features in Sino-Japanese intellectual interchange and Tokugawa intellectual history. First, Chinese concepts did not always fit neatly into the Tokugawa system, and thus they were subject to localization through reinterpretation and revision. Second, the Tokugawa system provided sufficient intellectual space for historians to creatively develop their own historical views. By redefining legitimacy, Tokugawa historical writings rationalized the establishment and authority of the Edo shogunate, the *bakuhan* system, the delicate *bakufu*-court relations, and the political implications of Shinto.

EPILOGUE

The imagination of China in the Tokugawa period was multifaceted, complicated, and ambiguous, and Tokugawa Japanese were often caught in a love-hate relationship with China. The line between Sinophilia and Sinophobia was never clear-cut among Tokugawa intellectuals. China was perceived as a combination of model and "the Other." Sinophiles did not forget Japan's own cultural heritage and their Japanese identity, whereas nativists studied Chinese classics and absorbed Chinese culture.

The purpose of this study was to explore a new perspective of Sino-Japanese relations and to find a new role for China in Japanese history beyond that of a role model and "the Other." It has demonstrated that the main function of China in Tokugawa Japan was not to introduce a more advanced culture, but to serve as a set of building blocks for the Japanese to develop their thought and culture. In the process of localization, Chinese culture often lost its original meanings and values, and only retained its shape in the form of terminology, ceremony, clothing, and folklore. Since Tokugawa Japanese borrowed Chinese forms to express Japanese ideas and feelings, the same things could have different meanings in China and Japan. The Japanese have called this kind of cultural appropriation *wakon kansai* (Japanese spirit, Chinese learning).[1] Using the three major important cultural forms, namely, Chinese legends, Confucian classics, and historical terms, as a point of reference, this study has investigated how the Japanese in the Tokugawa period employed Chinese elements as building blocks to express their indigenous spirit and values.

Chinese historical figures, such as Wu Taibo, Xu Fu, and Yang Guifei, have acquired new stories and identities in Japan. The Japanese seemed to have a stronger interest in these Chinese figures than their Chinese counterparts. Some Tokugawa Japanese believed that the three found second lives in ancient Japan and played an important role in Japanese history. Wu Taibo, Xu Fu, and Yang Guifei were regarded as ancestor of the imperial family, disseminator of advanced culture, and Japanese deity, respectively. These imaginative associations were the products of nativism, and were different ways of using Chinese legends to glorify Japan. Japan was thought to be a great nation because it was founded by an ancient sage, preserved the sagely way, and was under the protection of the deities.

Confucian classics and their commentaries were imported to Tokugawa Japan via Nagasaki, and reading Chinese books was a standard form of cultivation among Japanese intellectuals. The importation of Chinese books is commonly viewed as an expansion of the Confucian cultural sphere. This perspective can easily overlook the fact that Chinese elements were selectively absorbed and extensively modified to express indigenous ideas. The reading of Chinese classics among Tokugawa Japanese was unorthodox, but highly creative. Consciously or not, texts were often reinterpreted or distorted. For example, in the reading of the *Xiaojing*, most Tokugawa Confucians put loyalty before filial piety. Nakae Tōju, being relatively faithful to the original teaching of the text, represented merely an alternative voice. The *Yijing*, in the hands of the Hirata Atsutane and his followers, was turned into a Shinto text. Perhaps no Chinese text was more loosely interpreted and heavily twisted than the *Mengzi*, used by such loyalists as Yoshida Shōin to promote conservative ideology.

Chinese historical terms were used extensively in Tokugawa writings, but their usages and meanings were no longer the same as in China. Chinese political ideas were loosely interpreted to justify the Tokugawa system or elaborate upon Japanese political values. The localization of Chinese terminology took three different forms. First, there was the appropriation of names originally used for China, such as *Chūgoku* (Central Kingdom), and the imperial court, such as *chōtei* (central court government), to Japan and the *bakufu* (military government). Second, there was the reinterpretation of Chinese concepts, such as *tenmei* (heaven's mandate) and *kakumei* (revolution). Third, there was the creation of new concepts, such as the imperial regalia theory of legitimacy, and terms, such as *Seido* (Western Land). Chinese Confucian political thought did not fit into the Tokugawa system without major modification.

Although Japan was an integral part of the Sinosphere, it was never subordinate to China, politically or culturally. Chinese thought, culture, and language had their own lives in Japan. For example, classical Chinese or literary Sinitic has been used by the Japanese in their own unique way for a long time since its introduction to Japan. Chinese literary forms were used to express indigenous feelings and sense of beauty.[2] Similarly, this study has indicated that Tokugawa Japanese had a very strong nativist consciousness when it came to absorbing Chinese culture. To them, China was important not because it represented a more advanced culture for Japan to follow, but because it provided building blocks for the Japanese to express their own thinking.

I hope this study can break down the longstanding dichotomies between model and "the other," civilization and barbarism, and center and periphery in defining Sino-Japanese cultural exchange, so that the entire field of study can move into another dimension and level. Japanese culture was by no means an extended version of Chinese culture and thus China and Japan should be treated on equal terms. In the study of Tokugawa intellectual history, one should not overemphasize Chinese influence or see Japan merely as a member of the Chinese Confucian order. Likewise, the differences found in Japan's uses and interpretations of Chinese elements should not be condemned as deviations from the original teachings. Unless the Sinocentric perspective is replaced by a cross-cultural perspective, Tokugawa intellectual history will hardly be able to move on to a more sophisticated level of scholarship, and this study represents a step forward in this direction.

NOTES

INTRODUCTION

1. Wang Yong has advocated the concept of a "book road" that allegedly existed between China and Japan in ancient times. See Wang Yong, "Sichou-zhilu yu shujizhilu" [The Silk Road and the Book Road], *Zhejiang daxue xuebao (renwen shehui kexueban)* 33, no. 5 (September 2013): 5–12. I believe that the "book road" became a "book highway" in the early modern period. See Ōba Osamu, *Edo jidai ni okeru tōsenmochiwatarisho no kenkyū* [A Study of the Importation of Books by Chinese Ships in the Tokugawa Period] (Suita: Kansai daigaku tōzai gakujutsu kenkyūjo, 1967).

2. See Benjamin A. Elman, "Sinophiles and Sinophobes in Tokugawa Japan: Politics, Classicism and Medicine during the Eighteenth Century," *Eastern Asian Science, Technology and Society* 2, no. 1 (2008): 93–121.

3. Hayashi Razan, *Seika sensei gyōjō* [Life of Master Seika], *Hayashi Razan bunshū* 40 [Collected Writings of Hayashi Razan, vol. 40], ed. Kyōtō shisekikai (Kyoto: Kyōtō shisekikai, 1930), p. 463.

4. Kumazawa Banzan, *Shūgi gaisho* [Extra Writings on Accumulating Righteousness], *Banzan zenshū* 2 [Collected Works of Banzan, vol. 2], ed. Masamune Atsuo (Tokyo: Meicho shuppan, 1978), p. 25.

5. Kaibara Ekken, *Shinshiroku* [Record of Careful Thoughts], *Ekiken zenshū* 2 [Complete Collection of Ekken, vol. 2], ed. Ekiken Kai (Tokyo: Ekiken zenshū kankōbu, 1910), p. 49.

6. Hiraishi Naoaki, ed. *Soraishū, Soraishū shūi* [Collected Essays of Sorai and Supplement] (Tokyo: Perikansha, 1985), p. 314.

7. Ogyū Sorai, *Bendō* [Distinguishing the Way], *Nihon shisō taikei* 36, *Ogyū Sorai* [Books Series on Japanese Thought, vol. 36, Ogyū Sorai], annot. Yoshikawa Kōjirō (Tokyo: Iwanami shoten, 1973), p. 256. In addition, Sorai called Nagasaki "a land where Eastern barbarians meet the people of the

Central Civilization." See Olof G. Lidin, *The Life of Ogyū Sorai, a Tokugawa Confucian Philosopher* (Lund, Sweden: Studentlitt, 1973), p. 120.

8.   See Tian Shimin, *Jinshi Riben ruli shijian de yanjiu* [A Study of the Implementation of Confucian Etiquette in Early Modern Japan] (Taipei: Taiwan daxue chubanzhongxin, 2012).

9.   The disdain that many Tokugawa Japanese had for Qing politics and scholarship was not always fair. The *Tō-fūsetsugaki* (Reports of Rumors from the Chinese) that the Chinese captains submitted to *bakufu* officials in Nagasaki introduced regional rebellions and chaos rather than the achievements of Qing China. Few Tokugawa scholars, perhaps with the exception of Yoshida Kōton (1745–98) and Ōta Kinjō (1765–1825), took Qing culture seriously.

10.   In this book, *nativism* is used as a generic term referring to all kinds of indigenous discourse. It includes, but is not limited to, the intellectual movement or school called *kokugaku*. See Mark Teeuwen, "*Kokugaku* vs. Nativism," *Monumenta Nipponica* 61, no.2 (2006): 227–42.

11.   For a large number of examples, see Marius Jansen, *China in the Tokugawa World* (Cambridge, MA: Harvard University Press, 1992), ch. 2, pp. 53–92, and Tsujimoto Masashi, *Kinsei kyōiku shisōshi no kenkyū* [History of Education Thought in the Early Modern Period] (Kyoto: Shibunkaku shuppan, 1990).

12.   Wai-ming Ng, *The I Ching in Tokugawa Thought and Culture* (Honolulu: University of Hawai'i Press, 2000), pp. 66–67.

13.   The West Lake became a symbol of nostalgic imagination in Tokugawa thinking. See Kim Moonkyong, "Xihu zai Zhong Ri Han" [West Lake in China, Japan, and Korea], in *Dongya wenhua yixiang zhi xingsu* [The Making of Cultural Images of East Asian Culture], ed. Shi Shouqian and Liao Zhaocheng (Taipei: Yunchen wenhua shiye, 2011), pp. 141–66.

14.   For the craze of *hanshi* among Tokugawa intellectuals, see Ivo Smits, "Minding the Gaps: An Early Edo History of Sino-Japanese Poetry," in *Uncharted Waters: Intellectual Life in the Edo Period*, ed. Anna Beerens and Mark Teeuwen (Leiden: Brill, 2012), pp. 93–108.

15.   Wong Tin, "Hanmo qingyuan liangdeqian: Jindai Riben xiang Hua xueshu shuyao" [Connecting the Two Nations by Calligraphy: An Outline of Japanese Going to China to Learn Calligraphy in the Modern Period], in *Zai Riben xunzhao Zhongguo: Xiandaixing ji shenfen rentong de Zhong–Ri hudong*

[Searching for Japan in China: Modernity and Identity in Sino-Japanese Interactions], ed. Wai-ming Ng (Hong Kong: Zhongwen daxue chubanshe, 2013), pp. 4–7.

16.   Ishizaki Matazō, *Kinsei Nihon ni okeru Shina zokugo bungakushi* [A History of Chinese Vernacular Literature in Early Modern Japan] (Tokyo: Kōbundō shobō, 1940), pp. 56–60.

17.   Hayashi Rokurō, *Nagasaki Tōtsūji: Daitsūji Hayashi Dōei to sono shūhen* [Chinese Interpreters in Nagasaki: The Great Interpreter Hayashi Dōei and His Surroundings] (Nagasaki: Nagasaki bunkensha, 2010), p. 6.

18.   Yamaga Sokō, *Chūchō jujitsu* [True Facts Concerning the Middle Kingdom], *Yamaga Sokō zenshū: Shisōhen* 13 [Complete Works of Yamaga Sokō: His Thought, vol. 13], ed. Hirose Yutaka (Tokyo: Iwanami shoten, 1940), p. 225.

19.   Tokugawa Mitsukuni, *Seizankō zuihitsu* [Miscellaneous Writings of Mitsukuni], *Dai Nihon shisō zenshū* 18 [Complete Collection on Japanese Thought, vol. 18], ed. Uemura Katsuya (Tokyo: Dai Nihon shisō zenshū kankōkai, 1933), p. 357.

20.   Kamo Mabuchi, *Kokuikō* [Reflections on the Meaning of Our Nation], *Nihon shisō taikei* 39, *Kinsei shintōron zenki kokugaku* [Book Series on Japanese Thought, vol. 39, Shinto and Early *Kokugaku* in the Early Modern Period], ed. Taira Shigemichi and Abe Akio (Tokyo: Iwanami shoten, 1972), p. 383.

21.   Motoori Norinaga, *Naobi no mitama* [The Rectifying Spirit; 1711], *Shintō taikei: Ronsetsuhen* 25, *fukko shintō* 3 [Book Series on Shinto: Theories 25 Fukko Shinto 3], annot. Umezawa Isezō and Takahashi Miyuki (Tokyo: Shintō taikei hensankai, 1982), pp. 17–18.

22.   Sasaki Takanari, *Ben bendōsho* [Debating Bendōsho; 1736], *Dai-Nihon bunko shintō hen: Suika shintō* 3 [Collection of Books on Great Japan: Shinto, Suika Shinto 3], annot. Saeki Ariyoshi (Tokyo: Shunyōdō shoten, 1937), p. 299.

23.   Fukagawa Yūei, *Seidōron* [Discourse on the Right Way; 1776], *Kinnō bunko* 2 [Collection of Books on Royalism, vol. 2], ed. Arima Sukemasa (Tokyo: Dai-Nihon meidōkai, 1919), p. 409.

24.   Harry D. Harootunian, "The Functions of China in Tokugawa Thought," in *The Chinese and the Japanese: Essays in Political and Cultural Interactions*, ed. Akira Iriye (Princeton, NJ: Princeton University Press, 1980), pp. 9–36.

25. Peter Nosco, "The Place of China in the Construction of Japan's Early Modern World View," *Taiwan Journal of East Asian Studies* 4, no. 1 (June 2007): 27–48.

26. Han Dong-yu, *Cong "tuoru" dao "tuoya": Riben jinshi yilai "qu zhong xin hua" zhi sixiang guocheng yanjiu* [From De-Confucianism to De-Sinicization: A Study of the Process of Decentralization in Japan since the Early Modern Period] (Taipei: Taiwan daxue chuban zhongxin, 2009), pp. 339–84.

27. Naitō Konan, "Nippon bunka towa nani zoya" [What is Japanese Culture?], in *Naitō Konan zenshū* 9 [Complete Works of Naitō Konan, vol. 9] (Tokyo: Chikuma shobō, 1969), p. 14.

28. Ibid.

29. Takeuchi Yoshio, "Nihon no jukyō" [Japanese Confucianism], in *Takeuchi Yoshio zenshū* 4 [Complete Works of Takeuchi Yoshio, vol. 4] (Tokyo: Kadokawa shoten, 1979), p. 246.

30. Bitō Masahide, *Nihon bunka no rekishi* [History of Japanese Culture], (Tokyo: Iwanami shoten, 2000), ch. 11.

31. Inoue Tetsujirō, *Nihon shushigakuha no tetsugaku* [The Philosophy of the Zhu Xi School in Japan] (Tokyo: Fuzanbō, 1909), pp. 29–30.

32. Kurozumi Makoto, *Fukusūsei no Nihon shisō* [Plurality in Japanese Thought] (Tokyo: Perikansha, 2006), pp. 255–68.

33. Kumazawa Banzan, *Miwa monogatari* [The Tale of Miwa], *Nihon tetsugaku zensho* 4, *Shintōhen, Jukyōhen* [Anthology of Writings on Japanese Philosophy, vol. 4, Shinto, Confucianism], ed. Saigusa Hiroto (Tokyo: Daiichi shobō, 1936), p. 155.

34. Ibid., pp. 144–45.

35. Matsushita Kenrin, *Ishō Nihonden* [Treatises on Japan under Foreign Titles], in *Shiseki shūran* 20 [Collection of Historical Sources, vol. 20], ed. Kondō Heijō (Tokyo: Kondō shuppanbu, 1926), p. 9.

36. Yokoyama Shigeru, annot., *Ko jōruri shōhonshū* 3 [Original Scripts of Old Jōruri, vol. 3] (Tokyo: Kadokawa shoten, 1964), play 4, pt. 4, pp. 312–13. This diaologue was obviously fabricated, as Emperor Xuanzong died before Bai Juyi was born.

37. Quoted in Kondō Haruo, *Chōgonka Biwagyō no kenkyū* [A Study of The Song of Everlasting Sorrow and The Pipa Tune] (Tokyo: Meiji shoin, 1981), p. 162.

38.   Yoshida Shōin, *Kō-Mō yowa* [Additional Notes in Explanation of the *Mencius*] (Tokyo: Iwanami shoten, 1943), p. 47.

39.   See Martin Collcutt, "The Legacy of Confucianism in Japan," in *The East Asian Region: Confucian Heritage and Its Modern Adaptation*, ed. Gilbert Rozman (Princeton, NJ: Princeton University Press, 1991), pp. 133–34.

40.   Hirata Atsutane, *San'eki yuraiki jō* [The Origins of the Three Versions of the *Yijing*, part 1] (Tokyo: Ibukinoya, 1835), pp. 1–2, digital collection of National Diet Library of Japan, request no. 848-173.

41.   Yamaga Sokō, *Chūchō jujitsu*, in Hirose, ed. *Yamaga Sokō zenshū: Shisōhen* 13, p. 225.

42.   Fujita Tōko, *Kōdōkanki jutsugi* [A Commentary on *The Record of Kōdōkan*], *Nihon shisō taikei* 53, *Mitogaku*, ed. Imai Usaburō et al. (Tokyo: Iwanami shoten, 1973), p. 298.

43.   Tokugawa Harutoshi, *Shin Dai Nihonshi hyō* [The Memorial on *The Great History of Japan*)], quoted in Yamazaki Tōkichi and Horie Hideo, *Nanbokuchō seijun ronsan* [Discourse on the Southern and Northern Courts Controversy over Legitimacy] (Tokyo: Kōtenkōkyūjo Kokugakuin daigaku shuppantoshohanbaijo, 1911), p. 158.

44.   Yoshida, *Kō-Mō yowa*, p. 47. The term *yiyanfayan* is from the *Mengzi*, referring to the evil against evil situation.

CHAPTER I

1.   Modern scholars of Xu Fu in Japan and China have heretofore examined this issue mainly from archaeological and philological perspectives to discuss whether Xu Fu actually landed in Japan or not. For representative works, see Wang Xiangrong, "Xu Fu: Riben de Zhongguo yimin" [Xu Fu and Chinese Immigrants in Japan], in *Riben de Zhongguo yimin* [Chinese Immigrants in Japan], ed. Zhongguo Zhong–Ri guanxishi yanjiuhui (Beijing: Sanlian shudian, 1987); and *Jofuku densetsu o saguru* [Investigating the Xu Fu Legend], ed. An Shibin et al. (Tokyo: Shōgakukan, 1990). However, this chapter looks into the Xu Fu legend in Japan from an intellectual and textual perspective. It will not discuss whether Xu Fu actually landed in Japan or not. My area of concern rests solely with the intellectual significance of the Xu Fu discourse in Tokugawa history and Sino-Japanese relations.

2.   Hayashi Razan, *Honchō jinjakō* [A Study of Shinto Shrines in Japan] (Tokyo: Kaizōsha, 1942), p. 180.

3.   Reprinted in Kyoto by Iida Chūbei in 1669, the *Shishi liutie* was widely read by Tokugawa intellectuals.

4.   See Gi So (Yi Chu), *Giso rokujō* (*Yichu liutie*) (Kyoto: Hōyu shoten, 1979), p. 459.

5.   Gentō, *Sangoku denki* 1 (Tokyo: Koten bunko, 1982), p. 52.

6.   Wu Lai, *Yuanyingji* 4 (Beijing: Zhonghua shuju, 1985), p. 9.

7.   Quoted in Hada Buei, *Jofuku roman: Yayoi jidai no furontia* [Romance of Xu Fu: The Frontier of the Yayoi Period] (Tokyo: Aki shobō, 1993), pp. 155–56.

8.   Joshua A. Fogel, *The Literature of Travel in the Japanese Rediscovery of China, 1862–1945* (Stanford, CA: Stanford University Press, 1996), p. 31.

9.   Zekkai Chūshin, "Yingzhi fu sanshan" [Composing Poems on the Three Mountains at the Request of the Emperor], in *Gozan bungakushū, Edo kanshishū* [Collection of Literature of the Five Mountains, Collection of Chinese Poetry in the Edo Period], *Nihon koten bungaku taikei* 89 [Series on Japanese Classical Literature, vol. 89] (Tokyo: Iwanami shoten, 1966), p. 116.

10.   Shin Suk-ju, *Haedong jegukgi* (Seoul: Taeyang Sojok, 1972), p. 64.

11.   Quoted in Yamamoto Noritsuna, *Nihon ni ikiru Jofuku no denshō* [The Transmission of the Xu Fu Legend in Japan] (Tokyo: Kenkōsha, 1979), p. 104. Yamamoto traces the origins of the Penglai belief in Atsuta to the late Heian period.

12.   Ishō, *Tōkai keikashū*, in *Gozan bungaku shinshū* 2 [New Collection of Literature of the Five Mountains, vol. 2], ed. Tamamura Takeji (Tokyo: Tōkyō Daigaku shuppankai, 1968), p. 825.

13.   In contrast, some medieval Japanese suggested that the ancient Chinese prince Wu Taibo was the ancestor of the Japanese imperial family. This idea faced severe criticism and suppression.

14.   See Wai-ming Ng, "The Forgery of Books in Tokugawa Japan," *East Asian Library Journal* 9, no. 2 (2000): 19–45.

15.   Hayashi Razan, *Heishin kikō*, in *Nikki kikōshū* [Collection of Travel Diaries], annot. Tsukamoto Tetsuzō (Tokyo: Yūhōdō shoten, 1936), pp.179–80.

16.   Quoted in Hada Buei, *Jofuku roman: Yayoi jidai no furontia*, pp. 55–56.

17.   Daimyōjin is a title for Shinto deity and Jofuku is the Japanese name of Xu Fu.

18.   Quoted in Luo Qixiang and Iino Takahiro, eds., *Jofuku: Yayoi no kōsen* [Xu Fu: The Rainbow of Yayoi] (Tokyo: Tōkyō shoseki, 1988), p. 200. Tachibana Nankei (1754–1806) introduced this legend in detail in his *Hokusō sadan* (Brief Conversations through a Northern Window; 1825). See Tachibana Nankei, *Hokusō sadan*, in *Nihon zuihitsu taisei*, ser. 2, vol. 15, ed. Nihon zuihitsu taisei henshūbu (Tokyo: Yoshikawa kōbunkan, 1974), pp. 273–74.

19.   According to the *Nihon santai jutsuroku* [Records of Japan in the Three Reign Eras; 901], Mount Fuji erupted in 864. Tomonoatai Masada, allegedly a descendant of Xu Fu, built Sengen Shrine on Lake Kawaguchi to pacify Mount Fuji.

20.   Quoted in Luo Qixiang and Iino Takahiro, eds., *Jofuku: Yayoi no kōsen*, pp. 201, 206.

21.   For Tokugawa texts that mention Xu Fu in Kumano, see Tsuji Shiho, *Jofuku ron: Ima o ikiru densetsu* [Discourse on Xu Fu: A Living Legend] (Tokyo: Shintensha, 2004), pp. 120–30; Yamamoto Noritsuna, *Jofuku tōrai densetsu kō* [An Investigation of the Legend of Xu Fu in Japan] (Tokyo: Kenkōsha, 1975), pp. 238–53.

22.   The exact origins of these sites and traditions are difficult to ascertain; some probably already existed before the Tokugawa period. For instance, Shimada Masao believes that the Xu Fu Tomb was built in the late Muromachi period. See Shimada Masao, "Jofuku denshō seiritsu no kiban" [The Foundation of the Transmission of the Xu Fu Legend], in *Wakayamaken: rekishi* [History of Wakayama Prefectre], ed. Chihōshi kenkyūjo (Tokyo: Chihōshi kenkyūjo, 1957), pp. 260–74.

23.   See Lin Jiantong, "Qin Xufu shiji zhi yanjiu" [A Study of the History of the Qin Chinese Xu Fu], in *Xu Fu yu Riben* [Xu Fu and Japan], ed. Lin Jiantong and Zhu Zhensheng (Hong Kong: Xianggang Xufu hui, 1976), p. 13.

24.   Kyōtō shisekikai, ed., *Hayashi Razan bunshū* 1 (Tokyo: Perikansha, 1979), p. 1.

25.   Kitabatake Kakusai, *Kumano yūki* 2, pp. 10–11, digital collection of Waseda University Library, request no. ル04_03162.

26.   Takizawa Bakin, *Gendō hōgen* [1818], in *Nihon zuihitsu taisei*, ser. 1, vol. 5, ed. Nihon zuihitsu taisei henshūbu (Tokyo: Yoshikawa kōbunkan, 1975), p. 94. Regarding the medicine for immortality, some Tokugawa Japanese suggested *konbu* (a kind of seaweed that grows in cool waters), abalone, and aggregata (a species of flowering plant that is used in herbal medicine). See

Sasaki Sadataka, *Kansō sadan* [1841], in *Nihon zuihitsu taisei*, ser. 1, vol. 12, ed. Nihon zuihitsu taisei henshūbu (Tokyo: Yoshikawa kōbunkan, 1975), p. 416.

27.   Takizawa Bakin, *Chinsetsu yumiharizuki*, part 2, section 17, in *Nihon koten bungaku taikei* 60, annot. Gotō Tanji (Tokyo: Iwanami shoten, 1958), pp. 254–55.

28.   Quoted in Yamamoto, *Nihon ni ikiru Jofuku no denshō*, p. 107.

29.   Atsuta Jingū gūchō, ed., *Atsuta Jingū shiryō: Chōshū zasshi* 24 (Nagoya: Atsuta Jingū gūchō, 1969), pp. 1–2.

30.   See Iki Ichirō, *Jofuku shūdan torai to kodai Nihon* [The Coming of the Xu Fu Group and Ancient Japan] (Tokyo: Sanichi shobō, 1996), pp. 82, 126–28.

31.   Yamamoto, *Nihon ni ikiru Jofuku no denshō*, pp. 44–48.

32.   Hada, *Jofuku roman: Yayoi jidai no furontia*, p. 73. The most recent festival was held in 1980.

33.   Luo Qixiang and Iino Takahiro, eds., *Jofuku: Yayoi no kōsen*, pp. 199–200.

34.   The legend about Mount Kanmuri-dake can be traced to the Muromachi period. The Zen monk Keian Genju (1427–1508), in a poem called "Tōin gyoshō" (Fisherman Songs of Genju; 1478), associated this mountain with Xu Fu. It reads: "Xu Fu came from overseas. He realized that Japan was Penglai.... This divine man took off his hat. The beauty of the scenes touched the heavens." *Zoku gunsho ruijū* 12, no. 2 [Collection of Books by Catalogue, Sequel]ed. Hanawa Hokiichi (Tokyo: Zoku gunsho ruijū kanseikai, 1959), p. 657. The *Sangoku meishō zue* [Illustrative Explanation of the Scenic Attractions in the Three Nations; 1843] states: "One theory is that in the reign of Emperor Kōgen, the Qin Chinese Xu Fu came. He left his jade hat, and thus it is called Kanmuri-dake." Godai Hidetaka and Hashiguchi Kenpei, *Sangoku meishō zue* 1 (Tokyo: Minami Nihon shuppan bunka kyōkai, 1966), pp. 305–6.

35.   The origins of this view in Japan can be traced to Kitabatake Chikafusa's (1293–1354) *Jinnō shōtōki* [Records of the Legitimate Succession of the Divine Sovereigns; rev. 1339]. Concerning the era of Emperor Kōrei, it reads: "In the forty-fifth year of Yimao, the First Emperor of Qin ascended the throne. The First Emperor believed in the immortals and looked for the medicine for immortality in Japan. Japan wanted to acquire the books of the Three Sovereigns and Five Emperors. The First Emperor sent them to Japan. Thirty-five years later, that nation burned books and buried Confucians. The complete

collection of Confucian classics has survived in Japan." *Jinnō shōtōki, Masu kagami, Nihon koten bungaku taikei* 87, ed. Iwasa Masashi and Tokieda Motoki (Tokyo: Iwanami shoten, 1965), p. 71.

36.   Hayashi, *Honchō tsugan* 3 (Tokyo: Kokusho kankōkai, 1919), p. 55.

37.   Hayashi, *Hayashi Razan bunshū* 1, p. 1.

38.   The "Ribendao ge" reads: "Its ancestor Xu Fu tricked the men of Qin. In search of herbs, he tarried till the boys had grown old. With him, he took the hundred craftsmen and the five grains. To this day, the country's crafts are marked by great skill. From time to time these people brought tribute to the former dynasty. Their scholars were often clever with verse. When Xu Fu made his voyage, the *Book of Documents* had not been burned, so the complete hundred sections must be preserved in Japan. But their strict laws will not allow it to be sent to China, where indeed there is no one who can read the ancient texts." Translated by Burton Watson in his translation of Yoshikawa Kōjirō's *Sōshi gaisetsu* as, *An Introduction to Sung Poetry* (Cambridge, MA: Harvard University Press, 1967), pp. 10–12. Ouyang Xiu's conjecture was also adopted by Kitabatake Chikafusa in his *Jinnō shōtōki*.

39.   Hayashi, *Hayashi Razan bunshū, zuihitsu* 70, in *Kojiruien* 3 [Encyclopedia of Ancient Matters], ed. Jingūshichō (Kyoto: Kojiruien kankōkai, 1931), p. 773.

40.   See Tsunoda Ryūsaku, William Theodore de Bary, and Donald Keene, eds., *Sources of Japanese Tradition* (New York: Columbia University Press, 1958), pp. 357–60.

41.   Regarding the nationalistic attitude toward Confucianism among Tokugawa Confucians, see Kate Nakai, "The Naturalization of Confucianism in Tokugawa Japan: The Problem of Sinocentrism," *Harvard Journal of Asiatic Studies* 40, no. 1 (June 1980): 157–99.

42.   Kumazawa Banzan, *Miwa monogatari* [The Tale of Miwa], *Nihon tetsugaku zensho* 4, *Shintōhen, Jukyōhen*, ed. Saigusa Hiroto (Tokyo: Daiichi shobō, 1936), pp. 144–45.

43.   Hakuseki's views of Xu Fu were inconsistent from time to time and from text to text. In the *Koshitsū wakumon* [Questions on *The Survey of Ancient History*; 1716], he had reservations about the Xu Fu legend in Japan, arguing that Yi Zhou (a legendary island in the East China Sea) was not Japan and Xu Fu was not the first Chinese immigrant to Japan. He did not entertain the idea that the Japanese imperial family had originated on the continent. See

Arai Hakuseki, *Koshitsū wakumon*, in *Nihon no meicho* 15: *Arai Hakuseki*, ed. Kuwabara Takeo (Tokyo: Chūō kōronsha, 1969), p. 292.

44.   Arai Hakuseki, *Dōbun tsūkō* (Tokyo: Benseisha, 1979), p. 125.

45.   Iki, *Jofuku shūdan torai to kodai Nihon*, pp. 68–70.

46.   Tokugawa Mitsukuni, ed., and Hiraizumi Kiyoshi, annot., *Dai Nihonshi* (Tokyo: Shunyōdō shoten, 1937), vol.1, *hongi 1* [Annals, part 1], "Kōrei tennō."

47.   Tachibana Nankei, *Tōzaiyūki, Hokusō sadan* (Tokyo: Yūhōdō shoten, 1922), p. 350.

48.   Ibid.

49.   Ibid., p. 351.

50.   Momoi Tōu, *Kyūai zuihitsu, Nihon zuihitsu taisei*, ser. 2, vol. 12, ed. Nihon zuihitsu taisei henshūbu (Tokyo: Yoshikawa kōbunkan, 1974), p. 101.

51.   Ibid., p. 98–99.

52.   Satō Shigehiro, *Chūryō manroku* [The Prose Writings of Chūryō; 1826], *Nihon zuihitsu taikei*, ser. 3, vol. 3 (Tokyo: Yoshikawa kōbunkan, 1975), p. 138.

53.   Iwagaki Matsunae, *Kokushi ryaku*, in *Shinyaku kokushi ryaku* [New Translation of *Kokushi ryaku*], trans. Ōmachi Keigetsu (Tokyo: Shiseidō shoten, 1921), p. 26.

54.   Matsushita Kenrin, *Ishō Nihonden*, in *Shiseki shūran* 20 [Collection of Historical Sources, vol. 20], ed. Kondō Heijō (Tokyo: Kondō shuppanbu, 1926), p. 9.

55.   Ibid., p. 13. Liu refers to Liu Zhongda's *Liushi hongshu* (1611). The *Yuanshi mishu* was a sourcebook compiled by Zhu Quan (1378–1448).

56.   See Kanzawa Tokō, *Okingusa* [Writings of an Old Man], in *Nihon zuihitsu taikei*, ser. 3, vol. 21 (Tokyo: Yoshikawa kōbunkan, 1978), p. 134.

57.   Ono Takakiyo, *Hyakusō tsuyu* [Dew of the Hundred Plants], in *Nihon zuihitsu taisei*, ser. 3, vol. 11 (Tokyo: Yoshikawa kōbunkan, 1978), pp. 41–42.

58.   This text can be found in the *Jofuku kenshōhi* in Jofuku Kōen in Shingū.

59.   Quoted in Lin Jiantong, "Qin Xufu shiji zhi yanjiu," p. 11.

60.   In Kaibara Ekken, *Chikuzen kuni zoku fudoki* [The Topography of the Chikuzen Province, a Sequel], in *Ekken zenshū* 4 [Complete Collection of Ekken, vol. 4], ed. Ekken Kai (Tokyo: Ekken zenshū kankōbu, 1910), pp. 200–201.

61.   Amano Sadakage, *Shioshiri, Nihon zuihitsu taisei*, ser. 3, vol. 16, ed. Nihon zuihitsu taisei henshūbu (Tokyo: Yoshikawa kōbunkan, 1976), p. 170.

62.   Yamagata Bantō, *Yume no shiro* [In Place of Dreams], *Nihon keizai sōsho* 25, ed. Takimoto Seiichi (Tokyo: Nihon keizai sōsho kankōkai, 1916), p. 124.

63.   Ibid., p. 551.

64.   The *Tensho* was a history book attributed to Fujiwara Hamanari (724–90).

65.   Hirata Atsutane, *Kanna hifumi den* [Treatise on the Script of the Gods; 1819] (Edo: Ikukinoyajuku, 1824), pp. 6–8.

66.   These ideas can also be found in his *Sansenzan yokō* [Additional Investigation of the Three Sacred Mountains].

67.   Senke Takazumi, *Sakura no hayashi* [Sakura Forest], *Nihon zuihitsu taisei*, ser. 2, vol. 11, ed. Nihon zuihitsu taisei henshūbu (Tokyo: Yoshikawa kōbunkan, 1974), p. 137.

68.   Ise Sadatake, *Ansai zuihitsu* 1, ed. Imaizumi Teisuke (Tokyo: Yoshikawa kōbunkan, 1929), p. 243.

69.   Ibid., p. 401.

70.   Some modern Chinese scholars allege that Xu Fu was the ancestor of the Japanese imperial family. The Hong Kong scholar Wei Ting-sheng (1890–1977) jump-started the academic debate by arguing that the real identity of Emperor Jimmu was Xu Fu in his *Riben Shenwu kaiguo xinkao: Xu Fu ru Riben jianguo kao* [A New Investigation of the Founding of Japan by Emperor Jimmu: Xu Fu Moving to Japan and Building a Nation] (Hong Kong: Hong Kong Commercial Press, 1950). This book has a Japanese edition entitled *Jimmu Tennō=Jofuku densetsu no nazo* [Emperor Jimmu: The Secrets of the Legend of Xu Fu] (Tokyo: Shinjinbutsu ōraisha, 1977). Wei's theory was challenged by a number of Japanese scholars, including Ienaga Saburō (1913–2002). The Taiwanese scholar Peng Shuang-song wrote *Xu Fu jishi Shenwu Tianhuang* [Xu Fu Was Emperor Jimmu] (Miaoli: Fuhui tushu chubanshe, 1983) to support Wei.

71.   See Watanabe Hiroshi, *Kinsei Nihon shakai to Sōgaku* [Early Modern Japanese Society and Song Learning] (Tokyo: Tōkyō daigaku shuppankai, 1995).

CHAPTER 2

1.   See Masako Nakagawa Graham, *The Yang Kuei-fei Legend in Japanese Literature* (Lewiston, NY: Edwin Mellen Press, 1998), chs. 2–5.

2.   According to the *Jiu Tang shu* [Old Book of the Tang Dynasty], Yang was strangled to death by the eunuch Gao Lishi (684–762) in a Buddhist temple.

3.   According to Chinese mythology that originated in the state of Qi in the pre-Qin period, the Penglai Palace was located on Mount Penglai, where the immortals lived. According to the *Shanhaijing* (Classic of Mountains and Seas), Mount Penglai is located at the eastern end of the Bohai Sea. From the medieval period onwards, some Japanese believed that Mount Penglai was located in Japan, where Xu Fu and Yang Guifei landed and spent the rest of their lives. See Tanaka Hiroshi, *Tōkai ni hōraikoku ari: Jofuku den* [There Was a Penglai Kingdom in the Eastern Sea: The Story of Xu Fu] (Fukuoka: Kaichōsha, 1991), pp. 1–348.

4.   Translation is from Rewi Alley, *Bai Juyi: 200 Selected Poems* (Beijing: New World, 1983), p. 212.

5.   The Japanese monk Egaku was the first to bring the *Baishi wenji* (Collected Works of Bai Juyi, which includes the "Chang hen ge") to Japan from China in 847. See Graham, *The Yang Kuei-fei Legend in Japanese Literature*, p. 66.

6.   Thomas Rimer and Jonathan Chaves, trans. and annot., *Chinese and Japanese Poems to Sing: The Wakan Rōei Shū* (New York: Columbia University Press, 1997), p. 232.

7.   The *Chang hen ge zhuan* is a short novel describing Yang Guifei's stay on Mount Penglai in the Eastern Sea written by Chen Hong, a friend of Bai Juyi. Regarding the relationship between the *Genji monogatari* and "Chang hen ge," see David Pollack, *The Fracture of Meaning: Japan's Synthesis of China from the Eighth through the Eighteenth Centuries* (Princeton, NJ: Princeton University Press, 1986), ch. 2, pp. 55–76.

8.   Other representative works of the Heian period, such as the *Makura no sōshi* (Pillow Book; by Sei Shōnagon), *Sarashina nikki* (Sarashina Diary; by Sugawara Takasue Musume), and *Hamamatsu Chūnagon monogatari* (The Tale of the Hamamatsu Counselor; by Sugawara Takasue Musume), were also indebted to the "Chang hen ge." This poem was further popularized by the creation of editions translated into Japanese prose and waka verse in late Heian times in such works as the *Kara monogatari* (Tales of China) and *Shūigusō* (Gleanings of Worthless Grasses; 1216) by Fujiwara Sadaie (1162–1241).

9.   Military tales of the Kamakura and Muromachi periods, such as the *Heike monogatari* (Tale of Heike), *Hōgen monogatari* (Tale of Hōgen), and *Taiheiki* (Chronicle of Grand Peace), cited the "Chang hen ge" and *Chang hen ge zhuan*. Konparu Zenchiku (1405–1470?) wrote the *nō* drama *Yōkihi* to retell the story of Emperor Xuanzong searching for Yang Guifei in Japan. For a textual analysis of *Yōkihi* in medieval literary and *nō* traditions, see Leo Shing Chi Yip,

Reinventing China: Cultural Adaptation in Medieval Japanese Nō Theatre (PhD diss., Ohio State University, 2004), pp. 146–73. This play is still performed in contemporary Japan.

10.   See C. Andrew Gerstle, trans., *Chikamatsu: 5 Late Plays* (New York: Columbia University Press, 2001), p. 67.

11.   See Shane McCausland and Matthew McKelway, *Chinese Romance from a Japanese Brush: Kano Sansetsu's Chōgonka Scrolls in the Chester Beatty Library* (London: Scala, 2009); Muraki Keiko, "Chōgonka-e no henyō: Nara-e-kei Chōgonka emaki o tegakari ni" [The Transformation of the Scroll Paintings of *The Song of Everlasting Sorrow*: Using *Chōgonka emaki* of the Nara–e School as a Clue], *Bigaku geijutsugaku* 25 (2009): 50–69.

12.   For the popularization of the legend of Yang Guifei in Tokugawa Japan, see Graham, *The Yang Kuei-fei Legend in Japanese Literature*, pp. 195–250. See also Ikeda Mariko, "Nihon ni okeru Gensō Yōkihi-zu: Kinsei shoki no gadai to zuyō" [The Paintings of Xuanzong and Yang Guifei in Japan: Themes and Patterns in the Early Modern Period], *Bijutsu–shi kenkyū* 41 (2003): 43–64.

13.   In the poem, Emperor Xuanzong returns to the imperial palace in Chang'an after the An Lushan Rebellion. He misses Yang day and night and thus asks a Taoist priest to look for her soul in the spiritual world, but he does so in vain. This Taoist priest hears that there is a fairy lady named Taizhen living in the Eastern Sea who might be Yang Guifei. Sent by Emperor Xuanzong to the Eastern Sea, the Taoist priest finally finds Yang there in the Penglai Palace. This story may have stimulated the imagination of the Japanese about Yang's escape to Japan. The legend was also associated with a Shinto belief about the manifestation of Atsuta Daimyōjin. See Stuart D. B. Picken, *Historical Dictionary of Shinto* (Lanham, MD: Scarecrow, 2011), p. 34.

14.   This story is mentioned in two Tokugawa texts kept in Nison-in, but is not supported by other historical sources. According to official records, Abe Nakamaro never returned to Japan after the An Lushan Rebellion. He became a senior official in the Tang government and died in Chang'an in 770.

15.   It is said that these two books about Yang are unpublished records kept in Nison-in. They are mentioned in a number of secondary sources, but few modern scholars seem to have actually read the original sources.

16.   This paragraph can also be found in the inscription on Yang's tomb. Quoted in Izumi Hideki, ed., *Rekishi jinbutsu, igai na densetsu* [Historical Figures, Surprising Legends] (Tokyo: PHP, 2010), p. 258.

17.   Quoted in Nakae Katsumi, *Nipponshi nazo no jinbutsu no igai na shōtai* [Mysterious People in Japanese History and Their Surprising Real Identities] (Tokyo: PHP, 1999), p. 186. Yagi was a courtier family that can be traced back to the Nara period. The grandmother of Kibi no Makibi (695–775) was also named Yagi. See Ōmi Shōji, "Yōki-shi boshi no kenkyū" [A Study of the Yagi Epitaph], *Nihon rekishi* 211 (1962): 32–52.

18.   Nihon zuihitsu taisei henshūbu, ed., *Nihon zuihitsu taisei*, ser. 3, vol. 15 (Tokyo: Yoshikawa kōbunkan, 1995), p. 119.

19.   See Watanabe Ryūsaku, *Yōkihi kōden* [Sequel to the Biography of Yang Guifei] (Tokyo: Shūeishobō, 1980), chs. 9–10. This story is quite unreliable, as the capital during that time was Nara, not Kyoto.

20.   Zou shuang-shuang, "Densetsu kara genjitsu e yomigaetta Yōkihi no shosō: Amakusa-shi Shinwa-chō no Yōkihi o chūshin ni" [Facets of Yang Guifei from Legend to Fact: Highlighting the Legend of Yang Guifei in Shin-wa-chō, Amakusa-shi], *Amakusashotō no bunka kōshō–gaku kenkyū* [Study of Cultural Interchange in the Amakusa Islands], 2(March 2011): 153–62.

21.   Takebe Ayatari, *Honchō suikoden* (Tokyo: Iwanami shoten, 1992), *Shin Nihon koten bungaku taikei* 79, pp. 283–86.

22.   Takemura Noriyuki, "Chikushi ni utsurisunda Yōkihi: *Honchō suikoden* no Yōkihi koji ni tsuite" [Yang Guifei Moving to Live in Chikushi: The Story of Yang Guifei in Honchō suikoden], *Bungaku kenkyū* 101 (March 2004): 63–76.

23.   See Atsuko Sakaki, *Obsessions with the Sino-Japanese Polarity in Japanese Literature* (Honolulu: University of Hawai'i Press, 2006), pp. 55–64

24.   It is believed that Atsuta Myōjin transformed into Yamato-Takeru-no-Mikoto. In the *Kojiki*, Yamato-Takeru-no-Mikoto was a legendary hero who dressed like a young woman to kill his enemy in Kyūshū. For the relationships among Atsuta Myōjin, Prince Yamato-Takeru-no-Mikoto, and Yang Guifei, see Picken, *Historical Dictionary of Shinto*, pp. 48–49.

25.   Kōshū, *Keiran shūyōshū*, in *Taishō shinshū daizōkyō* 76 [The Chinese Buddhist Canon; The Taishō New Edition, vol. 76], ed. Takakusu Junjirō (Tokyo: Taishō issaikyō kankōkai, 1931), p. 518.

26.   Yang Guifei was enshrined in the Uchiten Shrine within Atsuta Shrine. Both the *Senden shūi* and *Gyōfūshū* were preserved in the Uchiten Shrine; they outline Sino-Japanese relations in the early Tang era from the reigns of Gaozong (628–83) to Xuanzong. When the early Tokugawa

Confucian-Shintoist Hayashi Razan wrote *Honchō jinjakō*, he used the *Gyōfūshū* as a reference. Although Razan introduced the myth about Yang being a manifestation of Atsuta Myōjin, he did not believe it.

27.   Quoted in Katō Kei, *Yōkihi hyōchaku densetsu no nazo* [The Mystery about the Drifting and Landing of Yang Guifei] (Tokyo: Jijūkokuminsha, 1987), p. 31.

28.   Watase Junko, "Atsuta no Yōkihi densetsu: *Soga monogatari* makini Gensō kōtei no koto o tansho to shite" [The Yang Guifei Legend in Atsuta: As Seen from the Second Scroll of *Soga Monogatari*, "Gensō kōtei no koto"], *Nihon bungaku* 54, no. 12 (December 2005): 21–29.

29.   Ichiko Teiji and Ōshima Takehiko, annot., *Soga monogatari* 2 (Tokyo: Iwanami shoten, 1966), p. 108.

30.   Kamichikama Shrine was officially dedicated to the worship of Otoyo-no-Mikoto, the governing deity of Owari.

31.   Hanawa Hokiichi, ed., *Gunsho ruijū* 11 (Tokyo: Keizai shinbunsha, 1892), p. 1007.

32.   Tani Sōboku, *Tōgoku kikō* [Records of My Travel to Eastern Provinces; 1544], *Gunsho ruijū, Kikōbu* [Collection of Books by Catalogue, Travels], vol. 14, scroll 340, ed. Hanawa Hokiichi (Tokyo: Nihon bunka shiryō sentā, 1983), p. 3.

33.   Kiyohara Nobukata, *Chōgonka narabini Biwagyō hisho* [Secret Commentary on the "Chang hen ge" and "Pipaxing"], p. 54, Kyoto University Library image database, http://edb.kulib.kyoto-u.ac.jp/exhibit/ca8/image/ca8shf/ca8sh0028.html.

34.   Izawa Banryō, *Kōeki zokusetsuben*, annot. Shiraishi Toshio (Tokyo: Heibonsha, 1989), p. 35. Banryū himself did not believe in this legend.

35.   The authorship of the *Biyō zakki* remains controversial; candidates include Mizuno Sadanobu, Mizuno Moritoshi, and Mizuno Tōshū. The author did not express his own position on this story.

36.   Hayashi Razan, *Honchō jinjakō, Jinjakō shōsetsu* (Tokyo: Gendai shichōsha, 1980), p. 181.

37.   Amano, *Shiojiri*, in *Nihon zuihitsu taisei*, ser. 3, vol. 15, p. 161.

38.   Naitō Tōho, *Chōshū zasshi* [Miscellaneous Notes on Owari; 1770–78] (Nagoya: Atsuta jingū kyūchō, 1969), p. 3.

39.   Yokoyama Shigeru, annot., *Ko jōruri shōhonshū* 3 [Original Scripts of Old Jōruri, vol. 3] (Tokyo: Kadokawa shoten, 1964), play 4, pt. 4.

40.   See Masako Nakagawa Graham, "The Consort and the Warrior: Yokihi Monogatari," *Monumenta Nipponica* 45, no. 1 (Spring 1990): 1–26.

41.   Yokoyama, annot., *Ko jōruri shōhonshū* 3:312–13.

42.   Ibid. This story is contradicted by the historical record, as Bai Juyi was born ten years after the death of Emperor Xuanzong. Masako Nakagawa Graham believes that this plot borrowed from the medieval *nō* drama, *Haku Rakuten* by Zeami Motokiyo (c. 1363–c. 1443). In the drama, Bai leads troops to Japan and has a heated debate with Sumiyoshi Myōjin, the god of Japanese poetry. He returns to China after losing the debate. See Graham, *The Yang Kuei-fei Legend in Japanese Literature*, pp. 173, 237.

43.   Asai Ryōi, *Yōkihi monogatari*, in *Yōkihi monogatari, Koten bunko* 478, annot. Kurashima Toshihisa (Tokyo: Koten bunkō, 1986), pp. 127–29.

44.   Quoted in Kondō, *Chōgonka Biwagyō no kenkyū*, p. 162.

45.   Quoted in Torii Fumiko, "Tosa jōruri no kyakushoku–hō, 10, Tō no Gensō" [The Adaptation of Tosa Jōruri for the Stage (10) Xuanzong of the Tang], *Tōkyō joshi daigaku kiyō ronshū* 38, no. 2 (March 1988): 47–71.

46.   Ki Kaion, *Gensō kōtei hōrai tsuru*, in *Nihon shomin bunka shiryō shūsei* 7, *Ningyō jōruri*, ed. Geinōshi kenkyūkai (Tokyo: Sanichi shobō, 1975), p. 636.

47.   Regarding *honji suijaku*, see Murayama Shūichi, *Honji suijaku* (Tokyo: Yoshikawa kōbunkan, 1974).

48.   Takafuji Harutoshi, "Honji suijaku setsu no tenkai o megutte: Shinpon shinjaku setsu kara shinpon butsujaku setsu he" [On the Development of the *Honji Suijaku* Theory: From *Shinpon Shinjaku* to *Shinpon Butsujaku*], *Shintōgaku*, no. 113 (May 1982): 1–31.

49.   Song Lian, *Luoshanji*, scroll 4, quoted in Liu Yuzhen, "Yang Guifeng," in *Rizhong wenhua jiaoliushi congshu* 10, *renwu*, ed. Nakanishi Susumu and Wang Yong [Book Series on the History of Sino-Japanese Cultural Interaction, vol. 10, Historical Figures] (Tokyo: Taishūkan shoten, 1996), p. 417. Yuhuan was another name for Yang.

50.   Ōsen Keisan, *Shōho enshi* [A Revision to Love Poems], quoted in Yoshizawa Katsuhiro, "Sennōka: Muromachi bunka no yokō" [Sennōka: The Remaining Glory of the Muromachi Culture], *Kikan Zenbunka*, no. 187 (2003): 150.

51.   Shinozaki Tōkai, *Narubeshisanchū, Nihon zuihitsu taisei*, ser. 2, vol. 15, ed. Nihon zuihitsu taisei henshūbu (Tokyo: Yoshikawa kōbunkan, 1974), p. 87.

52.   Wai-ming Ng, *The I Ching in Tokugawa Thought and Culture* (Honolulu: University of Hawai'i Press, 2000), pp. 106–13.

CHAPTER 3

1.   The family name of Taibo was not Wu, but Ji. Regarded as the ancestor of the Wu regime in southern China, however, he is commonly referred to as Wu Taibo in Chinese sources.

2.   Confucius, in the *Lunyu*, regarded him as one of the two perfect sages. He praised him, saying, "Tai Bo achieved the ultimate virtue, having abandoned the throne three times. People could not find the right words to praise him." Translated from Mao Zishui, annot., *Lunyu jinzhu jinyi* [Modern Commentary on the *Lunyu*] (Taipei: Shangwu yinshuguan, 2009), p. 112. Sima Qian, in the *Shiji*, listed Taibo at the top of thirty prominent houses. Zhu Xi, in his commentary on the *Lunyu*, lauded Taibo for achieving the ultimate virtue: "The virtue of Taibo, in the Shang and Zhou periods, was good enough to make the nobles surrender and to rule the nation. He gave up the opportunity and left. How absolute his virtue was!" Translated from Zhu Xi, *Sishi zhangju jizhu* [Commentary on the Four Books] (Beijing: Zhinghua shuju, 1983), p. 108.

3.   The quotations are translated from Wada Sei and Ishihara Michihiro, annot., *Gishi wajinden, gokanjo waden, sōsho wakokuden, zuisho wakokuden* [Japan in Wei, Late Han, Song, and Sui Histories] (Tokyo: Iwanami shoten, 1951), pp. 19, 92.

4.   Kitabatake Chikafusa, *Shinchū jinnō shōtōki* [A New Commentary on the *Jinnō shōtōki*], annot. Saitō Jinnosuke (Tokyo: Aoyamadō shobō, 1927), pp. 45–46.

5.   *Shinsen shōjiroku, Gunsho ruijū* 17, ed. Hanawa Hokiichi (Tokyo: Keizaizasshisha, 1894), p. 196. The *Shinsen shōjiroku* was compiled at the order of the Nara court, following the style of the *Shizuzhi* (Records of Families) by Gao Shilian (575–647). Of the 1,182 clans listed in the book, about one-fourth, or more precisely 326, originated in China and Korea. Some claimed to be the descendants of Chinese emperors such as Hata (Qin Shi Huang, the first Qin emperor), Uzumasa Kimi (the grandson of Qin Shi Huang), Bun (Han Gaozu), and Musa (Sun Quan, the first emperor of the state of Wu).

6.   Kuroita Katsumi, ed., *Shinteizōho kokushi taikei* 8 [Series on National History, New Edition, vol. 8] (Tokyo: Yoshikawa kōbunkan, 1965), p. 11.

7.   Yamaguchi Kamekichi, ed., *Yabataishi senjimon benkai taizen* [A Complete Explanation of "Yabataishi" in One Thousand Words] (Tokyo: Senshodō, 1894), p. 10.

8.   Urabe Kanekata, *Shaku Nihongi, Kokushi taikei* 7 [Series on National History, vol. 7], ed. Nihon keizaisha (Tokyo: Keizai zasshisha, 1901), p. 521.

9.   See Mark J. Hudson, *Ruins of Identity: Ethnogenesis in the Japanese Islands* (Honolulu: University of Hawai'i Press, 1999), p. 25.

10.   Quoted in Ono Takakiyo, *Hyakusōro* [Dew of the Hundred Plants], *Nihon zuihitsu taisei* [Anthology of Japanese Prose Writings], ser. 3, vol. 11, ed. Nihon zuihitsu taisei henshūbu (Tokyo: Yoshikawa kōbunkan, 1978), p. 82.

11.   The theory of Taibo as the ancestor of the Japanese was widespread in the early decades of the Tokugawa period. Even foreigners heard about this theory in Japan. For instance, Fukansai Habian (1565–1621) and Joao Rodrigues (1561–1634) mentioned it in their writings.

12.   Fujiwara Seika, *Baison saihitsu* [Writings in the Plum Village], *Nihon zuihitsu taisei*, ser. 1, vol. 1, ed. Nihon zuihitsu taisei henshūbu (Tokyo: Yoshikawa kōbunkan, 1975), p. 4.

13.   Hayashi Razan, *Razan bunshū* 25 [Collected Essays of Hayashi Razan, vol. 25], *Nihon zuihitsu taisei*, ser. 3, vol. 11, ed. Nihon zuihitsu taisei henshūbu (Tokyo: Yoshikawa kōbunkan, 1977), p. 40.

14.   Ibid., p. 41.

15.   Ibid., pp. 40–41.

16.   Modified from Tsunoda Ryūsaku, William Theodore de Bary, and Donald Keene, eds., *Sources of Japanese Tradition* (New York: Columbia University Press, 1958), p. 359.

17.   See Yamamoto Shichihei, *Arahitogami no sōsakushatachi* [The Creators of the Living God] (Tokyo: Bungei shunjū, 1983), p. 21.

18.   For instance, in his article "Taihaku" (Taibo), Razan criticized the Taibo legend from a Shinto perspective: "Confucius said that Taibo achieved the ultimate virtue. Later generations saw our nation as his descendants, praising us as the Nation of Ji in the Eastern Sea. How ridiculous they were! Our nation is the nation of deities. Why must we regard him as our ancestor?" In Kyōto shisekikai, ed., *Hayashi Razan bunshū* 36 (Kyoto: Kyōto shisekikai 1930), p. 11.

19.   See *Razan bunshū, in Kojiruien, seimeibu* 47 [Dictionary of Ancient Matters, Section on Names, vol. 47], ed. Kojiruien kankōkai (Tokyo: Kojiruien kankōkai, 1932), p. 411; also John S. Brownlee, *Japanese Historians and the National Myths, 1600–1945: The Age of the Gods and Emperor Jinmu* (Vancouver: University of British Columbia Press, 1997), pp. 25–27.

20.   See Sakamoto Tarō, *Shūshi to shigaku* [Compilation of History and Historiography] (Tokyo: Yoshikawa kōbunkan, 1989), p. 226; Noguchi Takehiko, *Edo no rekishika* [Historians in Edo Japan] (Tokyo: Chikuma shobō, 1979), pp. 30–36; and Hori Isao, *Hayashi Razan* (Tokyo: Yoshikawa kōbunkan, 1964), pp. 366–73.

21.   Hayashi Gahō, *Honchō tsugan enpenbatsu* (Afterword for the First Half of the *Honchō tsugan*), quoted in Tokutomi Iichirō, *Kindai Nihon kokumin: Tokugawa bakufu kamiki gekan shisōhen* [History of Modern Japanese: The First Stage of the Tokugawa Bakufu, Pt. 2: Thought] (Tokyo: Meiji shoin, 1936), p. 505. Shaokang was the sixth emperor of the Xia Dynasty. It is said that his descendants moved to Guiji and lived among the tribes in Southern China.

22.   Hayashi Gahō, *Gi taisakubun* (A Draft on Policies), quoted in Tokutomi, *Kindai Nihon kokumin: Tokugawa bakufu kamiki gekan shisōhen*, p. 499.

23.   Ibid.

24.   Ibid., pp. 500–501.

25.   Ibid., p. 501.

26.   Ibid., p. 502.

27.   Kinoshita Junan, *Taihakuron*, in *Zokuzoku gunsho ruijū* 13 [Classified Anthology of Books, Sequel 2, vol. 13] (Tokyo: Kokusho kankōkai, 1909), p. 190.

28.   Muro Kyūsō, "Yusa Jirō Zaemon ni kotafuru daisansho" [Third Reply to Yusa Jirō], *Nihon shisō taikei* 34 *Kaibara Ekken, Muro Kyūsō*, ed. Araki Kengo and Inoue Tadashi (Tokyo: Iwanami shoten, 1970), p. 246.

29.   Hori Keizan, *Fujingen* [Words Unexpressed], *Shin Nihon koten bungaku taikei* 99 (Anthology of Classical Japanese Literature, New Edition, vol. 99), ed. Hino Tatsuo (Tokyo: Iwanami shoten, 2000), p. 197.

30.   For instance, Rokumon Mochitsuki (1697–1769), a *kogaku* (ancient learning) scholar who studied under Hattori Nankaku (1683–1759), believed that Taibo and his people came to Japan in ancient times to disseminate the way of the sages. See Rokumon Mochitsuki, *Rokumon zuihitsu* [The Prose

Works of Rokumon], *Nihon geirin sōsho* 2 [Anthology of Writings by Japanese scholars, vol. 2], ed. Hamano Chizaburō et al. (Tokyo: Rokugōkan, 1928), p. 45.

31.   Their discussions of Taibo can be found in the following texts: Nakae Tōju, *Okina mondō* [Questions from an Old Man], *Nihon shisō taikei* 29, *Nakae Tōju*, ed. Yamashita Yū and Bitō Masahide (Tokyo: Iwanami shoten, 1974), p. 143; Kumazawa Banzan, *Miwa monogatari* [The Tale of Miwa], *Nihon tetsugaku zensho* 4, *Shintōhen, Jukyōhen*, ed. Saigusa Hiroto (Tokyo: Daiichi shobō, 1936), pp. 141–58; Kumazawa Banzan, *Genji monogatari Banzan shō* [Commentary on the *Genji monogatari* by Banzan] (Tokyo: Kogeisha, 1935).

32.   Kumazawa, *Miwa monogatari*, p. 155.

33.   Ibid., pp. 147–55.

34.   Ibid., 156. Modified from James McMullen's translation of Banzan's commentary on the *Genji monogatari*, in *Sources of Japanese Tradition* Part 2, comp. William Theodore de Bary et al. (New York: Columbia University Press, 2001), pp. 420–21.

35.   Kumazawa Banzan, *Kōkyō shōkai* [Simple Explanation of *The Classic of Filial Piety*], in *Kōkyō daigaku chūyō rongo* 1, ed. Waseda daigaku shuppanbu (Tokyo: Waseda daigaku shuppanbu, 1926), p. 31.

36.   Tō Teikan, *Shōkōhatsu* [On the Tip of My Tongue; 1781], pp. 3–4, digital collection of Waseda University, request no. ﾉ05_05003.

37.   Yamazaki Ansai, *Taihakuron, Shushigaku taikei* 12, *Chōsen no Shushigaku, Nihon no Shushigaku* [Series on the Zhu Xi School, vol. 12, The Zhu Xi School in Korea; The Zhu Xi School in Japan], ed. Kobayashi Hideo (Tokyo: Meitoku shuppansha, 1977), pp. 179–80. Ansai's explanation of Jishiguo was borrowed from Ichijō Kanera's *Nihon shoki sanso*.

38.   Quoted in Kurokawa Dōyū, *Enpekiken ki, Nihon zuihitsu taisei*, ser. 1, vol. 10, (Tokyo: Yoshikawa kōbunkan, 1975), p. 11.

39.   Ono, *Hyakusōro*, p. 42.

40.   Ibid.

41.   See Nishi Junzō and Maruyama Masao, annot., *Nihon shisō taikei* 31, *Yamazaki Ansai gakuha* (Tokyo: Iwanami shoten, 1980), pp. 204–10, 214–27.

42.   Asami Keisai, *Kōyūsō furoku* [Appendix to the *Juyou cao*], in ibid., p. 206.

43.   Andō Tameakira, *Nenzan kibun* [Records of Hearsay by Nenzan], in Ono, *Hyakusōro*, pp. 39–40. The same story was also told in Tachihara Suiken's

Seizan ibun (Hearings of Seizan) and Komiyayama Fūken's *Mito Gikō nenbu* (The Chronicles of Gikō of Mito Domain).

44.   Fujita Tōko, *Kōdōkan kijutsugi* [Records of Kōdōkan], in *Tōko zenshū* [Complete Works of Tōko], ed. Kikuchi Kenjirō (Tokyo: Hakubunkan, 1940), pp. 175–76.

45.   It is said that Mitsukuni was not well-behaved in his adolescence. Having read the story of Wu Taibo in the *Shiji* at the age of seventeen, he decided to live a moral life. See Kate Nakai, "Tokugawa Confucian Historiography: The Hayashi, Early Mito School and Arai Hakuseki," in *Confucianism and Tokugawa Culture*, ed. Peter Nosco (Princeton, NJ: Princeton University Press, 1984), pp. 74–75.

46.   Asaka Tanpaku, *Tōgen iji*, in *Gikō sōsho* [Collection of Gikō], ed. Chiba Shinji (Sendai: Hayakawa kappanjo, 1909), p. 45.

47.   In Ono, *Hyakusōro*, p. 83.

48.   Ibid.

49.   Arai Hakuseki, *Koshitsū*, *Nihon no meicho* 15 *Arai Hakuseki* [Japanese Classics, vol. 15, Arai Hakuseki], ed. Kuwabara Takeo (Tokyo: Chūō kōronsha, 1969), p. 260.

50.   Arai Hakuseki, *Koshitsū* (Tokyo: Shōzandō, 1871), p. 8.

51.   Arai Hakuseki, *Koshitsū wakumon* [Questions Regarding the *Koshitsū*], *Nihon no meicho* 15, *Arai Hakuseki*, p. 291.

52.   Ise Sadatake, *Ansai zuihitsu* 1, ed. Imaizumi Teisuke (Tokyo: Yoshikawa kōbunkan, 1929), p. 243.

53.   Ibid., p. 401.

54.   Yamaga Sokō, *Chūchō jujitsu* [The True Facts Concerning the Central Kingdom], in *Yamaga Sokō zenshū* 13 [Complete Works of Yamaga Sokō, vol. 13] (Tokyo: Iwanami shoten, 1941), p. 370.

55.   Ibid., p. 366.

56.   Nishikawa Joken, *Nihon suidokō*, in *Nishikawa Joken isho* 9 [The Testament of Nishikawa Joken, vol. 9], ed. Nishikawa Tadasuke (Tokyo: Nishikawa Tadasuke, 1907), p. 4.

57.   Ogyū Sorai, *Benmei* [Distinguishing Names], *Nihon shisō taikei* 36, *Ogyū Sorai*, annot. Yoshikawa Kōjirō (Tokyo: Iwanami shoten, 1973), p. 572.

58.   Ogyū Sorai, *Kenen zatsuwa* [Conversations at Kenen], 74, digital collection of Waseda University Library, request no. イ17 02304.

59.   Seiō, *Kochōan zuihitsu*, *Nihon zuihitsu taisei*, ser. 2, vol. 17, ed. Nihon zuihitsu taisei henshūbu (Tokyo: Yoshikawa kōbunkan, 1974), p. 142.

60.   Yamagata Bantō, *Yume no shiro*, *Nihon keizai sōsho* 25, ed. Takimoto Seiichi (Tokyo: Nihon keizai sōsho kankōkai, 1931), p. 218. The translation is modified from Brownlee, *Japanese Historians and the National Myths, 1600–1945: The Age of the Gods and Emperor Jinmu*, p. 52.

61.   Motoori Norinaga, *Kenkyōjin*, in *Motoori Norinaga zenshū* 5 [Complete Collection of Motoori Norinaga, vol. 5], annot. Motoori Toyokai (Tokyo: Yoshikawa kōbunkan, 1926), p. 529.

62.   In Ono, *Hyakusōro*, p. 42.

63.   In the Tokugawa period, for example, places claiming some Xu Fu legacy could be found across the whole of Japan, with the exception of Hokkaido. See Yamamoto Noritsuna, *Nihon ni ikiru Jofuku no denshō* [The Transmission of the Xu Fu Legend in Japan] (Tokyo: Kenkōsha, 1979). There are only two places in Japan that claimed to have Taibo's legacies. Morotsukayama (also named Mount Taibo) in Hyūga (now Miyazaki Prefecture) has a Taibo tomb and Kagoshima Shrine in Kirishima worships Taibo. The origins of their Taibo worship remain unknown.

64.   Chang Kun-chiang, "Riben Dechuan shidai shenru jianshe xuezhe dui shendao rudao de jieshi tese" [The Characteristics of Confucian-Shintoist Thinkers' Interpretations of Confucianism and Shintoism in Tokugawa Japan], *Taida wenshi zhexuebao* (NTU Humanitas Taiwanica), no. 58 (March 2003): 141–80.

65.   Hayashi Razan, "Yamatofu," [An Essay on Yamato; 1612], in *Hayashi Razan bunshū* 1, ed. Kyōto shisekikai (Tokyo: Perikansha, 1979), p. 1.

66.   See Watanabe Hiroshi, *Kinsei Nihon shakai to Sōgaku* (Tokyo: Tōkyō daigaku shuppankai, 1995).

CHAPTER 4

1.   Yoshida Shōin became a kind of national hero in modern Japan. Perceived and portrayed differently in the Meiji, early Shōwa, and postwar eras, he was used to promote various ideologies and political agendas. In the Meiji era (1868–1912), Tokutomi Sohō (1863–1957) wrote *Yoshida Shōin* (Tokyo: Minyūsha, 1893) to underline Shōin's role in the Meiji Restoration, praising him as a champion of the Meiji Revolution (*ishin kakumei kenji*). The study of

Shōin became a boom in the 1930s and early 1940s, when about forty books
on him were published, including such provocative works as Fukumoto Giryō's
Yoshida Shōin no saigo: Shisei junkoku [The Last Moments of Yoshida Shōin:
Dying for the Nation with Utmost Sincerity] (Tokyo: Seibundō shinkōsha,
1940) and Suyama Tsutomu's *Yoshida Shōin no seishin* [The Spirit of Yoshida
Shōin] (Tokyo: Daiichi shobō, 1941). Most works of this period served as pro-
paganda for the militarist government. Postwar studies on Shōin have been
more multidimensional, scholarly, and well balanced. About one hundred
books have been published, and some are very original and valuable, including
Morita Yoshihiko's *Heigakusha Yoshida Shōin: Senryaku jōhō bunmei* [Yoshida
Shōin as a Strategist: Strategy, Information, and Civilization] (Tokyo: Wejji,
2011) and Yamanaka Tetsuzō's *Yoshida Shōin no Shisō* [Poems by Yoshida
Shōin] (Tokuyama: Tokuyama daigaku sōgō keizai kenkyūjo, 1983).

2.   This work is also called *Kō-Mō satsuki* (Notes on the *Mencius*). For this
research, three different editions of the text have been used. Hirose Yutaka, ed.,
Kō-Mō yowa (Tokyo: Iwanami shoten, 1942) is the most important. It covers
the entire text in its original language without annotations. Naramoto Tatsuya,
ed., *Nihon no shisō* 19, *Yoshida Shōin shū* [Japanese Thought, vol. 19, Works
of Yoshida Shōin], (Tokyo: Chikuma shobō, 1969) includes selected parts of
the text in both the original language and modern translation. It also includes
valuable correspondences between Yoshida and Yamagata Taika (1781–1866),
a Chōshū Confucian. Matsumoto Sannosuke, ed., *Nihon no meicho* 31, *Yoshida
Shōin* [Famous Writings of Japan, vol. 31, Yoshida Shōin] (Tokyo: Chūō
kōronsha, 1973) contains a modern translation of selected parts of the text.

3.   The terms *sonnō jōi*, *tennōsei*, and *bushidō* are commonly used by
modern Japanese scholars to discuss the Tokugawa and prewar Japanese discourses, and were not actually used by Yoshida Shōin and late Tokugawa Japanese. Shōin only used *kokutai* and *shidō* in his writings.

4.   See Huang Jun-jie, *Mengxue sixiang shilun* [Historical Discourse on
Mencian Thought] (Taipei: Institute of Chinese Literature and Philosophy,
Academia Sinica, 1997), pp. 13–53, 394.

5.   Tai Chen (1724–77), Chong Yagyong (1762–1836), and Kang Youwei
(1858–1927) also used the *Mencius* to express their own political ideas, but they
cannot compare with Yoshida Shōin in terms of level of appropriation of the text.

6.   For a historical overview of Mencian studies before the Tokugawa era,
see Inoue Junri, *Honpō chūsei made ni okeru Mōshi juyō shi no kenkyū* [A Study

of the Reception of the *Mencius* in Japan through the Medieval Period] (Tokyo: Kasama shobō, 1972).

7.   See Fukushima Kashizō, ed., *Kinsei Nihon no jugaku* [Confucianism in Early Modern Japan] (Tokyo: Iwanami shoten, 1939), pp. 1141–43.

8.   Inoue Junri, "Kinsei hōjin senjutsu Mōshi chūshakusho mokuroku" [Index of Commentaries on the *Mencius* by Early Modern Japanese], in *Tōyōgaku ronshū* [Collected Articles on East Asian Studies], ed. Ikeda Suetoshi hakushi koki kinen jigyōkai (Hiroshima: Ikeda Suetoshi hakushi koki kinen jigyōkai, 1980), pp. 903–42.

9.   Seo Kunio, ed., *Kōshi Mōshi ni kansuru bunken mokuroku* [List of Documents concerning Confucius and Mencius] (Tokyo: Hakuteisha, 1992).

10.   The most popular Confucian classics in the Tokugawa period were the *Yijing* and the *Lunyu*. For example, there were at least 1,085 Tokugawa commentaries on the *Yijing* by 416 authors. See Wai-ming Ng, *The I Ching in Tokugawa Thought and Culture* (Honolulu: University of Hawai'i Press, 2000), p. 23.

11.   According to the Ming text *Wuzazu* (Five Assorted Offerings), Tokugawa book dealers believed that any ship bringing the *Mencius* to Japan would sink. See Warren Smith, *Confucianism in Modern Japan: A Study of Conservatism in Japanese Intellectual History* (Tokyo: Hokuseido Press, 1973), p. 141. This idea was denied by Tsukada Taihō (1745–1832).

12.   See Inoue, *Honpō chūsei made ni okeru Mōshi juyōshi no kenkyū*, p. 513.

13.   See Che Xing-jian, "Shanjing ding jingji jiaokan de wenxian pingjie" [The Sources that Yamanoi Kanae Used in His Textual Criticism], *Jingxue yanjiu luncong* [Studies on the Chinese Classics] 1 (April 1994): 323–46.

14.   See Ōba Osamu, *Edo jidai no Nit-Chū hiwa* [Unknown Sino-Japanese Tales of the Edo Period] (Tokyo: Tōhō shoten, 1980), pp. 157–58.

15.   For a discussion of Jinsai's and Riken's interpretations of the *Mencius*, see Huang, *Mengxue sixiang shilun*, pp. 241–63; and Chun-chieh Huang, "Nakai Riken's Interpretation of the *Mencius*," in *The Book of Mencius and Its Reception in China and Beyond*, ed. Chun-chieh Huang, Gregor Paul, and Heiner Roetz (Wiesbaden, Germany: Harrassowitz Verlag, 2008), pp. 117–45.

16.   See Tetsuo Najita, *Visions of Virtue in Tokugawa Japan: The Kaitokudō Merchant Academy of Osaka* (Chicago: University of Chicago Press, 1987), pp. 25–36, 88. See also Robert N. Bellah, *Tokugawa Religion: The Values of Pre–Industrial Japan* (New York: Free Press, 1957), p. 160.

17.   Tokugawa scholars read the *Mencius* in the context of the political reality of their own time and place. One can find a parallel in Song scholars. See Wolfgang Ommerborn, "Mencius Theory of Renzheng (Human Politics) and Its Reception in the Song Dynasty," in Huang et al., *The Book of Mencius and Its Reception in China and Beyond*, pp. 21–36.

18.   Scholars of the Kimon school did not completely deny the political value of the *Mencius*. They only attacked those ideas that they deemed as going against Japan's political traditions and Suika Shintō. Their extensive writings on the text include Yamazaki Ansai's (1618–82) *Mōshi shūchū josetsu* (Introduction to the *Meng–tzu chi–chu*; 1667), Asami Keisai's (1652–1711) *Mōshi kōgi* (Lectures on the *Mencius*), and Miyake Shōsai's (1662–1741) *Mōshi hikki* (Notes on the *Mencius*).

19.   Certain Zhu Xi scholars defended the *Mencius* in a roundabout manner. They argued that Dazai misread the *Mencius* and wrongly accused Mencius for ideas that he did not advocate. Yabu Kosan (1735–1802) criticized Dazai's *Mōshiron* in his *Sū Mō* (Revering Mencius; 1775). Nakayama Jōsan (1763–1837) and Hattori Rissai (1736–1800) wrote commentaries on the *Sū Mō*. They are included in Rai Tsutomu, annot., *Nihon shisō taikei 37, Sorai gakuha* (Tokyo: Iwanami shoten, 1972), pp. 356–80. See also Chang Kun-chiang, *Riben Dechuan shidai guxuepai zhi wangdao zhengzhi lun* [The Concept of the Kingly Way in the School of Ancient Learning in Tokugawa Japan] (Taipei: Taiwan daxue chuban zhongxin, 2004), pp. 195–97.

20.   See Yoshida, *Kō-Mō yowa* (Tokyo: Iwanami shoten, 1942), pp. 251, 322–23, 326.

21.   Ibid., p. 38.

22.   In Naramoto Tatsuya, ed., *Yoshida Shōin shū* (Tokyo: Chikuma shobō, 1969), p. 377.

23.   Yoshida, *Kō-Mō yowa*, pp. 151, 322–23.

24.   Shōin quoted the writings of some Kimon school scholars in the *Kō-Mō yowa*, but did not mention Dazai's *Mōshiron*. Nevertheless, the *Mōshiron* was a popular text, and it is likely that Shōin had read it.

25.   Scholars of the Kimon school discussed this topic at length. With the exception of Satō Naokata (1639–1719) and Miyake Shōsai, they disapproved of the Mencian concept of revolution, insisting that the subject had to obey the emperor even when the latter was a tyrant. See Nishi Junzō et al., annot.,

Nihon shisō taikei 31, *Yamazaki Ansai gakuha* (Tokyo: Iwanami shoten, 1980), pp. 200–242.

26. Dazai Shundai, *Mōshiron, Nihon shisō taikei* 37, *Sorai gakuha*, p. 153.

27. Yoshida, *Kō-Mō yowa*, pp. 159–60.

28. See Dazai, *Mōshiron, Nihon shisō taikei* 37, *Sorai gakuha*, pp. 153–56.

29. Naramoto, ed., *Yoshida Shōin shū*, pp. 271–72.

30. Noguchi Takehiko classifies Yoshida Shōin into the Wang Yangming school and regards Satō Issai's *Mōshi rangaisho* and Shōin's *Kō-Mō yowa* as the two representative commentaries on the *Mencius* of this school. See Noguchi Takehiko, "Edo Yōmeigaku to Mōshi" [Wang Yangming Studies in the Edo Period and the *Mencius*], *Bungaku* 49, no. 2 (1981): 97.

31. Yoshida, *Kō-Mō yowa*, pp. 217–18.

32. Ibid., p. 5.

33. Ibid., pp. 94–95.

34. Ibid., p. 314.

35. Ibid., pp. 360–62.

36. Naramoto, ed., *Yoshida Shōin shū*, pp. 271–72.

37. Yoshida, *Kō-Mō yowa*, p. 44.

38. Naramoto, ed., *Yoshida Shōin shū*, pp. 243.

39. Yoshida, *Kō-Mō yowa*, p. 134.

40. Naramoto, ed., *Yoshida Shōin shū*, p. 305.

41. Yoshida, *Kō-Mō yowa*, p. 21.

42. Shōin repeated the same idea in the *Yūshitsu bunkō* (Dark Room Manuscript; 1857): "Suppose that in our country our emperor oppresses us as King Jie of the Xia Dynasty and King Zhou of the Shang Dynasty have done. We can do nothing but offer our heads to them." Translation is modified from Henry van Straelen, *Yoshida Shōin: Forerunner of the Meiji Restoration* (Leiden: Brill, 1952), p. 87.

43. Yoshida, *Kō-Mō yowa*, p. 196.

44. Ibid., pp. 138–39.

45. Ibid., pp. 157–58.

46. Yoshida Shōin, *Noyama bunkō, Dai–Nippon shisō zenshū* 17, *Yoshida Shōin shū, Sakuma Shōzan shū*, ed. Uemura Katsuya (Tokyo: Dai–Nippon shisō zenshū kankōkai, 1932), p. 104.

47. Yoshida, *Kō-Mō yowa*, p. 90.

48. Naramoto, ed., *Yoshida Shōin shū*, p. 277.

49.   Yoshida, *Kō-Mō yowa*, p. 105.

50.   Ibid., pp. 331–33. For discussions of the Mencian concept of revolution in the Tokugawa period, see Noguchi Takehiko, *Ōdō to kakumei no aida: Nihon shisō to Mōshi mondai* [Between the Kingly Way and Revolution: Japanese Thought and Issues in the *Mencius*] (Tokyo: Chikuma shobō, 1986); and John Tucker, "Two Mencian Political Notions in Tokugawa Japan," *Philosophy East and West* 47, no. 2 (April 1997): 233–53.

51.   Yoshida, *Kō-Mō yowa*, p. 47.

52.   The separation of sovereignty and governance was considered a feature of Japan's *kokutai* among many Tokugawa intellectuals. Yoshida Shōin was not unique in this respect. For instance, Hayashi Razan applied the Mencian ideas of mandate of heaven and revolution to justify the founding of the Edo *bakufu* from the perspective of the right to govern. See Tucker, "Two Mencian Political Notions in Tokugawa Japan," pp. 237–38.

53.   See Kawakami Tetsutarō, *Yoshida Shōin: Bu to ju ni yoru ningenzō* [Yoshida Shōin: His Life as a Samurai and Confucian] (Tokyo: Bungei-shunjū, 1968), p. 92; Guo Lian-you, "Mengzi sixiang zai Riben" [Mencian Thought in Japan], *Zhong–Ri wenhua jiaoliushi daxi* 3, *Sixiang juan* (Series on Sino-Japanese Cultural Interchange, vol. 3: Thought), ed. Yan Shaodang and Minamoto Ryōen (Hangzhou: Zhejiang renmin chubanshe, 1996), p. 352.

54.   Yoshida, *Kō-Mō yowa*, pp. 118, 140.

55.   Ibid., pp. 234–35, 238, 301–2.

56.   Ibid., pp. 330–31.

57.   Ibid., p. 47.

58.   Ibid., p. 312.

59.   Naramoto, ed., *Yoshida Shōin shū*, p. 320.

60.   Yoshida, *Kō-Mō yowa*, pp. 77–78. Shōin also attacked the *bakufu* for being arrogant and wasteful, for not using talented people, and for not reducing taxation and punishments. He quoted the *Mencius* to ask the *bakufu* and the *daimyō* to carry out political, economic, and military reforms based on the politics of benevolence. See *Kō-Mō yowa*, pp. 178, 242, 148–49.

61.   Naramoto, ed., *Yoshida Shōin shū*, p. 345.

62.   Hayashi Razan and Muro Kyūsō (1658–1734) also used the *Mencius* to expound upon *bushidō*. See Tucker, "Two Mencian Political Notions in Tokugawa Japan," pp. 237–39.

63. Regarding the making of Shōin's *shishi* vision, see Thomas M. Huber, *The Revolutionary Origins of Modern Japan* (Stanford, CA: Stanford University Press, 1981), pp. 57–58.

64. Yoshida, *Kō-Mō yowa*, p. 339.

65. Ibid., p. 101.

66. Ibid., p. 101. The translation is modified from D. C. Lau, trans., *Mencius* (London: Penguin, 1970), p. 106.

67. Yoshida, *Kō-Mō yowa*, p. 336.

68. Ibid., p. 23.

69. Ibid., p. 193.

70. Ibid., pp. 111–12.

71. The *bakufu* at first had no plan to execute him, but Shōin revealed his plot to assassinate *bakufu* officials. See Albert M. Craig, *Chōshū in the Meiji Restoration* (Cambridge, MA: Harvard University Press, 1961), p. 162.

72. Yoshida Shōin, *Tōkō zen nikki* [Dairy of my Trip to the East], in *Yoshida Shōin zenshū* 9 [Complete Collection of Yoshida Shōin, vol. 9], ed. Yamaguchigen kyōikukai (Tokyo: Daiwa shobō, 1974), p. 574.

73. See Matsumoto Sannosuke, "Shisōka to shite no Yoshida Shōin" [Yoshida Shōin as a Thinker], *Nihon no meicho* 31, *Yoshida Shōin*, p. 8; and Chō Sobai, "Yoshida Shōin no ningenron" [Yoshida Shōin's View of Humanity], *Kikan Nihon shisō shi* 44 (1992): 104–26.

74. Yoshida, *Kō-Mō yowa*, p. 36. Modified from D. C. Lau, trans., *Mencius*, p. 58.

75. Yoshida, *Kō-Mō yowa*, pp. 60–63.

76. Ibid., p. 267.

77. Albert Craig believes that, more than any other figure, Shōin was responsible for the formation of *sonnō* ideology. See Craig, *Chōshū in the Meiji Restoration*, p. 162.

78. According to Chang Kun-chiang, Shōin replaced the space and time of Mencius and the *Mencius* with his own; in Shōin's hand it was no long the Chinese original, but the Japanese edition in the spirit of *kokutai* discourse. See his "Jitian songyin *jiangmeng yuhua* de quanshi tezhi jiqi pipan" [Interpretative Features and Criticisms of Yoshida Shōin's *Kō-Mō yowa*], *Hanxue yanjiu* 27, no. 1 (March 2009): 207–30.

79. Tanaka Akira, "Yoshida Shōin zō no hensen" [Changes in the Image of Yoshida Shōin]), *Nihon no meicho* 31, *Yoshida Shōin*, pp. 39–43.

80.   Ōba, *Edo jidai no Nit-Chū hiwa*, p. 14.

81.   See Smith, *Confucianism in Modern Japan*, pp. 141–56.

CHAPTER 5

1.   In the Meiji period, theories of *dōbun dōshu* (about Japan and China having "the same writing system and the same racial origins") emerged. In the 1950s, Kawano Rokurō (1912–98) coined the term *Kan bunka ken* (Chinese cultural sphere) to include China's neighboring countries. Kamei Takashi (1912–95) changed this into *Kanji bunka ken* (Chinese character cultural sphere). Western scholars used the term "Confucian cultural sphere" in the 1960s and 1970s. In the 1980s, it was applied to explain the economic success of Japan and the "four little dragons" (Singapore, Taiwan, South Korea, and Hong Kong).

2.   See Kate Wildman Nakai, "The Naturalization of Confucianism in Tokugawa Japan: The Problem of Sinocentrism," *Harvard Journal of Asiatic Studies* 40, no. 1 (June 1980): 157–99.

3.   For support from Japanese scholars, see Shima Kenji, *Shushigaku to Yōmeigaku* [Zhu Xi School and Wang Yangming School] (Tokyo: Iwanami shoten, 1967), pp. 28–29; Terao Yoshio, *Chūgoku bunka denrai jiten* [A Dictionary of the Importation of Chinese Culture] (Tokyo: Kawate shobō, 1982), pp. 446–48. Some Western scholars have expressed similar views. See Robert N. Bellah, *Tokugawa Religion* (New York: Free Press, 1957), p. 18; and Ruth Benedict, *The Chrysanthemum and the Sword: Patterns of Japanese Culture* (Boston: Houghton Mifflin, 1946), ch. 10, "The Dilemma of Virtue."

4.   See Nishi Shin'ichirō, *Chūkōron* [Discourse on Loyalty and Filial Piety] (Tokyo: Iwanami Shoten, 1931); Hirano Harue, *Chūkō no saikōsatsu* [A Reexamination of Loyalty and Filial Piety] (Tokyo: Shingidō shuppanbu, 1934); and Mori Shinzō, *Chūkō no shinri* [Truth about Loyalty and Filial Piety] (Tokyo: Meguro shoten, 1935). Takeuchi Yoshio (1886–1966) also supports this distinction. He adds that loyalty and filial piety have often been at odds in China, whereas they have been united in Japan. See Takeuchi Yoshio, "Jukyō hen 3" [Chapter on Confucianism, Number 3], *Takeuchi Yoshio zenshū* 4 [Complete Collection of Tekeuchi Yoshio, vol. 4] (Tokyo: Kadokawa shoten, 1979), p. 135. Regarding the formation of the *kokutai* and *tennōsei* (emperor system) discourses, see Carol Gluck, *Japan's Modern Myths: Ideology in the Late Meiji*

Period (Princeton, NJ: Princeton University Press, 1985), ch. 5; Wai-ming Ng, "Civil Morality in the Life and Thought of Inoue Tetsujirō (1855–1911)," *BC Asian Review* 9 (Winter 1995–96): 208–41.

5.　The most representative work was written by Shang Hui-peng, a professor of the University of Beijing, in his *Zhongguoren yu Ribenren: Shehui jituan, xingwei fangshi he wenhua xinli de bijiao yanjiu* [The Chinese and the Japanese: A Comparative Study of Social Organization, Behavior Patterns, and Cultural Psychology] (Beijing: Beijing daxue chubanshe, 1998). Other advocates include Cui Shiguang, Li Han, Xian Jianzhong, Chen Wenjing, and Bi Yanhong.

6.　According to Han Weizhi, the priority of loyalty and filial piety varied at different periods in China, and their respective advocates always coexisted and debated with each other. See Han Weizhi, *Shanggu wenxue zhong junchen shixiang de yanjiu* [A Study of Emperor-Minister Relations in Ancient Literature] (Shanghai: Shanghai guji chubanshe, 2006), ch. 4.

7.　Regarding this issue in Japan, see James McMullen, "Rulers or Fathers? A Casuistical Problem in Early Modern Japanese Thought," *Past and Present*, no. 116 (August 1987): 56–97; and Zhang Kunjiang, *Dechuan Riben "zhong" "xiao" gainian de xingcheng yu fazhan: Yi bingxue yu Yangming xue wei zhongxin* [The Formation and Development of the Concepts of Loyalty and Filial Piety in Tokugawa Japan: Using Military Studies and the Wang Yangming School as the Main References] (Shanghai: Huadong shifan daxue chubanshe, 2008). For its development in China, see Heiner Roetz, *Confucian Ethics of the Axial Age* (Albany: State University of New York Press, 1993), pp. 93–100.

8.　Kaji Nobuyuki and James McMullen disagree with this view. See Kaji Nobuyuki, "*Kōkyō keimō* no shomondai" [Questions about the *Kōkyō keimō*], *Nihon shisō taikei* 29 *Nakae Tōju*, annot. Yamanoi Yū and Yamashita Ryūji (Tokyo: Iwanami shoten, 1974), pp. 420, 429; and McMullen, "Rulers or Fathers?," pp. 56–97.

9.　In 1904, when the Ministry of Education launched the first batch of ethics textbooks, Nakae Tōju's life was included as one chapter in *Kōtō shōgaku shūshinsho* (Ethics Textbook for Elementary School). In prewar ethics textbooks, there were altogether seven chapters on Nakae Tōju, placing him among the eleven most frequently cited historical figures (Emperor Meiji was number one with nineteen and a half chapters). See Shiga daigaku fuzoku toshokan, ed., *Kindai Nihon no kyōkasho no ayumi: Meijiki kara gendai made* [A History of

Textbooks in Modern Japan: From the Meiji to the Present] (Hikone: Sanraizu shuppan, 2006), pp. 15–21.

10.   Regarding the appreciation of Nakae Tōju in modern Japanese scholarship, see Murai Gensai, *Ōmi seijin* [The Sage of Ōmi] (Tokyo: Hakubunkan, 1892); Uchimura Kanzō, *Daihyōteki Nihonjin* [Representatives of Japan] (Tokyo: Keiseisha shoten, 1908); and Shibata Jingorō, *Seijin Nakae Tōju* [Nakae Tōju the Sage] (Tokyo: Kōgakusha, 1937). Even now, people remain appreciative of Nakae Tōju's legacy. A museum dedicated to Tōju was built in his hometown, Takashi City of Shiga Prefecture. In 2004, the four-hundredth anniversary of his birth, a movie about him was screened, with special recommendation from the Ministry of Education, Culture, Sports, Science, and Technology.

11.   Yamanoi Yū and Yamashita, annot., *Tōju sensei nenpu, Nihon shisō taikei* 29, *Nakae Tōju*, pp. 283–84.

12.   Musaka San, annot., *Nakae Tōju bunshū* [Selected Works of Nakae Tōju] (Tokyo: Yūhōdō shoten, 1926), p. 430.

13.   Yamanoi Yū and Yamashita, annot., *Tōju sensei nenpu*, in *Nihon shisō taikei* 29, *Nakae Tōju*, p. 290.

14.   Nanzan Inshi, *Kindai seijin hyakubanashi* [The Hundred Tales of Modern Sages] (Tokyo: Daigakukan, 1910), p. 11.

15.   See Yamamoto Tsunetomo, *Hagakure*, trans. William S. Wilson (Tokyo: Kodansha, 1983), p. 109. The *Hagakure* does not take filial piety lightly. Being filial is one of the moral obligations of samurai. It stresses that, in normal times, loyalty and filial piety can coexist, but in crucial times, loyalty must come first.

16.   Matsuda Hidenao was a retainer of Hōjō Ujimasa (1538–90). He reported to Ujimasa about his father's plot in 1590. See Asami Keisai, *Chūkō ruisetsu*, pp. 1–17, digital collection of Waseda University Library, request no. イ04_00696. See also Kondō Keikō, "*Chūkō ruisetsu* no kōgai to kaisetsu" [Introduction to and Explanation of *Chūkō ruisetsu*], *Shintōshi kenkyū* 52, no. 2 (October 2004): 215–31.

17.   Nanzan, *Kindai seijin hyakubanashi*, pp. 156–57.

18.   Okada Tsuyoshi, *Tōju-sensei nenpu* (Kyoto: Yamaga Zenbei, 1893), p. 3.

19.   For instance, Zeng Shen, a disciple of Confucius, refused to accept a post so that he could look after his parents. Li Min (224–87) declined an offer from Emperor Wu of the Jin Dynasty on the grounds that he had to take care

of his grandmother. Zeng Guofan (1811–72), a Qing minister, left the battle-front to attend his mother's funeral.

20.   Zhu Shouchang's mother left him to remarry during his childhood. He later became an official of the central government. Having found clues to his mother's whereabouts, he quit his post and went to look for her in Shanxi. The *Er Shi Si Xiao* has different versions in China. One version replaced Zhu's story with Pan Yue's (247–300). Pan was a Western Jin official who quit his job to take care of his ailing mother. Tokugawa editions of the *Er Shi Si Xiao* adopted Zhu's story. See the 1646 edition (request no. ◻09_04446) and 1682 edition (request no. ◻09 04440) kept in the Waseda University's Central Library.

21.   For a review of the impact of the *Er Shi Si Xiao* on Tokugawa literature, see Tokuda Susumu, *Kōshi setsuwashū no kenkyū: Nijūshikō o chūshin ni, kinseihen* [A Study of Collected Tales of Filial Sons: Using the *Er Shi Si Xiao* as the Main Reference, Section on the Early Modern] (Tokyo: Kuresu shuppan, 2004); and Teruoka Yasutaka, "Kanshō no shiori" [Suggestions on Appreciation], in *Saikaku zenshū gendaigoyaku* 8 [Modern Translation of the Complete Collection of Saikaku, vol. 8], trans. Teruoka Yasutaka (Tokyo: Shōgakkan, 1976), pp. 214–18, 234–38.

22.   See Watanabe Hiroshi, *Kinsei Nihon shakai to Sōgaku* (Tokyo: Tōkyō daigaku shuppankai, 1985), pp. 4–6.

23.   Razan rated loyalty higher than filial piety, as he associated the former with public ethics. Having read a story in the *Mengzi* about Emperor Shun fleeing with his bloodstained father, Razan criticized Mencius for supporting Emperor Shun, who chose "private ethics at the expense of public justice." See Kyōto shisekikai, ed., *Hayashi Razan bunshū* 1 (Tokyo: Perikansha, 1979), p. 351.

24.   Nanzan, *Kindai seijin hyakubanashi*, p. 157.

25.   There were different voices within the Zhu Xi school circle. For example, Satō Naokata (1650–1719) put filial piety ahead of loyalty. See James McMullen, "Edo shoki ni okeru chū to kō no mondai ni tsuite" [Issues concerning Loyalty and Filial Piety in the Early Tokugawa Period], *Kikan Nihon shisōshi*, no. 31 (1988): 35–59.

26.   McMullen, "Rulers or Fathers?," p. 93.

27.   Asami Keisai, in his *Chūkō ruisetsu*, used eight cases of the loyalty–filial piety dilemma in Japanese and Chinese history to determine whether both virtues could be achieved at the same time. See Tajiri Yūichirō, "Riben

dui songmingxue de shourong yu bian rong" [The Adaptation and Change of Song-Ming Learning in Japan], in *Zhong-Ri wenhua jiaoliushi daxi 3 sixiang juan* [Series on the History of Sino-Japanese Cultural Interchange 3: Thought], ed. Yan Shaodang and Minamoto Ryōen (Hangzhou: Zhejiang renmin chubanshe, 1996), p. 233.

28.   His other writings about filial piety include the *Kōkyō kō* (An Investigation of the *Classic of Filial Piety*), *Kōkyō kōshaku kikigaki* (An Explanation of the *Classic of Filial Piety*), *Kana kōkyō* (*Classic of Filial Piety* in Japanese), and *Kagamigusa* (Mirror Plant).

29.   Nakae, *Okina mondō*, *Nihon shisō taikei* 29, *Nakae Tōju*, p. 25.

30.   Nakae, *Kōkyō keimō*, *Nihon shisō taikei* 29, *Nakae Tōju*, p. 257. This ritual might have been influenced by such Ming-Qing Confucians as Yu Chunxi (1553–1621) and Yang Qiyuan (1547–99). See Lu Miao–fen, "Zuowei yishixing wenben de *Xiaojing*: Ming-Qing shiren *Xiaojing* shijian de gean yanji" [The *Xiaojing* as a Ritual Text: A Case Study of the Application of the *Xiaojing* by Ming-Qing Literati], *Zhongyang yanjiuyuan jindaishi yanjiusuo jikan* [Bulletin of the Institute of Modern History, Academia Sinica] 60 (2008): 7–8.

31.   Nakae, *Okina mondō*, *Yōmeigaku taikei* 8, *Nihon no Yōmeigaku* 1 [Series on the Wang Yangming School, vol. 8, The Wang Yangming School in Japan, Pt.1] (Tokyo: Meitoku shuppansha, 1973), p. 28.

32.   Quoted in Tsunoda Ryusaku, William Theodore de Bary, and Donald Keene, eds., *Sources of Japanese Tradition* (New York: Columbia University Press, 1958), p. 375.

33.   Nakae, *Okina mondō*, in *Nihon shisō taikei* 29, *Nakae Tōju*, p. 28.

34.   Nakae, "Oku Morimura ko kikyō jo" [Farewell to Home-Returning Morimura, Preface], in *Nakae Tōju bunshū*, p. 447.

35.   Herman Ooms, *Tokugawa Ideology: Early Constructs, 1570–1680* (Princeton, NJ: Princeton University Press, 1985), p. 56.

36.   See Wai-ming Ng, *The I Ching in Tokugawa Thought and Culture* (Honolulu: University of Hawai'i Press, 2000), pp. 59–60.

37.   Ooms, *Tokugawa Ideology*, pp. 114–16.

38.   Regarding the five constant relations, the *Mengzi* places father and son ahead of emperor and minister, whereas the *Zhongyong* (The Doctrine of the Mean) reverses that order. Throughout Chinese history, most Confucians, particularly the Zhu Xi school scholars, adopted the order suggested by the *Mengzi*. See Roetz, *Confucian Ethics of the Axial Age*, p. 93.

39.   See Martin Collcutt, "The Legacy of Confucianism in Japan," in *The East Asian Region: Confucian Heritage and Its Modern Adaptation*, ed. Gilbert Rozman (Princeton, NJ: Princeton University Press, 1991), pp. 133–34. Regarding Razan's discussion of the five relations, see Maruyama Masao, *Studies in the Intellectual History of Tokugawa Japan*, trans. Mikiso Hane (Princeton, NJ: Princeton University Press, 1974), pp. 195–96, 212–13. On Ekken's view, see Mary Evelyn Tucker, *Moral and Spiritual Cultivation in Japanese Neo-Confucianism: The Life and Thought of Kaibara Ekken* (Albany: State University of New York Press, 1989), p. 404.

40.   Nakae, *Okina mondō, Nihon shisō taikei* 29, *Nakae Tōju*, p. 33.

41.   Ibid., p. 46.

42.   This theme can be found in *nō* drama. For example, a play called *Nishikido* portrays the loyalty of Izumi to Minamoto Yoshitsune (1159–89), as Izumi sacrificed his life to keep the promise he made to his father to support Yoshitsune. See Mae J. Smethurst, *Dramatic Representations of Filial Piety: Five Noh in Translation with an Introduction* (Ithaca, NY: Cornell University East Asia Program, 1998), pp. 147–63.

43.   Nakae, *Kōkyō keimō, Nihon shisō taikei* 29, *Nakae Tōju*, p. 259.

44.   Ibid., p. 190.

45.   See Bellah, *Tokugawa Religion*, pp. 90–94. *Bushidō* did not take filial piety lightly. Both the *Buke shohatto* (Regulations for Warrior Households) and *Hagakure* saw filial piety as an important virtue for the samurai. When a choice needed to be made between loyalty and filial piety, the samurai would choose loyalty.

46.   Nakae, *Kōkyō keimō, Nihon shisō taikei* 29, *Nakae Tōju*, p. 197.

47.   Ibid., p. 273.

48.   Ibid., pp. 211–18.

49.   Bellah, *Tokugawa Religion*, p. 82.

50.   Hayashi Hideichi, trans., *Kōkyō* (Tokyo: Meitoku shuppansha, 1984), p. 146, 177. With regard to the popularity and impact of the old-script edition in Tokugawa Japan, see Gu Yong-xin, "Riben chuan ben guwen *Xiaojing* hui chuan zhōngguo kao" [An Investigation of the Reverse Import of the Old-Script Edition of the *Xiaojing*], *Beijing daxue xuebao* [Journal of Peking University] 41, no. 2 (March 2004): 100–108.

51.   Nakae, *Kōkyō keimō, Nihon shisō taikei* 29, *Nakae Tōju*, p. 277.

52.   Ibid., pp. 275–76.

53.   Okada, *Tōju sensei nenpu*, *Nihon shisō taikei* 29, *Nakae Tōju*, p. 293.

54.   Nakae, "Oku Morimura ko kikyō jo," *Nakae Tōju bunshū*, p. 449.

55.   Nake, *Kōkyō keimō*, *Nihon shisō taikei* 29, *Nakae Tōju*, p. 269.

56.   See *Anshō shii Gendō ron* [On Anshō's Murder of Gendō; 1631] and *Hayash-ishi teihatsu juiben* [On Hayashi Receiving Tonsure to Acquire Official Status; 1631], *Nihon shisō taikei* 29, *Nakae Tōju*, pp. 8–17.

57.   Quoted in James McMullen, *Idealism, Protest and the Tale of Genji: The Confucianism of Kumazawa Banzan (1619–91)* (Oxford: Clarendon Press, 1999), p. 253.

58.   He simplified Chinese rites of filial piety to accommodate the customs of Japan.

59.   Morita Yasuo, *Ōshio Heihachirō to Yōmeigaku* [Ōshio Heihachirō and Wang Yangming School] (Tokyo: Izumi shoin, 2008), ch. 2; and Chang Kun-chiang, "Riben Yangming daxue Zhongjiang Tengshu yu Dayan Zhongzhai dui xiao zhi jieshi" [The Interpretations of Filial Piety by Japanese Wang Yangming School Scholars Nakae Tōju and Ōshio Heihachirō], *Taida lishi xuebao* [Bulletin of the Department of History, National Taiwan University] 29 (June 2002): 127–67.

60.   Nanzan, *Kindai seijin hyakubanashi*, p. 49.

61.   Ibid., p. 49.

CHAPTER 6

1.   Motoori Norinaga was a representative *kokugaku* scholar who built his national identity and developed his nativist ideas in opposition to Chinese culture. See Matsumoto Shigeru, *Motoori Norinaga no shisō to shinri: Aidentitī tankyū no kiseki* [The Thought and Mind of Motoori Norinaga: His Search for Identity] (Tokyo: Tōkyōdaigaku shuppankai, 1981). His *Naobi no mitama* (The Rectifying Spirit; 1771) puts Confucianism and Shinto on opposite sides. See Ogasawara Haruo, *Koku-ju ronsō no kenkyū: Naobi no mitama o kiten to shite* [A Study of the Conflict between *Kokugaku* and Confucianism: The *Naobi no mitama* as the Point of Departure] (Tokyo: Perikansha, 1988).

2.   Peter Nosco believes that, in the seventeenth century, *kokugaku* and Confucianism were basically not at odds with each other, and they only became more confrontational after the eighteenth century. He uses Kada Azumamaro (1699–1736), Kamo Mabuchi (1697–1769), and Motoori Norinaga as examples

to demonstrate this change. See Peter Nosco, *Remembering Paradise: Nativism and Nostalgia in Eighteenth-Century Japan* (Cambridge, MA: Council on East Asian Studies, Harvard University, 1990).

3.   See Chang Kun-chiang, "Riben Dechuan shidai shenru jianshe xuezhe dui shendao rudao de jieshi tese" [The Characteristics of Confucian-Shintoist Thinkers' Interpretation of Confucianism and Shintoism in Tokugawa Japan], *Taida wenshi zhexuebao* (NTU Humanitas Taiwanica), no. 58 (March 2003): 141–80. See also Herman Ooms, *Tokugawa Ideology: Early Constructs, 1570–1680* (Princeton, NJ: Princeton University Press, 1985), chs. 6–7.

4.   Wai-ming Ng, *The I Ching in Tokugawa Thought and Culture* (Honolulu: University of Hawai'i Press, 2000), ch. 6, pp. 96–113.

5.   Wai-ming Ng, "Cong *Bainaao* kan zhongshi Riben yixue de beddihua" [The Localization of *Yijing* scholarship in Medieval Japan: A Study of the *Hyakunōō*], *Xueshu yuekan*, no. 46 (2014): 162–67.

6.   Ng, *The I Ching in Tokugawa Thought and Culture*, pp. 14–15.

7.   Mabuchi and his school in Edo did not see Chinese Confucianism as something necessarily incompatible with Japanese tradition. See Mark McNally, *Proving the Way: Conflict and Practice in the History of Japanese Nativism* (Cambridge, MA: Harvard University Asia Center, 2005), p. 23. Nevertheless, Mabuchi criticized China's ancient sages for replacing natural law with human wisdom and endorsing the evil ideas of revolution and abdication of the throne. See Peter Flueckiger, *Imagining Harmony: Poetry, Empathy, and Community in Mid-Tokugawa Confucianism and Nativism* (Stanford, CA: Stanford University Press, 2011), pp. 155–65. This view had a strong impact on Norinaga. See also Nosco, *Remembering Paradise*, pp. 136–51. Azumamaro was critical of Confucianism and Chinese studies, but he employed *yin-yang wu-xing* theory to explain the *Nihon shoki*. See Nosco, *Remembering Paradise*, pp. 87, 91–93.

8.   Modified from Harry Harootunian, *Things Seen and Unseen: Discourse and Ideology in Tokugawa Nativism* (Chicago: University of Chicago Press, 1988), p. 99.

9.   Keizan was also interested in *kokugaku* and was befriended by Motoori Norinaga, Keichū (1640–1701), and Higuchi Munetake (1674–1754).

10.   Muraoka Tsunetsugu, *Motoori Norinaga* (Tokyo: Iwanami shoten, 1941), pp. 13, 21.

11.   Motoori Norinaga, *Kuzuka* [*Pueraria lobata*], in *Dai-Nippon shisō zenshū* 9, pt. 2, ed. Dai-Nippon shisō zenshū kankōkai (Tokyo: Dai-Nippon

shisō zenshū kankōkai, 1933), p. 166. Despite holding negative views of China, Norinaga read Chinese texts throughout his life.

12.   Regarding Razan and Nobuyoshi's attempts to apply the *yin-yang wu-xing* theory to explain Shinto, see Ng, *The I Ching in Tokugawa Thought and Culture*, pp. 97–98, 102–3. On Norinaga's criticism of Razan and Nobuyoshi in this regard, see Motoori Norinaga, *Kojikiden* [Commentary on the *Kojiki*], in *Shintō taikei: Ronsetsuhen 25, Fukko shintō 3, Motoori Norinaga*, annot. Umezawa Isezō and Takahashi Miyuki (Tokyo: Shintō taikei hensankai, 1982), pp. 331, 386.

13.   Motoori, *Kojikiden*, pp. 176–77; Shigeru Matsumoto, *Motoori Norinaga* (Cambridge, MA: Harvard University Press, 1970), p. 89.

14.   Motoori, *Kuzuka*, Pt. 2, p. 169.

15.   Motoori Norinaga, *Naobi no mitama*, in *Shintō taikei: Ronsetsuhen 25, fukko shintō 3, Motoori Norinaga*, pp. 17–18.

16.   Nosco, *Remembering Paradise*, pp. 186–89, 195–98. See also Susan L. Burns, *Before the Nation: Kokugaku and the Imagining of Community in Early Modern Japan* (Durham, NC: Duke University Press, 2003), pp. 95–97.

17.   Izumi Makuni, *Meidōsho* [Book to Explain the Way], *Nihon shisō taikei 51, Kokugaku undō no shisō* [The Thoughts of the Nativist Movement], annot. Haga Noboru and Matsumoto Sannosuke (Tokyo: Iwanami shoten, 1971), p. 151.

18.   Ibid., p. 186.

19.   He also wrote the *Ekikōsetsu* (An Investigation of the *Yijing*), *Ekisenkō* (An Investigation of the Divination of the *Yijing*), and *Ekisen mondō* (Questions and Answers about the *Yijing* Oracles).

20.   Ban Nobutomo, *Shūeki shiron, Ban Nobutomo zenshū 5* [Complete Writings of Ban Nobutomo, vol. 5], ed. Kokusho kankōkai (Tokyo: Kokusho kankōkai, 1909), p. 157.

21.   See Kiyohara Sadao, *Kokugaku hattatsushi* [A History of *Kokugaku*] (Tokyo: Unebi shobō, 1940), pp. 315–16.

22.   This theory first appeared in the *Zhouli* (The Rites of Zhou) and *Shanhaijing* (The Classic of Mountains and Seas) and became well-known in the *Chunqiu zhanguo* (Spring and Autumn and Warring States) period (770–221 BC). The Song scholar Zhu Yuansheng (?–1275) and the late Ming scholar Huang Daozhou (1585–1646) elaborated on this theory in the *Sanyi beiyi* (Supplementary Notes on the Three Versions of the *Yijing*) and *Sanyi dongji* (Revealing the Nature of the Three Versions of the *Yijing*), respectively.

23.   Seeing ancient Chinese sage-kings as the manifestations of Japanese deities and viewing ancient Chinese classics as works of Japanese deities were not original ideas of Atsutane. Motoori Norinaga, in his *Kojikiden*, suggested that Fu Xi, Shennong, Huang Di, Yao, and Shun were all manifestations of Sukunabikona-no-Kami, the Shinto deity of medicine, rain, crops, and wine. His view, based on the story in the *Kojiki* about this deity going to Tokoyo-no-kuni (Land of Immortality) from Kumano, was probably inspired by the Buddhist doctrine of *honchi suijaku* (Shinto deities as local manifestations of the Buddha). Norinaga's assertion was criticized by his fellow *kokugaku* scholar Ueda Akinari (1734–1809). Furthermore, Suika Shintoist Suzuki Teisai (?–1740) suggested that some Chinese classics were written by Shinto deities in the *Shingaku kokinben* (The Comparison of Shinto Schools: Past and Present). See Denki gakkai, ed., *Yamazaki Ansai to sono monryū* [Yamazaki Ansai and His School] (Tokyo: Meiji shobō, 1933), p. 268.

24.   Hirata Atsutane, *Sango hongokukō* 1, p. 1, digital collection of the National Diet Library of Japan, request no. 839-28.

25.   Hirata Atsutane, *Taiko koekiden*, *Hirata Atsutane zenshū* 6 [Complete Works of Hirata Atsutane, vol. 6], ed. Hirata Moritane and Miki Ioe (Tokyo: Hōbunkan, 1935), p. 2.

26.   Hirata Atsutane, *Tama no mihashira*, *Nihon shisō taikei* 50, *Hirata Atsutane, Ban Nobutomo, Ōkuni Takamasa*, ed. Tahara Tsuguo (Tokyo: Iwanami shoten, 1973), pp. 33–34.

27.   Hirata Atsutane, *Kōshi seisetsukō* 1, pp. 1–2, digital collection of the National Diet Library of Japan, request no. 848-143.

28.   Hirata Atsutane, *Sekiken taikoden seibun* [The Text of The Legend of Ancient China] (Tokyo: Ibukinoya, 1870), p. 1, digital collection of the National Diet Library of Japan, request no. 131-135.

29.   Hirata, *Sango hongokukō* 1, p. 13.

30.   Hirata Atsutane, *Daifusō kokukō* 2 [An Investigation of the Great Nation of Fusō] (Tokyo: Ibukinoya, 1836), p. 14, digital collection of Kyoto University Library, request no. ル3429-2.

31.   Hirata Atsutane, *Saneki yuraiki* 1 (Tokyo: Ibukinoya), p. 36, digital collection of the National Diet Library of Japan, request no. 848-173.

32.   Amamoto Haruhi, *Nenka hassakuhō: Hirata Atsutane no ekigaku kenkyū* [Eight Diagrams for Yearly Divination: The *Yijing* Scholarship of Hirata Atsutane] (Tokyo: Bungeisha, 2005), pp. 32–33.

33.   Hirata, *Taiko koekiden*, p. 6.

34.   Hirata, *Saneki yuraiki* 1, pp. 1–2.

35.   Hirata, *Sango hongokukō* 1, p. 24.

36.   Hirata Atsutane, *Seiseki gairon* 1 [An Introduction to Western (Chinese) Books; 1858], p. 27, digital collection of the National Diet Library of Japan, request no. 838-20.

37.   Hirata, *Daifusō kokukō* 2, p. 30.

38.   Hirata, *Saneki yuraiki* 1, pp. 15–16.

39.   Ibid., pp. 46–47.

40.   Ibid., pp. 8, 11, 19–20.

41.   Ibid, pt. 2, pp. 6–8.

42.   Muraoka Tsunetsugu, *Norinaga to Atsutane* (Tokyo: Sōbunsha, 1957), pp. 170–75.

43.   Regarding the divination method suggested by Atsutane, see Amamoto, *Nenka hassakuhō: Hirata Atsutane no ekigaku kenkyū.*

44.   Hirata, *Kōshi seisetsukō* 1, pp. 3–4.

45.   Hirata, *Saneki yuraiki* 2, p. 10.

46.   Furukawa Tetsushi and Ishida Ichirō, eds., *Nihon shisōshi kōza* 4, *Kinsei no shisō* 1 [Lectures on Intellectual History of Japan, vol. 4, Early Modern Thought, pt. 1] (Tokyo: Yūzankaku, 1976), p. 235.

47.   Many students of Atsutane came from the Akita domain. Morimura, a retainer of the Akita domain, specialized in the divination and numerology of the *Yijing*. Morimura studied under Atsutane in Akita. He wrote extensively on the *Yijing*, and his works include the *Ekiden seigiben* (Debating the Right and Suspicious Things in the Yichuan), *Eki koshin* (The Old and New Things about the *Yijing*; 1864), *Ekisen mondō* (Questions and Answers about the Divination of the *Yijing*), *Fukko hakka hōi ben* (Debating the Position of the Eight Trigrams in the Original *Yijing*; 1865), and *Hakka kō* (An Investigation of the Eight Trigrams). Michishige, a *machi-bugyō* (town magistrate) of the Akita domain, was the author of the *Koekimei zukai* (Illustrative Explanation of Fate in the Ancient *Yijing*), *Sanzu shinekiben* (An Explanation of Divine *Yijing* in Three Diagrams), and *Shineki ben ōbi* (An Explanation of the Ultimate Secret of the Divine *Yijing*). Ietane, a Confucian-turned-*kokugaku* scholar from the Akita domain, wrote the *Ekigaku shikō* (My Own Investigation of the *Yijing*). Kanetane, Atsutane's adopted son, and his younger brother, Midorikawa Yoshihisa, did not leave any specific writings on the *Yijing*. Amamoto Haruhi believes that

Ikuta Yorozu and Aratame Michishige were influenced by Atsutane in their application of the *Taichi*, *yin-yang*, *wu-xing*, and eight trigrams to explain the Age of the Gods. See *Nenka hassakuhō: Hirata Atsutane no ekigaku kenkyū*, pp. 65–66. As a matter of fact, Ōkuni Takamasa was also influenced in this regard.

48. See Ng, *The I Ching in Tokugawa Thought and Culture*, pp. 85–88.

49. Ikuta Yorozu, *Taneki seigi*, in *Ikuta Yorozu zenshū* 3 [Complete Works of Ikuta Yorozu, vol. 3], ed. Haga Noboru (Tokyo: Kyōiku shuppan sentā, 1986), p. 469.

50. Ikuta, *Taneki seigi* 2, p. 30, digital collection of the National Diet Library of Japan, request no. 848-128.

51. Ikuta, *Koeki taishōkyō den* 1, pp. 2–3, digital collection of the National Diet Library of Japan, request no. 847-103).

52. Ibid., pp. 19–20.

53. Preface to *Koeki taishōkyō den*, *Ikuta Yorozu zenshū* 2, pp. 412–13.

54. Ikuta, *Taneki seigi* 1, p. 3.

55. Ibid., pt. 2, pp. 38–39.

56. He believed that Western science came from the Japanese deity Sukunabikona-no-Kami. See John Breen, "Accommodating the Alien: Ōkuni Takamasa and the Religion of the Lord of Heaven," in *Religion in Japan: Arrows to Heaven and Earth*, ed. Peter Kornicki and James McMullen (Cambridge, MA: Cambridge University Press, 1996), pp. 179–97.

57. See Fujii Sadafumi, *Edo kokugaku tenseishi no kenkyū* [A Study of the History of the Transformation of *Kokugaku* in the Edo Period] (Tokyo: Yoshikawa kōbunkan, 1987), p. 37.

58. He wrote: "All nations in this world were founded by Susanoo-no-Mikoto and his descendants. This view is supported by ancient texts. Huang Di in China was the visiting spirit of Ōkuninushi-no-Kami. Cangjie, the creator of writing characters, was the visiting spirit of Kuebiko." Ōkuni Takamasa, *Koden tsūkai* 3 (Tokyo: Yao shoten, 1897), p. 2.

59. Ōkuni Takamasa, *Gakutō benron* [Debating the Intellectual Lineage], *Nihon shisō taikei* 50, *Hirata Atsutane, Ban Nobutomo, Ōkuni Takamasa*, p. 487.

60. Ibid., p. 489.

61. Hirata, *Tama no mihashira* 2, p. 84.

62. Ōkuni Takamasa, *Shōuchū shinji sen* [Commentary on the *Shinjigen*] (Tokyo: Jingū kyōin, 1873), p. 12. His view on the evolution of writing system was further elaborated by his student Ōhata Harukuni (1818–75), who

explained how Chinese characters were developed from scripts of the Age of the Gods in his *Kanjigen* (Origins of Chinese Characters).

63.   Ōkuni Takamasa, *Koden tsūkai*, *Ōkuni Takamasa zenshū* 7 (Complete Works of Ōkuni Takamasa, vol. 7), annot. Nomura Denshirō (Tokyo: Yūkōsha, 1938), pp. 1–12.

64.   On the difference between Norinaga and Atsutane and the nature of the new *kokugaku* founded by Atsutane, see McNally, *Proving the Way*, ch. 5.

65.   See Okino Iwasaburō, *Hirata Atsutane to sono jidai* [Hirata Atsutane and His Times] (Tokyo: Kōseikaku, 1943); Donald Keene, "Hirata Atsutane and Western Learning," *T'oung Pao* 42, no. 5 (1954): 353–80.

CHAPTER 7

1.   The region under the Han race was the first definition. For instance, in the *Chunqiu*, the word *Zhongguo* was used to underline the concept of *huay-izhibian* (the distinction between the Han and barbarians). According to Wang Ermin, in 145 (83%) of the 178 instances of its use in pre-Qin texts, *Zhongguo* referred to the region under the Han. See Wang Ermin, *Zhingguo jindai six-iangshulun* [Comments on Intellectual History of Modern China] (Taipei: Huashi chubanshe, 1977), p. 442.

2.   Joshua A. Fogel, "On Japanese Expressions for 'China,' " *Sino-Japanese Studies* 2, no. 1 (December 1989): 5.

3.   Using Great Tang (*Dai-Tō*) would cause problems in terms of national identity and political independence. One way to solve this dilemma used by Heian Japanese was to read the Chinese characters with their Japanese native reading method (*kunyomi*). By reading *Dai-Tō* as *Morokoshi*, literally the importation of miscellaneous goods, they thus reduced the Sinocentric flavor of the term in favor of a more transnational dimension. See Kishi Toshio, *Nihon kodai bunbutsu no kenkyū* [A Study of Cultural Relics of Ancient Japan] (Tokyo: Hanawashobō, 1988), ch. 15, pp. 425–50.

4.   See Maeno Michiko, "Kokugō ni miru Nihon no jiko ishiki." [Self-Consciousness of Being Japan as Seen from National Titles], *Gengo bunka kenkyū sōsho* [Language and Culture Research Series] 5 (2006): 26–62.

5.   Quoted in Ishizaki Zenjirō, *Ikeda Mitsumasa kō den* [Biography of Duke Ikeda Mitsumasa] (Tokyo: Ishizaki Senjirō, 1932), p.1324. See also Kitajima Manji, *Toyotomi seiken no taigai ninshiki to Chōsen shinryaku*

[Knowledge of International Affairs and the Invasion of Korea during the Toyotomi Regime] (Tokyo: Azekura shobō, 1990), p. 106.

6. Names for Japan also became more diversified in the Tokugawa period. Common names were *Nihon* (used by Hayashi Razan, Asami Keisai, Kumazawa Banzan, Dazai Shundai, Tokugawa Mitsukuni, Arai Hakuseki, Nishikawa Joken, and Hayashi Shihei), *honchō* (used by Hayashi Razan, Yamazaki Ansai, Yamaga Sokō, Watarai Nobuyoshi, Dazai Shundai, Keichū, and Hayashi Shihei), *Nihonkoku* (used by Hayashi Razan and Hayashi Shihei), *Wagakuni* (used by Hayashi Razan, Yamazaki Ansai, and Watanabe Kazan), *Wagachō* (used by Hayashi Razan, Asami Keisai, Rai Sanyō, and Ishida Baigan), and *Kōkoku* (used by Motoori Norinaga, Ueda Akinari, Tachibana Moribe, Izumi Makuni, Katsu Kaishū, and Satō Nobuhiro). Less common terms were *Dai-Nihon* (used by Nakai Chikuzan and Tokugawa Mitsukuni), *Honpō* (used by Yoshida Shōin), *Yamato* (大和, used by Kaibara Ekken), *Kōchō* (used by Ikuta Yorozu), *Tenchō* (used by Yoshida Shōin and Aizawa Seishisai), *Shinkoku* (used by Hayashi Razan, Fujita Tōko, and Aizawa Seishisai), *Shinshū* (used by Fujita Tōko and Aizawa Seishisai), *Shinpō* (used by Sakuma Taika), *Yamato* (倭, used by Dazai Shundai), *Yashima* (used by Asami Keisai and Rai Sanyō), *Ashihara Nakatsukuni* (used by Yamazaki Ansai), and *Kōwa* (used by Rai Sanyō).

7. The three-nation worldview remained influential in Buddhist circles in the Tokugawa period. Nevertheless, the role of China in the worldview of Tokugawa Japanese became increasingly marginalized. See Peter Nosco, "The Place of China in the Construction of Japan's Early Modern World View," *Taiwan Journal of East Asian Studies* 4, no. 1 (June 2007): 27–48.

8. Terajima Ryōan, *Wakan sansai zue* 13 (Tokyo: Chūgai shuppansha, 1901), p. 259.

9. Hayashi Razan, *Seika sensei gyōjō* [Life of Master Seika], in *Hayashi Razan bunshū*, ed. Kyōto shisekikai (Tokyo: Perikansha, 1979), p. 463.

10. Kumazawa Banzan, *Shūgi gaisho* [Extra Writings on Accumulating Righteousness], *Nihon rinri ihen* 2, ed. Inoue Tetsujirō and Kanie Yoshimaru (Tokyo: Ikuseikai, 1901), p. 61.

11. See Satō Saburō, *Kindai Nitchū kōshōshi no kenkyū* [A Study of the History of Sino-Japanese Interaction in the Modern Period] (Tokyo: Yoshikawa kōbunkan, 1984), pp. 26–33.

12.   Amano Sakakage, *Shioshiri*, *Nihon zuihitsu taisei* (Collection of Japanese Essays), ser. 3, vol. 16, ed. Nihon zuihitsu taisei henshūbu (Tokyo: Yoshikawa kōbunkan, 1976), p. 80.

13.   Both *Shina* and *Shintan* were translated from *Cina*, the Sanskrit for Qin. *Shina* was primarily used by Buddhist monks, including Kūkai (774–835), Kokan Shiren (1278–1346), Banri Shūku (1428–?), and Mangen Shiban (1626–1710). In the mid-Tokugawa period, *Shina* was introduced to Japan a second time through the translation of the Dutch term *China* by Arai Hakuseki (1657–1725). Mid- and late Tokugawa scholars who used *Shina* included Motoori Norinaga, Sugita Genpaku, Ōtsuki Gentaku, Tominaga Nakamoto, Kaiho Seiryō, Satō Nobuhiro, Terajima Ryōan, and Takano Chōei. None of them used it in a negative tone. *Shina* became more frequently used in the *bakumatsu* period. For instance, Yoshida Shōin (1830–59) and Takasugi Shinsaku (1839–67) used it to refer to China, and negative implications were added to the term. *Shina* became increasingly negative in the Meiji period (1868–1912), particularly after the Sino-Japanese War (1894–1895) and Russo-Japanese War (1904–5).

14.   See Haga Noboru, *Nikkan bunka kōryūshi no kenkyū* [A Study of Japan-Korea Cultural Interaction] (Tokyo: Yūzankaku shuppan, 1986), ch. 2.

15.   Satō, *Kindai Nitchū kōshōshi no kenkyū*, pp. 25–66.

16.   See Harry Harootunian, "The Functions of China in Tokugawa Thought," in *The Chinese and the Japanese: Essays in Political and Cultural Interactions*, ed. Akira Iriye (Princeton, NJ: Princeton University Press, 1980), pp. 9–36; Marius Jansen, *China in the Tokugawa World* (Cambridge, MA: Harvard University Press, 1992), pp. 82–83.

17.   Kumazawa Banzan, *Shūgi gaisho*, *Banzan zenshū* (Complete Collection of Banzan), ed. Masamune Atsuo (Tokyo: Meicho shuppan, 1978), p. 25.

18.   The translation is modified from Paul Varley, *A Chronicle of Gods and Sovereigns: Jinno Shotoki of Kitabatake Chikafusa* (New York: Columbia University Press, 1980), p. 49.

19.   Quoted in Kajiyama Takao, "Fujita Yūkoku no *Boku yoku-hen jo*" [Preface to the *Boku yoku-hen* by Fujita Yūkoku], posted on his blog, November 17, 2012, http://edosakio.cocolog-nifty.com/blog/2012/11/post-df96.html.

20.   In Fujita Tōko et al., *Keimō kōdōkanki jutsugi* [A Brief Explanation of *Kōdōkanki*] (Tokyo: Ryūeiken, 1885), p. 7, digital collection of the National Diet Library, request no. toku 35-216.

21.   Fujita Tōko, *Kōdōkanki-jutsugi*, *Tokugawa Mitsukuni shū, Fujita Tōko shū, Hashimoto Sanai shū, Dai-Nihon shisō zenshū* 18 (Tokyo: Dai-Nihon shisō zenshū kankōkai, 1933), p. 293.

22.   Ibid., pp. 202–3.

23.   Yamaga Sokō, *Haisho zanpitsu* [Writings in Exile], *Yamaga Sokō zenshū: shisōhen* 8 (Complete Collection of Yamaga Sokō: Thought, vol. 8), ed. Hirose Yutaka (Tokyo: Iwanami shoten, 1940), pp. 591–93.

24.   Watarai Nobuyoshi, *Jingū hiden mondō* [Secret Transmission of Shinto: Question and Answer], *Shintō taikei: Ronsetsuhen 7 Ise shintō* pt. 2, annot. Nishikawa Masatami (Tokyo: Shintō taikei hensankai, 1982), p. 74.

25.   Goi Ranshū, *Jūyakuron* (Discourse on Ten Misfortunes), quoted in Tao De-min, *Kaitokudō shushigaku no kenkyū* [A Study of the Zhu Xi school in the Kaitokudō Academy] (Suita: Ōsaka daigaku shuppankai, 1994), p. 271.

26.   Motoori Norinaga, *Naobi no mitama* [The Rectifying Spirit], *Shintō taikei: Ronsetsuhen 25, fukko shintō* 3 [Series on Shinto, Lectures 25, Fukko Shinto 3], annot. Umezawa Isezō and Takahashi Miyuki (Tokyo: Shintō taikei hensankai, 1982), pp. 17–18.

27.   Motoori Norinaga, *Kakaika* [Reproving the Reed Cutter; 1786], in *Motoori Norinaga zenshū* 8 [Complete Works of Motoori Norinaga, vol. 8], annot. Ōno Susumu and Ōkubo Tadashi (Tokyo: Chikuma shobō, 1972), p. 404.

28.   Izumi Makuni, *Meidōsho* [A Book to Clarify the Way; 1804], *Nihon shisō taikei* 51, *Kokugaku undō no shisō* [Series on Japanese Thought, vol. 51, The Thought of the *Kokugaku* Movement], annot. Haga Noboru and Matsumoto Sannosuke (Tokyo: Iwanami shoten, 1971), p. 186.

29.   Regarding the impact of the fall of the Ming and the rise of the Manchu dynasty on the worldview of Tokugawa Japanese, see Han Dong-yu, *Cong "tuoru" dao "tuoya": Riben jinshi yilai "qu zhong xin hua" zhi sixiang guocheng yanjiu* [From De-Confucianism to De-Sinicization: A Study of the Process of Decentralization in Japan since the Early Modern Period] (Taipei: Taiwan daxue chuban zhongxin, 2009), pp. 162–67. On the change of worldview caused by Dutch learning, see Grant Goodman, *Japan: The Dutch Experience* (London: Athlone Press, 1986); and Marius B. Jansen, *Japan and Its World* (Princeton, NJ: Princeton University Press, 1980).

30.   Bitō Nichū, *Seiki yohitsu* [Writings in My Seclusion], *Nihon jurin sōsho* 2 [Series on Japanese Confucianism, vol. 2], ed. Seki Giichirō (Tokyo: Ōtori shuppan, 1971), p. 10.

31.   Satō Issai, *Genshiroku* [Records of My Aspirations], *Nihon shisō taikei* 46: *Ōshio Chūsai, Satō Issai*, annot. Sagara Tōru, Mizoguchi Yūzō, and Fukunaga Mitsuji (Tokyo: Iwanami shoten, 1980), p. 31.

32.   Goi Ranshū, *Sago* [Trifle Talks], *Nihon jurin sōsho* 1, ed. Seki Giichirō (Tokyo: Ōtori shuppan, 1971), p. 44.

33.   Motoori Norinaga, *Tamakatsuma* [Jeweled Comb Basket; 1795–1812], in *Tamakatsuma*, pt. 2, annot. Muraoka Tsunetsugu (Tokyo: Iwanami shoten, 1943), p. 57.

34.   Izawa Banryō, *Zokusetsu zeiben* [Detailed Discussion on Common Views] (Tokyo: Kokumin bunko kankōkai, 1912), p. 591.

35.   Ise Sadatake, *Ansai zuihitsu* 1 [Discursive Essays by Ansai, vol. 1] (Tokyo: Yoshikawa kōbunkan, 1929), p. 401.

36.   See Tokugawa Mitsukuni, ed., *Dai Nihonshi* [Great History of Japan], vol. 117.

37.   Gan Huai-zhen, "Shanlu Suxing *Zhongchao shishi* zhong de Tianxia yu zhongguo gainian" [The Ideas of Tenka and Chūgoku in Yamaga Sokō's *Chūchō jijitsu*], in *Jianghu shidai Riben Hanxue yanjiu zhumianxiang: Sixiang wenhua pian* [Various Facets of Chinese Learning in Tokugawa Japan: Intellectual and Cultural Aspects], ed. Ye Guoliang and Xu Xingqing (Taipei: Taiwan daxue chuban zhongxin, 2009), p. 123.

38.   Yamaga Sokō, *Chūchō jijitsu*, *Yamaga Sokō zenshū: Shisōhen* 13, ed. Hirose Yutaka (Tokyo: Iwanami shoten, 1940), p. 239.

39.   Arai Hakuseki, *Koshitsū wakumon* [Questions about the *Koshitsū*], *Nihon no meicho* 15, *Arai Hakuseki* (Great Books of Japan 15, Arai Hakuseki), ed. Kuwabara Takeo (Tokyo: Chūō kōronsha, 1969), p. 282. In addition, he also pointed out that ancient Japan was called Nakatsukuni 中津国 (Central Kingdom) in the *Jinnō shōtōki*.

40.   Amemori Hōshū, *Taharegusa, Dai Nihon shisō zenshū 7* [Compete Collection of Great Japanese Thought, vol. 7], ed. Uemura Katsuya (Tokyo: Dai Nihon shisō zenshū kankōkai, 1933), p. 411.

41.   Yamazaki Ansai, *Bunkai hitsuroku* [Written Records of Encounters with Scholars], *Yamazaki Ansai zenshū 1* [Complete Collection of Yamazaki Ansai, vol. 1], ed. Nihon koten gakkai (Tokyo: Perikansha, 1978), p. 373.

42.   Ono Takakiyo, *Hyakusōro, Nihon zuihitsu taisei*, ser. 3, vol. 11 (Tokyo: Yoshikawa kōbunkan, 1978), p. 72.

43.   Asami Keisai, *Satsuroku* [Collections of Notes], *Nihon shisō taikei* 31, *Yamazaki Ansai gakuha* [Series on Japanese Thought, vol. 31, The School of

Yamazaki Ansai], annot. Nishi Junzō, Abe Ryūichi, and Maruyama Masao (Tokyo: Iwanami shoten, 1980), p. 377.

44.   Asami Keisai, *Chūgoku ben* [About the Central Kingdom], *Nihon shisō taikei* 31, *Yamazaki Ansai gakuha*, p. 416.

45.   Katō Naokata, *Chūgoku ronshū* [Collection of Essays on the Central Kingdom], *Nihon shisō taikei* 31, *Yamazaki Ansai gakuha*, p. 420. Naokata himself did not fully accept this view. He believed that the central kingdom should be based on geographic location and thus the Japanese should not be disappointed for not being born in the central kingdom.

46.   Sasaki Takanari, *Ben bendōsho* [Debating *Bendōsho*; 1736], *Dai-Nihon bunko shintō hen: Suika shintō* 3, annot. Saeki Ariyoshi (Tokyo: Shunyōdō shoten, 1937), p. 299.

47.   Watarai Jōshō, *Shintō meiben* [Clarifying Shinto], in *Kinnō bunko 2* [Collection of Books on Royalism, vol. 2], ed. Arima Sukemasa (Tokyo: Dai-Nihon meidōkai, 1919), p. 115.

48.   Fukagawa Yūei, *Seidōron* [Discourse on the Right Way; 1776], Arima, ed. *Kinnō bunko 2*, p. 409.

49.   Tokugawa Mitsukuni, *Seizankō zuihitsu* [Discursive Writings of Mitsukuni], *Dai Nihon shisō zenshū* 18, ed. Uemura Katsuya (Tokyo: Dai Nihon shisō zenshū kankōkai, 1933), p. 357.

50.   Sugita Genpaku, *Kyōi no gen* [Words of a Crazed Doctor], in *Nihon shisō taikei* 64, *Yōgaku* 1, annot. Numata Jirō (Tokyo: Iwanami shoten, 1976), p. 230.

51.   Ōtsuki Gentaku, *Rangaku kaitei* [Introduction to Dutch Learning], *Nihon shisō taikei* 63, *Yōgaku* 1, annot. Numata Jirō, p. 339.

52.   Chun-chieh Huang, "The Idea of 'Zhongguo' and Its Transformation in Early Modern Japan and Contemporary Taiwan," *Journal of Kanbun Studies in Japan* 2 (March 2007): 398–408.

53.   It should be noted that Yamaga Sokō used *Chūgoku* and *honchō* (our dynasty) to refer to China and Japan respectively in his early writings such as the *Seikyō yōroku* (Digest of Sacred Teachings; 1666) and *Yamaga gorui* (The Classified Sayings of Yamaga). This serves as a footnote to show that his perception of names for China and Japan underwent tremendous changes at different stages of his life. See Tahara Tsuguo and Morimoto Junichirō, annot., *Nihon shisō taikei* 32, *Yamaga Sokō* (Tokyo: Iwanami shoten, 1970), p. 8.

54. Yamaga Sokō, *Chūchō jijitsu*, in *Yamaga Sokō zenshū: Shisōhen* 13, p. 225.

55. Ibid.

56. Ibid., p. 234.

57. Rai Sanyō, *Shinsaku*, in *Dai-Nihon shisō zenshū* 15 *Rai Sanyō shū*, ed. Uemura Katsuya (Tokyo: Dai Nihon shisō zenshū kankōkai, 1933), p. 131.

58. Fujita Tōko, *Kōdōkan kijutsugi*, *Dai-Nihon shisō zenshū* 18, p. 267.

59. Ibid., p. 268.

60. Ibid., p. 219.

61. See Bob Tadashi Wakabayashi, *Anti-Foreignism and Western Learning in Early Modern Japan: The New Theses of 1825* (Cambridge, MA: Harvard University Press, 1986), p. 9.

62. Aizawa Seishisai, *Shinron*, annot. Okamura Rihei (Tokyo: Meiji shoten, 1939), p. 25.

63. Ibid., p. 29.

64. Ibid., p. 23. It should be noted that Seishisai's view of the distinction between civilized and barbarian was multidimensional. See Lan Hong-yue, "Shenzhou, zhongguo, diiguo: Huizezhengzhizhai de guojia xiangxiang yu shijiu shiji Riben zhi Yazhou lunshu," [*Shenzhou, zhongguo, diiguo*: Nation in Aizawa Seishisai's Thinking and His Discourses on Asia in Nineteenth–Century Japan], in *Xinshixue* [New History] 22, no. 3 (September 2011): 87–90.

65. Regarding the notion of "cultural China," see Wei-ming Tu, "Cultural China: Periphery as the Center," *Daedalus* 120, no. 2 (Spring 1991): 1–32.

66. Some *kokugaku* and Shinto scholars condemned Confucians for using *jōkoku* and *Chūchō* for China. However, I have not yet found any example of this in my reading of Tokugawa texts.

CHAPTER 8

1. Kenneth Pyle, *The Making of Modern Japan* (Lexington, MA: D. C. Heath, 1978), p. 189.

2. Preface to Watanabe Hiroshi, *Higashi Ajia no ōken to shisō* [East Asian Kingly Authorities and Ideologies] (Tokyo: Tōkyō daigaku shuppankai, 1997), pp. 1–6. He uses *go-kōgi* and *kubō-sama* to refer to the Edo *bakufu* and *shōgun*,

respectively. This instantly stimulated a lively exchange of ideas in 1998 among scholars of Tokugawa studies. Luke Roberts and Wai-ming Ng presented papers on this issue at the International Convention of Asian Scholars in June 1998. Roberts translated the preface as "About Some Japanese Historical Terms," in *Sino-Japanese Studies* 10, no. 2 (April 1998): 32–42.

3.   See Jeffrey P. Mass, *Antiquity and Anachronism in Japanese History* (Stanford, CA: Stanford University Press, 1992), p. 158.

4.   *Mufu* first appeared in the *Li Mu chuan* (Biography of Li Mu) of the *Shiji* (Records of the Grand Historian), referring to the office of the general. The Song dynasty historical encyclopedia *Cefu yuangui* (Prime Tortoise of the Record Bureau; 1005–13), suggests that *mufu* already existed in the Warring States period (403–221 BCE). It reads: "In the Warring States period, the office of the general began to be called *mufu*." For the origins of *mufu* and its transformation in China, see Guo Run-tao, "Zhongguo mufu zhide de tezheng xingtai ji bianqian" [The Characteristics, Forms and Transformation of the *Mufu* System in China], *Zhongguoshi yanjiu* [Journal of Chinese Historical Studies], no. 1 (1997): 3–14.

5.   See Shi Yun-tao, *Tangdai mufu zhide yanjiu* [A Study of the *Mufu* System of the Tang Period] (Beijing: Zhongguo shehui kezue chubanshe, 2003).

6.   *Bakufu*, as an administrative post, cannot be found in medieval Japanese officialdom. It is not recorded in the *Kojiruien* (The Encyclopedia of Ancient Matters) either. See *Kojiruien* 14–17, *Kanibu* [Part on Officialdom] (Tokyo: Kojiruien kankōkai, 1932).

7.   *Konoefu* was the imperial guard unit. In the Nara period, it was called *jutōei* (sword-bearing imperial guards). In the early Heian period, *jutōei* became *chōefu* (central imperial guard) and *konoefu*, and they were later renamed *sa-konoefu* and *u-konoefu* (left and right *konoefu*), respectively. The head of the two *konoefu* was called *taishō* (general) or *urin taishōgun* (general of the feathered forest imperial guard) in Tang Chinese terminology. See Sasayama Haruo, *Nihon kodai eifu seido no kenkyū* [A Study of the Imperial Guard System in Ancient Japan] (Tokyo: Tōkyōdaigaku shuppankai, 1985).

8.   For a dissenting view, see Mass, *Antiquity and Anachronism in Japanese History*, pp. 159–61. Mass argues that the term *bakufu* had not developed beyond its original Heian meanings during the Kamakura period.

9.   Quoted in Mihashi Tokugen, *Mihashi Tokugen Chosakushū* [Collected Writings of Mihashi Tokugen] (Tokyo: Zoku gunshoruijū kanseikai, 1999), p. 82.

10.   Tōkyō daigaku shiryōhensansho, ed., *Dai Nihon shiryō* 10 [Historical Sources of Great Japan, no. 10] (Tokyo: Tōkyō daigaku shiryōhensansho, 2009), p. 45

11.   Tōkyō daigaku shiryōhensansho, ed., *Dai Nihon shiryō* 4, no. 5, p. 86.

12.   Kojiruien kankōkai, ed., *Kojiruien 35, Kanibu, Kamakura Shōgun* (Tokyo: Kojiruien kankōkai, 1932), p. 650.

13.   Tōkyō daigaku shiryōhensansho, ed., *Dai Nihon shiryō* 6, no. 29, p. 84.

14.   Kokusho kankōkai, ed., *Azuma kagami* 2, (Tokyo: Kokusho kankōkai, 1923), p. 306.

15.   Hakubankan, ed., *Taiheiki* (Tokyo: Hakubankan, 1899), p. 43.

16.   See Watanabe Hiroshi, "Goikō to shōchō: Tokugawa seiji taisei no ichi sokumen" [Authority and Symbolism: As Aspect of Tokugawa System], *Shisō*, no. 740 (February 1986): 132–54.

17.   There are several exceptions. First, Hayashi Razan (1583–1657), in a private record, referred to Tokugawa Ieyasu (1542–1616) as *bakufu* several times. See "Hayashi sensei bunshū," [The Collection of the Literary Works of Master Hayashi], *Nihon shisō taikei* 28, *Fujiwara Seika, Hayashi Razan*, ed. Ishida Ichiryō and Kaneya Osamu (Tokyo: Iwanami shoten, 1975), pp. 228–30. Second, Muro Kyūsō (1658–1734), in his *Akō gijin roku* (Records of the Righteous Men of Akō Domain; 1703), used *bakufu* once in a footnote. It reads: "The descendants of former noble families have lost their domains for a long time. The *bakufu* [also called the central government (*chōtei*)] chooses the most prominent of them, giving them titles and special treatments in promotion. These families are called the high families." Muro handled this footnote with extra care and put a special annotation after the term *bakufu* to show that he acknowledged the Edo *bakufu* as the legitimate regime. In this context, *bakufu* by no means contained any negative implications. See Muro Kyūsō, *Akō gijin roku, Nihon shisō taikei* 27, *Kinsei buke shisō*, ed. Ishii Shirō (Tokyo: Iwanami shoten, 1974), pp. 274–75, 343. Third, Rai Sanyō (1780–1832), in his *Nihon gaishi* (An Unofficial Japanese History; 1829), referred to Tokugawa Ieyasu as *bakufu*. See Rai Sanyō, *Nihon gaishi* 2, ed. Tsukamoto Tetsuzō (Tokyo: Yūhōdō shoten, 1921), pp. 1016, 1022. For other examples, see Watanabe, *Higashi Ajia no ōken to shisō*, p. 2.

18.   The *Kokusho sōmokuroku* (A Complete Index of Japanese Books) alone carries 97 titles with the term *bakufu*. See *Kokusho sōmokuroku* 16 (Tokyo: Iwanami shoten, 1968), pp. 582–84. I have checked a dozen of them at the

University of Tokyo General Library and found that all of these titles were given by post-Tokugawa Japanese when they compiled or hand-copied the original texts.

19.   See Herman Ooms, *Tokugawa Ideology: Early Constructs, 1570–1680* (Princeton, NJ: Princeton University Press, 1985), pp. 26–29.

20.   For a brief discussion on the names for the Tokugawa *bakufu*, see Watanabe, *Higashi Ajia no ōken to shisō*, pp. 1–6.

21.   See Yoshida Tsunekichi and Satō Seiszaburō, eds., *Nihon shisō taikei 56, Bakumatsu seiji ronshū* [Collection of Political Discourses in the Late Tokugawa] (Tokyo: Iwanami shoten, 1976), pp. 334–35. In early Tokugawa times, the *shōgun* and emperor were on equal footing in their meetings. However, when Iemochi met Emperor Kōmei in Kyoto, he was in a subordinate position. See Shimohashi Yukiosa, *Bakumatsu no kyūtei* [The Imperial Court in Late Tokugawa Times] (Tokyo: Heibonsha, 1979), pp. 219–22.

22.   Nakane Yukie, *Zoku saimu kiji* 2 [Records of My Dream, Sequel, vol. 2] (Tokyo: Nihon shiseki kyōkai, 1921), entry of 28 February 1884, pp. 366–68.

23.   Yoshida and Satō, eds., *Nihon shisō taikei 56, Bakumatsu seiji ronshū*, p. 251. During the Six Dynasties (220–589) in China, the office of military leader and local king was called *hafu* (霸府). The term was borrowed by imperial loyalists in late Tokugawa Japan to belittle the *bakufu*.

24.   Ibid., p. 199.

25.   Ibid., p. 449.

26.   Ibid., p. 549.

27.   Shimohashi, *Bakumatsu no kyūtei*, p. 49.

28.   For the controversy over this term, see Ronald Toby, "Reopening the Question of Sakoku: Diplomacy in the Legitimation of the Tokugawa Bakufu," *Journal of Japanese Studies* 3, no. 2 (Summer 1977): 347–55. See also David Earl, *Emperor and Nation in Japan: Political Thinkers of the Tokugawa Period* (Seattle: University of Washington Press, 1964), p. 196. After the Meiji Restoration, *Ōkimi* was applied to emperors on unofficial occasions.

29.   *Tennō* was not used in the Tokugawa period to refer to the emperor. Aside from *kinchū*, other popular names for the emperors in the Tokugawa period were *kinri* (literally, inside the palace), *tenshi* (son of heaven), *tōgin* (emperor in reign), *gosho* (person in the palace), *gojō* (my lord), *kintei* (inner palace), *kyōomo* (common lord), and *shujō* (supreme lord). Retired and deceased emperors were called *in* 院, as in the case of Gomizunoo-in. *Jōkō* (former

emperor) and *gosho* 御所 were also used. See Watanabe, *Higashi Ajia no ōken to shisō*, p. 7.

30.   Hayashi Jussai, *Kisa kankin* [Picking Gold from Sand] (Tokyo: Zoku gunshoruijū kanseikai, 1977), pp. 385–86.

31.   This work is included in Tokinoya Masaru, ed., *Sonjō shūei* [Gathering Elites to Repel the Barbarians] (Tokyo: Tōyōbunka kenkyūkai, 1943), electronic collection of Kyoto University, file #0177900.

32.   In the *Hou Hanshu* (History of the Later Han), the general Feng Yi (?–34) was called *dashu jiangjun* (big tree general). For a discussion of the origins of this term, see Ise Sadatake, *Teijō zakki* [Miscellaneous Writings of Sadatake] (Tokyo: Yoshikawa kōbunkan, 1928), p. 153.

33.   Okada Takehiko, ed., *Bakumatsu ishin Shushigakusha shokanshū, Shushigaku taikei* 14 [Collection of Letters by Zhuxi Scholars in the Late Tokugawa and Restoration Periods, Series on the Zhuxi School, vol. 14] (Tokyo: Meitoku shuppansha, 1974), pp. 77–78.

34.   The idea of *seimei* is from the chapter 13 of the *Lunyu*. It reads: "When names are not correct, what is said will not sound reasonable; when what is said does not sound reasonable, affairs will not culminate in success; when affairs do not culminate in success, rites and music will not flourish; when rites and music do not flourish, punishments will not fit the crimes; when punishments do not fit the crimes, the common people will not know where to put hand and foot." Translation is from D. C. Lau, *Confucius, the Analects* (Harmondsworth, UK: Penguin Books Ltd, 1979), p. 118. Applying this idea to politics and morality, the Song school made the idea of *seimei* the theoretical basis for the *wulun* (five constant relationships).

35.   Dazai Shundai, *Keizairoku, Nihon shisō taikei* 37, *Sōrai gakuha*, ed. Rai Tsutomu (Tokyo: Iwanami shoten, 1972), p. 11.

36.   See Yamagata Daini, *Ryūshi shinron* (Tokyo: Iwanami shoten, 1943), p. 308

37.   Quotation is from Bob Tadashi Wakabayashi, *Japanese Loyalism Reconstrued: Yamagata Daini's Ryūshi Shinron of 1759* (Honolulu: University of Hawai'i Press, 1995), p. 132.

38.   Fujita Yūkoku, *Seimeiron, Nihon shisō taikei* 53: *Mitogaku*, annot. Imai Usaburō, Seya Yoshihiko, and Bitō Masahide (Tokyo: Iwanami shoten, 1973), p. 13.

39.   Ibid., p. 298.

CHAPTER 9

1.   For an analysis of the localization of Chinese ideas and terms in Japanese historical writings, see David Pollack, *The Fracture of Meaning: Japan's Synthesis of China from the Eighth through the Eighteenth Centuries* (Princeton, NJ: Princeton University Press, 1986), esp. chs. 1–2. Regarding the adaptation of Chinese concepts of political legitimacy in the *Kojiki* and *Nihon shoki*, see Qiao Zhi-zhong, "Lun Zhong-Ri liangguo chuantong shixue zhi zhengtonglun guannian de yitong" [A Comparison of Legitimacy in Historical Writings in China and Japan], *Qiushi xuekan* [Seeking Truth], no. 2 (2005): 109–16.

2.   Herman Ooms, *Tokugawa Ideology: Early Constructs, 1570–1680* (Princeton, NJ: Princeton University Press, 1985), pp. 50–62; Sonehara Satoshi, *Tokugawa Ieyasu shinkakuka e no michi* [The Way to the Deification of Tokugawa Ieyasu] (Tokyo: Yoshikawa kōbunkan, 1996).

3.   Victor J. Koschmann, *The Mito Ideology: Discourse, Reform, and Insurrection in Late Tokugawa Japan, 1790–1864* (Berkeley: University of California Press, 1987), p. 45.

4.   See Rao Zong-yi (Jao Tsung-I), *Zhongguo shixue shang zhi zhengtonglun* [Legitimacy in Chinese Historiography] (Shanghai: Shanghai yuandong chubanshe, 1996), pp. 74–80. He traces the development of the discourse of legitimacy from Han to Qing, paying special attention to ethnicity and morality.

5.   Unification and legitimacy are closely tied. See Yuri Pines, "Name or Substance? Between *Zhengtong* and *Yitong*," *History: Theory and Criticism* 2 (May 2001): 105–37. The internal conflict between unification and legitimacy can be seen in Zhu Xi's disagreement with Sima Guang over the Three Kingdoms. While Sima Guang regarded Wei as the legitimate regime because it was responsible for finally unifying the nation, Zhu Xi claimed legitimacy for Shu because of its proper bloodline and righteous motives. See Naitō Konan, "Cong Songdai shixue kan Zhongguo zhengtong lun" [Legitimacy in China as seen from Song Historiography], trans. Wai-ming Ng, *History: Theory and Criticism* 2 (May 2001): 161–67.

6.   Gu Jie-gang, *Wude zhongshi shuo xia de zhengzhi he lishi* [Politics and History under the Doctrine of the Rotation of the Five Virtues] (Hong Kong: Longmen shudian, 1970).

7.   Wai-ming Ng, *The I Ching in Tokugawa Thought and Culture* (Honolulu: University of Hawai'i Press, 2000), ch. 4. There are a few

exceptions. For instance, the preface of the *Kojiki* uses the *wu-xing* theory to comment on Emperor Tenmu (631–86) as follows: "Having grasped the celestial seals, he was paramount over the Six Cardinal Points; having obtained the heavenly supremacy, he annexed the Eight Wildernesses. He held the mean between the Two Essences, and regulated the order of the Five Elements." See Basil Hall Chamberlain, trans., *Kojiki: Records of Ancient Matters* (Tokyo: Tuttle, 1981), p. 3. The use of *wu-xing* is merely decorative.

8.   Kate Wildman Nakai, "The Naturalization of Confucianism in Tokugawa Japan: The Problem of Sinocentrism," *Harvard Journal of Asiatic Studies* 40, no. 1 (June 1980): 157–99.

9.   Wai-ming Ng, "The Forgery of Books in Tokugawa Japan," *East Asian Library Journal* 9, no. 2 (2000): 19–45.

10.   Rai Sanyō, *Nihon gaishi* 2, ed. Tsukamoto Tetsuzō (Tokyo: Yūhōdō, 1921), p. 555. The *Mikawa motogatari* (Tale of Mikawa; 1622) even traces the origin of Tokugawa Ieyasu to the Shinto deity, Kuni-no-tokotachi: "The ancestors of the Great Minister Ieyasu came from Tsushima in Aki, Japan, descended from Kuni-no-tokotachi." *Nihon shisō taikei* 26, *Mikawa motogatari, hagakure*, annot. Ōkubo Tadataka, Saiki Kazuma et al. (Tokyo: Iwanami shoten, 1974), p. 14.

11.   John Tucker, "Two Mencian Political Notions in Tokugawa Japan," *Philosophy East and West* 47, no. 2 (April 1997): 233–53. See also Chen Wei-fen, *Jindai Riben hanxue de guanjianci yanjiu* [A Study of Key Words in Chinese Studies in Modern Japan] (Taipei: Taiwan daxue chuban zhongxin, 2005), ch. 4.

12.   Arai Hakuseki regarded the Edo *bakufu* as a new dynasty that combined sovereignty and governance, a position close to the Chinese definition of "revolution." Daizai Shundai insisted that the Kamakura *bakufu*, Muromachi *bakufu*, and Edo *bakufu* were all independent dynasties and that the *shōgun* should carry the title of "King of Japan." Theirs were, nevertheless, alternative views.

13.   The terms *tendō* (*tiandao* in Chinese) and *tenmei* (*tianming* in Chinese) first appeared in the *Shujing*. It reads: "Worship heaven's way [*tendō*] and keep heaven's mandate [*tenmei*]." Buddhism has the idea of *tendō* as one of the six realms of existence, but it is not related to politics.

14.   Ozawa Eiichi, *Kinsei shigaku shisō shi kenkyū* [A Study of Ideas in Early Modern Japanese Historiography] (Tokyo: Yoshikawa kōbunkan, 1974), pp.

15–17. Likewise, the late Zhou period saw the rise of ideas about "following the Way rather than the emperor," and "heaven's mandate is ever-changing. We can only count on morality." See Chen Wei-fen, "Tiandao tianming wangdao gainian zai Riben de jicheng he zhuanhua" [The Continuity and Change of the Ideas of the Heavenly Way, Mandate of Heaven and Kingly Way], *Zhongguo wenzhe yanjiu jikan* [Bulletin of the Institute of Chinese Literature and Philosophy] 23 (September 2003): 239.

15.　Asaka Tanpaku, *Dai Nihonshi sansō* [Appraisal of the *Dai Nihonshi*], in *Nihon shisō taikei* 48, *Kinsei shi ronshū* [Collection of Early Modern Historical Writings], annot. Matsumoto Sannosuke and Ogura Yoshihiko (Tokyo: Iwanami shoten, 1974), p. 297.

16.　Yoshida Shōin, *Kōmō yowa* [Additional Notes on the Explanation of Mencius], *Yoshida Shōin zenshū* 2 [Compete Collection of Yoshida Shōin, vol. 2], ed. Yamaguchi-ken kyōikukai (Tokyo: Iwanami shoten, 1982), p. 279.

17.　Hayashi Gahō, *Honchō tsugan*, vol. 55 (Tokyo: Hakubunkan, 1897), p. 1. Hayashi Gahō also expressed this argument in the *Nihon ōdai ichiran* (Survey of the Sovereigns of Japan).

18.　Wang Wen-xue, *Zhengtong lun* [On Legitimacy] (Xian: Shaanxi renmin chubanshe, 2002), pp. 136–70.

19.　Hayashi Gahō, *Honchō tsugan* 1 (Tokyo: Kokusho kankōkai, 1920), p. 8.

20.　Matsumoto and Ogura, annot., *Nihon shisō taikei* 48, *Kinsei shi ronshū*, p. 263.

21.　Paul Varley, *Imperial Restoration in Medieval Japan* (New York: Columbia University Press, 1971), pp.147–49. The *Masukagami* (The Clear Mirror), a Japanese historical tale written in the early Muromachi period, also used the three regalia to support the legitimacy of the Southern Court.

22.　See Matsumoto Sannosuke, "Kinsei ni okeru rekishi jōjutsu to sono shisō" [Historical Narrative and Thought in the Early Modern Period], *Nihon shisō taikei* 48, *Kinsei shi ronshū*, annot. Matsumoto and Ogura, p. 603.

23.　Quoted in Yamazaki Tōkichi and Horie Hideo, *Nanbokuchō seijun ronsan* [Discourse on the Southern and Northern Courts Controversy over Legitimacy] (Tokyo: Kōtenkōkyūjo Kokugakuindaigaku shuppantoshohanbaijo, 1911), p. 147.

24.　Matsumoto and Ogura, annot., *Nihon shisō taikei* 48, *Kinsei shi ronshū*, p. 263.

25.   Takasu Yoshijirō, ed., *Mitogaku zenshū* 5 (Tokyo: Nittō shoin, 1933), pp. 16–18.

26.   Quoted in Yamazaki and Horie, *Nanbokuchō seijun ronsan*, p. 158.

27.   Ozawa, *Kinsei shigaku shisō shi kenkyū*, pp. 282–86.

28.   Quoted in Yamazaki and Horie, *Nanbokuchō seijun ronsan*, p. 158.

29.   Ibid., 127.

30.   *Kokushikan nichiroku* (The Diary of the National History Compilation Office), quoted in Kate Nakai, "Tokugawa Confucian Historiography: The Hayashi, Early Mito school and Arai Hakuseki," in *Confucianism and Tokugawa Culture*, ed. Peter Nosco (Princeton, NJ: Princeton University Press, 1984), p. 81.

31.   Quoted in Yamazaki and Horie, *Nanbokuchō seijun ronsan*, pp. 215–16.

32.   Referring to the Northern Court as "an illegitimate regime controlled by the Ashikaga," Hakuseki was sympathetic to the Southern Court. However, he criticized the Southern Court for being too weak and marginalized, making it so that "no one knew the existence of the imperial family." He believed that the imperial family, both the Southern line and the Northern line, lost the mandate of heaven to the warrior houses.

33.   Wai-ming Ng, "Political Terminology in the Legitimation of Tokugawa Japan," *Journal of Asian History* 34, no. 2 (2000): 138–48.

34.   Hayashi Gahō, *Honchō tsugan* 81 (Tokyo: Hakubunkan, 1897), p. 67.

35.   The Hayashi family was mild and implicit in its historical critique. While upholding the legitimacy of the Northern Court and the Edo *bakufu*, it respected the Southern Court and the imperial family in Kyoto. See John S. Brownlee, *Japanese Historians and the National Myths, 1600–1945: The Age of the Gods and Emperor Jimmu* (Vancouver: University of British Columbia Press, 1997), pp. 20–21.

36.   John S. Brownlee, *Political Thought in Japanese Historical Writing: From Kojiki (712) to Tokushi Yoron (1712)* (Waterloo, ON: Wilfrid Laurier University Press, 1991), pp. 116–28.

37.   Arai Hakuseki, *Tokushi yoron*, *Nihon shisō taikei* 35, *Arai Hakuseki*, annot. Matsumura Akira, Bitō Masahide, and Katō Shūichi (Tokyo: Iwanami shoten, 1975), p. 184.

38.   See Wai-ming Ng, *The I Ching in Tokugawa Thought and Culture*, pp. 69, 225; introduction to *Lessons from History: The Tokushi Yoron by Arai Hakuseki*, trans. Joyce Ackroyd (St. Lucia, Australia: University of Queensland

Press, 1982), pp. ix–liv; and Katō Shūichi, "Arai Hakuseki no sekai" [The World of Arai Hakuseki], *Nihon shisō taikei 35, Arai Hakuseki*, annot. Matsumura et al., pp. 534–35.

39.   Noguchi Takehiko, *Edo no rekishika* [Historians of the Tokugawa Period] (Tokyo: Chikuma shobō, 1979), p.116.

40.   "Bairi sensei hi" [Epigraph of Mr. Bairi (Mitsukuni)], in *Mito gikō zenshū* [Complete Works of Mitsukuni], ed. Tokugawa Kuniyuki (Tokyo: Iwanami shoten, 1970), p. 193.

41.   Miki Miyuki, *Tōgen iji* [Forgotten Stories about Mitsukuni], in *Mitogaku no tassei to tenkai* [The Making and Development of the Mito School], by Nagoya Tokimasa (Mito: Mito shigakkai, 1992). It is said that Mitsukini, on New Year's Day, put on a court costume and worshipped in the direction of Kyoto, shouting: "My lord is the emperor. The present *shōgun* is the head of my family." See Brownlee, *Japanese Historians and the National Myths, 1600–1945*, p. 32.

42.   Quoted in Noguchi, *Edo no rekishika*, p.143.

43.   Fujita Yūkoku, *Seimeiron*, in *Nihon shisō taikei 53: Mitogaku*, annot. Imai Usaburō, Seya Yoshihiko, and Bitō Masahide (Tokyo: Iwanami shoten, 1973), p. 371.

44.   See Hongō Takamori, "Tengtian Yougu Zhengming lun de lishi diwei" [The Historical Role of Fujita Yūkoku's *Seimeiron*], in *Dechuan shidai Riben ruxueshi lunji* [Collected Articles on the History of Tokugawa Confucianism], ed. Zhang Bao-san and Xu Xing-qing (Taipei: Taiwan daxue chuban zhongxin, 2004), pp. 203–42.

45.   See Takasu Yoshijirō, *Mito gakuha no sonnō oyobi keirin* [The Royalism in Mito School and Its History] (Tokyo: Yūzankaku, 1936), pp. 371–77.

46.   Koschmann, *The Mito Ideology*, p. 46.

47.   Rai Sanyō, *Nihon gaishi ronsan* [Commentary on the *Nihon Gaishi*], *Dai Nihon shisō zenshū 15, Rai Sanyō shū*, ed. Dai Nihon shisō zenshū kankōkai (Tokyo: Dai Nihon shisō zenshū kankōkai, 1933), pp. 76–78.

48.   Rai, *Nihon gaishi* 2, pp. 1001–2.

49.   Rai, *Nihon gaishi ronsan*, p.13.

50.   Rai, *Nihon gaishi*, p. 1045. This remark serves as a reminder of the "arrogant dragon [who] has cause to repent," an undesirable status mentioned in the *Yijing*.

51.   Whether the end statement of the *Nihon gaishi* contains loyalist implications has been a subject of debate among modern Japanese scholars. Some think it was a subtle way to express the idea of "the arrogant dragon has cause to repent" expounded in the *Yijing*. See Kizaki Aikichi, *Rai Sanyō* (Tokyo: Shinchōsha, 1941). Others question whether the *Nihon gaishi* was loyalist in nature. See Noguchi, *Edo no rekishika*, p. 16, 149–50.

52.   Kate Nakai, "Tokugawa Confucian Historiography: The Hayashi, Early Mito School and Arai Hakuseki," pp. 62–91; Kate Nakai, *Shogunal Politics: Arai Hakuseki and the Premises of Tokugawa Rule* (Cambridge, MA: Harvard University Press, 1988).

53.   Hayashi, *Honchō tsugan* 1, p. 7.

54.   Arai, *Tokushi yoron*, in *Nihon shisō taikei* 35, *Arai Hakuseki*, annot. Matsumura et al., p. 368.

55.   Imai Usaburō et al., *Nihon shisō taikei* 53, *Mitogaku*, p. 371.

56.   See Bitō Masahide, "Arai Hakuseki no rekishi shisō" [Historical Thought of Arai Hakuseki], in *Nihon shisō taikei* 35: *Arai Hakuseki*, pp. 563–65; and Mizubayashi Takeshi, *Tennōsei shiron: Honshitsu kigen tenkai* [The History of the Emperor System: Nature, Origin, and Development] (Tokyo: Iawanami shoten, 2006), pp. 227–28.

57.   *Tokushi yoron, Nihon shisō taikei* 35: *Arai Hakuseki*, p. 369.

EPILOGUE

1.   The term *wakon kansai* appeared for the first time in the Muromachi period work, *Kanke ikai* (The Last Instructions of Sugawara Michizane). In the late Tokugawa period, nativist scholars from the Hirata school built a stone monument to *wakon kansai* at Tenmangū in Dazaifu. The monument includes this sentence: "What *kokugaku* wants to know is everything in this world from past to present. Without Japanese spirit and Chinese learning, we cannot gain access to the innermost mystery." See Haruyama Ikujirō, *Gesshō monogatari* [Tale of Moonshine] (Tokyo: Kateidō, 1927), pp. 83–85. The Kimon school scholar Tani Jinzan (1663–1718) and *kokugaku* scholar Kurokawa Mayori (1823–1906) also advocated *wakon kansai*.

2.   See Brian Steininger, *Chinese Literary Forms in Heian Japan: Poetics and Practice* (Cambridge, MA: Asia Center at Harvard University, 2017).

BIBLIOGRAPHY

Aizawa Seishisai. *Shinron*, annotated by Okamura Rihei. Tokyo: Meiji shoten, 1939.

Alley, Rewi. *Bai Juyi: 200 Selected Poems*. Beijing: New World, 1983.

Amamoto Haruhi. *Nenka hassakuhō: Hirata Atsutane no ekigaku kenkyū*. Tokyo: Bungeisha, 2005.

Amano Sadakage. *Shioshiri. Nihon zuihitsu taisei*, ser. 3, vol. 16. Tokyo: Yoshikawa kōbunkan, 1976.

Amemori Hōshū. *Taharegusa. Dai Nihon shisō zenshū 7*, edited by Uemura Katsuya. Tokyo: Dai Nihon shisō zenshū kankōkai, 1933.

An Shibin, ed. *Jofuku densetsu o saguru*. Tokyo: Shōgakukan, 1990.

Andō Tameakira. *Nenzan kibun*. In *Hyakusōro, Nihon zuihitsu taisei*, ser. 3, vol. 11. Tokyo: Yoshikawa kōbunkan, 1977.

Arai Hakuseki. *Dōbun tsūkō*. Tokyo: Benseisha, 1979.

———. *Koshitsū*. Tokyo: Shōzandō, 1871.

———. *Koshitsū. Nihon no meicho 15: Arai Hakuseki*, edited by Kuwabara Takeo. Tokyo: Chūō kōronsha, 1969.

———. *Koshitsū wakumon. Nihon no meicho 15: Arai Hakuseki*, edited by Kuwabara Takeo. Tokyo: Chūō kōronsha, 1969.

———. *Lessons from History: The Tokushi Yoron by Arai Hakuseki*, translated by Joyce Ackroyd. St. Lucia, Australia: University of Queensland Press, 1982.

———. *Tokushi yoron. Nihon shisō taikei 35: Arai Hakuseki*, annotated by Matsumura Akira, Bitō Masahide, and Katō Shūichi. Tokyo: Iwanami shoten, 1975.

Asai Ryōi. *Yōkihi monogatari*. In *Yōkihi monogatari, Koten bunko 478*, annotated by Kurashima Toshihisa. Tokyo: Koten bunkō, 1986.

Asaka Tanpaku. *Dai Nihonshi sansō. Nihon shisō taikei 48: Kinsei shi ronshū*, annotated by Matsumoto Sannosuke and Ogura Yoshihiko. Tokyo: Iwanami shoten, 1974.

———. *Tōgen iji.* In *Gikō sōsho*, edited by Chiba Shinji. Sendai: Hayakawa kappanjo, 1909.

Asami Keisai. *Chūgoku ben. Nihon shisō taikei 31: Yamazaki Ansai gakuha*, annotated by Nishi Junzō, Abe Ryūichi, and Maruyama Masao. Tokyo: Iwanami shoten, 1980.

———. *Chūkō ruisetsu.* Digital collection of Waseda University Library, request no. イ04_00696.

———. *Satsuroku. Nihon shisō taikei 31: Yamazaki Ansai gakuha*, annotated by Nishi Junzō, Abe Ryūichi, and Maruyama Masao. Tokyo: Iwanami shoten, 1980.

Atsuta Jingū gūchō, ed. *Atsuta Jingū shiryō: Chōshū zasshi* 24. Nagoya: Atsuta Jingū gūchō, 1969.

Ban Nobutomo. *Shūeki shiron. Ban Nobutomo zenshū* 5, edited by Kokusho kankōkai. Tokyo: Kokusho kankōkai, 1909.

Bellah, Robert N. *Tokugawa Religion: The Values of Pre-industrial Japan.* New York: Free Press, 1957.

Benedict, Ruth. *The Chrysanthemum and the Sword: Patterns of Japanese Culture.* Boston: Houghton Mifflin, 1946.

Bitō Masahide. "Arai Hakuseki no rekishi shisō." *Nihon shisō taikei 35: Arai Hakuseki*, annotated by Matsumura Akira, Bitō Masahide, and Katō Shūichi. Tokyo: Iwanami shoten, 1975.

———. *Nihon bunka no rekishi.* Tokyo: Iwanami shoten, 2000.

Bitō Nichū. *Seiki yohitsu.* In *Nihon jurin sōsho* 2, edited by Seki Giichirō. Tokyo: Ōtori shuppan, 1971.

Breen, John. "Accommodating the Alien: Ōkuni Takamasa and the Religion of the Lord of Heaven." In *Religion in Japan: Arrows to Heaven and Earth*, edited by P. F. Kornicki and I. J. McMullen. Cambridge, UK: Cambridge University Press, 1996.

Brownlee, John S. *Japanese Historians and the National Myths, 1600–1945: The Age of the Gods and Emperor Jinmu.* Vancouver: University of British Columbia Press, 1997.

———. *Political Thought in Japanese Historical Writing: From Kojiki (712) to Tokushi Yoron (1712)*. Waterloo, ON: Wilfrid Laurier University Press, 1991.

Burns, Susan L. *Before the Nation: Kokugaku and the Imagining of Community in Early Modern Japan*. Durham, NC: Duke University Press, 2003.

Chamberlain, Basil Hall, trans. *Kojiki: Records of Ancient Matters*. Tokyo: Tuttle, 1981.

Chang Kun-chiang. *Dechuan Riben "zhong" "xiao" gainian de xingcheng yu fazhan: Yi bingxue yu Yangming xue wei zhongxin*. Shanghai: Huadong shifan daxue chubanshe, 2008.

———. "Jitian songyin jiangmeng yuhua de quanshi tezhi jiqi pipan." *Hanxue yanjiu* 27, no. 1 (March 2009): 207–30.

———. *Riben Dechuan shidai guxuepai zhi wangdao zhengzhi lun*. Taipei: Taiwan daxue chuban zhongxin, 2004.

———. "Riben Dechuan shidai shenru jianshe xuezhe dui shendao rudao de jieshi tese." *Taida wenshi zhexuebao*, no. 58 (March 2003): 141–80.

———. "Riben Yangming daxue Zhongjiang Tengshù yu Dayan Zhongzhai dui xiao zhi jieshi." *Taida lishi xuebao* 29 (June 2002): 127–67.

Che Xing-jian. "Shanjing ding jingji jiaokan de wenxian pingjie." *Jingxue yanjiu luncong* 1 (1994): 323–46.

Chen Wei-fen. *Jindai Riben hanxue de guanjianci yanjiu*. Taipei: Guoli Taiwan daxue chuban zhongxin, 2005.

———. "Tiandao tianming wangdao gainian zai Riben de jicheng he zhuanhua." *Zhongguo wenzhe yanjiu jikan* 23 (September 2003).

Chō Sobai. "Yoshida Shōin no ningenron." *Kikan Nihon shisō shi* 44 (1992): 104–26.

Collcutt, Martin. "The Legacy of Confucianism in Japan." In *The East Asian Region: Confucian Heritage and Its Modern Adaptation*, edited by Gilbert Rozman. Princeton, NJ: Princeton University Press, 1991.

Craig, Albert M. *Chōshū in the Meiji Restoration*. Cambridge, MA: Harvard University Press, 1961.

Dazai Shundai. *Keizairoku. Nihon shisō taikei* 37, *Sōrai gakuha*, edited by Rai Tsutomu. Tokyo: Iwanami shoten, 1972.

De Bary, William Theodore, et al., comps. *Sources of Japanese Tradition*. Pt. 2, 2nd ed. New York: Columbia University Press, 2001.

Denki gakkai, ed. *Yamazaki Ansai to sono monryū*. Tokyo: Meiji shobō, 1933.

Earl, David Magarey. *Emperor and Nation in Japan: Political Thinkers of the Tokugawa Period*. Seattle: University of Washington Press, 1964.

Elman, Benjamin A. "Sinophiles and Sinophobes in Tokugawa Japan: Politics, Classicism, and Medicine during the Eighteenth Century." *Eastern Asian Science, Technology and Society* 2, no. 1 (2008): 93–121.

Flueckiger, Peter. *Imagining Harmony: Poetry, Empathy, and Community in Mid-Tokugawa Confucianism and Nativism*. Stanford, CA: Stanford University Press, 2011.

Fogel, Joshua A. *The Literature of Travel in the Japanese Rediscovery of China, 1862–1945*. Stanford, CA: Stanford University Press, 1996.

———. "On Japanese Expressions for 'China.' " *Sino-Japanese Studies* 2, no. 1 (December 1989): 5–16.

Fujii Sadafumi. *Edo kokugaku tenseishi no kenkyū*. Tokyo: Yoshikawa kōbunkan, 1987.

Fujita Tōko. *Kōdōkan kijutsugi. Tokugawa Mitsukuni shū, Fujita Tōko shū, Hashimoto Sanai shū, Dai-Nihon shisō zenshū* 18. Tokyo: Dai-Nihon shisō zenshū kankōkai, 1933.

———. *Kōdōkan kijutsugi. Tōko zenshū*, edited by Kikuchi Kenjirō. Tokyo: Hakubunkan, 1940.

———. *Kōdōkan kijutsugi. Nihon shisō taikei* 53: *Mitogaku*, edited by Imai Usaburō, Seya Yoshihiko, and Bitō Masahide. Tokyo: Iwanami shoten, 1973.

Fujita Tōko et al. *Keimō kōdōkan kijutsugi* 1. Tokyo: Ryūeiken, 1885. Digital collection of the National Diet Library, request no. 35-216.

Fujita Yūkoku. *Seimeiron. Nihon shisō taikei* 53: *Mitogaku*, annotated by Imai Usaburō, Seya Yoshihiko, and Bitō Masahide. Tokyo: Iwanami shoten, 1973.

Fujiwara Seika. *Baison saihitsu. Nihon zuihitsu taisei*, ser. 1, vol. 1. Tokyo: Yoshikawa kōbunkan, 1975.

Fukagawa Yūei. *Seidōron*. In *Kinnō bunko* 2, edited by Arima Sukemasa. Tokyo: Dai-Nihon meidōkai, 1919.

Fukushima Kashizō, ed. *Kinsei Nihon no jugaku*. Tokyo: Iwanami shoten, 1939.

Furukawa Tetsushi and Ishida Ichirō, eds. *Nihon shisōshi kōza 4: Kinsei no shisō* 1. Tokyo: Yūzankaku, 1976.

Gan Huai-zhen. "Shanlu Suxing *Zhongchao shishi* zhong de *Tianxia* yu zhongguo gainian." In *Jianghu shidai Riben Hanxue yanjiu zhumianxiang: Sixiang wenhua pian*, edited by Ye Guoliang and Xu Xingqing. Taipei: Taiwan daxue chuban zhongxin, 2009.

Gentō. *Sangoku denki* 1. Tokyo: Koten bunko, 1982.

Gerstle, C. Andrew, trans. *Chikamatsu: 5 Late Plays*. New York: Columbia University Press, 2001.

Gi So (Yi Chu). *Giso rokujō*. Kyoto: Hōyu shoten, 1979.

Gluck, Carol. *Japan's Modern Myths: Ideology in the Late Meiji Period*. Princeton, NJ: Princeton University Press, 1985.

Godai Hidetaka and Hashiguchi Kenpei. *Sangoku meishō zue* 1. Tokyo: Minami Nihon shuppan bunka kyōkai, 1966.

Goi Ranshū. *Sago. Nihon jurin sōsho* 1, edited by Seki Giichirō. Tokyo: Ōtori shuppan, 1971.

Goodman, Grant. *Japan: The Dutch Experience*. London: Athlone Press, 1986.

Graham, Masako Nakagawa. "The Consort and the Warrior: *Yokihi Monogatari*." *Monumenta Nipponica* 45, no. 1 (Spring 1990): 1–26.

———. *The Yang Kuei-fei Legend in Japanese Literature*. (Lewiston, NY: Edwin Mellen Press, 1998).

Gu Jie-gang. *Wude zhongshi shuo xia de zhengzhi he lishi*. Hong Kong: Longmen shudian, 1970.

Gu Yong-xin. "Riben chuan ben guwen Xiaojing hui chuan zhōngguo kao." *Journal of Peking University* (Philosophy and Social Sciences) 41, no. 2 (March 2004): 100–108.

Guo Lian-you. "Mengzi sixiang zai Riben." In *Zhong-Ri wenhua jiaoliushi daxi 3: Sixiang juan*, edited by Yan Shaodang and Minamoto Ryōen. Hangzhou: Zhejiang renmin chubanshe, 1996.

Guo Run-tao. "Zhongguo mufu zhide de tezheng xingtai ji bianqian." *Zhongguoshi yanjiu*, no. 1 (1997), 3–14.

Hada Buei. *Jofuku roman: Yayoi jidai no furontia*. Tokyo: Aki shobō, 1993.

Haga Noboru. *Nikkan bunka kōryūshi no kenkyū*. Tokyo: Yūzankaku shuppan, 1986.

Han Dong-yu. *Cong "tuoru" dao "tuoya": Riben jinshi yilai "qu zhong xin hua" zhi sixiang guocheng yanjiu*. Taipei: Taiwan daxue chubanzhongxin, 2009.

Han Wei-zhi. *Shanggu wenxue zhong junchen shixiang de yanjiu*. Shanghai: Shanghai guji chubanshe, 2006.

Hanawa Hokiichi, ed. *Gunsho ruijū* 11. Tokyo: Keizai shinbunsha, 1892.

Hanawa Hokiichi, ed. *Zoku gunsho ruijū* 12. Tokyo: Zoku gunsho ruijū kanseikai, 1959.

Harootunian, Harry D. "The Functions of China in Tokugawa Thought." In *The Chinese and the Japanese: Essays in Political and Cultural Interactions*, edited by Akira Iriye. Princeton, NJ: Princeton University Press, 1980.

———. *Things Seen and Unseen: Discourse and Ideology in Tokugawa Nativism* Chicago: University of Chicago Press, 1988.

Haruyama Ikujirō. *Gesshō monogatari*. Tokyo: Kateidō, 1927.

Hayashi Gahō. *Gi taisakubun*. In *Kindai Nihon kokumin: Tokugawa bakufu kamiki gekan shisōhen*, by Tokutomi Iichirō. Tokyo: Meiji shoin, 1936.

———. *Honchō tsugan enpenbatsu*. In *Kindai Nihon kokumin: Tokugawa bakufu kamiki gekan shisōhen*, by Tokutomi Iichirō. Tokyo: Meiji shoin, 1936.

———. *Honchō tsugan* 1. Tokyo: Kokusho kankōkai, 1920.

———. *Honchō tsugan* 55. Tokyo: Hakubunkan, 1897.

———. *Honchō tsugan* 81. Tokyo: Hakubunkan, 1897.

Hayashi Hideichi, trans. *Kōkyō*. Tokyo: Meitoku shuppansha, 1984.

Hayashi Jussai. *Kisa kankin*. Tokyo: Zoku gunshoruijū kanseikai, 1977.

Hayashi Razan. "Hayashi sensei bunshū." In *Nihon shisō taikei* 28, *Fujiwara Seika, Hayashi Razan*, annotated by Ishida Ichiryō and Kaneya Osamu. Tokyo: Iwanami shoten, 1975.

———. *Hayashi Razan bunshū* 1. Kyoto: Kyōtō shisekikai, 1930.

———. *Hayashi Razan bunshū, zuihitsu* 70. In *Kojiruien*, vol. 3, Kyoto: Kojiruien kankōkai, 1931.

———. *Honchō jinjakō*. Tokyo: Kaizōsha, 1942.

———. *Honchō jinjakō, Jinjakō shōsetsu*. Tokyo: Gendai shichōsha, 1980.

———. *Razan bunshū*. In *Kojiruien, seimeibu* 47. Tokyo: Kojiruien kankōkai, 1932.

———. *Razan bunshū* 25. *Nihon zuihitsu taisei*, ser. 3, vol. 11. Tokyo: Yoshikawa kōbunkan, 1977.

———. *Seika sensei gyōjō*. *Hayashi Razan bunshū*, edited by Kyōtō shisekikai. Tokyo: Perikansha, 1979.

———. *Seika sensei gyōjō*. *Hayashi Razan bunshū* 40, edited by Kyōtō shisekikai. Kyoto: Kyōtō shisekikai, 1930.

———. "Yamatofu." *Hayashi Razan bunshū* 1, edited by Kyōtō shisekikai. Tokyo: Perikansha, 1979.

Hayashi Razan and Hayashi Gahō. *Honchō tsugan*. Tokyo: Kokusho kankōkai, 1919.

Hayashi Razan "Heishin kikō." In *Nikki kikōshū*, annotated by Tsukamoto Tetsuzō. Tokyo: Yūhōdō shoten, 1936.

Hayashi Rokurō. *Nagasaki Tōtsūji: Daitsūji Hayashi Dōei to sono shūhen*. Nagasaki: Nagasaki bunkensha, 2010.

Hiraishi Naoaki, ed. *Soraishū, Soraishū shūi*. Tokyo: Perikansha, 1985.

Hirano Harue. *Chūkō no saikōsatsu*. Tokyo: Shingidō shuppanbu, 1934.

Hirata Atsutane. *Daifusō kokukō* 2. Tokyo: Ibukinoya, 1836.

———. *Kanna hifumi den*. Edo: Ikukinoyajuku, 1824.

———. *Kōshi seisetsukō* 1. Digital collection of the National Diet Library of Japan, request no. 848-143.

———. *San'eki yuraik* 1. Tokyo: Ibukinoya, 1835. Digital collection of National Diet Library of Japan, request no. 848-173.

———. *Sango hongokukō* 1. Digital collection of the National Diet Library of Japan, request no. 839-28.

———. *Seiseki gairon* 1. Digital collection of the National Diet Library of Japan, request no. 838-820.

———. *Sekiken taikoden seibun*. Tokyo: Ibukinoya, 1870..

———. *Taiko koekiden*. *Hirata Atsutane zenshū* 6, edited by Hirata Moritane and Miki Ioe Tokyo: Hōbunkan, 1935.

———. *Tama no mihashira*. *Nihon shisō taikei 50: Hirata Atsutane, Ban Nobutomo, Ōkuni Takamasa*, annotated by Tahara Tsuguo. Tokyo: Iwanami shoten, 1973.

Hirose Yutaka, ed. *Kō-Mō yowa*. Tokyo: Iwanami shoten, 1942.

Hongō Takamori. "Tengtian Yougu *Zhengming lun* de lishi diwei." In *Dechuan shidai Riben ruxueshi lunji*, edited by Zhang Bao-san, Xu Xing-qing. Taipei: Taiwan daxue chuban zhongxin, 2004.

Hori Isao. *Hayashi Razan*. Tokyo: Yoshikawa kōbunkan, 1964.

Hori Keizan. *Fujingen. Shin Nihon koten bungaku taikei* 99, edited by Hino Tatsuo. Tokyo: Iwanami shoten, 2000.

Huang Chun-chieh. "Nakai Riken's Interpretation of the *Mencius*." In *The Book of Mencius and Its Reception in China and Beyond*, edited by Chun-chieh

Huang, Gregor Paul, and Heiner Roetz. Wiesbaden, Ger.: Harrassowitz
Verlag, 2008.

———. "The Idea of 'Zhongguo' and Its Transformation in Early Modern
Japan and Contemporary Taiwan." *Journal of Kanbun Studies in Japan* 2
(March 2007): 398–408.

Huang Jun-jie. *Mengxue sixiang shilun*. Taipei: Institute of Chinese Literature
and Philosophy, Academia Sinica, 1997.

Huber, Thomas M. *The Revolutionary Origins of Modern Japan*. Stanford, CA:
Stanford University Press, 1981.

Hudson, Mark J. *Ruins of Identity: Ethnogenesis in the Japanese Islands*.
Honolulu: University of Hawai'i Press, 1999.

Ichiko Teiji and Ōshima Takehiko, annot. *Soga monogatari* 2. Tokyo: Iwanami
shoten, 1966.

Ikeda Mariko. "Nihon ni okeru Gensō Yōkihi-zu: Kinsei shoki no gadai to
zuyō." *Bijutsu-shi kenkyū* 41 (2003): 43–64.

Iki Ichirō. *Jofuku shūdan torai to kodai Nihon*. Tokyo: Sanichi shobō, 1996.

Ikuta Yorozu. *Koeki taishōkyō den* 1. Digital collection of the National Diet
Library of Japan, request no. 847-103.

———. *Taneki seigi*. Digital collection of the National Diet Library of Japan,
request no. 848-128.

———. *Taneki seigi. Ikuta Yorozu zenshū* 3, edited by Haga Noboru. Tokyo:
Kyōiku shuppan sentā, 1986.

Inoue Junri "Kinsei hōjin senjutsu Mōshi chūshakusho mokuroku." In
Tōyōgaku ronshū, edited by Ikeda Suetoshi hakushi koki kinen jigyōkai.
Hiroshima: Ikeda Suetoshi hakushi koki kinen jigyōkai, 1980.

———. *Honpō chūsei made ni okeru Mōshi juyō shi no kenkyū*. Tokyo: Kasama
shobō, 1972.

Inoue Tetsujirō. *Nihon shushigakuha no tetsugaku*. Tokyo: Fuzanbō, 1909.

Ise Sadatake. *Ansai zuihitsu* 1. Edited by Imaizumi Teisuke. Tokyo: Yoshikawa
kōbunkan, 1929.

———. *Teijō zakki*. Tokyo: Yoshikawa kōbunkan, 1928.

Ishizaki Matazō. *Kinsei Nihon ni okeru Shina zokugo bungakushi*. Tokyo:
Kōbundō shobō, 1940.

Ishizaki Senjirō. *Ikeda Mitsumasa ko den* 3. Tokyo: Ishizaki Senjirō, 1932.

Ishō. *Tōkai keikashū*. In *Gozan bungaku shinshū* 2, edited by Tamamura Takeji.
Tokyo: Tōkyō Daigaku shuppankai, 1968.

Iwagaki Matsunae. *Kokushi ryaku.* In *Shinyaku kokushi ryaku,* translated by
Ōmachi Keigetsu. Tokyo: Shiseidō shoten, 1921.

Iwasa Masashi and Tokieda Motoki, eds. *Jinnō shōtōki, Masu kagami, Nihon
koten bungaku taikei* 87. Tokyo: Iwanami shoten, 1965.

Izawa Banryō. *Zokusetsu zeiben.* Tokyo: Kokumin bunko kankōkai, 1912.

Izumi Hideki, ed. *Rekishi jinbutsu, igai na densetsu.* Tokyo: PHP, 2010.

Izumi Makuni. *Meidōsho.* In *Nihon shisō taikei* 51: *Kokugaku undō no shisō,*
annotated by Haga Noboru and Matsumoto Sannosuke. Tokyo:
Iwanami shoten, 1971.

Jansen, Marius B. *China in the Tokugawa World.* Cambridge, MA: Harvard
University Press, 1992.

———. *Japan and Its World: Two Centuries of Change.* Princeton, NJ:
Princeton University Press, 1980.

Kaibara Ekken. *Chikuzen kuni zoku fudoki. Ekken zenshū* 4, edited by Ekken
Kai. Tokyo: Ekken zenshū kankōbu, 1910.

———. *Shinshiroku. Ekiken zenshū* 2, edited by Ekiken Kai. Tokyo: Ekiken
zenshū kankōbu, 1910.

Kaji Nobuyuki. *Kōkyō keimō no shomondai.* In *Nihon shisō taikei* 29 *Nakae
Tōju,* annotated by Yamanoi Yū and Yamashita Ryūji. Tokyo: Iwanami
shoten, 1974.

Kamo Mabuchi. *Kokuikō. Nihon shisō taikei* 39, *Kinsei shintōron zenki kokugaku,*
annotated by Taira Shigemichi and Abe Akio. Tokyo: Iwanami shoten,
1972.

Kanzawa Tokō. *Okingusa.* In *Nihon zuihitsu taikei,* ser. 3, vol. 21. Tokyo:
Yoshikawa kōbunkan, 1978.

Katō Kei. *Yōkihi hyōchaku densetsu no nazo.* Tokyo: Jijukokuminsha, 1987.

Katō Naokata. *Chūgoku ronshū. Nihon shisō taikei* 31: *Yamazaki Ansai gakuha,*
annotated by Nishi Junzō, Abe Ryūichi and Maruyama Masao. Tokyo:
Iwanami shoten, 1980.

Katō Shūichi. "Arai Hakuseki no sekai." *Nihon shisō taikei* 35: *Arai Hakuseki,*
annotated by Matsumura Akira, Bitō Masahide, and Katō Shūichi.
Tokyo: Iwanami shoten, 1975.

Kawakami Tetsutarō. *Yoshida Shōin: Bu to ju ni yoru ningenzō.* Tokyo:
Bungeishunjū, 1968.

Keene, Donald. "Hirata Atsutane and Western Learning." *T'oung Pao* 42, no. 5
(1954): 353–80.

Ki Kaion. *Gensō kōtei hōrai tsuru. Nihon shomin bunka shiryō shūsei 7, Ningyō jōruri*, edited by Geinōshi kenkyūkai. Tokyo: Sanichi shobō, 1975.

Kim Moonkyong. "Xihu zai Zhong Ri Han." In *Dongya wenhua yixiang zhi xingsu*, edited by Shi Shouqian and Liao Zhaocheng. Taipei: Yunchen wenhua shiye, 2011.

Kinoshita Junan. *Taihakuron*. In *Zokuzoku gunsho ruijū* 13. Tokyo: Kokusho kankōkai, 1909.

Kishi Toshio *Nihon kodai bunbutsu no kenkyū*. Tokyo: Hanawashobō, 1988.

Kitabatake Chikafusa. *Shinchū jinnō shōtōki*. Annotated by Saitō Jinnosuke. Tokyo: Aoyama shobō, 1927.

Kitabatake Kakusai. *Kumano yūki* 2. Digital collection of Waseda University Library, request no. ﾙ04_03162.

Kitajima Manji. *Toyotomi seiken no taigai ninshiki to Chōsen shinryaku*. Tokyo: Azekura shobō, 1990.

Kiyohara Nobukata. *Chōgonka narabini Biwagyō hisho*. Kyoto University Library: http://edb.kulib.kyoto-u.ac.jp/exhibit/ca8/image/ca8shf/ca8sh0028.html.

Kiyohara Sadao. *Kokugaku hattatsushi*. Tokyo: Unebi shobō, 1940.

Kizaki Aikichi. *Rai Sanyō*. Tokyo: Shinchōsha, 1941.

Kondō Haruo. *Chōgonka Biwagyō no kenkyū*. Tokyo: Meiji shoin, 1981.

Kondō Keiko. "*Chūkō ruisetsu* no kōgai to kaisetsu." *Shintōshi kenkyū* 52, no. 2 (October 2004): 215–31.

Koschmann, J. Victor. *The Mito Ideology: Discourse, Reform, and Insurrection in Late Tokugawa Japan, 1790-1864*. Berkeley: University of California Press, 1987.

Kōshū. *Keiran shūyōshū*. In *Taishō shinshū daizōkyō* 76, edited by Takakusu Junjiō. Tokyo: Taishō issaikyō kankōkai, 1931.

Kumazawa Banzan. *Genji monogatari Banzan shō*. Tokyo: Kogeisha, 1935.

———. *Kōkyō shōkai*. In *Kōkyō daigaku chūyō rongo*. Tokyo: Waseda daigaku shuppanbu, 1926.

———. *Miwa monogatari*. *Nihon tetsugaku zensho* 4, *Shintōhen, Jukyōhen*, edited by Saigusa Hiroto. Tokyo: Daiichi shobō, 1936.

———. *Shūgi gaisho*. *Nihon rinri ihen* 2, edited by Inoue Tetsujirō and Kanie Yoshimaru. Tokyo: Ikuseikai, 1901.

———. *Shūgi gaisho*. *Banzan zenshū*, edited by Masamune Atsuo. Tokyo: Meicho shuppan, 1978.

Kuroita Katsumi, ed. *Kokushi taikei: shinteizōho* 8. Tokyo: Yoshikawa kōbunkan, 1965.

Kurokawa Dōyū. *Enpekiken ki. Nihon zuihitsu taisei*, ser. 1, vol. 10. Tokyo: Yoshikawa kōbunkan, 1975.

Kurozumi Makoto. *Fukusūsei no Nihon shisō*. Tokyo: Perikansha, 2006.

Kyōto shisekikai, ed. *Hayashi Razan bunshū* 36. Osaka: Kōbunsha, 1930.

Kyōto shisekikai, ed. *Hayashi Razan bunshū* 1. Tokyo: Perikansha, 1979.

Lan Hong-yue. "Shenzhou, zhongguo, diiguo: Huizezhengzhizhai de guojia xiangxiang yu shijiu shiji Riben zhi Yazhou lunshu." *Xinshixue* 22, no. 3 (September 2011): 87–90.

Lau, D. C., trans. *Confucius: The Analects*. Harmondsworth, UK: Penguin, 1979.

———, trans. *Mencius*. London: Penguin, 1970.

Lidin, Olof G. *The Life of Ogyū Sorai, a Tokugawa Confucian Philosopher*. Lund, Sweden: Studentlitt, 1973.

Lin Jiantong. "Qin Xufu shiji zhi yanjiu." In *Xu Fu yu Riben*, edited by Lin Jiantong and Zhu Zhensheng. Hong Kong: Xianggang Xufu hui, 1976.

Liu Yuzhe. "Yang Guifeng," in *Rizhong wenhua jiaoliushi congshu 10 renwu*, edited by Nakanishi Susumu and Wang Yong. Tokyo: Taishūkan shoten, 1996.

Lu Miao-fen. "Zuowei yishixing wenben de Xiaojing: Ming-Qing shiren *Xiaojing* shijian de gean yanji." *Zhongyang yanjiuyuan jindaishi yanjiusuo jikan* 60 (2008): 7–8.

Luo Qixiang, Iino Takahiro, eds. *Jofuku: Yayoi no kōsen*. Tokyo: Tōkyō shoseki, 1988.

Maeno Michiko. "Kokugō ni miru Nihon no jiko ishiki." *Gengo bunka kenkyū sōsho* 5 (2006): 26–62.

Mao Zishui, annot. *Lunyu jinzhu jinyi*. Taipei: Shangwu yinshuguan, 2009.

Maruyama Masao. *Studies in the Intellectual History of Tokugawa Japan*. Translated by Mikiso Hane. Princeton, NJ: Princeton University Press, 1974.

Mass, Jeffrey P. *Antiquity and Anachronism in Japanese History*. Stanford, CA: Stanford University Press, 1992.

Matsumoto Sannosuke, "Kinsei ni okeru rekishi jōjutsu to sono shisō," *Nihon shisō taikei* 48: *Kinsei shi ronshū*, annotated by Matsumoto Sannosuke and Ogura Yoshihiko. Tokyo: Iwanami shoten, 1974.

———, ed. *Nihon no meicho* 31, *Yoshida Shōin*. Tokyo: Chūō kōronsha, 1973.

Matsumoto Shigeru. *Motoori Norinaga no shisō to shinri: Aidentitī tankyū no kiseki*. Tokyo: Tōkyōdaigaku shuppankai, 1981.

———. *Motoori Norinaga*. Cambridge, MA: Harvard University Press, 1970.

Matsushita Kenrin. *Ishō Nihonden*. In Kondō Heijō, ed., *Shiseki shūran* 20, edited by Kondō Heijō. Tokyo: Kondō shuppanbu, 1926.

McCausland, Shane, and Matthew McKelway. *Chinese Romance from a Japanese Brush: Kano Sansetsu's Chōgonka Scrolls in the Chester Beatty Library*. London: Scala, 2009.

McMullen, James. "Edo shoki ni okeru chū to kō no mondai ni tsuite." *Kikan Nihon shisōshi* 31 (1988): 35–59.

———. *Idealism, Protest, and the Tale of Genji: The Confucianism of Kumazawa Banzan (1619–91)*. Oxford: Clarendon Press, 1999.

———. "Rulers or Fathers? A Casuistical Problem in Early Modern Japanese Thought." *Past and Present*, no. 116 (August 1987): 56–97.

McNally, Mark. *Proving the Way: Conflict and Practice in the History of Japanese Nativism*. Cambridge, MA: Harvard University Asia Center, 2005.

Mihashi Tokugen. *Mihashi Tokugen Chosakushū*. Tokyo: Zoku gunshoruijū kanseikai, 1999.

Miki Miyuki. *Tōgen iji*. In *Mitogaku no tassei to tenkai*, by Nagoya Tokimasa. Mito: Mito shigakkai, 1992.

Mito Mitsukuni. "Bairi sensei hi." In *Mito Mitsukuni no Bairi sensei hi*, edited by Miyata Masahiko. Mito: Mito shigakkai, 2004.

Mizubayashi Takeshi. *Tennōsei shiron: Honshitsu kigen tenkai*. Tokyo: Iawanami shoten, 2006.

Momoi Tōu. *Kyūai zuihitsu*. *Nihon zuihitsu taisei*, ser. 2, vol. 12. Tokyo: Yoshikawa kōbunkan, 1974.

Mori Shinzō. *Chūkō no shinri*. Tokyo: Meguro shoten, 1935.

Morita Yasuo. *Ōshio Heihachirō to Yōmeigaku*. Tokyo: Izumi shoin, 2008.

Morita Yoshihiko. *Heigakusha Yoshida Shōin: Senryaku jōhō bunmei*. Tokyo: Wejji, 2011.

Motoori Norinaga. *Kakaika*. In *Motoori Norinaga zenshū* 8, annotated by Ōno Susumu and Ōkubo Tadashi. Tokyo: Chikuma shobō, 1972.

———. *Kenkyōjin*. *Motoori Norinaga zenshū*, annotated by Motoori Toyokai. Tokyo: Yoshikawa kōbunkan, 1926.

———. *Kojikiden*. *Shintō taikei: Ronsetsuhen 25, Fukko shintō 3, Motoori*

Norinaga, annotated by Umezawa Isezō and Takahashi Miyuki. Tokyo: Shintō taikei hensankai, 1982.

———. *Kuzuka. Dai-Nippon shisō zenshū 9*, part 2, edited by Dai-Nippon shisō zenshū kankōkai. Tokyo: Dai-Nippon shisō zenshū kankōkai, 1933.

———. *Naobi no mitama. Shintō taikei: Ronsetsuhen 25, fukko shintō 3*, annotated by Umezawa Isezō and Takahashi Miyuki. Tokyo: Shintō taikei hensankai, 1982.

———. *Tamakatsuma* 11. In *Tamakatsuma*, pt. 2, annotated by Muraoka Tsunetsugu. Tokyo: Iwanami shoten, 1943.

Murai Gensai. *Ōmi seijin*. Tokyo: Hakubunkan, 1892.

Muraki Keiko. "Chōgonka e no henyō: Nara-e-kei *Chōgonka emaki* o tegakari ni." *Bigaku geijutsugaku* 25 (2009): 50–69.

Muraoka Tsunetsugu. *Norinaga to Atsutane*. Tokyo: Sōbunsha, 1957.

Murayama Shūichi. *Honji suijaku*. Tokyo: Yoshikawa kōbunkan, 1974.

Muro Kyūsō. *Akō gijin roku. Nihon shisō taikei 27, Kinsei buke shisō*, edited by Ishii Shirō. Tokyo: Iwanami shoten, 1974.

———. "Yusa Jirō Zaemon ni kotafuru daisansho." *Nihon shisō taikei 34 Kaibara Ekken, Muro Kyūsō 34*, annotated by Araki Kengo and Inoue Tadashi. Tokyo: Iwanami shoten, 1970.

Musaka San, annot. *Nakae Tōju bunshū*. Tokyo: Yūhōdō shoten, 1926.

Naitō Konan. "Cong Songdai shixue kan Zhongguo zhengtong lun." Translated by Wai-ming Ng. *History: Theory and Criticism* 2 (May 2001): 161–67.

———. "Nippon bunka towa nani zoya." *Naitō Konan zenshū 9*. Tokyo: Chikuma shobō, 1969.

Naitō Tōho. *Chōshū zasshi*. Nagoya: Atsuta jingū kyūchō, 1969.

Najita Tetsuo. *Visions of Virtue in Tokugawa Japan: The Kaitokudō Merchant Academy of Osaka*. Chicago: University of Chicago Press, 1987.

Nakae Katsumi. *Nipponshi nazo no jinbutsu no igai na shōtai*. Tokyo: PHP, 1999.

Nakae Tōju. *Okina mondō. Nihon shisō taikei 29, Nakae Tōju*, annotated by Yamashita Yū and Bitō Masahide. Tokyo: Iwanami shoten, 1974.

———. *Okina mondō. Yōmeigaku taikei 8, Nihon no Yōmeigaku 1*. Tokyo: Meitoku shuppansha, 1973.

Nakai, Kate Wildman. *Shogunal Politics: Arai Hakuseki and the Premises of*

Tokugawa Rule. Cambridge, MA: Harvard University Press, 1988.

———. "The Naturalization of Confucianism in Tokugawa Japan: The Problem of Sinocentrism." *Harvard Journal of Asiatic Studies* 40, no. 1 (June 1980): 157–99.

———. "Tokugawa Confucian Historiography: The Hayashi, Early Mito School and Arai Hakuseki." In *Confucianism and Tokugawa Culture*, edited by Peter Nosco. Princeton, NJ: Princeton University Press, 1984.

Nakane Yukie. *Zoku saimu kiji* 2. Tokyo: Nihon shiseki kyōkai, 1921.

Nanzan Inshi. *Kindai seijin hyakubanashi*. Tokyo: Daigakukan, 1910.

Naramoto Tatsuya, ed. *Yoshida Shōin shū*. Tokyo: Chikuma shobō, 1969.

Ng Wai-ming. "Civil Morality in the Life and Thought of Inoue Tetsujirō (1855–1911)." *BC Asian Review* 9 (Winter 1995–96): 208–241.

———. "Cong Bainaao kan zhongshi Riben yixue de beddihua." *Xueshu yuekan*, no. 46 (2014): 162–67.

———. "Political Terminology in the Legitimation of Tokugawa Japan." *Journal of Asian History* 34, no. 2 (2000): 138–48.

———. "The Forgery of Books in Tokugawa Japan." *East Asian Library Journal* 9, no. 2 (2000): 19–45.

———. *The I Ching in Tokugawa Thought and Culture*. Honolulu: University of Hawai'i Press, 2000.

Nihon zuihitsu taisei henshūbu, ed. *Nihon zuihitsu taisei*, ser. 3, vol. 15. Tokyo: Yoshikawa kōbunkan bunkan, 1995.

Nishi Shin'ichirō. *Chūkōron*. Tokyo: Iwanami Shoten, 1931.

Nishikawa Joken. *Nihon suidokō*. In *Nishikawa Joken isho* 9, edited by Nishikawa Tadasuke. Tokyo: Nishikawa Tadasuke, 1907.

Noguchi Takehiko. *Edo no rekishika*. Tokyo: Chikuma shobō, 1979.

———. "Edo Yūmeigaku to Mōshi." *Bungaku* 49, no. 2 (1981): 97

———. *Ōdō to kakumei no aida: Nihon shisō to Mōshi mondai*. Tokyo: Chikuma shobō, 1986.

Nosco, Peter. "The Place of China in the Construction of Japan's Early Modern World View." *Taiwan Journal of East Asian Studies* 4, no. 1 (June 2007): 27–48.

———. *Remembering Paradise: Nativism and Nostalgia in Eighteenth-Century Japan* Cambridge, MA: Council on East Asian Studies, Harvard University, 1990.

Noya Masaru, ed. *Sonjō shūei*. Tokyo: Tōyōbunka kenkyūkai, 1943. Electronic collection of Kyoto University, file #0177900.

Ōba Osamu. *Edo jidai ni okeru tōsenmochiwatarisho no kenkyū*. Suita: Kansai daigaku tōzai gakujutsu kenkyūjo, 1967.

———. *Edo jidai no Nit-Chū hiwa*. Tokyo: Tōhō shoten, 1980.

Ogasawara Haruo. *Koku-ju ronsō no kenkyū: Naobi no mitama o kiten to shite*. Tokyo: Perikansha, 1988.

Ogyū Sorai. *Bendō*. *Nihon shisō taikei 36 Ogyū Sorai*, annotated by Yoshikawa Kōjirō. Tokyo: Iwanami shoten, 1973.

———. *Benmei*. In *Nihon shisō taikei 36 Ogyū Sorai*, annotated by Yoshikawa Kōjirō. Tokyo: Iwanami shoten, 1973.

———. *Kenen zatsuwa*. Digital collection of Waseda University Library, request no. イ17 02304.

Okada Takehiko, ed. *Bakumatsu ishin Shushigakusha shokanshū, Shushigaku taikei*, 14. Tokyo: Meitoku shuppansha, 1974.

Okada Tsuyoshi. *Tōju-sensei nenpu*. Kyoto: Yamaga Zenbei, 1893.

Okino Iwasaburō. *Hirata Atsutane to sono jidai*. Tokyo: Kōseikaku, 1943.

Ōkubo Tadataka, Saiki Kazuma, et al., annot. *Nihon shisō taikei 26: Mikawa motogatari, hagakure*. Tokyo: Iwanami shoten, 1974.

Ōkuni Takamasa. *Gakutō benron*. *Nihon shisō taikei 50: Hirata Atsutane, Ban Nobutomo, Ōkuni Takamasa*, annotated by Tahara Tsuguo. Tokyo: Iwanami shoten, 1973.

———. *Koden tsūkai*. *Ōkuni Takamasa zenshū 7*, annotated by Nomura Denshirō. Tokyo: Yūkōsha, 1938.

———. *Koden tsūkai 3*. Tokyo: Yao shoten, 1897.

———. *Shōuchū shinji sen*. Tokyo: Jingū kyōin, 1873.

Ōmi Shōji. "Yōki-shi boshi no kenkyū." *Nihon rekishi*, no. 211 (1962): 32–52.

Ommerborn, Wolfgang. "Mencius Theory of *Renzheng* (Human Politics) and Its Reception in the Song Dynasty." In *The Book of Mencius and Its Reception in China and Beyond*, edited by Chun-chieh Huang, Gregor Paul, and Heiner Roetz. Wiesbaden, Ger.: Harrassowitz Verlag, 2008.

Ōno Susumu et al., eds. *Iwanami kogo jiten*. Tokyo: Iwanami shoten, 1974.

Ono Takakiyo. *Hyakusōro*. *Nihon zuihitsu taisei*, ser. 3, vol. 11. Tokyo: Yoshikawa kōbunkan, 1978.

Ooms, Herman. *Tokugawa Ideology: Early Constructs, 1570–1680*. Princeton, NJ: Princeton University Press, 1985.

Ōtsuki Gentaku. *Rangaku kaitei. Nihon shisō taikei 63, Yōgaku* 1, annotated by Numata Jirō. Tokyo: Iwanami shoten, 1976.

Ozawa Eiichi. *Kinsei shigaku shisō shi kenkyū*. Tokyo: Yoshikawa kōbunkan, 1974.

Peng Shuang-song. *Xu Fu jishi Shenwu Tianhuang*. Miaoli: Fuhui tushu chubanshe, 1983.

Picken, Stuart D. B. *Historical Dictionary of Shinto*. Lanham, MD: Scarecrow, 2011.

Pines, Yuri. "Name or Substance? Between *Zhengtong* and *Yitong*." *History: Theory and Criticism* 2 (May 2001): 105–37.

Pollack, David. *The Fracture of Meaning: Japan's Synthesis of China from the Eighth through the Eighteenth Centuries*. Princeton, NJ: Princeton University Press, 1986.

Pyle, Kenneth. *The Making of Modern Japan*. Lexington, MA: D. C. Heath, 1978).

Qiao Zhi-zhong. "Lun Zhong-Ri liangguo chuantong shixue zhi zhengtonglun guannian de yitong." *Qiushi xuekan*, no. 2 (2005): 109–16.

Rai Sanyō. *Nihon gaishi* 2, edited by Tsukamoto Tetsuzō. Tokyo: Yūhōdō shoten, 1921.

———. *Nihon gaishi ronsan, Dai Nihon shisō zenshū 15: Rai Sanyō shū*. Tokyo: Dai Nihon shisō zenshū kankōkai, 1933.

———. *Shinsaku. Dai-Nihon shisō zenshū 15, Rai Sanyō shū*, annotated by Uemura Katsuya. Tokyo: Dai Nihon shisō zenshū kankōkai, 1933.

Rai Tsutomu, annot. *Nihon shisō taikei 37, Sorai gakuha*. Tokyo: Iwanami shoten, 1972.

Rao Zong-yi (Jao Tsung-I). *Zhongguo shixue shang zhi zhengtonglun*. Shanghai: Shanghai yuandong chubanshe, 1996.

Rimer, Thomas and Jonathan Chaves, trans. and annot. *Chinese and Japanese Poems to Sing: The Wakan rōei shū*. New York: Columbia University Press, 1997.

Roetz, Heiner. *Confucian Ethics of the Axial Age*. Albany: State University of New York Press, 1993.

Rokumon Mochitsuki. *Rokumon zuihitsu*. In *Nihon geirin sōsho* 2, edited by Hamano Chizaburō et al. Tokyo: Rokugōkan, 1928.

Tsunoda Ryūsaku, William Theodore De Bary, and Donald Keene, eds. *Sources of Japanese Tradition*. New York: Columbia University Press, 1958.

Sakaki Atsuko. *Obsessions with the Sino-Japanese Polarity in Japanese Literature.* Honolulu: University of Hawai'i Press, 2006.

Sakamoto Tarō. *Shūshi to shigaku.* Tokyo: Yoshikawa kōbunkan, 1989.

Sasaki Sadataka. *Kansō sadan.* In *Nihon zuihitsu taisei*, ser. 1, vol. 12. Tokyo: Yoshikawa kōbunkan, 1975.

Sasaki Takanari. *Ben bendōsho.* In *Dai-Nihon bunko shintō hen: Suika shintō* 3, annotated by Saeki Ariyoshi. Tokyo: Shunyōdō shoten, 1937.

Sasayama Haruo. *Nihon kodai eifu seido no kenkyū.* Tokyo: Tōkyōdaigaku shuppankai, 1985.

Satō Issai. *Genshiroku. Nihon shisō taikei 46: Ōshio Chūsai, Satō Issai*, annotated by Sagara Tōru, Mizoguchi Yūzō, and Fukunaga Mitsuji. Tokyo: Iwanami shoten, 1980.

Satō Saburō. *Kindai Nitchū kōshōshi no kenkyū.* Tokyo: Yoshikawa kōbunkan, 1984.

Satō Shigehiro. *Chūryō manroku*, in *Nihon zuihitsu taikei*, ser. 3, vol. 3. Tokyo: Yoshikawa kōbunkan, 1975.

Seiō. *Kochōan zuihitsu*, in *Nihon zuihitsu taisei*, ser. 2, vol. 17. Tokyo: Yoshikawa kōbunkan, 1974.

Senke Takazumi. *Sakura no hayashi. Nihon zuihitsu taisei*, ser. 2, vol. 11. Tokyo: Yoshikawa kōbunkan, 1974.

Seo Kunio, ed. *Kōshi Mōshi ni kansuru bunken mokuroku.* Tokyo: Hakuteisha, 1992.

Shang Hui-peng. *Zhongguoren yu Ribenren: Shehui jituan, xingwei fangshi he wenhua xinli de bijiao yanjiu.* Beijing: Beijing daxue chubanshe, 1998.

Shi Yun-tao. *Tangdai mufu zhide yanjiu.* Beijing: Zhongguo shehui kezue chubanshe, 2003.

Shibata Jingorō. *Seijin Nakae Tōju.* Tokyo: kōgakusha, 1937.

Shiga daigaku fuzoku toshokan, ed. *Kindai Nihon no kyōkasho no ayumi: Meijiki kara gendai made.* Hikone: Sanraizu shuppan, 2006.

Shima Kenji. *Shushigaku to Yōmeigaku.* Tokyo: Iwanami shoten, 1967.

Shimada Masao. "Jofuku denshō seiritsu no kiban." In *Kumano*, edited by Chihōshi kenkyūsho. Tokyo: Geirinsha, 1974.

Shimohashi Yukiosa. *Bakumatsu no kyūtei.* Tokyo: Heibonsha, 1979.

Shin Suk-ju. *Haedong jegukgi.* Seoul: Taeyang Sojok, 1972.

Shinozaki Tōkai. *Narubeshisanchū. Nihon zuihitsu taisei*, ser. 2, vol. 15. Tokyo: Yoshikawa kōbunkan, 1974.

Shiraishi Toshio, annot. *Kōeki zokusetsuben.* Tokyo: Heibonsha, 1989.

Smethurst, Mae J. *Dramatic Representations of Filial Piety: Five Noh in Translation with an Introduction*. Ithaca, NY: Cornell University East Asia Program, 1998.

Smith, Warren. *Confucianism in Modern Japan: A Study of Conservatism in Japanese Intellectual History*. Tokyo: Hokuseido Press, 1973.

Smits, Ivo. "Minding the Gaps: An Early Edo History of Sino-Japanese Poetry." In *Uncharted Waters: Intellectual Life in the Edo Period*, edited by Anna Beerens and Mark Teeuwen. Leiden: Brill, 2012.

Sonehara Satoshi. *Tokugawa Ieyasu shinkakuka e no michi*. Tokyo: Yoshikawa kōbunkan, 1996.

Steininger, Brian. *Chinese Literary Forms in Heian Japan: Poetics and Practice*. Cambridge, MA: Harvard University Asia Center, 2017.

Straelen, Henry van. *Yoshida Shōin: Forerunner of the Meiji Restoration*. Leiden: Brill, 1952.

Sugita Genpaku. *Kyōi no gen*. *Nihon shisō taikei* 64, *Yōgaku* 1, annotated by Numata Jirō. Tokyo: Iwanami shoten, 1976.

Tachibana Nankei. *Hokusō sadan*. *Nihon zuihitsu taisei*, ser. 2, vol. 15, edited by Nihon zuihitsu taisei henshūbu. Tokyo: Yoshikawa kōbunkan, 1974.

———. *Tōzaiyūki, Hokusō sadan*. Tokyo: Yūhōdō shoten, 1922.

———. *Japanese Loyalism Reconstrued: Yamagata Daini's Ryūshi Shinron of 1759*. Honolulu: University of Hawai'i Press, 1995.

Tahara Tsuguo and Morimoto Junichirō, annot. *Nihon shisō taikei 32: Yamaga Sokō*. Tokyo: Iwanami shoten, 1970.

Tajiri Yūichirō. "Riben dui songmingxue de shourong yu bian rong." In *Zhong-Ri wenhua jiaoliushi daxi. 3 sixiang juan*, edited by Yan Shaodang and Minamoto Ryōen. Hangzhou: Zhejiang renmin chubanshe, 1996.

Takafuji Harutoshi. "Honji suijaku setsu no tenkai o megutte: Shinpon shinjaku setsu kara shinpon butsujaku setsu he." *Shintōgaku*, no. 113 (May, 1982): 1–31.

Takasu Yoshijirō, ed. *Mitogaku zenshū* 5. Tokyo: Nittō shoin, 1933.

———. *Mito gakuha no sonnō oyobi keirin*. Tokyo: Yūzankaku, 1936.

Takebe Ayatari. *Honchō suikoden* (Tokyo: Iwanami shoten, 1992).

Takemura Noriyuki. "Chikushi ni utsurisunda Yōkihi: *Honchō suikoden* no Yōkihi koji ni tsuite." *Bungaku kenkyū* 101 (March 2004): 63–76.

Takeuchi Yoshio. "Jukyō hen 3." *Takeuchi Yoshio zenshū* 4. Tokyo: Kadokawa shoten, 1979.

———. "Nihon no jukyō." *Takeuchi Yoshio zenshū* 4. Tokyo: Kadokawa shoten, 1979.

Takizawa Bakin. *Chinsetsu yumiharizuki. Nihon koten bungaku taikei* 60, annotated by Gotō Tanji. Tokyo: Iwanami shoten, 1958.

———. *Gendō hōgen. Nihon zuihitsu taisei,* ser. 1, vol. 5, edited by Nihon zuihitsu taisei henshūbu. Tokyo: Yoshikawa kōbunkan, 1975.

Tanaka Hiroshi. *Tōkai ni hōraikoku ari: Jofuku den.* Fukuoka: Kaichōsha, 1991.

Tani Sōboku. *Tōgoku kikō.* In *Gunsho ruijū, Kikōbu,* vol. 14, scroll 340, edited by Hanawa Hokiichi. Tokyo: Nihon bunka shiryō sentā, 1983.

Tao De-min. *Kaitokudō shushigaku no kenkyū.* Suita: Ōsaka daigaku shuppankai, 1994.

Teeuwen, Mark. "*Kokugaku* vs. Nativism." *Monumenta Nipponica* 61, no. 2 (2006): 227–42.

Terajima Ryōan. *Wakan sansai zue* 13. Tokyo: Chūgai shuppansha, 1901.

Terao Yoshio. *Chūgoku bunka denrai jiten.* Tokyo: Kawate shobō, 1982.

Teruoka Yasutaka. "Kanshō no shiori." In *Saikaku zenshū gendaigoyaku* 8, translated by Teruoka Yasutaka. Tokyo: Shōgakkan, 1976.

Tian Shimin. *Jinshi Riben ruli shijian de yanjiu.* Taipei: Taiwan daxue chuban zhongxin, 2012.

Tō Teikan. *Shōkōhatsu.* Digital collection of Waseda University, request no. リ05_05003.

Toby, Ronald. "Reopening the Question of Sakoku: Diplomacy in the Legitimation of the Tokugawa Bakufu." *Journal of Japanese Studies* 3, no. 2 (Summer 1977): 347–55.

Tokuda Susumu. *Kōshi setsuwashū no kenkyū: Nijūshikō o chūshin ni, kinseihen.* Tokyo: Kuresu shuppan, 2004.

Tokugawa Harutoshi. *Shin Dai Nihonshi hyō.* In *Nanbokuchō seijun ronsan,* by Yamazaki Tōkichi and Horie Hideo. Tokyo: Kōtenkōkyūjo Kokugakuin daigaku shuppantoshohanbaijo, 1911.

Tokugawa Mitsukuni, ed. *Dai Nihonshi,* annotated by Hiraizumi Kiyoshi. Tokyo: Shunyōdō shoten, 1937.

———. *Seizankō zuihitsu. Dai Nihon shisō zenshū* 18, edited by Uemura Katsuya. Tokyo: Dai Nihon shisō zenshū kankōkai, 1933.

Tōkyō daigaku shiryōhensansho, ed. *Dai Nihon shiryō.* Tokyo: Tōkyō daigaku shiryōhensansho, 2009.

Torii Fumiko. "Tosa jōruri no kyakushoku-hō, 10, Tō no Gensō." *Tōkyō Joshi Daigaku kiyō ronshū* 38, no. 2 (March 1988): 47–71.

Tsuji Shiho. *Jofuku ron: Ima o ikiru densetsu*. Tokyo: Shintensha, 2004.

Tsujimoto Masashi. *Kinsei kyōiku shisōshi no kenkyū*. Kyoto: Shibunkaku shuppan, 1990.

Tsunetsugu, Muraoka. *Motoori Norinaga*. Tokyo: Iwanami shoten, 1941.

Tu, Wei-ming. "Cultural China: Periphery as the Center." *Daedalus* 120, no. 2 (Spring 1991): 1–32.

Tucker, John Allen. "Two Mencian Political Notions in Tokugawa Japan." *Philosophy East and West* 47, no. 2 (April 1997): 233–53.

Tucker, Mary Evelyn. *Moral and Spiritual Cultivation in Japanese Neo-Confucianism: The Life and Thought of Kaibara Ekken, 1630–1714*. Albany: State University of New York Press, 1989.

Uchimura Kanzō. *Daihyōteki Nihonjin*. Tokyo: Keiseisha shoten, 1908.

Urabe Kanekata. *Shaku Nihongi*. In *Kokushi taikei*, Tokyo: Keizai zasshisha, 1901.

Varley, H. Paul, trans. *A Chronicle of Gods and Sovereigns: Jinno Shotoki of Kitabatake Chikafusa*. New York: Columbia University Press, 1980.

———. *Imperial Restoration in Medieval Japan*. New York: Columbia University Press, 1971.

Wada Sei and Ishihara Michihiro, annot. *Gishi wajinden, gokanjo waden, sōsho wakokuden, zuisho wakokuden*. Tokyo: Iwanami shoten, 1951.

Wakabayashi, Bob Tadashi. *Anti-Foreignism and Western Learning in Early-Modern Japan: The "New Theses" of 1825*. Cambridge, MA: Harvard University Press, 1986.

Wang Ermin. *Zhingguo jindai sixiangshulun*. Taipei: Huashi chubanshe, 1977.

Wang Wen-xue. *Zhengtong lun*. Xian: Shaanxi renmin chubanshe, 2002.

Wang Xiangrong. "Xu Fu: Riben de Zhongguo yimin." In *Riben de Zhongguo yimin*, edited by Zhongguo Zhong-Ri guanxishi yanjiuhui. Beijing: Sanlian shudian, 1987.

Wang Yong. "Sichouzhilu yu shujizhilu." *Zhejiang daxue xuebao* 33, no. 5 (September 2013): 5–12.

Watanabe Hiroshi. "About Some Japanese Historical Terms." Translated by Luke Roberts. *Sino-Japanese Studies* 10, no. 2 (April 1998): 32–42.

———. "Goikō to shōchō: Tokugawa seiji taisei no ichi sokumen." *Shisō*, no. 740 (February 1986): 132–54.

———. *Higashi Ajia no ōken to shisō*. Tokyo: Tōkyō daigaku shuppankai, 1997.

———. *Kinsei Nihon shakai to Sōgaku*. Tokyo: Tōkyō daigaku shuppankai, 1995.

Watanabe Ryūsaku. *Yōkihi kōden.* Tokyo: Shūeishobō, 1980.

Watarai Jōshō. *Shintō meiben.* In *Kinnō bunko 2,* edited by Arima Sukemasa. Tokyo: Dai-Nihon meidōkai, 1919.

Watarai Nobuyoshi. *Jingū hiden mondō. Shintō taikei: Ronsetsuhen 7, Ise shintō part 2,* annotated by Nishikawa Masatami. Tokyo: Shintō taikei hensankai, 1982.

Watase Junko. "Atsuta no Yōkihi densetsu: *Soga monogatari* makini Gensō kōtei no koto o tansho to shite." *Nihon bungaku* 54, no. 12 (December 2005): 21–29.   Webb ?

Wei Ting-sheng. *Riben Shenwu kaiguo xinkao: Xu Fu ru Riben jianguo kao.* Hong Kong: Hong Kong Commercial Press, 1950.

Wong Tin. "Hanmo qingyuan liangdeqian: Jindai Riben xiang Hua xueshu shuyao." In *Zai Riben xunzhao Zhongguo: Xiandaixing ji shenfen rentong de Zhong-Ri hudong,* edited by Wai-ming Ng. Hong Kong: Zhongwen daxue chubanshe, 2013.

Wu Lai. *Yuanyingji 4.* Beijing: Zhonghua shuju, 1985.

Yamaga Sokō. *Chūchō jujitsu. Yamaga Sokō zenshū: Shisōhen 13,* edited by Hirose Yutaka. Tokyo: Iwanami shoten, 1940.

———. *Haisho zanpitsu. Yamaga Sokō zenshū: Shisōhen 8,* edited by Hirose Yutaka. Tokyo: Iwanami shoten, 1940.

Yamagata Bantō. *Yume no shiro. Nihon keizai sōsho 25,* edited by Takimoto Seiichi. Tokyo: Nihon keizai sōsho kankōkai, 1916.

Yamagata Daini. *Ryūshi shinron.* Tokyo: Iwanami shoten, 1943.

Yamaguchi Kamekichi, ed. *Yabataishi senjimon benkai taizen.* Tokyo: Senshodō, 1894.

Yamamoto Noritsuna. *Jofuku tōrai densetsu kō.* Tokyo: Kenkōsha, 1975.

———. *Nihon ni ikiru Jofuku no denshō.* Tokyo: Kenkōsha, 1979.

Yamamoto Shichihei. *Arahitogami no sōsakushatach.* Tokyo: Bungei shunjū, 1983.

Yamamoto Tsunetomo. *Hagakure.* Translated by William S. Wilson. Tokyo: Kodansha, 1983.

Yamanaka Tetsuzō. *Yoshida Shōin no Shisō.* Tokuyama: Tokuyama daigaku sōgō keizai kenkyūjo, 1983.

Yamazaki Ansai, *Bunkai hitsuroku. Yamazaki Ansai zenshū 1,* edited by Nihon koten gakkai. Tokyo: Perikansha, 1978.

———. *Taihakuron. Shushigaku taikei 12, Chōsen no Shushigaku, Nihon no Shushigaku,* edited by Kobayashi Hideo. Tokyo: Meitoku shuppansha, 1977.

Yamazaki Tōkichi and Horie Hideo. *Nanbokuchō seijun ronsan*. Tokyo: Kōtenkōkyūjo Kokugakuindaigaku shuppantoshohanbaijo, 1911.

Yip, Leo Shing Chi. *Reinventing China: Cultural Adaptation in Medieval Japanese Nō Theatre*. PhD diss., Ohio State University, 2004.

Yoshizawa Katsuhiro. "*Sennōka*: Muromachi bunka no yokō." *Kikan Zenbunka*, no. 187 (2003): 150.

Yokoyama Shigeru, annot. *Ko jōruri shōhonshū* 3. Tokyo: Kadokawa shoten, 1964.

Yoshida Shōin. *Kō-Mō yowa*. Tokyo: Iwanami shoten, 1943.

———. *Kōmō yowa. Yoshida Shōin zenshū* 2, edited by Yamaguchi-ken kyōi-kukai. Tokyo: Iwanami shoten, 1982.

———. *Noyama bunkō. Dai-Nippon shisō zenshū 17: Yoshida Shōin shū, Sakuma Shōzan shū*, edited by Uemura Katsuya. Tokyo: Dai-Nippon shisō zenshū kankōkai, 1932.

———. *Tōkō zen nikki. Yoshida Shōin zenshū* 9, edited by Yamaguchigen kyōi-kukai. Tokyo: Daiwa shobō, 1974.

Yoshida Tsunekichi and Satō Seiszaburō, eds. *Nihon shisō taikei 56, Bakumatsu seiji ronshū*. Tokyo: Iwanami shoten, 1976.

Yoshikawa Kōjirō. *An Introduction to Sung Poetry*. Cambridge, MA: Harvard University Press, 1967.

Zekkai Chūshin. "Yingzhi fu sanshan." *Gozan bungakushū, Edo kanshishū, Nihon koten bungaku taikei* 89, edited by Yamagishi Tokuhei. Tokyo: Iwanami shoten, 1966.

Zhu Xi. *Sishi zhangju jizhu*. Beijing: Zhinghua shuju, 1983.

Zou shuang-shuang. "Densetsu kara genjitsu e yomigaetta Yōkihi no shosō: Amakusa-shi Shinwa-chō no Yōkihi o chūshin ni." *Amakusashotō no bunka kōshō-gaku kenkyū*, no. 2 (2011): 153–62.

INDEX